Transforming the U.S. Financial System

Transforming the U.S. Financial System

Equity and Efficiency for the 21st Century

Gary A. Dymski
Gerald Epstein
Robert Pollin
Editors

M.E. Sharpe
Armonk, New York
London, England

Library of Congress Cataloging-in-Publication Data

Transforming the U.S. financial system: equity and efficiency for the
21st century / Gary A. Dymski, Gerald Epstein, Robert Pollin, editors
p. cm. — (Economic Policy Institute)
Includes bibliographical references and index.
ISBN 1-56324-268-0. — ISBN 1-56324-269-9 (pbk.)
1. Finance—United States. 2. Monetary policy—United States.
I. Dymski, Gary. II. Epstein, Gerald A. III. Pollin, Robert.
IV. Title: Transforming the U.S. financial system.
V. Series: Economic Policy Institute (Series)
HG181.T7   1993
332.1′0973—dc20
93-23796
CIP

Printed in the United States of America

The paper used in this publication meets the minimum requirements of American
National Standard for Information Sciences—Permanence of Paper for Printed
Materials, ANSI Z39.48-1984

Recommended citation for this book is as follows:
Dymski, Gary A., Gerald Epstein, and Robert Pollin, editors,
*Transforming the U.S. Financial System: Equity and Efficiency for the 21st
Century.* Economic Policy Institute Series. Armonk: M.E. Sharpe, Inc., 1993.

MV (c) 10   9   8   7   6   5   4   3   2   1
MV (p) 10   9   8   7   6   5   4   3   2   1

CONTENTS

PART II: BANKING AND FINANCIAL REGULATION

PART III: FINANCIAL MARKETS AND PRODUCTIVE INVESTMENT

TABLES AND FIGURES

Tables

Figures

ACKNOWLEDGMENTS

This book is an outgrowth of the energetic efforts of the Economic Policy Institute to promote progressive thinking in macroeconomics, monetary policy, and financial regulation, areas that, for some time, have been largely neglected by progressive economists. The immediate inspiration came from a January 1991 conference organized by the Economic Policy Institute, during which many of the ideas developed in the volume were subject to lively debate. Following that meeting, we editors approached EPI about transforming these discussions into a more tangible product. The result is this book.

We therefore first thank the leadership at EPI—Jeff Faux, Larry Mishel, and Roger Hickey—for supporting our idea and providing us with the financial and institutional wherewithal for seeing the project through. We also thank the many members of the EPI staff for their efforts. In particular, we must single out Eileen Appelbaum and Dean Baker. They dug into all the grubby details and, with their dirty hands, high energy, and good humor, made the project happen.

EPI organized two conferences around this book, in June of both 1991 and 1992. The discussions at these meetings substantially improved the quality of this volume, and we wish to acknowledge those who participated at the two events along with the volume's authors and EPI staff: Patrick Bond, Deepak Borghana, Paul Burkett, John Caskey, Sherry Ettleson, Carla Feldpausch, Sheldon Friedman, Donald Harris, Dorene Isenberg, Michael Mandler, Robert McCauley, Rick McGahey, Hyman Minsky, Tom Palley, Howard Wachtel, Michael Waldman, Jeanne Wells, Robin Wells, and Herb Whitehouse.

Richard Bartel of M. E. Sharpe has enthusiastically supported this project from its inception, in addition to his active participation at the June 1991 meeting. We also wish to thank Linda Frede-Tripicco at M. E. Sharpe for moving this project to a timely completion.

—The Editors

Transforming the U.S. Financial System

CHAPTER ONE

Introduction

GARY A. DYMSKI, GERALD EPSTEIN, AND ROBERT POLLIN

The U.S. financial and monetary system is broken and needs to be fixed. The collapse and bailout of the savings and loan industry—which, as of the latest government estimate, will cost U.S. taxpayers $300 billion and has crippled what was once the most accessible source of housing credit for nonwealthy households—is the most visible sign of failure. But problems in our financial system are far more extensive than this. The banking industry, for example, has also experienced unprecedented instability. Over the 1980s, banks failed at an average annual rate of 78 per 10,000, whereas for the period 1947–1979, the annual failure rate averaged 4 per 10,000. These weaknesses in lending institutions have been matched by rising levels of defaults and bankruptcies by nonfinancial businesses and households. Real interest rates, meanwhile, were sustained at historically high levels throughout the 1980s and early 1990s. From 1980 through 1989, long-term rates averaged 7.2 percent, whereas from 1947 through 1979, the average figure was 1.2 percent. Even between 1875 and 1941, an era prior to the development of extensive government stabilization policies, the average long-term rate of 4.4 percent was significantly lower than for the most recent period.[1]

More important still, our poorly functioning financial system has had a major impact on the overall performance of the economy. It affects our job prospects and chances for starting businesses. It is a major determinant of our income level, our opportunities to obtain decent housing, and the security of our retirement. It affects the long-term growth and stability of the economy and, thereby, the prospects for our children and future generations. It also has a major influence on who gets what from the economy—whether economic well-being will be distributed widely and fairly or, as has been the recent trend, increasingly concentrated among the wealthy few.

For generations, prevailing economic theory claimed that the financial structure was irrelevant to the performance of the overall economy. We argue just the opposite. The financial structure is the economy's circulatory system: it transmits material sustenance through the economy just as our bloodstream distributes oxygen, hormones, and cell-building nutrients through our body.

This book seeks to accomplish two basic tasks: to explain the underlying problems of our financial system and to propose a new policy approach for addressing these problems in ways that will promote fairness, efficiency, and a more productive economy. The book ranges widely in pursuing these ends. The first section examines monetary policy. It considers how monetary policy has contributed to the high interest rates and instability of recent years. It also explores the prospects for pursuing a monetary policy focused on restoring a low-interest-rate environment rather than concentrating almost exclusively, as it has in recent years, on controlling inflation.

The second section examines banks and other intermediaries as well as the government programs that regulate these institutions. In the 1930s, the U.S. developed an ambitious and largely successful regulatory system. But this regulatory structure is now in shambles. We explain how this breakdown has occurred and propose new approaches to regulation.

The final section focuses on the relationship between the financial structure and nonfinancial productive investment. It considers the mergers, buyout, and takeover movements of the 1980s as an important experience for understanding how an unregulated financial structure is capable of dramatically misallocating investment funds and thus inhibiting the growth of productive activity. It also considers the role of pension funds in fostering long-term investment and discusses the role the Federal Reserve can play in promoting financial stability, long-term investment, and increasing accountability within the financial system.

The volume offers a broad approach to policy, though not a uniform set of proposals. The chapters focus on various questions, and the proposals that flow from each therefore vary in emphasis and sometimes in substance. Nevertheless, seen from a wider angle, the essays do offer a consistent set of proposals. In the rest of this introduction, we summarize the main analytic points and policy approaches that form the core ideas of this book.

What Are the Problems?

The fundamental economic problem in the United States is that living standards for the majority have stagnated or declined for the past two decades. As a first approximation, we can cite five basic reasons for this decline in living standards:

• Low productivity growth and declining ability of the economy to generate good jobs;
• Decaying living conditions in our major cities;
• Worsening inequality of income, wealth, and opportunity;
• Increased debt dependency by corporations, households, and the federal government and;
• The declining ability of the government to control the destructive cycles of boom and bust.

All of these problems, in turn, are closely associated with weaknesses in our financial system. Consider the following connections: First, the private financial structure is biased against financing productive investment in favor of unproductive expenditures, such as corporate mergers and buyouts and real estate speculation. This leads to inadequate and inappropriate public and private investment, which contributes to low productivity growth. Moreover, by contributing to excessive debt dependence and speculation, this bias in the financial system also leads to more severe cyclical fluctuations of recession and unsustainable expansion.

Second, the financial structure reflects the highly inequitable distribution of wealth and power in our society and itself contributes to wealth inequality. Through redlining and other forms of discrimination and neglect, the financial system biases credit flows against communities that have relatively few resources but can use funds productively. At the same time, the system showers credit on the well-off, who already have more than enough, even when they have no productive use for the funds. This contributes to worsening living conditions in cities and worsening inequality.

Third, the Federal Reserve's monetary policy adds to these problems by helping to keep real interest rates inefficiently high. These high interest rates contribute to low rates of productive investment, high budget deficits, continuing dependence on debt, and worsening inequality by redistributing income to those who already have the most wealth.

Fourth, the financial regulatory system has at best failed to help solve these problems and increasingly has contributed to them. For example, the system of pension fund regulation has inhibited the channeling of pension money toward projects that would yield higher-paid and more productive jobs within the U.S. economy. And as is by now well known, bank regulators stood by while real estate speculation swept the country in the 1980s. Taxpayers are now paying the price of this neglect through the savings and loan fiasco, with the prospect of a similar bailout of the banking system threatening on the horizon. Such bailouts in turn contribute to the federal budget deficit, diverting scarce public funds away from education, health, and the public infrastructure.

Not all economists will agree that private financial institutions are responsible for these difficulties. Indeed, many regard the government's involvement in the financial sector as the problem and financial deregulation as the solution. But we know that government regulators did not force U.S. institutions into a reckless lending boom to Latin America in the 1970s; or into throwing egregious sums of money at real estate speculators, who overbuilt office towers and luxury condominiums; or into paying Drexel, Burnham, Lambert's "junk bond" king Michael Milken $500 million in one year (1987) to engineer mergers and leveraged buyouts that left nonfinancial corporations overburdened with debt. Private institutions accomplished these ends on their own.

Free market purists acknowledge that private institutions make mistakes. A free market system, in the purists' view, simply requires that those who err be punished: market participants must be forced to sink or swim. The problem with this argument is that if too many financial institutions sink, then we all drown with them. The reason is that the activities of banks and other financial institutions almost always have a far wider impact than the activities of firms in nonfinancial industries: they both hold our life's savings and lend these savings to others, whose investments will construct our economic future. The bank runs that helped to produce the 1930s Depression and the bank-financed real estate boom and bust of the 1980s, leading to the long recession of the 1990s, both demonstrate the capacity of destabilizing private financial activity to reverberate powerfully throughout the economy. This is why the financial system must be regulated and the public must have some protection from the private market's mistakes.

The problem we face, however, is that the financial regulatory system we now have—created in the Depression, beginning with the passage of the Glass-Steagall act in 1932—no longer works. Conditions have changed dramatically in the past 60 years, but the regulatory environment has never been renovated properly to keep up with those changes. The Glass-Steagall system was designed to promote financial stability and efficiency by limiting competition and by offering public protection. But this approach was based on a set of conditions—including low interest rates, low inflation, low global integration, and relative lack of financial innovation—that prevailed in the 1930s but that no longer exists today. What is needed now is neither deregulation nor a mere defense of the old regulatory approach. Nor do we simply need more regulations. We rather need *better* regulations and, more broadly, a new approach to financial restructuring. The aim of the new approach should be not simply more credit for more people, but a more equitable and efficient allocation of credit—an allocation that promotes socially productive rather than wasteful and destructive ends.

The individual chapters in this volume present critiques of a variety of restructuring proposals that are bound to fail, either because they overestimate the efficiency of private markets or because they rely excessively on the existing regulatory framework. Most important, we also advance our alternative policy agenda. In many ways, our proposals break decisively with conventional approaches to reform. At the same time, we have taken care to offer ideas that are feasible and workable within the existing set of political and regulatory institutions.

Our agenda is built on the following four principles:

• *Rig markets but do not smother them.* We support vigorous private activity in financial markets and also recognize that there are limits to what governments can administer competently. We therefore favor proposals that would, at most, require insignificant increases in administration as well as low levels of public outlay. Our purpose is to reorient the main currents, but not every eddy, of existing market practices.

• *Accountability from below.* We recognize that government agencies can be readily captured by the institutions they are supposed to regulate and that the more there is at stake, the greater will be the efforts of the regulated to control the regulators. The only mechanism to control for this is to establish broad and ongoing institutions of democratic accountability.

• *Level the playing field upward.* One of the primary problems of the Glass-Steagall system was that unequal regulatory demands were placed on different types of institutions. The result was that business flowed from highly regulated intermediaries to less regulated ones. One obvious approach to resolving this problem is deregulation, that is, leveling the playing field downward. This approach has been tried since 1980; the dismal results are before us. The logical alternative is to create consistent regulations for all institutions.

• *Renew the social contract.* The activities of financial institutions have a large impact not only on their depositors and shareholders but also on the communities in which they operate and on the overall economic environment. In exchange for receiving public protection such as publicly insured deposits, financial institutions must take more responsibility for the effects they have on communities. In particular, when public funds are used to support or stabilize private financial institutions, the public must receive clear and direct benefits from its investment.

Let us now sketch out the way we apply these principles in the three areas of monetary policy, banking and regulatory policy, and the financing of investment.

Monetary Policy

The operations of the U.S. financial system are intimately bound up with the Federal Reserve's monetary policy. Most simply put, a healthy financial system is unattainable without an effective monetary policy, but achieving an effective monetary policy is more difficult when the financial structure is unstable. With the federal deficit having immobilized fiscal policy as a macroeconomic policy instrument, monetary policy has become the federal government's primary policy weapon. Monetary policy errors have thus become very costly. In the late 1980s, for example, an excessively tight monetary policy instigated the long recession of the early 1990s.

The experience of the 1980s also showed how an unhealthy financial system undermined the Federal Reserve's ability to conduct monetary policy. In the mid-1980s, when monetary policy was loosened somewhat to encourage an economic expansion, much of the credit created failed to support productive investments. Instead, a substantial share of new funds flowed to hostile takeovers and real estate speculation. This weakened the link between expansionary monetary policy and economic growth.

Then, in the early 1990s, when monetary policy was loosened to fight the recession, the excessive debts that nonfinancial firms and banks accumulated in the 1980s became an obstacle to expansionary policy. Rather than lend to firms, banks tried to rebuild their capital, and, rather than borrow to invest in new plant and equipment, nonfinancial firms used the low interest rates to work the debts off their balance sheets.

Given the structural imbalances in the financial system in the 1980s and early 1990s, including of course the burgeoning federal deficit, even the best monetary policy would not have been good enough. However, what actually happened is that the Federal Reserve only contributed to the system's structural problems through its policy errors. The Federal Reserve's most basic mistake, as James Galbraith emphasizes in Chapter 2, is that for most of the 1980s, the Federal Reserve single-mindedly focused on fighting inflation, neglecting all other considerations.

However, the Fed's tight money policies have at best reduced inflation at the cost of periodic recessions and sluggish long-term growth without, as Galbraith shows, addressing the underlying sources of inflationary pressure. In addition, as Steven Fazzari makes clear in Chapter 3, these restrictive policies have actually contributed to inflationary problems by discouraging investment and thereby lowering the growth rate of productivity.

Finally, as Galbraith points out, the Fed's obsession with inflation-fighting undermined its credibility when it came time, in 1990, to try reviving the economy from the recession it had helped to create. Galbraith argues that the Fed's lack of credibility as a recession fighter helps to explain why, for example, long-term interest rates remained high in the early 1990s even as short-term rates fell sharply: the markets believed that the Federal Reserve would quickly raise interest rates again at the first signs of renewed inflationary pressures.

Fazzari's chapter clarifies an important mechanism through which restrictive monetary policies such as those pursued in the 1980s can have broad negative consequences. Fazzari develops a new, but increasingly accepted, approach to understanding the transmission mechanism between monetary policy and the macroeconomy. His approach emphasizes the special role played by banks as assessors all of credit risk and needs as well as credit suppliers. The banks in this approach are a key link in transmitting the effects of monetary policy throughout the economy.

According to this approach, banks are important suppliers of credit to firms that want to invest but may face difficulties obtaining sufficient financing for their projects. Such firms, in other words, are "credit rationed." Often, the credit-rationed firms are smaller businesses that are among the most technologically progressive in the economy. Restrictive monetary policy raises short-term interest costs to the banks, which in turn pass on these costs to their borrowers. This reduces profit prospects for the small firms, which inhibits their ability to obtain credit and expand. Conversely, more expansionary monetary policy lowers short-term interest rates, which increases profit prospects for the smaller firms. This encourages banks to make more credit available to the smaller firms, enabling these firms to undertake more rapid expansion.

Fazzari's chapter has several important lessons for this volume. First, banks play a special role in our financial system as suppliers of credit to important nonfinancial firms. This role needs to be preserved. Second, Fazzari illustrates well the point made earlier: that successful monetary policy depends on the effective operations of banks and other financial institutions. Finally, tight monetary policy can worsen underlying stagflation problems. This is because tight money will undermine the productive investment plans of the most technologically progressive firms, slowing these firms' ability to reduce their production costs. This inhibits the firms' ability to cut prices.

Why then has the Federal Reserve been pursuing such self-defeating tight-money policies? A generous explanation is that, with the Congress and President having abandoned responsibility for macroeconomic policy, the Fed is the only institution seriously concerned with controlling inflation. But even this interpretation cannot explain why the Fed would not adopt a more balanced approach between controlling inflation and preventing recessions.

According to Gerald Epstein (Chapter 4) and Galbraith, the crux of the matter is that the Federal Reserve is insufficiently accountable to the Congress and to citizens generally, but it is excessively accountable to major financial interests. These financial powers tend to be particularly phobic about inflation, which explains the corresponding excessive inflationary fears of the Fed. More generally then, we see here a problem that will emerge frequently in this volume: the issue of accountability of financial institutions to "stakeholders" in the economy, namely, the households, communities, and workers who do not exercise power through owning companies or holding substantial wealth but whose well-being nevertheless depends on how efficiently and equitably the financial system functions.

How can monetary policy operate more effectively? Galbraith and Epstein argue that the Federal Reserve needs to be insulated from the influence of the large banks and financial institutions. Different authors in this volume propose alternative ways to achieve this end. Galbraith supports the proposal of U.S. Representative Lee Hamilton and U.S. Senator Paul Sarbanes to remove the Federal Reserve regional bank presidents from the Federal Open Market Committee, the main policymaking body of the Fed. The regional bank presidents typically have close ties to local private bankers. Galbraith's second suggestion is to maintain the current level of institutional power of the regional bank presidents, but to make the regional officers accountable to a broader constituency. One possibility is to have state governments appoint the regional presidents. Robert Pollin suggests in Chapter 12, which we discuss below, that the regional bank directors be directly elected. Still another approach is to give Congress more oversight over policy by ensuring the prompt release of Open Market Committee decisions (Galbraith) or by having Congress exercise direct control over appointments to the Federal Reserve (Epstein). By whatever method, reducing the power of private financial institutions over Federal Reserve policy is an important structural reform with which all the aforementioned authors mentioned agree.

Second, the mandate of the Federal Reserve should be changed. The Federal Reserve should no longer be solely responsible for price stability. New strategies, including a long-run decline in the (properly defined) structural federal deficit, must be found to deal with the problem of persistent inflationary pressures. The Federal Reserve could then focus more on keeping interest rates low (Galbraith) or on improving credit allocation toward productive investment projects (Pollin).

A final important structural reform, suggested by Epstein and Galbraith, is to improve the coordination between monetary and fiscal policy. The two policies must be coordinated so as to ensure that they support rather than undermine each other. Both reducing the accountability of the Fed to financial institutions and shifting its policy focus away from inflation control will contribute to this process.

In Chapter 4, Epstein confronts a number of possible objections to these policy proposals. Critics suggest that there are three major barriers to pursuing a monetary policy oriented more toward sustaining lower interest rates and promoting productive investment. These three barriers are the danger of inflation (the "inflation constraint"); the international integration of financial markets, which prohibits interest rates from falling below international levels (the "external constraint"); and highly liquid and expectations-oriented financial markets, which can nullify the Federal Reserve's efforts at lowering real long-term interest rates (the "financial constraint").

Epstein argues that, in assessing these constraints, it is important to distinguish between economic and political obstacles. Economic obstacles refer to adverse changes in output or the economic undermining of policies, whereas political obstacles involve the effects on income distribution and therefore the political undermining of policies. Epstein presents evidence that moderate rates of inflation have few, if any, economic costs. He also argues that the extent to which the external constraint is binding depends on the context within which macroeconomic policy occurs—most important, that the international financial markets have a sense that policy is under control. The force of the financial market constraints also depends heavily on the attitudes of financial markets toward the stability of a policy regime. Epstein suggests that complementary policies to overcome these constraints may be needed at times. But Epstein also argues that the strictly economic barriers to expansionary monetary policy are generally exaggerated. In fact, political barriers to expansionary policy—that is, the struggle for income shares—often masquerade as constraints on economic growth.

For this reason, policies to reduce the Federal Reserve's accountability to powerful financial interests and increase that to communities will help to separate the economic from the political barriers to a new policy approach. Redistributing the relative influence over Federal Reserve decisions away from the financial community will have the additional benefit of fostering initiatives toward increased complementarity between fiscal and monetary policy. Finally, restructuring the Federal Reserve will make it politically easier to reform the financial and banking system. Heretofore, as Galbraith notes, the Federal Reserve has been among the most powerful opponents of constructive monetary and financial reform.

Banking and Financial Regulation

The collapse of the savings and loan industry and the accelerating rate of bank failures leave no doubt that the system of financial intermediation—encompassing banks, savings and loan associations (S&Ls), and "nonbank intermediaries" such as insurance and finance companies—needs to be transformed. The increasing instability of the intermediaries has also diminished their willingness and ability to provide credit for poorer communities and smaller businesses. This also reinforces the need for a fundamental overhaul of the industry.

Few observers disagree with the need for transforming the system of banking and intermediation via some type of reconstruction of the regulatory environment surrounding these institutions. The question is not whether, but how, structural change should be accomplished.

Unfortunately, most proposals for restructuring simply will not work: they will not restore stability and they will not broaden access to credit. Some proposals rely substantially on maintaining the old Glass-Steagall approach even though the conditions needed for these regulations to work have long since ceased to exist. Worse, however, are the free market proponents who favor laissez-faire policies based on financial and economic conditions that have never existed. What is needed is a new set of regulatory principles that build from a realistic understanding of contemporary financial markets.

Gary Dymski, drawing from the contributions of the other chapters in this section, provides an overview of how the contemporary U.S. financial market operates. In particular, Dymski describes several characteristics of the markets that demonstrate the need for effective public regulation (see also James Crotty and Don Goldstein, Chapter 10).

As Dymski emphasizes, four characteristics of contemporary financial markets generate inherent tendencies toward inefficiency, instability, and inequality. These are the pervasiveness of imperfect information or uncertainty; herding behavior among market participants; the contagion effects of market trends; and spillover effects, or externalities, from market activity to the broader economy.

As Dymski argues, informational problems make it difficult to assess which types of investments are most profitable: this is particularly important in credit relations because lending is based on future prospects about which, in some cases, very little can be known. When there is an absence of hard information about profitable and efficient investments, financial markets tend to follow the herd in making investments. As John Maynard Keynes said:

> A 'sound' banker, alas! is not one who foresees danger and avoids it, but one who, when he is ruined, is ruined in a conventional and orthodox way along with his fellows, so that no one can really blame him. (1963, p. 176)

The lending booms to Latin America in the 1970s and to domestic real estate developers in the 1980s are costly examples of herds stampeding beyond the abyss.

This herding behavior is reinforced by contagion and spillover effects, in both a positive and a negative sense. For example, a series of loans to a poor community can create a generalized increase in prosperity in that community, which will allow the initial loans to be repaid. Such contagion effects may then spill over to the community as a whole, bringing more credit, better jobs, and rising overall prosperity. A vibrant community may result from this combination of contagion and spillover effects. The corollary is that the absence of contagion and spillover effects can be devastating when the herd refuses to invest.

On their own, private financial institutions will not take account of spillover effects in their calculations. Nor are they capable of avoiding the lure of the herd or the spread of contagion. It therefore falls on public institutions to channel these market forces away from destructive outcomes and toward socially desirable ends. As Dymski notes, markets are made, not given; their essential characteristics therefore depend on the nature of public intervention.

Martin Wolfson, in Chapter 6, describes the basic features of the system of public intervention designed in the 1930s, the remnant of which is still in place today. The system was organized around two principles. The first was restriction of competition among financial institutions, which involved ceiling interest rates on deposits, separation of commercial and investment banking, and general compartmentalization of financial institutions. Such policies were designed to promote the profitability of institutions in their designated lines of business and to discourage herding across market segments. They also sought to prevent contagion effects from disrupting credit flows to sectors of the economy, such as housing, that were designated to receive preferential access to funds.

The second principle was government protection from the financial instability that would result from herding, contagion, and spillover effects. This involved federally guaranteed deposit insurance and a commitment to lender-of-last-resort interventions by the Federal Reserve.

However, as was mentioned earlier, the 1930s regulatory approach was predicted on four features of financial markets: low inflation, low interest rates, low debt levels, and a financial system relatively insulated from international competition. The steady disappearance of these conditions since the 1960s meant that the old regulatory approach was increasingly unable to fulfill its stabilizing functions.

For example, government protection from the effects of financial instability has become much more costly as corporate and household debt levels have risen. Rising private-sector debt dependency has fostered a fragile financial structure. This fragility has created the conditions for financial crises. When crises emerge, the government is forced to bail out the markets through deposit insurance guarantees and lender-of-last-resort interventions. The S&L bailout represents merely the best publicized and most expensive of a long string of such bailouts beginning in the late 1960s.

In addition, higher inflation and interest rates in the late 1960s and 1970s encouraged financial innovations among unregulated nonbank intermediaries, allowing them to compete successfully with the regulated banks and S&Ls. The restrictions on competition, which initially enhanced stability and profitability among banks and S&Ls, had by the 1970s put them at a disadvantage against unregulated institutions that could offer virtually the same services.

Jane D'Arista and Tom Schlesinger, in Chapter 7, present a detailed case study of the emergence of nonbank intermediaries—what they call the "parallel banking system." The most important such institutions are finance companies, which lend to both households and businesses and are linked to major nonfinancial corporations but are subject to virtually no regulations. Their ability to function on commercial banks' terrain free of regulatory costs has allowed them to erode the market share and profitability of the banks. Thus, from 1980 to 1990, finance company assets rose from 12.4 percent to 21.3 percent of commercial bank assets.

This erosion of the commercial banks' competitive position may have been one factor encouraging the banks to pursue speculative lending in real estate and corporate takeovers. At the same time, as D'Arista and Schlesinger show, the finance companies have also made highly risky loans, leaving them vulnerable to some of the same problems as commercial banks. As a result, these unregulated institutions could themselves confront the government and taxpayers with another bailout bill.

Hence, this case study shows that the old regulatory system of restrictions on competition generates an uneven playing field that no longer protects either the banks or the public. At the same time, because of the need for public protection from the effects of financial crises, the government may be forced to act as a lender of last resort at public expense for a set of financial institutions over which it exercises little control.

What should be done to redress these problems? We do not consider either a free market approach or the preservation of the outmoded Glass-Steagall framework as a viable alternative. Equally unsatisfactory, however, is the fact that these two poles—preservation or elimination of the existing system—have largely defined the boundaries of the discussion over financial reform.

Wolfson suggests a more useful approach to evaluating reform proposals, which is their stance on two issues—public regulation and public protection. Thus, for example, the so-called Treasury proposal of the former Bush administration would have abandoned most competitive restrictions. It sought to create a level regulatory playing field by essentially eliminating the field. At the same time, the Bush Treasury proposal would have maintained the existing amount of public protection through deposit insurance and lender-of-last-resort policies. This combination of little public regulation but strong public protection is an invitation to disaster, because the message to intermediaries is: "Proceed as you wish; the government will absorb the consequences."

Another proposal, developed by Robert E. Litan of the Brookings Institution, would create "narrow banks," which alone could offer government-insured deposits. The asset portfolios of narrow banks would then be restricted to safe government securities. No other financial institution would be subject to either public regulation or public protection. D'Arista/Schlesinger and Fazzari oppose this idea because of concerns that it would reduce the ability of banks to act as retail suppliers of credit. Wolfson argues that eliminating regulation of most intermediaries would encourage financial instability and lead to the need for renewed public protection.

Can we envision a strategy that strikes a better balance between public regulation and protection? In their chapter, D'Arista and Schlesinger propose a new framework for regulation based on the principle of leveling the playing field upward. The authors would implement, among other things, a uniform licensing system for all intermediaries—among which they would include all institutions that accept deposits from the public and make loans or purchase equity with those funds. The virtue of this approach is that it would bring all financial institutions under a common regulatory umbrella so that none would have a competitive advantage as a result of disparate regulations. At the same time, the approach recognizes that public control is necessary. Contrary to the Bush Treasury proposal, we see here that the logic of regulatory consistency need not imply deregulation.

Upward leveling of the regulatory playing field goes far to address issues of public regulation but provides much less guidance in the area of public protection. A central component of any public protection policy must be government-guaranteed deposit insurance, and in D'Arista's single-authored contribution to the volume (Chapter 8), she offers an innovative proposal that conforms to her and Schlesinger's principle of consistency in the realm of public regulation.

There are two main components to her proposal. The first is that deposit insurance would be applied directly to individuals as depositors rather than, as is now done, to institutions that accept deposits. Individual depositors would receive a specified amount of deposit insurance—say, up to $100,000—for which they would pay a compulsory fee out of their interest earnings. The insurance could then be used to cover funds up to the maximum held at any government-regulated institution. In this way, the public protection function of deposit insurance is clearly separated from the public regulation of intermediaries.

The second feature of the proposal is that business transaction balances—the funds needed to meet current payrolls, purchases, bills, and other current obligations—should be protected in unlimited amounts. As with the insurance for individuals, all government-regulated institutions would be eligible to accept and administer these transaction balances as long as they continued to hold them in safe investments.

D'Arista's concern is that a maximum amount of insurance coverage of, say, $100,000 would be too small to cover the transaction balances of even small businesses. Thus, the ripple effects of a bank failure for businesses would be powerful, involving widespread losses to workers and suppliers and inviting a chain reaction of bankruptcies and business insolvencies. Insuring all transaction balances in full will therefore bring equal protection throughout the economy against failures of banks or other intermediaries. Protection is selective under current arrangements. It depends first on whether a business holds its transaction balances in insured or uninsured institutions and, second, on the Federal Reserve's discretion in applying lender-of-last-resort protection to failing institutions.

D'Arista's proposal raises several provocative questions. For example, given that the individual's portable insurance coverage can cover funds held by any regulated financial institution, will this enable institutions to offer premiums to accept insured deposits, then use these insured funds to make especially risky loans? Certainly this is not the intent of the proposal, but it may be its outcome unless further restrictions are placed on institutions accepting insured deposits.

Similarly with transaction balances receiving full coverage: will this allow intermediaries to hold funds in nontransaction accounts that can earn higher interest, with the proviso that the intermediary provide an automatic transfer service from the higher-yielding account to the transaction balance? Transfers would occur either when businesses need to draw funds or if the intermediary is threatened with failure. This way, intermediaries could circumvent the investment restrictions on the transaction accounts while still offering the mandatory insurance coverage.

Finally, to the extent that the spirit of D'Arista's proposal is successfully followed, would that then reduce the willingness of banks to make risky loans to less established businesses? Fazzari's chapter, for example, raises concerns about any measures that would reduce deposit insurance coverage for banks below its present level because of his view that banks play a unique role as credit suppliers to small, innovative firms. Within a limited space, D'Arista's proposal could not possibly answer each of these and related questions. Still, her proposal offers useful guidance on how to specify the essential principle, advanced by herself and Schlesinger, of leveling upward the regulatory playing field.

Their contribution also then raises another question: once the playing field has been leveled and raised, what else is needed to improve prospects that the game will be played fairly? Here we return to another one of our basic principles: renewing the social contract. In Chapter 9, James Campen provides a clear description of how the social contract—in the form of community reinvestment—has been systematically violated by banks and bank regulators alike. As Campen describes, there are abundant unmet banking needs in poor communities. These unmet banking needs have serious spillover effects: without appropriate banking services and credit availability, poor communities find it much more difficult to attract the new businesses, investments, and jobs necessary to raise the local living standards.

Campen argues that in failing to offer credit to these communities, banks in fact are missing profitable opportunities. In part, banks are following the herd instinct here. But more specifically, as Campen documents well, these missed opportunities also result from a systematic pattern of racial discrimination.

Since the early 1970s, community activists have fought for laws that would force banks to accept their end of the social contract. In 1975 and again in 1977, they succeeded in getting the federal government to pass two important pieces of legislation. The Home Mortgage Disclosure Act required increased disclosure of information on bank performance, and the Community Reinvestment Act (CRA) formally established banks' affirmative obligation to help meet the credit needs of the local communities in which they are chartered. However, as Campen describes, these laws have not been adequately enforced by regulators. Campen offers several specific proposals for improving enforcement and generally increasing adherence to the principles that motivate these laws. First, consistent with the idea of a level playing field, he argues that community reinvestment obligations should be extended to nonbank financial institutions. Second, he supports establishing community-oriented not-for-profit banks. Finally, as measures to improve performance for all relevant institutions, he favors enhanced enforcement of laws prohibiting racial discrimination, mandated provision of affordable basic banking services, improvements in the CRA examination and evaluation process, material incentives for improved bank performance, and increased disclosure of information on CRA-related lending.

Note that Campen's proposals, considered as a whole, incorporate not only the ideas of leveling upward and renewing the social contract but also the other two guidelines of financial restructuring that we have proposed, namely, rigging markets and accountability from below. Creating material incentives for compliance with the CRA is an example of rigging the market toward a desired goal, and increasing the disclosure laws will improve the capacity of community organizations to monitor the banks and thus strengthen their ability to demand compliance with the laws.

These are surely viable guidelines for increasing the level of productive activity and improving opportunities in poor communities. At the same time, these proposals are targeted at a particular sector of the economy. For the economy as a whole, we still need to ask the question that Campen has posed for poor communities: What structural changes are needed to correct the financial system's tendency to misallocate credit, providing insufficient funds for socially useful investments and generating a persistent tendency toward financial instability? This is the question to which we now turn.

Financial Markets and Productive Investment

The 1980s saw one of the most extraordinary efforts at market-led financial restructuring in the history of the U.S. We refer, of course, to the corporate merger and takeover movement. The financial resources devoted to this project were enormous. For example, as James Crotty and Don Goldstein point out in their chapter, the total volume of corporate mergers between 1984 and 1989 averaged $184 billion per year, approximately $100 billion more *per year* than the total spent in the United States on investment in new productive assets. Almost all of this merger activity was financed with credit, in particular through the use of low-grade corporate junk bonds—the financial innovation that, until he began his two-year prison sentence in 1991, made Michael Milken of Drexel Burnham Lambert the wealthiest and most powerful U.S. financier at least since J. P. Morgan.

The excesses of the merger and takeover movement have been well chronicled in such popular books as *Den of Thieves*, *Barbarians at the Gate*, *Predator's Ball*, and *America: What Went Wrong*. But contrary to the impressions conveyed by such popular literature, much, if not the majority, of academic research on the topic has argued that the net effects of the merger movement have been quite beneficial. Led by Professor Michael Jensen of the Harvard Business School, this view argues first that the merger movement generated enormous gains for the shareholders of the targeted companies and more modest gains—but certainly not losses—for the acquiring firms' shareholders. In addition, this view holds that the merger movement forced substantial increases in the productive efficiency both of firms that were involved in mergers and among U.S. corporations generally. The Jensen argument is that there is an enormous "principal/agent" problem in U.S. corporate structure. The "principals" of firms—their shareholders—have been badly served by their "agents"—self-seeking managers, who, through the organizational structure of the modern corporation, can pursue their own interests even when they conflict with those of shareholders. Jensen regards the merger and takeover movement as a market-based mechanism for shaking managers out of their torpor and restoring legitimate control to shareholders.

Crotty's and Goldstein's careful survey of this literature agrees that there is much to criticize in contemporary U.S. corporate management practices. Nevertheless, Crotty and Goldstein find the Jensenite perspective almost completely without merit, despite the formidable volume of evidence marshaled by its proponents. Building from arguments developed by a range of critics, Crotty and Goldstein instead found that the merger movement has produced two principal effects. The first is "financial pollution," wherein highly risky junk bonds were spread throughout the financial system as a result of mergers, takeovers, and related activities, contributing to financial instability. The second is "corporate anorexia." This refers to the practice in which, to boost short-term cash flow and meet debt obligations, acquiring firms cut deeply into spending on employment, investment, and research and development. In the long term, such cuts have substantial negative consequences for the firms themselves and for the firms' stakeholders, meaning, the workers and communities whose lives are bound up with the firms. Overall, Crotty's and Goldstein's study, like the Campen chapter, offers a vivid application of the problems of herding, contagion, and spillover effects that are pervasive in financial markets.

Crotty and Goldstein cite substantial evidence to show that the deregulated financial markets of the 1980s proved to be egregiously inefficient as credit allocators. The authors propose several avenues for promoting the productive uses of credit, including taxing short-term security gains and all secondary market trading, giving legal power to corporate stakeholders and encouraging shareholder activism, and ending the tax advantages of corporate debt financing.

Any program for transforming the process of credit allocation in the United States has to give special attention to the role of pension funds. This is because pension funds, with more than $4 trillion in assets, are now the largest single source of funds for the U.S. financial market. Moreover, the way in which these funds are allocated for investment represents a manifest case of "principal/agent" conflict in the financial market.

As Randy Barber and Teresa Ghilarducci explain in their chapter, since the 1974 enactment of the Employee Retirement Income Security Act, pension fund managers have been obliged to treat their fiduciary responsibility as equivalent to that for incompetent heirs. That is, the fiduciary's duty is to obtain risk-adjusted maximum rates of return in capital markets that are assumed to be free and efficient. But Barber and Ghilarducci argue that this approach fails to recognize fund participants' whole identities as workers needing employment, citizens of communities, and parents concerned with their children's future as well as their own.

As a result, pension fund managers and regulators have not taken account of how the allocation of pension funds affects employment, community development, and long-term investment. Indeed, pension funds were major financiers of the 1980s merger movement and other speculative excesses in those years.

Barber and Ghilarducci also point to a second underrepresented "principal" in pension fund allocational decisions—the U.S. taxpayer. As tax-exempt savings vehicles, pension funds are in large part creations of the tax code. In 1992 alone, the funds' tax-exempt status was worth $51 billion in foregone revenue for the U.S. Treasury, making it among the largest tax expenditures in the federal code. Because of this status, it is reasonable to expect that pension fund investments support economic policy goals beyond simply the narrow pursuit of maximizing quarterly returns.

To increase both the "life-cycle" concerns of pension fund contributors and the public-purpose aims of the funds, a movement developed in the late 1970s and early 1980s for pension funds to pursue "economically targeted investments." Barber and Ghilarducci survey the development and current status of this movement. They recognize that the initial conception of targeted investments was flawed and that mistakes were made in its early implementation. Nevertheless, they argue that substantial advances have been achieved over the past decade, both analytically and in practice, such that economically targeted investment strategies can now be effectively used by pension funds to promote employment, community, and productivity-enhancing activities. More generally, Barber and Ghilarducci offer a series of proposals, consistent with those of Crotty and Goldstein, to encourage the productive deployment of pension funds.

The Crotty/Goldstein and Barber/Ghilarducci chapters, as well as discussions in previous sections of the book, make clear the need for an economy-wide approach for addressing the problems of persistent financial instability, bias toward short-term speculative investments, and the present inadequate forms of accountability within financial markets. Outlining a broad-gauged policy framework is the theme of Robert Pollin's chapter, which concludes the volume.

Pollin advances a comprehensive restructuring program for the Federal Reserve System, giving it broad authority in the area of credit allocation. In addition, Pollin argues that the proposal offers a vehicle for addressing two somewhat separate, but equally serious, questions. The first is the need to undertake two long-term processes of industrial conversion—out of military production on the one hand and into environmentally benign production techniques on the other. The second is to confront the persistent downward wage pressures resulting from the globalization of U.S. labor and financial markets.

The specific features of Pollin's restructuring proposal are drawn entirely from programs that have been used or at least seriously considered by the U.S. or other market economies. The first major proposal, mentioned earlier, is to increase democratic accountability within the Federal Reserve through direct election of the directors of the 12 Federal Reserve district banks. The second is to increase the role of discount-window reserve creation relative to open market operations. This will give district banks more direct regulatory authority over the lending activities of private intermediaries, enabling them to promote financial stability and the productive uses of funds. It will also redistribute downward Federal Reserve decisionmaking power, creating more effective channels for accountability. The third suggestion is to establish differential asset reserve requirements for all U.S. intermediaries. Preferred uses of credit, such as loans for productivity-enhancing equipment or environmentally benign technologies, will thus become significantly less costly than nonpreferred uses of funds, such as mergers and takeovers.

Pollin addresses the practicality of these proposals in terms of historical experiences with government credit allocation policies, in the United States and elsewhere. In particular, he derives important lessons both from the U.S. experience with such policies as those that have supported single-family housing since the 1930s and from Japan, France, and South Korea, where credit allocation policies were central levers within an overall development strategy.

Pollin argues that, working within the existing Federal Reserve structure, credit allocation policies would be both feasible and effective at promoting financial stability, domestic productive investment, and democratic accountability. Moreover, they would place minimal demands on the federal budget while maintaining substantial flexibility for the private sector in financial markets.

Conclusion

We realize, of course, that whether the Pollin proposal or any of the others in the volume is feasible may have little to do with its success in receiving a serious hearing. Throughout the volume, we take pains to develop a concrete policy agenda flowing from a well-specified analysis of how the current-day U.S. financial markets actually operate. But we know that both our analyses and our proposals are at sharp variance with predominant viewpoints on current economic questions.

Along with prevailing opinion, we recognize that markets are necessary and often enormously effective modes of economic organization. But our reading of history, and certainly the experiences of the past 15 years, also inform us that markets produce unfair, damaging, and irrational outcomes when left on their own. In particular, we reject the idea that a deregulated U.S. financial market is capable of functioning to the benefit of the majority.

Governments, of course, are just as capable as markets of harmful and irrational practices. Yet governments can also perform important economic tasks well if their purposes are nurtured by well-informed and mobilized political institutions. The U.S. government, in particular, has the capacity to influence the broad directions of our financial market far more effectively than the invisible hand if it operates as the organized expression of the democratic will rather than the captured mouthpiece of the wealthy and well connected. That is why we are careful in this volume to specify not only the technical features of our restructuring program but also the democratic mechanisms through which our proposals would be executed.

The fact that our proposals represent a dramatic departure from the status quo is of course deliberate. The status quo that we contemplate in the following pages includes interest rates that have been sustained at a higher level than at any time in U.S. history; a financial market that spectacularly rewards speculation while neglecting productive investments; an outmoded system of public protections and regulations that finances, among other things, an indulgent safety net for S&L operators; and a maldistribution of wealth and opportunity reinforced by the allocational biases of banks, pension funds, and other financial institutions. We see little in this situation that encourages complacency. To disturb the complacency of the status quo's defenders is, unambiguously, one aim of this volume. But, more ambitiously, we also hope to provide both a beam of clarity for the dissatisfied but confused and a usable instrument for those already committed to greater equality and efficiency in our economic system.

Note

1. The banking industry and interest rate data are drawn from Pollin and Dymski (1993).

Bibliography

Keynes, John Maynard (1963), *Essays in Persuasion*, New York: W. W. Norton.
Pollin, Robert and Gary Dymski (1993), "The Costs and Benefits of Financial Instability: Big Government Capitalism and the Minsky Paradox," in Dymski and Pollin eds., *New Perspectives in Monetary Macroeconomics: Explorations in the Tradition of Hyman P. Minsky*, Ann Arbor, MI: University of Michigan Press.

PART I
Monetary Policy and Interest Rates

CHAPTER TWO

The Federal Reserve under Clinton[1]

JAMES K. GALBRAITH

CHAPTER SUMMARY

The recession that began in 1990 and the failure of interest rate cuts to generate a strong recovery by the end of 1992 ought to trigger a new movement for change at the Federal Reserve. This chapter describes the failure of the Volcker-Greenspan monetary regime and makes the case for comprehensive reform.

Introduction

Monetary policy has remained outside politics in recent years, as critics of the Reagan-Bush economic policies focused on deficits in budgets and trade. But the recession was triggered largely by tight money from 1987 to 1990, and from 1991 to 1992, the Federal Reserve assumed the main responsibility for bringing on a recovery, by lowering interest rates.

In this task, the Federal Reserve faced major obstacles. Past accumulations of debt blocked demand for new loans, as did an enormous excess capacity in commercial office space and residential housing. But also, interest rate cuts came too late, were too gradual, and were too easily reversed with every uptick in economic statistics. As a result, the Federal Reserve—having spent a decade fixated on the disappearing threat of inflation—never gained credibility as an agent of economic growth. Short-term interest rates fell, but long-term and real interest rates remained high, and a strong credit-based recovery did not take hold. The recovery that did occur was slow, uncertain, and anemic, and it did not achieve at least one of its ostensible objectives, that of placing President Bush's reelection beyond challenge.

To dwell on this point, however, is to miss an even more serious one. Politically motivated or not, Greenspan's policy from 1989 onward was a fundamental departure from the rulebook that was supposed to have been established for monetary policy 10 years before. It was the final, final end of the Volcker era, the final failure of the conservative monetary policy dream, and it ought to open a new debate over what has been since 1979 a politically closed subject.

To recall: in October 1979, the Federal Reserve's then chairman Paul Volcker imposed anti-inflation shock therapy: supertight money and super-high interest rates. That "October surprise," even more than the other one, ruined the Democratic Party. It contributed to President Jimmy Carter's re-election defeat and set the stage both for the deep recession of 1981 to 1982 and for the strong, noninflationary but debt-ridden recovery that carried Ronald Reagan to reelection triumph in 1984.

Although Volcker's actions had clear political consequences, he was never accused of a political motivation. On the contrary, even his sharpest critics gave him credit for a deeper purpose, based in part on the advanced academic economics of that time. This was to use a temporary bout of very tight money not only to cut the rate of inflation but also to change the image of the Federal Reserve, to establish once and for all that inflation would not be tolerated, and so to drive inflation expectations out of the system. With inflation expectations tamed, the theory went, sustained growth without renewed inflation would again be possible, and the pain would be justified by benefits over the long run.[2]

As late as 1986 or 1987, one might have believed that Volcker had succeeded. Inflation did fall, and even with recovery stayed below half its former peak. U.S. economic performance was good, especially in international perspective. The United States had apparently reconciled real economic growth rates between 3 and 4 percent per year, with stable inflation of about the same amount. We had also reduced unemployment from 10 to 6 percent, creating 13 million new jobs (by 1987). Eventually the expansion became the longest on the postwar record.

But could it continue? Had inflation truly been driven out of the system? Or were the gains merely temporary, provisional, an interim of stability at the price of chaos later on? The conservative theory held that permanent stability had been reached. Today we know better. Volcker's expansion could continue only so long as the government chose to tolerate what had quickly become an overvalued dollar and then an unsustainable deficit in the balance of trade. When the dollar came down, consumer price inflation gradually edged up, reaching 6.1 percent in 1990 (with help from Iraq's Saddam Hussein). Greenspan's monetary policy reacted to this rising inflation in the old style, with tight money and high interest rates leading inexorably to recession. It thus abandoned, in deed though not in word, the pretext that the Volcker formula had been successful.

In reality, then, the gains from Volcker's war on inflation were not once and for all. Rather, the battle must be waged again and again, over the same scarred terrain of unemployment, human misery, industrial dislocation, and social decay. Greenspan's recovery—if it came—would be from Greenspan's own recession, and the only prospect it holds out is for yet another recession later on. It is perhaps time to ask whether we need new tactics, some new weapons, and also some new generals with which to fight this war.

The Deficit and Monetary Politics

Of course, throughout the 1980s, many people believed that economic policy was on the road to ruin. But attention focused mainly on the budget deficit and not on the Federal Reserve. In this view, the Federal Reserve was mainly an innocent bystander; the real villains were big spenders and antitaxers who together tolerated deepening budget imbalance. Investment bankers, politicians, foreign central bankers, business journalists, and some professional economists formed a Greek chorus on the irresponsibility of it all. They insisted that the prosperity was merely borrowed, and they warned sternly that cutting "entitlements"—a code word for Social Security—or raising taxes would be necessary to avoid national financial ruin.

This argument virtually exempted the Federal Reserve from responsibility for any eventual debacle. It also overlooked two facts: that interest on the public debt, an item not insensitive to high interest rates, was the fastest-growing element of public expenditure and that tight monetary policy constricted both private incomes and tax collections. Given these facts, it is not surprising that the deficit diversion drew support from Volcker himself, for whom it could serve as a scapegoat if (more likely, when) things went wrong.

The budget deficit was also associated with another, and more important, phenomenon: rapid economic globalization. With rising trade in manufactured goods, a flood of imports rolled in after 1983. It was easy to correlate deficits in budgets and trade, but to do so was fundamentally misleading. The "twin deficits" argument, of which Volcker was especially fond, ignored the role of tight money in generating a higher dollar and the conditions for a huge trade deficit from 1980 forward—even before the tax cuts and economic expansion of the middle 1980s. It also both underplayed the structural role of the trade deficit and misstated the appropriate cure.

It was globalization, prompted in part by the extraordinary tightness of monetary policy, that really delayed inflation during the 1980s expansion. Cheap foreign labor costs in low-technology industries split apart the wage structure. Cost competition held down wage increases in vulnerable industries, in particular labor- and materials-intensive sectors, from textiles to cars. At the same time, the high dollar killed export markets in more advanced sectors, holding down wage increases in industries such as aerospace and communications that would ordinarily have little trouble competing.

The effect was to substitute a large trade deficit and rising international debt for rising inflation. In the policy arena, trade issues tended to crowd out discussion of inflation. Yet, it remained true that when policy finally moved to reduce the trade deficit, with progressive dollar depreciation after 1985, a rising rate of inflation would eventually follow so long as the economy were to be allowed room to grow.

Paul Volcker seems to have suspected that his miracle was unsustainable when he resigned in the summer of 1987, as I wrote then, "in the nick of time." Thus it was that Alan Greenspan, the man who wanted in the worst way to be a central banker, got his wish. Since the economy at the moment of his appointment was not yet in crisis, he could hardly have called for a state of emergency and the draconian measures on which central bankers build their legends. Nor could Greenspan hope to sustain a noninflationary expansion through the whole of his term in office. Once policy set out to reduce the trade deficit, Greenspan's only choice was between a recession before an inflation crisis, or after.

Greenspan's Choice

Greenspan chose to slow the economy, raising interest rates and tightening money to hold inflation in check. Already in 1989, real economic growth was less than the growth of population, and the economy was stagnant. By mid-1990, stagnation had turned into recession, and by late 1991, hopes for recovery, once quite strong, had actually faded. They did not return until heroic end-of-year cuts in interest rates brought them back in the spring of 1992—only to fade again by summer. There would be no inflation crisis for one simple reason: the fire fighters flooded the house before the fire began. Meanwhile, the trade balance had, of course, improved, even though the structural deterioration of manufacturing continued, virtually ensuring that trade deficits would be even worse when recovery finally got under way.

Thus the 1990–92 recession punctured the myth—the Reagan-Volcker myth— that sustained stable growth without inflation can be achieved by the magic of monetary policy alongside laissez-faire in all other domains. If the recovery does take hold, then either a collapsing dollar and rising prices or a rising dollar and rising trade deficit are expected. And neither can be tolerated for long.

As the Federal Reserve sought recovery in 1991 and 1992, short-term interest rates were cut repeatedly. But the spread between short- and long-term rates, nearly the highest in memory, tells us that the financial markets did not believe in the recession "cure." Rather, the markets appeared to be convinced that short-term interest rates would go up again once the beginnings of recovery were established—or, perhaps, merely after the presidential election in 1992.

Is this the only way to live? Is there no way to keep this grim cycle from repeating? Might we not prefer a monetary strategy that is less disruptive, that destroys fewer lives and livelihoods, that maintains a higher average standard of living? Couldn't we now be prepared to talk about serious reform in this area?

Projects for Reform: Straitjackets or Democratic Accountability?

Monetary reformers on both the left and the right call for stable growth fueled by low real interest rates. They often argue that institutional reform of the role and structure of the Federal Reserve is a necessary means to this end.

Monetarist economists, led at least spiritually by Milton Friedman, continue to argue that the road to monetary stability requires placing the Federal Reserve on automatic pilot. They claim that a fixed rule to dictate the rate of money growth is required. But with technical monetarism in more disarray than usual (over, as ever, how best to define the concept of money), this idea has now gone somewhat out of fashion.

In its place, we now have proposals to give the Federal Reserve a clear and single-minded mandate to seek a zero-inflation outcome. These proposals are rooted in the New Classical economics that has displaced monetarism in academic life. They have strong support from Federal Reserve Governor Wayne Angell and even a perfunctory endorsement from Chairman Greenspan.

A zero-inflation mandate would free the Federal Reserve from obligations even of lip service to the goals of full employment and full production contained in the Humphrey-Hawkins Act of 1978. Since there is no way for zero inflation to be achieved except by putting the economy through the wringer, it is a prescription for a return to the shock therapies of 1979–1981, with a vengeance. A new recession would, with luck, eliminate the remaining market power of workers—labor markets would be made truly competitive by the simple device of crippling the industries that are presently competitive, in the other sense, on world markets. Meanwhile, construction and other cyclical workers would lie idle, and those in open competition with Third World products would see their wages fall even more. And as inflation rates fell while interest rates rose, business bankruptcies, mortgage foreclosures, and bank failures would rise. It is easy to see why the call for a zero-inflation policy remains hypothetical and why even Alan Greenspan has refrained from issuing an enthusiastic endorsement.

Progressives and populists, from the money radicals of the late-19th century to Wright Patman to latter-day populists like William Greider, have coupled calls for easy money and low interest rates with demand for a more democratic and politically accountable central bank. They make this link for the plausible reason that the structure of the Federal Reserve system presently reflects the power of creditors who prefer "sound" money and slow growth to any risk of inflation or increased bargaining power on the part of workers. This, of course, reflects compromises that were made at the very beginning of the Federal Reserve in 1914.

There are really two separate ideas on the left. One is to rationalize the process of monetary policymaking by making it more responsive to, and better coordinated with, the other economic policies of the executive branch. The other is to make monetary policy more open and accountable to the people, in part by improving oversight procedures in Congress and in part simply by making monetary policymaking more transparent.

Lowercase "d" democrats can find plenty of flaws in the Federal Reserve's structure. The composition of its principal decisionmaking body, the Federal Open Market Committee (FOMC), is probably unconstitutional, since the five regional Federal Reserve bank presidents who rotate on and off this committee are not "officers of the United States" under the appointments clause of the constitution. The Federal Reserve's own budget remains uniquely immune from congressional appropriations. Rather, the Federal Reserve "earns" its budget as interest on the portfolio of national debt it holds, subtracts what it needs for its own purposes, and returns the remainder as "surplus" to the Treasury. Or again, the FOMC and the Board of Governors are unusually shielded from normal federal sunlight requirements.

Fixing these defects would on many grounds be a good thing. But the question must be, What difference would it make for policy? Some reformers have championed the subordination of the Federal Reserve to the Department of the Treasury. The administrative structure of such proposals varies from placing a Treasury representative on the Board (the secretary of the Treasury once sat there ex officio) to moving the whole institution into the executive branch. The argument for this is that an "integrated" central bank would tend to pursue an easier policy, accepting higher inflation on average and achieving a lower rate of unemployment.

But is there a divergence of interest or a failure of policy coordination between the Federal Reserve Board, or the FOMC, and the Administration?

At best the answer is not clear. For Republican administrations, as well as for financially orthodox Democrats (of whom there are many), there may be no fundamental conflict between Federal Reserve policy and Administration desires. On the contrary, the nominal independence of the Federal Reserve is often a political convenience. It enables the president to pretend both to insulate himself from the fallout of tight policies and to espouse an easier monetary policy than he favors in fact.

Putting the Federal Reserve under the Treasury would have the main merit of ensuring that monetary policy changes course when an administration changes hands. It would force an austerity-minded administration to invent another bogey (for a model, see the role now played by the German Bundesbank in, say, France or Britain). On the other hand, it is doubtful that the independence of the Federal Reserve has fooled voters; they remain resolutely willing to punish an incumbent administration for stagnation (1970, 1974, 1980, 1982, and 1992) and to reward it for growth (1964, 1972, and 1984). Republican presidents know this (Democrats have been known to forget) and, therefore, generally do not allow the Federal Reserve to escape from partisan control. Changing Federal Reserve policy, in other words, is distinct from and more important than changing the perceived locus of control.

Proposals to make the Federal Reserve more accountable to Congress reflect a slightly different argument, namely, that sometimes there are strong reasons the institutional interests of the Federal Reserve and the executive branch differ from those of Congress. Congress, compared with the executive branch, is a stable institution that likes a stable economy. Representatives make a career of their job; they face their constituents every weekend and their voters every two years. They therefore do not like recessions, and especially not off-year recessions geared to producing reelection booms two years ahead. To the Congress, there are no off-year elections.

Increasing Federal Reserve exposure to the Congress thus has the practical effect of turning up the volume of congressional criticism of the Federal Reserve during recession years. This criticism generally has a stabilizing influence on policy. Increased congressional oversight was the purpose of a series of actions beginning in 1975 and continuing through the Federal Reserve Act amendments in the Humphrey-Hawkins Act (1978). In that case, and not by accident, Congress framed regular reporting requirements to encourage a more stable demand policy. The design of the oversight was flawed and the implementation weak, but the intent did reflect a true congressional desire for stability that actual Federal Reserve policy has not displayed.

Today, the single most useful reform on behalf of congressional accountability would require immediate public announcement of all FOMC directives, which make monetary policy. The practical effect of these directives is almost always largely transparent to the markets, and their concealment has only one real purpose—to blunt their impact as news and therefore their vulnerability to criticism from the public and Congress. The present practice of releasing an old directive only after a new one has replaced it kills the news value of the FOMC's decisions and makes it all but impossible for Congress to make monetary policy a subject of current policy debate. Milton Friedman himself long ago suggested the proper procedure: to make and implement the Open Market decision on Friday, releasing the directive itself to the media on Monday morning.

Even so, the generic difficulty with congressional oversight of monetary policy would remain, which is that it offers little political mileage and at least some political risks for members of Congress. Someone has to care enough to ask the questions. Representative Henry Reuss, chairman of the House Banking Committee until 1981, was such a person, but monetary oversight in the House has since fallen on hard times. In the Senate, oversight has suffered from the departure of Senator William Proxmire.

The more tractable structural issue therefore may be not whether the Federal Reserve system can be brought under the control of the Treasury and Congress, but whether it can be more effectively detached from the present institutional influences of the largest banks. These influences are now built into the system and account in part for important policy results, among them the fact that the extraordinary fall in bank deposit rates in 1991–92 was not accompanied by a parallel decline in lending rates.

A reform package could do worse than to work to remove the influences behind such outcomes. For example, Congress could pass the Hamilton-Sarbanes proposal to remove the five banker-influenced regional Federal Reserve bank presidents from their voting role on the Open Market Committee. (The regional presidents often take strongly conservative ideological positions. Rumor has it that the Federal Reserve Board in Washington would not be unhappy to see them go.) To achieve true regionalism without the present nominal private bank ownership of the regional Federal Reserve banks, the boards of directors of those regional Federal Reserve banks, which now include local bankers by statute, could be reconstituted as state government appointments. The budget of the whole system should be brought into the federal budget.

These actions would abolish the visible symbols of private affiliation that the system now has. They might make it easier to pursue fundamental reforms of the way that deposit insurance, regulation, and lender-of-last-resort functions now work, so that the necessary business of supporting the banking system is not hostage to the fate of particular private banks. Such fundamental reforms will become urgent, it might be noted, if, as seems possible, a comprehensive policy of flattening the yield curve reveals that some large banks were actually being kept afloat by the tenuous, and untenable, lifeline of that very spread between longer and shorter rates.

It should be clear, though, that institutional changes in the Federal Reserve are at best necessary but not sufficient. Under a progressive administration committed to high growth and structural reform, subordination of a hostile Federal Reserve Board would be essential. But what does a high-growth path require of monetary policy?

Sustaining Low Interest Rates

Nobody doubts anymore that the Federal Reserve does control short-term interest rates. Long-term rates are another story, and without lower interest rates across the spectrum, even Alan Greenspan's best efforts of 1992 remained only partly effective. Low short-term rates are effective especially in lowering the dollar and relieving business debt burdens. But only low long-term rates can unleash the kind of capital spending essential to a major rebuilding of America's manufacturing capacity and infrastructure.

The key problem is evidently not the present budget deficit, which crowds out nothing in a recession and is financed anyway at least as much in short-term markets as in long—which fact did not prevent short-term interest rates from falling. Nor is it plausibly future deficits, since future deficits do decline with economic growth and since the fall in those anticipated deficits over the expansion of the mid-1980s failed to reduce long-term interest rates. Nor can it be a fear of inflation. If it were true that a serious fear of future rates of 6 or 7 or 8 percent inflation underlay long-term interest rates at present, the real interest rate would be low, not high, and the high nominal long-term rates would not pose the obstacle to renewed investment that they evidently do.

Rather, the key problem appears to be that old conservative bugbear, policy credibility. If long-term lenders believed, as they evidently have not believed, that short-term rates were going to stay down—so that a series of short-term borrowings could plausibly substitute for a single long bond issue—then long-term rates would have to come down. Arbitrage and the operation of efficient financial markets would certainly achieve this result in theory. The question is how to achieve the precondition in practice.

Part of the answer is that Alan Greenspan could not achieve it. For long rates to come down, investors must believe that short rates will stay down. But this belief is something that a right-wing, antigrowth, rentier-dominated, "stagnationist" board cannot deliver—not to mention one with a reputation for being easily panicked into raising interest rates to defend the dollar. Only a new administration, in explicit alliance with a new Federal Reserve Board, can make the credible precommitment to sustained low short-term interest rates and appropriate fiscal policies that a climate of low long-term interest rates will require.

Such an alliance, made explicitly as part of a broader package of economic policy reforms, is therefore the essential first step. Once the alliance is in place, policy can then take certain additional steps to reinforce its resolve. For instance, the Treasury could suspend the issue of long-maturity bonds pending an interest rate drop, as recommended by Professor James Tobin and others. And the Federal Reserve could act to buy back long bonds in the open market, thus raising their price and reducing their yield.[3]

There may be a second reason, going beyond ideology and macroeconomics, why the Federal Reserve has been unable or unwilling to deliver a flatter yield curve. This is the effect of the steep yield curve on bank profits. It may well be that the rise in bank profitability in the second and third quarters of 1992 stemmed largely from the increased spread between short-term deposit rates and the high rates that banks could continue to earn on loans and investments in long-term government bonds. To the extent that the financial viability of key banks may have actually depended on this spread, policy may have become, in effect, hostage to it. And if this is true, then measures to deliver low interest rates across the spectrum of yields may require, as a precondition, alternative measures in order to reform and stabilize the banking sector.

With an across-the-spectrum fall in interest rates, demand for bank lending for long-term capital investment would presumably revive. Such lending was virtually absent on net in the 1980s, as nonfinancial businesses relied almost entirely on retained earnings for their investments, and bank lending went off instead into mergers, acquisitions, and real estate speculation.[4] If banks could be persuaded to meet this demand—another uncertainty that will perhaps require its own policy attention—then a capital investment boom would follow.

In most respects, a capital investment boom would be a very good thing.

Alongside new public investment, the nation needs affordable houses and an accelerated renewal of its industrial capital stock. In recent years, the construction sector has substantially downsized; apartment construction, in particular, is down by nearly half. Construction equipment, farm equipment, and machinery manufacturing of all kinds took a vicious beating in the early 1980s. A good capital boom (though it might have to rely on imports at first) might help to restore these sectors, particularly if policy directed the new construction at many of the regions not overbuilt in the various regional construction binges of the 1980s.

A low-interest-rate policy would also have progressive distributive effects. The middle classes would benefit mightily from a reduction in interest on their consumer and mortgage debts. But the biggest and most systematic gainer from a low-interest-rate policy would be the government itself and, therefore, the taxpayer. Low interest rates and capital investment boom would cut government expenditure and raise revenue. Every macroeconomic model verifies that lower interest rates would powerfully rectify the financial problems of the government. (Indeed, artificially projecting lower future interest rates has been for years a favorite trick of budgeteers who wished to disguise the size of future deficits.)

Yet there are risks. The main one is that a simple credit boom is inherently unstable. Those who fear that the low-rate environment will not last may borrow in advance of their own needs, in the hope of capitalizing on a subsequent rise in interest rates. These speculative movements in credit demand, which tend to grow if expectations of a rate rise increase, can put immense strain on a low-rate policy.

For this reason, a sustained low-interest-rate policy presupposes renewed regulatory safeguards on credit flows in order to discourage speculative moves against the policy itself. Even quick examination of sustained low-interest policies in other countries, such as Japan and France from the 1950s through the 1970s, reveals that such quantity safeguards, whether in the form of light-handed "guidance" from the central bank to the commercial banking system in Japan or the strict quantitative limits on new lending of the French, were almost always in effect. Without such regulation, the ability of a low-interest policy to withstand speculation is doubtful.

Conservatives are aware of all this, which explains their opposition to a low-interest-rate policy. To the extent that American financial politics, and particularly the Republican Party, remain dominated by a rentier class, enriched under Reagan and Bush and protective of the sources of its wealth (of which clipping coupons is a major part and speculating on asset prices not a small one), then getting to a stable, low, short-rate policy will not be easy. To the extent that these forces remain a potent opposition under a progressive administration (and especially so long as they retain control at the Federal Reserve itself), maintaining a drive toward low interest rates will not be easy either.

But assuming that political obstacles and speculation can be overcome, a more progressive government must also be prepared to meet by other means the main economic contingencies that might cause its low-interest-rate policy to be abandoned. Chief among these, once again, is the eventual return of inflation.

Inflation is not an immediate risk. Excess capacity, foreign imports, and the generally cowed character of the labor markets will keep inflation at bay. But it is likely that the move toward sustained low interest rates will trigger dollar devaluation, thus raising import prices in advanced product lines (those imported from industrial countries against whose currencies the dollar would fall) and strengthening the bargaining hand of the strongest elements of American labor. Asset and commodity prices would also tend to rise. Over three to five years, it is likely that a low-interest policy would accelerate modestly the rise in inflation that had already been under way in the late 1980s.

Granted, some inflation can be tolerated, and some occurs as the result of external shocks that cannot always be avoided. But some inflation risks—two in particular—can and must be managed. These are (1) cost-push inflation resulting from higher growth and the spillover of wage increases from high- to low-productivity-growth sectors and (2) the spillover from asset-market speculation into the prices of currently produced goods. Dealing with these risks could require measures of credit regulation and an incomes policy—a return, in short, to the unpleasant politics of inflation control. Since the record of U.S. authorities in these matters is not good, a measure of imagination in the design of a new incomes policy and a new and effective social contract will be essential.

There is time for a fuller discussion of these issues. But the raising of this disagreeable topic illustrates a broader point, which is that the low-interest-rate agenda presented here for the Federal Reserve cannot be sustained on its own. It must be embedded in a larger project—a comprehensive project—of progressive reform.

Comprehensive Progressive Reform

Comprehensive progressive reform is consistent with much of the low-interest-rate and democracy/accountability programs, but it goes far beyond them. It demands not only a reconsideration of the Federal Reserve's structure and responsibilities but also a systematic integration of international and domestic economic policies.

The larger program for sustained growth cannot be discussed here.[5] It begins with an immediate emergency recovery program based on capital grants to states and localities and perhaps tax relief. It continues with an export growth and public investment strategy to sustain growth and competitiveness over the long term. It must, as noted earlier, include the design of new policies to stabilize growth, to reduce inequality, and to bring the fiscal position of the federal government into better balance as the economy grows. Taken together, the hope is to reconcile three economic objectives that have been in increasing conflict for 20 years: high growth, balanced trade, and reasonably stable prices.

Once the broad strategy has been defined, the role of monetary policy virtually follows. The Federal Reserve must establish the credibility of a sustained program of low and stable interest rates. It must commit to the competitiveness of the dollar and so support both private investment and export demand. And it must return to the business of restoring order and discipline to the financial system, especially tending, through means other than the yield curve, to the stability of the banks.

Above all, the Federal Reserve must cooperate with the Administration. It cannot continue to arrogate to itself, as it has for 13 years, sole and independent responsibility for fighting inflation. Nor can the Administration afford to cede this responsibility to the Federal Reserve. A program of comprehensive economic reforms will not work unless the Federal Reserve cooperates by keeping interest rates low. A low-interest-rate policy can be sustained only when other policies for growth and financial stability are in place. In a program of comprehensive progressive reform, the Federal Reserve had better accustom itself to playing on the team.

Notes

1. An earlier version of this article appeared as "Monetary Policy: The Federal Reserve." In Mark Green, ed., *Changing America: Blueprints for a New Administration,* 1992, and *The American Prospect*, Summer 1992.

2. Volcker's 1979 actions were precipitated by warnings that international capital was about to dump the dollar. They were presented and defended, however, as an anti-inflationary regime shift.

3. The idea here is not "Operation Twist," which raised short-term rates and lowered long rates simultaneously. Rather, it is to proceed with open-market purchases across the spectrum of maturities—an antidepression measure recommended in the 1930s by Keynes.

4. See the chapter by Robert Pollin in this volume.

5. See, for example, James K. Galbraith and Michael Mandler, "Economic Overview." In Mark Green, ed., *Changing America: Blueprints for a New Administration*, 1992.

Bibliography

Galbraith, James K. and Michael Mandler. "Economic Overview." In Mark Green, ed., *Changing America: Blueprints for a New Administration*. New York: New Market Press, 1992.

CHAPTER THREE

Monetary Policy, Financial Structure, and Investment[1]

Steven M. Fazzari

CHAPTER SUMMARY

Analysts from all parts of the political spectrum see capital investment as central to current policy debates. Because of the many links between investment and financial markets, a complete discussion of monetary and financial policy options must address the impact of policy on investment.

Monetary policy is widely believed to have an important influence on the course of macroeconomic fluctuations. The research presented here makes clear that investment cannot be divorced from the state of the economy. Lower sales reduce the need to expand capacity. A weak economy lowers profits, reducing firms' internal means of financing investment. Tighter lending requirements that emerge as profits and sales fall (the recent "credit crunch," for example) also limit investment. These channels must be taken into account in assessing the impact of monetary decisions.

Although these macroeconomic effects are very strong empirically, interest rates constitute the primary link between money and investment in most accounts. That is, changes in the money supply affect investment because they change interest rates. Yet, measuring the sensitivity of investment to interest rates has been the subject of years of controversy in the empirical literature. It is by no means obvious that interest rates play a particularly significant role in explaining fluctuations of investment. Indeed, the empirical study presented here fails to find a reliable impact of interest rates on investment spending.

Recent research, however, has resurrected earlier ideas that the availability of finance, either through firms' internal cash flow or from external debt, plays a fundamental role in determining the course of private investment. These "finance effects" on investment are separate from the traditional interest-rate/cost-of-capital channel, and they are possibly more potent. The effects of monetary policy on the *cost* of credit may not be particularly important for investment, but the effect of monetary policy and, more broadly, the institutional structure of the financial system may be

35

significant for the *availability* of credit. Therefore, if one focuses on interest rates alone, one could underestimate the importance of monetary policy for investment.

More concretely, one consequence of using tight monetary policy to fight inflation may be weak investment, not necessarily because tight money raises interest rates but because of its macroeconomic impact on firms' profits, cash flow, and credit availability. In addition, the research presented here applies to policies that affect the financial structure of firms. For example, the leveraged-buyout wave raised debt and substantially weakened balance sheets. The affected firms will be less able to maintain investment and innovative activity in a downturn, hurting productivity and inhibiting economic recovery. Therefore, we must look hard at policies that encourage debt (the tax deductibility of interest, for example). A high debt environment is less likely to provide the stable financial base necessary for capital expansion.

Finally, the new view of the investment-finance interaction implies that all firms and all investment projects are not equally affected by financial conditions. Mature firms may be able to replace internal funds or bank credit with some other form of funding during a monetary tightening. These substitution possibilities may not be available to firms in new, growth industries. Evidence presented here supports the conclusion that tight credit conditions are likely to disproportionately affect smaller, fast-growing firms in new, relatively high technology industries. The result is that monetary policy could have an inadvertent impact on the allocation of investment, not simply on its level.

Introduction: Some Broad Themes

Investment is central to modern discussions of monetary policy for at least two reasons. First, investment provides a means by which money affects demand. If the state of aggregate demand matters for fluctuations in output, then the money-investment-demand relationship explains one channel through which monetary policy affects the course of the business cycle. Second, over a longer horizon, capital investment is a significant determinant of labor productivity, wages, and the standard of living of the population. To the extent that monetary policy influences investment, it will affect the capital stock and the performance of the economy over a long horizon.

This chapter critically examines the theoretical and empirical foundations for the link between monetary policy and capital investment. In most accounts, the components of the cost of capital, interest rates in particular, constitute the primary link between money and investment. That is, changes in the money supply affect investment because they change interest rates. Yet, measuring the sensitivity of investment to interest rates has been the subject of years of controversy in the empirical literature. It is by no means obvious that interest rates play a particularly significant role in explaining fluctuations of investment. Examining the existing empirical work leads to mixed conclusions. If investment is not much affected by interest rates, then the mechanism by which monetary policy matters for investment, if it matters at all, comes into question.

Indeed, the empirical work presented here fails to find a reliable impact of interest rates on investment spending. But this observation does not necessarily mean that monetary policy, and the structure of the financial system more broadly, is not important for investment. Recent research has resurrected older ideas in the literature, relating investment to different channels through which monetary policy and financial structure may operate. Investment may not be sensitive to the market *cost* of finance (the interest rate), but policy may ultimately affect the *quantity* of finance that firms can obtain and therefore may influence investment.

The distinction between the cost and quantity of finance becomes important if capital markets are not "perfect." In a perfect capital market, in which the interest rate equates the supply and demand for funds, it does not make much difference to investing firms whether they finance their projects internally (implicitly causing their owners to forgo the opportunity cost[2] of internal funds) or whether they borrow to finance investment at market interest rates. A large number of modern empirical studies, however, reject the common assumption that capital markets are perfect. These results imply that firms cannot obtain external funds on the same terms as the opportunity cost they face for internal finance. The wedge that seems to exist between the cost of internal versus external funds may be an important channel through which monetary policy affects investment. These "finance effects" on investment are logically and empirically separate from the traditional interest-rate/cost-of-capital channel discussed earlier, and they are potentially more potent.

More specifically, suppose that banks or other providers of investment finance ration credit by controlling the quantity of credit that they provide for borrowers rather than simply by adjusting the interest rate on loans in response to changes in supply and demand. Monetary policy can affect the cost of lending for these institutions and the *quantity* of credit they offer. But the interest rate on investment loans to firms—the effective *price* of credit—need not change in response to changes in monetary policy, even though centralized money market rates move. Therefore, if one focuses on interest rates alone, one can underestimate the importance of monetary policy for investment. The following considers the impact of these results in the literature for the money-investment link, along with some new empirical evidence on the relative importance of interest rates and the availability of finance.

Finance effects on investment lead to broader implications for the investment-monetary link. Much recent research identifies a strong impact of firms' internal cash flow on their capital spending, presumably because internal finance provides a less risky and lower-cost source of finance and because firms must pay a premium in the market for external credit. Internal cash flow, of course, correlates closely with profits. To the extent that monetary policy effectively limits downside variation in the economy, it will help sustain profits and internal finance with positive effects on investment. Conversely, one of the consequences of using tight monetary policy to fight inflation may be weak investment, not necessarily because tight money raises interest rates but because of tight money's indirect macroeconomic impact on profits and cash flow. Again, an exclusive focus on the interest rate channel for monetary effects on investment may understate the true importance of money for capital accumulation.

The broader perspective about the determination of investment emphasized here extends to another major concern of this volume: the institutional structure of the financial system. In a world of perfect capital markets, financial intermediaries (such as banks) simply suck up funds from savers and distribute them to borrowers. They may enhance allocational efficiency by centralizing the intermediation process and reducing transaction costs, in contrast to a system in which savers and borrowers deal with each other directly; but this is a secondary consideration in perfect capital markets. If the costs of external finance are well above the opportunity costs of internal funds, however, the financial intermediation process plays a fundamental role in determining the level and distribution of credit. Effective intermediation gives firms access to investment funds that they could not obtain in impersonal, centralized credit markets. Banks and related institutions *are* special. Their effective operation attenuates constraints on external investment finance and therefore supports investment and the health of the economy. This point is often ignored in discussion of financial restructuring. Its relevance for current policy debates will be developed here.

Finally, the new view of the investment-finance interaction implies that all firms and all investment projects are not equally affected by financial conditions. Mature firms with well-established credit records and well-known investment prospects may be able to replace internal funds or bank credit with some other form of funding during a monetary tightening. These substitution possibilities may not be available to firms in new, growth industries in which prospects are not as well understood by providers of investment finance. The result is that monetary policy could have an inadvertent impact on the allocation of investment, not simply on its level. Tight money can disproportionately impair the ability of the financial system to channel funds to the firms that depend most on bank finance: small and innovative companies, often located in the most growth oriented sectors of the economy. Such heterogeneity is not recognized by analyses that focus exclusively on the conventional link between the cost of capital and investment.

Taken together, the existence of strong, complex links between finance and investment, largely ignored in many discussions of monetary policy, can increase the social costs of monetary policy narrowly focused on driving inflation to zero. These costs may be higher than one would expect from a perspective that focuses on the cost of capital as the exclusive channel through which money affects investment. Perhaps more important, tight money policies can affect the allocation of investment in ways that are not evident when analysis considers only the cost-of-capital channel. These points support the case that the conduct of monetary policy, and the broader process of financial reform, must be better informed about how the financial system interacts with investment.

Do We Need More Investment?

This paper examines the link between monetary policy and investment. Yet, a background issue must be addressed, at least briefly, before proceeding. Should monetary policy be specifically structured to stimulate investment in the United States at this time? Obviously, the answer to this question is basic to the policy analysis pursued here.

Statistics show that investment has been particularly weak. Figure 3.1 plots net private fixed investment as a percentage of gross domestic product (GDP) for the past 40 years. The ratio varies widely with the business cycle. But recent experience still stands out as unusual. After hitting a local peak in early 1985, the investment:GDP ratio declined, well in advance of the official beginning of the recession in mid-1990. During the recent slow growth and recession period, the investment percentage has fluctuated around its lowest levels in post-Depression experience. Its level in late 1991 was below the trough reached following the 1973–74 recession, which was widely believed to be more severe than the recent downturn.

There is surprising agreement from nearly every part of the political spectrum that policy should attempt to reverse this trend, in spite of sharp differences over the best way to pursue this goal. Professor Benjamin Friedman, a strong critic of the Reagan-Bush fiscal policies, argues that as a result of low investment in the 1980s, "productivity gains have continued to be disappointing and wages have lagged" (Friedman, 1991, p. 150). Murray Weidenbaum, Ronald Reagan's first chairman of the Council of Economic Advisors, has called for a temporary investment tax credit on "productivity-enhancing equipment for manufacturing companies" (Youngblood, 1992).

Yet, in spite of this agreement, there is some intellectual justification for questioning whether the pursuit of policies that stimulate investment enhances social well-being. For given output, an increase of investment necessarily involves the sacrifice of some resources that could have been used for current consumption. It is not entirely obvious, therefore, that more investment is good. That is, the future benefits to society from higher investment may not be great enough to justify the sacrifice of current consumption.

For several reasons, however, I believe that under current circumstances in the United States, policy should attempt to increase private investment. The most obvious of these is that the economy is far from the full employment of its productive resources.3 Higher investment spending will increase demand and output. Therefore, in the current situation, the premise necessary for the conclusion that higher investment requires a sacrifice of current consumption is false

Figure 3.1. **Net Nonresidential Investment, 1952–1992**

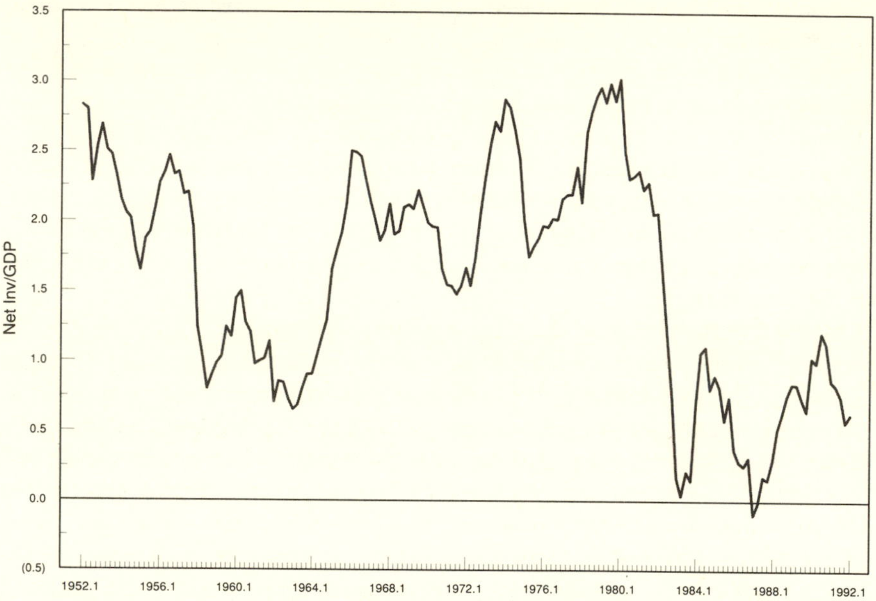

Source: National Income and Product Accounts, adjusted in Fair, 1992.

because output is not fixed at a given level. Higher investment will increase output and employment, speeding economic recovery.

A longer-term concern also supports the conclusion that the United States would benefit from higher private investment. The 1990 report of the Social Security Administration predicts that the ratio of Social Security beneficiaries to employed workers who pay Social Security taxes will rise from 0.3 in 1990 to 0.5 about 40 years later.[4] This widely discussed change, caused by the aging of the baby-boom generation, will either greatly increase the burden borne by workers to support retirees or lead to substantial cuts in the benefits paid to retirees. Much has been written about the need to build up reserves in anticipation of this potentially serious intergenerational conflict in the next century.

The popular understanding of the Social Security problem, however, is clouded by a fallacy of composition. The obvious solution for an individual who wants to provide for retirement is to save while working and then to use accumulated savings to finance consumption during retirement. Through their saving, people see themselves as transferring resources from the present to the future, and from their individual perspective, this view is correct. But no such transfer of the actual goods that retirees want to consume occurs in the society taken as a whole. Baby-boom retirees will want to drive nice cars, eat good food, and consume high-quality medical care that will be the products of the future economy. No one accumulates stocks of such goods in massive warehouses, planning to take them out for use when they retire in the third decade of the next century! The goods that the baby boomers will consume when they retire must come from the production of society at that time.

The best thing, therefore, that we can do today to provide for the retirement of the baby boomers is to enhance the ability of the economy to produce goods and services in the future. This objective requires higher investment. With these demographic realities in mind, the downward trend of investment in recent years is particularly discouraging. Investment should be rising as a share of output. One of the challenges for monetary policy and financial reform in the 1990s, therefore, must be to facilitate capital investment.

What Do We Know About the Determinants of Investment?

To meet the objective of creating a monetary and financial environment conducive to investment, we need a clear view of how investment decisions are made. With some risk of oversimplification, the determinants of investment studied in the voluminous academic literature on the subject can be divided into three broad categories: the cost of capital, output or sales variables, and measures of firms' access to finance. We shall now consider each of these categories in some detail.

The Cost of Capital and the Neo-classical Investment Model

Early empirical work emphasized all three categories of investment determinants.[5] In the 1960s, however, Dale Jorgenson developed what became the dominant view of investment: the neo-classical investment model.[6] According to this theory, firms make employment, investment, and production decisions to maximize their profits (more precisely, the present value of profits over time). The only constraints on firms' choices arise from market prices (which they cannot affect under the perfectly competitive assumptions of the Jorgenson model) and technology (which determines the amount of output a firm can produce from given inputs). Within this theoretical framework, then, investment is determined by technology and the full spectrum of prices, including, but not limited to, interest rates.

The direct role played by monetary policy in this framework is clear and narrowly delimited: monetary policy matters for investment only to the extent that it affects the real cost of capital, largely through its influence on interest rates.[7] In most of the literature based on the neo-classical investment model, the interest rate effects are assumed to be quite large.

This model constitutes a theory. Although the theory is logically coherent, it is based on some strong assumptions. For example, most versions assume that firms can purchase all the inputs and sell all the output they want to at given prices (firms operate in "perfectly competitive" markets). In addition, if firms do not have sufficient funds to finance a desirable investment project themselves, they can obtain all the finance they need externally by issuing new shares at a fair market price or by borrowing at an economy-wide interest rate. There is little doubt that these strong assumptions are violated to some degree in reality. The more important question for policy analysis, however, is whether the theory based on these assumptions nevertheless adequately describes the most important aspects of the way that firms make investment decisions. This question must be answered by empirical tests of the theory.

Tests of the neo-classical investment model immediately run up against an important problem. The role played by technology is clear and very general in the theoretical model, but in practice the true structure of firms' technology and its impact on the demand for investment is unobservable. Researchers must make some additional assumptions about the nature of technology to test the theory. The character of these assumptions is important for policy purposes, because they usually introduce firms' sales or output as determinants of investment along with the cost of capital. Some of these models explain investment very well, but it is not clear that their explanatory power is driven by the cost of capital and therefore related to policy-driven changes in interest rates. The success of these empirical neo-classical models could be the result of including sales, which may have little to do with the neo-classical theory, an issue we shall take up momentarily.[8] Thus, there is uncertainty about the standard influences of policy on investment through the cost of capital. We shall try to resolve some of this uncertainty with the new empirical research reported in the next section. First, however, we must consider some alternative perspectives on investment. And although these views have not been subject to anything like the volume of research surrounding the neo-classical model, their relevance to current policy issues may be significant.

Sales and the Accelerator

In most versions of the neo-classical model, firms choose how much output they want to produce under the assumption that they can sell all they want to at the given price. The only limitations they perceive on their production arise from their technology and market prices. This "perfectly competitive" environment, however, does not adequately describe the circumstances of firms in most U.S. industries. Typically, firms have at least some control over the price they charge, and the sales they can make at a given price are limited by the strength of demand for their products. Under these conditions, one would expect that firms' expectations of future sales would have an important impact on their investment spending. High sales, currently and in the recent past, will likely cause expectations of higher sales in the future and will give firms the incentive to invest in new productive capacity. Low sales will reduce the incentives to invest.

This kind of intuition underlies one of the oldest and most empirically successful investment models: the accelerator, which relates investment to recent changes in sales.[9] Various versions of the accelerator have been used in empirical investment studies for decades with excellent results. As mentioned previously, accelerator effects have clouded the empirical evaluation of the neo-classical model, because many versions of the neo-classical approach allow the cost of capital to affect investment only through variables that also include sales or output. Therefore, one often cannot determine the separate impact of sales and the cost of capital, and it is difficult to evaluate the independent importance of the interest-rate channel and the effect of monetary policy.

Some studies, however, in order to explain investment, have compared the separate effects of sales and the cost of capital. In an extensive recent survey, Robert Chirinko (1991, p. 14) writes, "Although empirical results with versions of the Neoclassical Model differ widely, they suggest to this author that output (or sales) is clearly the dominant determinant of investment spending with the [cost of capital] having a modest effect." Therefore, there is doubt about the important implicit assumption, largely unquestioned in policy circles, that changes in the cost of capital will be the dominant policy variable affecting investment. New empirical evidence to address this problem is presented in the following section.

If sales dominate the cost of capital as a determinant of investment, and if sales are determined in part by macroeconomic conditions, then the links between monetary policy and capital spending are significantly different from those of the neo-classical model summarized previously. For under these circumstances, the indirect impact of monetary policy on the general state of the economy may well be more important for investment than its direct impact on the cost of capital. Indeed, there is little doubt that monetary policy has important effects on economic activity as a whole.[10] The following discusses some possible explanations for these results, even when investment is not sensitive to the cost of capital.

In mainstream economics, this discussion must be qualified in an important way. On one hand, the strong effects of the accelerator are widely viewed as temporary, applying to the (it is hoped) transient circumstances when the economy is operating below full employment of its labor and capital resources. On the other hand, the cost-of-capital effects, although they are certainly weaker empirically, are permanent, and they affect the desired stock of capital even at full employment. However, mainstream models also predict that monetary policy does not have a permanent impact on the real interest rates that enter the cost of capital. In fact, if inflation nonneutralities resulting from the tax system increase the cost of capital as is widely believed, then conventional long-run analysis would suggest that expansionary monetary policy will hurt investment over a long horizon as it adds to the inflation rate (Lindsey, 1992). This point provides yet another reason for discounting the interest-rate/cost-of-capital channel as a major influence on investment.

There are several important reasons, however, why such a focus could be seriously misleading for effective policy design. At this writing, the economy has suffered an extended period during which resources were far from fully utilized.

The sacrifice in terms of material standard of living and, perhaps more important, national sense of well-being has been substantial. An important objective of investment policy over the short-to-medium horizon must be to invigorate the economy by creating jobs, improving productivity, and increasing incomes. To the extent that expansionary monetary policy can boost economic activity, the strong accelerator effect will stimulate investment.

Indeed, the argument in favor of a focus on the accelerator may go even deeper because it is not clear that the effects are necessarily short term. The conventional view that investment stimulus through the accelerator is temporary relies on the assumption that the economy will inevitably converge to a full-employment equilibrium as a result of its own natural adjustment mechanisms. Moreover, the output and employment forthcoming in this equilibrium are largely independent of the way the economy has performed in the recent past. There are good reasons to question both of these critical assumptions.

The natural stabilizing forces in the economy that are usually assumed to restore full employment can be quite weak, and they may be dwarfed by destabilizing channels.[11] If this is the case, investment stimulus due to monetary policy could have a prolonged effect by pushing the economy toward full employment when it otherwise may have continued to stagnate. In addition, even if the economy were to get to a long-run, full-employment equilibrium on its own, the short-run strength of the economy may have an impact on the character of such long-run equilibrium. These effects arise because short-run performance affects the extent of technical progress (which is also tied to the level of investment), the productivity of labor, and "learning-by-doing" effects. As Frank Hahn has written, "We do not have to settle for the historical determinism entailed by unique steady state growth rates" (1990, p. 35). We must not, therefore, discount the importance of what are usually viewed as "short-term" fluctuations of investment or employment because we believe that all will be well in some long-run steady state, the character of which is independent of the short-run path of the economy. Short-run macroeconomic weakness can have long-run consequences.

Finance and Investment

Recent developments in the research on capital markets and investment also suggest a need to reexamine the economic foundations of the link between monetary policy and investment. Much of the mainstream empirical research on the determinants of investment is based on the assumption that firms can obtain financing for any investment project they believe is profitable (when the project is evaluated at a cost of capital based on market interest rates). New theoretical and empirical research, however, has made important advances in studying what are often called "financial constraints." The idea that the access to finance may pose a constraint on investment, independent of traditional determinants such as interest rates, taxes, and technology, now has wide (though not universal) support among economists.[12]

Suppose a firm does not have sufficient internal cash to undertake a desirable investment project. It must then seek funds from external sources—either new borrowing or stock issues. External finance, however, may be more costly than internal funds for a variety of reasons.[13] Undoubtedly, there are transaction costs associated with external finance because of the need to deal with financial intermediaries, who must cover their costs and make a profit on the deal. Estimates of these costs can be quite substantial, especially for new stock issues. Therefore, an investment project that would be undertaken when the firm has sufficient internal cash to finance it may be postponed, or not undertaken at all, if the firm must rely on more costly external funds.

Recent literature has emphasized even deeper reasons why financial constraints on investment may arise. Many of the problems center on different ("asymmetric") information available to borrowers and lenders that can lead to many nontraditional results. For example, credit may be rationed, meaning that interest rates do not equate the supply and demand for loans. Then, firms that are quite willing to borrow to finance investment at prevailing interest rates may be unable to obtain loans. Furthermore, firms' access to funds can depend on their financial condition. Specifically, the ability of a firm to undertake an investment project can depend not only on the market and the technological characteristics of the project under consideration (the project's "fundamental" value, in the jargon of the literature) but also on the firm's financial condition, such as its indebtedness or the collateral it can provide for new loans. Again, projects in which a firm would invest if it had sufficient internal funds might not be undertaken if the firm must raise external funds to finance the project.

This research program has led to new empirical work that strongly supports the idea that access to finance matters for investment. In particular, recent work has demonstrated the link between investment and internal funds, variations in which are determined largely by profits. Moreover, this link is most important for relatively small, fast-growing firms that are likely concentrated in the most progressive sectors of the U.S. economy. This heterogeneity is not surprising. We would expect information gaps between firms and potential lenders to be the widest for small firms in new industries. Therefore, if information problems are at the root of finance constraints that prevent some firms from obtaining external finance for profitable projects, these constraints are likely the tightest for more progressive firms, and the investment of these firms will be the most dependent on the availability of internal finance.[14]

These developments open a new channel for monetary effects on investment. The effects of monetary policy on the *cost* of credit may not be particularly important for investment, but the effect of monetary policy and, more broadly, the institutional structure of the financial system may be significant for the *availability* of credit. If capital markets were "perfect," no distinction would

Table 3.1

Selected Nominal Interest Rates

Period	Baa Bond Yield (%)	Commerical Paper Rate (%)	Average Prime Rate (%)
1989 Q1	10.64	9.45	11.08
1989 Q2	10.37	9.29	11.50
1989 Q3	9.89	8.39	10.83
1989 Q4	9.81	8.06	10.50
1990 Q1	10.10	8.08	10.08
1990 Q2	10.31	8.19	10.00
1990 Q3	10.42	7.83	10.00
1990 Q4	10.60	7.68	10.00
1991 Q1	10.40	6.60	9.33
1991 Q2	9.92	6.06	8.75
1991 Q3	9.68	5.83	8.42
1991 Q4	9.40	4.91	7.58

Source: *Economic Report of the President*, 1992, p. 379. Averages of monthly data.

arise between the cost and availability of credit: firms that wanted to borrow more would simply have to pay a higher cost. But if credit is rationed, as explained by Stiglitz and Weiss (1981), lenders may be unwilling to provide more funds even though firms offer to pay higher rates of interest. Theoretically, rationing can occur among firms that are in all observable ways equivalent to ones that get loans. The more common result in practice is likely to be that the largest borrowers with the most established credit records and the best collateral will receive credit. Rationing is likely to affect smaller firms with less of a track record and less collateral.

These theoretical ideas link to recent U.S. experience with the "credit crunch" that is widely viewed as partly responsible for poor macroeconomic performance in the early 1990s. If the credit market cleared on the basis of interest rates, one would expect that complaints of credit tightness would be accompanied by rising interest rates. But interest rates have been quite low and falling during this weak period, as shown in Table 3.1. Therefore, at least casual observation suggests that something like credit rationing is at work.[15]

Furthermore, as mentioned previously, the credit crunch is not likely to hit all firms equally. This point was even acknowledged by the Bush administration in its 1992 *Economic Report of the President*, the last such report it issued. The report stated that "the lagged effects of a relatively tight monetary policy coupled with problems in the availability of credit, *especially for small- and medium-sized businesses*, dampened economic growth" (emphasis added). Econometric evidence presented elsewhere and in the next section supports this conclusion that tight credit conditions are likely to affect disproportionately smaller, fast-growing firms in new, relatively high technology industries. But presumably, these firms are the most important in providing employment growth and enhancing U.S. international competitiveness, and therefore they deserve special attention in policy discussion.

How is the extent of credit rationing and of the severity of a "credit crunch" affected by monetary policy? By increasing the reserves of the banking system, the Fed reduces the cost of funds for banks. In standard market-clearing models, this reduction in the cost of funds would open a gap between the profits on new loans and the costs of funding increased lending. Competitive banks would respond by cutting the cost of loans to attract new customers. The new loan market equilibrium would therefore involve lower interest rates and higher quantities of lending. The link between monetary expansion and higher lending works somewhat differently in rationed markets, however. Increases in reserves supplied by the Fed still reduce the cost of funds and open a gap between this cost and the expected profits of new lending. But there is no need for banks to lower their interest rates in order to attract new customers when there is credit rationing. They simply meet the credit demands of some borrowers who were previously rationed, expanding the quantity of credit offered even though the interest rates they charge remain the same.[16] This result, which follows the discussion in Stiglitz and Weiss (1981), implies that monetary policy may be important for the quantity of finance available for investment even though investment does not appear to be sensitive to changes in the interest rate.[17]

Financial effects on investment interact with the business cycle in another, more subtle way that has implications for a variety of policy debates. Profit, or more broadly, "cash flow," is not the only source of internal finance for investment. Firms can also temporarily finance capital spending by reducing the amount of other assets they hold. For example, if firms face a downturn in cash flow but want to maintain investment spending without resorting to new borrowing or stock issues, they can sell off (or simply not replace) inventories, reduce their cash holdings, or tighten their policies on collecting accounts receivable. The funds released by these reductions in liquid assets can be used to temporarily "smooth" a firm's investment spending.[18]

The extent to which this kind of behavior can occur depends on how liquid firms are as they go into a recession. Firms' ability to cushion investment against downturns in cash flow will be reduced if they hold fewer liquid assets or are more heavily indebted going into the recession. Again, this point is particularly relevant to current conditions. Coming into the early 1990s, U.S. corporations had lower inventory stocks and much higher debt than in recent history. Thus, their liquidity was low. And, as shown in Figure 3.1, investment as a percentage of output fell off much more in the recent slow growth and recession period than it did at any other time since the end of World War II. The debt overhang, therefore, and policies that contributed to it (the tax deductibility of interest and some kinds of financial deregulation, for example) have likely increased the sensitivity of investment to cyclical downturns. This metamorphosis of financial circumstances increases the importance of macroeconomic fluctuations for investment, and it correspondingly magnifies the role of policies that both create and contain the business cycle.

Empirical Evidence on the Determinants of Investment

Motivation and the Data

The theoretical analysis summarized in the previous section identifies a number of channels through which monetary and financial policy may affect investment. Many of the references previously cited provide empirical evidence that can be used to sort through the relative size of the various channels and thus to provide a quantitative basis for policy proposals. But this evidence tends to be fragmented, and various results are often inconclusive or contradictory.

Moreover, even though the analysis of investment determinants is fundamentally a microeconomic issue about the behavior of individual firms, the majority of the empirical studies on these issues are undertaken using aggregate data, often under the assumption that the entire economy behaves "as if" it could be described by a single "representative firm." Obviously, this approach precludes any evidence to support the view that heterogeneity among different kinds of firms is important for policy purposes. Although some studies do analyze firm-level data, they usually do not cover enough of the economy to support strong conclusions for macroeconomic policy.

For these reasons, this section presents some new empirical evidence on the determinants of investment to shed statistical light on the issues raised previously. An innovation in the new research reported here is the sample of firm data used. This sample is constructed from the "full coverage" files of the Standard and Poor's COMPUSTAT database. It provides information for more than 5,000 U.S. manufacturing firms from 1971 to 1990 (about 53,000 observations). During that period, total capital spending by these firms accounts for 42 percent of total U.S. fixed capital investment.[19] Therefore, this database captures a large part of the economy. This extent of macrocoverage is greater than any previous study of U.S. investment with firm-level data. It will be explained later how to generalize the results to the rest of the economy.

To measure the sensitivity of investment to the major determinants discussed previously, the investment regression contains three sets of variables: sales growth, firms' internal cash flow, and the cost of capital. The sales growth variables are suggested by the accelerator theory.[20] The effect of internal cash flow represents the importance of finance constraints: when firms have higher cash flow, they will have greater control over their investment spending because they depend less on external funds (new debt or stock issues) that may be excessively costly, or even impossible, to obtain.[21] The cost of capital variables consist of interest rates (adjusted for tax effects in some cases). They reflect the conventional channels for policy influence on investment.

The regression equations presented here are called "reduced forms" in the literature. That is, they simply relate the dependent variable—firm investment in this case—to various determinants suggested by theory without imposing any particular structure on the empirical relationship.[22] This approach has been criticized, especially for purposes of policy analysis, because new policies may change the empirical parameters estimated from data generated under the old policies. This problem is called in the literature the "Lucas critique," after Robert Lucas, whose work emphasized these issues. After obtaining results and considering their significance for policy, we should substantively consider how policy changes might affect the economic structure that generates the empirical results.[23] In addition, one should not base judgments on small or highly uncertain effects. Most of the analysis pursued here emphasizes results that are extremely strong from a statistical perspective. In this sense, the use of a large sample of firm data helps to overcome the problems because the size of the database greatly increases the statistical significance of the results relative to studies based on aggregate data.

Firm Heterogeneity

To address the possibility that the importance of various determinants of investment may not be the same for all firms, I have divided the sample into four groups based on each firm's average real sales growth during the period that it is part of the sample. This is only one of a number of possibly interesting sample splits, but it seems particularly appropriate for the purposes of this research. We are interested in the differential effects of investment policies across firms with different potential to contribute to the long-run growth of productivity, employment, and international competitiveness. Sales growth captures these characteristics. Fast-growing firms are the ones that have been successful at producing for changing markets. They are the ones that are most likely hiring new workers in the greatest numbers. They are most likely the ones to develop and adopt new technologies.

The details of the sales growth classification are given in the econometric appendix. Inflation-adjusted sales of the negative-growth firms contracted, on average, by 1 percent or more during the sample period. Table 3.2 shows that these firms accounted for almost 19 percent of the observations, but less than 4 percent of the total investment. Real sales for zero-growth firms grew between negative 1 percent and positive 2 percent. The highest proportion of the observations, the majority of investment, and the biggest firms fell into the moderate-growth class. These firms had real sales growth rates that averaged between 2 and 7 percent. The high-growth firms, with average growth rate above 7 percent, were expanding very fast indeed (average sales growth above 11 percent).

Table 3.2

Characteristics of Sample Firms by Sales-Growth Class

Variable	Growth Class			
	Negative Class	Zero Class	Moderate Class	High Class
Percentage of observations	19.1%	21.0%	36.8%	23.1%
Percentage of investment	3.8%	19.1%	64.6%	12.5%
Average capital (millions of 1982$)	$125	$420	$809	$175
Average sales growth	−4.3%	+0.6%	+4.3%	+11.2%
High-tech percentage	36.3%	40.8%	45.5%	64.8%
Average stock price growth	9.0%	9.2%	9.5%	11.6%
Average employment growth	0.6%	0.9%	4.5%	12.5%
Investment-to-capital ratio	0.117	0.153	0.196	0.319
R&D spending-to-capital ratio	0.091	0.087	0.124	0.264
Share of R&D in capital spending	27.4%	25.0%	29.1%	37.0%

Source: Author's calculations from COMPUSTAT manufacturing firm database. See the econometric appendix for further details.

Table 3.2 also provides statistics that highlight further differences between these groups of firms. Not only are the high-sales-growth firms expanding more quickly, but they are concentrated in high-technology industries.[24] The higher growth classes provided much more employment growth during the sample period, and their gross investment rate (plant and equipment spending divided by the capital stock) was much higher. The stock market value of firms in the highest growth class rose more quickly than that of the other firms. Finally, research and development (R&D) spending was much higher for the faster-growing classes. Together these statistics show that the moderate-growth firms, and especially the high-growth firms, represent the most progressive sectors of the U.S. economy. For this reason, their investment is likely crucial for productivity growth and international competitiveness.

Regression Results

Summary results of the investment regressions appear in Table 3.3.[25] As found by other studies, the sales growth (accelerator) effects are very strong. The cash flow effects that capture the impact of financial constraints are also quite important. Both the sales growth and cash flow effects are much stronger for the faster-growing firms, a result to be discussed in more detail in a moment. Further analysis of the statistical results (see the appendix for details) reinforces the impression that the accelerator and financial effects are quite powerful. One can overwhelmingly reject the hypothesis that these effects are in fact zero, with the positive estimated effect due simply to random variation. These results leave no

Table 3.3

Regression Estimates of Impact of Investment Determinants on the Investment-to-Capital Ratio by Sales-Growth Class

Growth Class	Sales Growth	Cash Flow	Real Interest Rates
Negative	0.158	0.134	−0.002
Zero	0.179	0.204	−0.002
Moderate	0.287	0.248	0
High	0.361	0.329	0

doubt of the importance of accelerator and financial effects for investment. In light of the Lucas critique (discussed earlier), it is hard to imagine any policy change that would remove these effects.

The impact of real interest rates on investment, however, is much less certain. The evidence suggests that higher real rates cause investment to fall only for the negative- and slow-growth firms. Even weaker effects are obtained when one uses a cost-of-capital measure adjusted for taxation (see the econometric appendix). The interest rate estimates are also much less precise, meaning that the econometric analysis cannot pin down the size of these effects with a great deal of certainty. On the one hand, there is no strong evidence that the interest rate effects are not zero. On the other hand, given the imprecise estimates, the effects could be negative and of a larger magnitude than those reported here. But we have no clear evidence of such effects, and it would be speculative to base policy on the assumption that interest rates drive investment to an important extent, especially for growing firms.

One possible reason for the imprecise estimates of the interest rate effects is that the regressions use rates determined in centralized securities markets (for example, the Baa corporate bond yield, in the case of the results in Table 3.3). The interest rates that firms face may well vary substantially from such centralized rates. If we could measure such rates, they may have more explanatory power for investment. While this point is of interest for economic theory, for policy purposes, such results are not particularly important. If monetary policy is to affect investment through interest rates, it certainly works through the interest rates set by the money markets. One expects monetary policy to move federal funds rates and short-term Treasury instrument yields, and these rates may affect long-term yields through the term structure of interest rates and various mechanisms of expectation. Such interest rates may not be directly available to most of the firms in our sample. But if these interest rates do not ultimately affect this sample, it is hard to see how monetary influences on interest rates would affect investment in this sample that accounts for over 40 percent of U.S. aggregate capital spending.[26]

Furthermore, it is unlikely that the firms that are not included in the sample will be more affected by centralized money market rates than the sample firms.

Table 3.4

Percentage Drop of Investment from Representative Changes in Investment Determinants

Growth Class	Sales Growth	Cash Flow	Real Intertest Rates
Negative	3.4%	1.4%	3.1%
Zero	3.1	3.7	2.5
Moderate	4.0	6.5	0
High	3.0	10.1	0

COMPUSTAT tracks the firms with the most interest to the investment community. Although the sample is extensive and contains much heterogeneity, one expects that the U.S. firms not included in the sample are smaller on average, with less access to centralized securities markets. Therefore, I conclude that if any policy-induced effects of interest rates on investment exist, they should be found in this sample.

Let us put these results into a more relevant perspective. How much variance of investment would these estimated equations predict as the result of recent events? The long-term trend of real final sales growth was 3.1 percent from 1970 to 1988. During the slow-growth period from the second quarter of 1989 to the fourth quarter of 1991, final sales growth dropped to 0.3 percent. We can compute the predicted drop of investment from the estimated model as a result of the drop in recent sales growth alone. This calculation appears in the Sales Growth column of Table 3.4. To estimate the effect of recent economic weakness on cash flow, note that after-tax real corporate profits through 1991 had dropped 30.3 percent from their 1988 peak. The impact of this drop on predicted investment from our estimated model is in the Cash Flow column of Table 3.4.[27]

Finally, let us consider interest rate effects. A 200-basis-point change in real (inflation-adjusted) interest rates that are relevant for investment would be a very large impact of monetary policy. Monetary actions in 1991 and 1992 have been credited with substantial reductions in short-term interest rates, but the long-term rates that probably matter the most for investment have fallen much less. Nevertheless, Table 3.4 presents the impact of a 200-basis-point drop in real interest rates predicted by the estimated investment model. The effects are zero for the moderate- and high-growth firms because the estimated coefficients on interest rates in their investment equations were zero. If we nonetheless assumed that these firms had the same interest rate coefficients that were estimated for the negative- and zero-growth classes, the percentage change of investment figures would be 2.0 and 1.2 percent for the moderate- and high-growth firms, respectively.

The statistics in Table 3.4 present a striking pattern. Most of the variables have a nonnegligible effect on investment, for at least some of the sales growth classes. For reference purposes, aggregate nonresidential investment fell by 7.5 percent in the 1982–83 recession; it fell by 6.5 percent from 1990 to 1991 during the recent downturn. Thus, the simulated effects presented in Table 3.4 can easily explain investment fluctuations as large as those we have observed. (Note that the full effect of the recession is the *sum* of the sales growth and cash flow effects, which roughly equals or exceeds the drop of investment observed in recent downturns.) Perhaps more important, there is a substantial difference in the determinants of investment across firms with different growth characteristics. Sales growth is important at roughly the same magnitude for all firms. But cash flow is nearly eight times more important for the high-growth firms than the contracting class. The opposite pattern arises for interest rates. There is a moderate effect of interest rates for contracting and stagnant firms. For the growing firms, however, there is no statistically reliable impact of interest rates on investment. The importance of heterogeneity in firm characteristics is clear in these results. Such differences must not be ignored in policy discussions about monetary and financial influences on investment, to which we now turn.

Policy Implications

The results presented here demonstrate the importance of cyclical and financial factors for the determination of investment. They suggest that the impact of interest rates and the cost of capital, which have received the most attention in discussions about the link between monetary policy and investment, are uncertain and possibly quite small. The analysis also shows clearly that the importance of the various channels of influence on investment varies across different firms. What messages can be taken from these findings for the conduct of monetary policy and the progress of financial reform?

First, it is clear that investment cannot be divorced from finance. The investment-finance research helps to understand and explain business cycles and has special relevance to the U.S. economy's current weakness. As the economy weakens, lower profits reduce internal cash flow and thus weaken investment. Lower sales reduce the need to expand capacity. Tighter lending requirements (the current "credit crunch," for example) that emerge as profits and sales fall also limit investment. Therefore, there is an endogenous process at work through investment that amplifies business-cycle fluctuations through channels often ignored in policy discussion. As monetary policy is widely believed to have an important impact on the course of macroeconomic fluctuations, these channels must be taken into account in assessing the impact of monetary decisions.

The literature summarized herein and the new research reported in this chapter also add an important new dimension to this point. The impact of financial factors on investment clearly appears different across different groups of firms. Specifically, the new results in this chapter show that finance effects are most important for the fastest-growing firms in the U.S. economy. Also, work by Charles Himmelberg and Bruce Petersen (1992) shows that research and development expenditures are especially likely to be limited by the availability of finance. Therefore, if monetary policy and financial reform affect the flows of finance in the economy, these effects will be most important for the most dynamic sectors of the economy. Aggregate investment is only part of the story. We must also pay attention to how policy affects the allocation of investment among different sectors.

Understanding these points highlights the importance for investment of maintaining stable macroeconomic conditions and financial relations. Failure to do so will magnify the severity of economic downturns, inhibit recovery from recessions that will undoubtedly occur regardless of the policies pursued, and constrain the long-term capital development of the economy. What specific kinds of policies should be pursued?

The insights developed here add perspective to the consequences of using monetary policy to fight inflation. For example, Lawrence Lindsey (1992, p. 3) states, "The case for disinflation in the 1990s is a strong one. While disinflation is not a costless process, most of the costs of reducing inflation have already been borne." No doubt there are important costs of inflation, but as the results here show, there also can be quite significant costs to investment if disinflationary monetary policy causes or exacerbates a profit-and-credit crunch. But Lindsey argues that disinflation would help investment by lowering the cost of capital. Indeed, he claims (1992, p. 2) that reducing inflation "from 4 percent to zero would induce nearly the same reduction in the after-tax cost of industrial equipment as a 3.5 percent investment tax credit." Calculations I carried out (using the cost-of-capital specification from Jorgenson and Yun, 1989) show that this kind of change would lower the effective, tax-adjusted cost of capital by about 20 basis points. This is one-tenth of the reduction assumed in the analysis presented earlier, which compared the cost-of-capital channel to the sales and internal funds effects. Even with a dramatically larger fall in the cost of capital than Lindsey's proposal would generate, the predicted effects on investment were small and disproportionately weighted toward stagnant firms.

In contrast, the negative impact of tight money on the course of the business cycle and credit conditions would seem at least as well established over short-to-medium horizons as its effect on inflation.[28] The empirical results here show that these negative results of tight money have much more certain and quantitatively significant effects on investment. Furthermore, they hurt investment the most for the kinds of firms that are most likely to contribute to long-term economic strength.

These points do not suggest that the Fed should necessarily ignore inflation in setting its policy goals. Those issues are addressed elsewhere in this volume. But the analysis here shows that simple rules for monetary policy are unlikely to be in the economy's best interest. The Fed has a difficult job to do; it must be well informed about the wide variety of channels through which its actions affect the real economy in general and investment in particular.

The results presented here also have implications for the assessment of policy toward corporate financial restructuring. Much economic analysis of leveraged buyouts and related transactions has focused on microeconomic efficiency issues and the "agency problems" in getting managers to act in shareholders' interest. Leveraged buyouts are widely thought to improve microeconomic performance of firms. The management of highly indebted companies must pay out earnings as interest on debt instead of keeping them under their own control and possibly using them to further the managers' interests rather than the long-term interests of the firms' shareholders. But the ideas discussed in this paper suggest a different dimension to the corporate takeover issue.

If these transactions raise debt and lead to substantially weaker balance sheets, the affected firms will be less able to maintain investment and innovative activity in a downturn, a situation that will hurt productivity and inhibit economic recovery. Therefore, we must look hard at policies that encourage debt (the tax deductibility of interest, for example). A high-debt environment is less likely to provide the stable financial base necessary for capital expansion.

This research program that links investment and finance also emphasizes a special role of banks—one that has been largely ignored in most mainstream policy discussions of financial reform. In the traditional view, banks are intermediaries that reduce the transaction costs of channeling funds from savers to borrowers. Banks may have a comparative advantage in performing these functions, but if the banking system is weakened by adverse exogenous circumstances (Third World debt, incorrect forecasts of oil or real estate prices, etc.), other institutions will fill the gap left by the collapse of banks or savings and loans with no first-order macroeconomic losses to the economy.

The alternative view of banking supported by much of the work presented here recognizes that banks are particularly well suited to overcome the finance constraints that firms face. Banks specialize in identifying good investment prospects and raising the financing for them. They establish personalized, long-term relations that are conducive to overcoming the inherent information problems that exist between agents in impersonal primary security markets. Banks are probably most important in funding activities in smaller, faster-growing firms that account for much of the economy's employment, innovation, and growth.

Historically, the banking system had access to a stable funding mechanism: government-insured deposits. There is no doubt that these insured liabilities also played a role in exacerbating the savings and loan and banking crises of the 1980s. But proposals to eliminate deposit insurance that focus exclusively on bank liabilities, ignoring banks' key and specialized role in financing capital investment, could damage investment in an attempt to fix perceived "moral hazard" problems with deposit insurance. In addition, the costs of such reform are likely to be greatest for the fastest-growing sectors of the economy.

For example, many analysts have proposed that the government insure only the deposits of "narrow banks" that hold only U.S. Treasury securities as assets. These banks would be prohibited from financing investment, and hence investment finance would be divorced from the stable funding base it has enjoyed historically as the result of government deposit insurance. Most narrow bank proposals argue that uninsured alternative institutions would arise to fund investment. But the liabilities of such institutions would be more unstable, which would reduce their ability to act as a cushion to provide financing for good investment projects, especially in unsettled macroeconomic circumstances. One suspects that the "lender-of-last-resort" function of the Fed will be called upon more often, and with it other moral hazard problems will arise. The social costs, therefore, of severely restricting deposit insurance may be much greater than they seem on the surface.

Monetary policy making and restructuring of the financial system are difficult jobs. Investment growth is only one dimension of the multiple goals that these policies must strive to achieve. But it is a particularly important dimension, given the challenges the U.S. economy faces as it moves into the next century. Whereas most policy analysis of the money-finance-investment link focuses exclusively on the cost of capital, this paper has argued that alternative channels are empirically stronger. Recognition of this point implies that monetary and financial policy affect investment in different ways from the ones often assumed, through the quantity of credit available to fund investment rather than the cost of credit. An exclusive focus on the cost of capital also masks the impact that the financial system has on the allocation of investment across firms with different characteristics. Failure to account for these alternative channels could result in underestimating the importance of money and finance for investment.

Econometric Appendix

Definition of Sales Growth Classes

To limit the effect of extreme observations in the classification of firms, annual real sales growth figures in each year were capped between negative 20 and positive 20 percent. These limited sales growth data were then averaged for each firm. Firms were put into the negative-growth class if their average was less than negative 1 percent. The zero-growth class includes averages from negative 1 percent to positive 2 percent. Moderate growth covers 2–7 percent, and high-growth firms had real sales growth that averaged higher than 7 percent.

Data Definitions

Investment (I) is capital spending on plant and equipment from the firms' sources and uses of funds statements. Sales (S) is total revenue from operations less discounts or returns. Cash flow (CF) includes after-tax profits, depreciation and amortization expense, extraordinary items, and deferred taxes. The sales data were deflated by the gross national product deflator. Cash flow and investment were deflated by the implicit deflator for nonresidential fixed investment.

The capital stock (K) calculations used estimates of capital price inflation and economic depreciation to calculate a replacement value of capital. The method used was similar to that reported in Fazzari, Hubbard, and Petersen (1988b), with modifications to better account for acquisitions and divestitures and to measure depreciation more robustly.

The interest rate data used in the regressions reported in the text are the average yields on corporate bonds carrying BAA ratings taken from the 1991 *Economic Report of the President*. To estimate real interest rates (RBAA), the actual rate of change of the deflator for gross domestic product was subtracted from the nominal Baa interest rates. Additional tests were conducted using federal funds rates (real and nominal). The results for these alternative variables indicated weaker cost-of-capital effects than those for the real Baa rates, and there was virtually no effect of using the alternative cost-of-capital variables on the other results reported in the text.

Regression Sample Selection Criteria

All available annual data from COMPUSTAT for manufacturing firms (SIC codes 20 to 39) were put into the initial sample. The version of COMPUSTAT used to construct the sample included information from 1971 through 1990. The 1971 and 1972 data were used to construct lags, and therefore the regression sample covers 1973–1990. Some observations were deleted because of major mergers or large inconsistencies in the accounting information. The regressions reported in the sample exclude outliers of the ratios used in the regressions defined as follows: investment to capital (I/K) exceeding 2.0; real sales growth (SG) less than −75 percent or greater than 200 percent in a given year; cash flow to capital (CF/K) less than −2.5 or greater than 2.5. These limitations reduced the sample by just over 5 percent. The regression results were much more robust after removing the outliers, especially for sales growth. The cash flow and cost-of-capital variables performed in similar ways in the full sample and in limited samples. Tighter sample limits did not change the results materially.

Regression Specification and Estimation

The estimated regression equations had the following form:

$$(I/K)_{jt} = a_j + (a_{10})\,SG_{jt} + (a_{11})\,SG_{jt-1} + (a_{12})\,SG_{jt-2}$$
$$+ (a_{20})\,(CF/K)_{jt} + (a_{21})\,(CF/K)_{jt-1} + (a_{22})\,(CF/K)_{jt-2}$$
$$+ (a_{30})\,RBAA_t + (a_{31})\,RBAA_{t-1} + (a_{32})\,RBAA_{t-2}$$

where the variables are defined as described earlier. The a symbols represent estimated coefficients. The j subscript indicates different firms; t indexes time periods. Because the intercept term was allowed to vary across firms, the estimator used captures time-series variation (the "within" fixed-effects estimator for panel data). The regression results reported in the text are the sum of the coefficients on the contemporaneous and two annual lags for each variable. The regression was estimated by ordinary least squares, although a two-stage least-squares estimator was used to test whether endogeneity of the current interest rates affects the results. The 2SLS results did not indicate any substantial change in any of the reported statistics.

Regression Results

Complete regression results for the specification analyzed in the text are as follows. The estimated t statistics for the null hypothesis that the coefficient on each variable is zero are in parentheses below the parameter estimates.

The adjusted R-squared figures do not include the explanatory power of the fixed effect. As mentioned in the text, it is clear that the statistical significance of the SG and CF/K variables is much stronger than the cost-of-capital variables. Specifications with different interest rates and different lag lengths led to quite similar results.

The results below are from a specification that uses a tax-adjusted cost-of-capital (COC) computed along the lines suggested by Jorgenson and Yun (1989) in place of the real interest rate variable. This variable corrects for the investment tax credit, tax deductions to due depreciation, corporate taxes, tax deductibility of interest, and the differential personal tax treatment of dividends and capital gains.

Appendix Table 1

Dependent Variable: (I/K)$_{jt}$

Independent Variable	Negative Growth	Zero Growth	Moderate Growth	High Growth
SG$_{jt}$	0.070	0.092	0.151	0.203
	(10.1)	(12.7)	(23.7)	(17.9)
SG$_{jt-1}$	0.057	0.068	0.090	0.111
	(8.3)	(9.7)	(14.6)	(10.6)
SG$_{jt-2}$	0.031	0.019	0.046	0.047
	(4.6)	(2.8)	(7.9)	(4.9)
CF/K$_{jt}$	0.033	0.061	0.068	0.110
	(6.7)	(11.0)	(14.0)	(14.5)
CF/K$_{jt-1}$	0.060	0.087	0.110	0.158
	(12.4)	(14.9)	(20.3)	(17.6)
CF/K$_{jt-2}$	0.041	0.056	0.070	0.061
	(9.2)	(9.9)	(13.0)	(6.5)
RBAA$_t$	−0.002	−0.001	0.002	0.005
	(2.2)	(1.2)	(1.9)	(3.0)
RBAA$_{t-1}$	0.002	0.001	0.0003	0.003
	(1.1)	(0.9)	(0.3)	(1.1)
RBAA$_{t-2}$	−0.002	−0.002	−0.002	−0.008
	(2.2)	(1.8)	(2.7)	(4.7)
Adjusted R-Squared	0.127	0.165	0.181	0.228

Appendix Table 2

Dependent Variable: (I/K)$_{jt}$

Independent Variable	Negative Growth	Zero Growth	Moderate Growth	High Growth
SG$_{jt}$	0.068	0.089	0.146	0.193
	(9.7)	(12.2)	(22.7)	(16.9)
SG$_{jt-1}$	0.034	0.070	0.087	0.105
	(8.7)	(9.9)	(14.2)	(10.0)
SG$_{jt-2}$	0.034	0.022	0.048	0.047
	(5.1)	(3.1)	(8.1)	(4.9)
CF/K$_{jt}$	0.035	0.063	0.069	0.111
	(7.1)	(11.4)	(14.2)	(14.6)
CF/K$_{jt-1}$	0.061	0.088	0.111	0.157
	(12.6)	(15.1)	(20.4)	(17.5)
CF/K$_{jt-2}$	0.043	0.059	0.071	0.063
	(9.5)	(10.4)	(13.2)	(6.7)
COC$_t$	0.002	0.002	0.002	0.005
	(2.8)	(2.3)	(3.4)	(3.9)
COC$_{t-1}$	−0.001	−0.0002	0.001	0.002
	(1.5)	(0.2)	(2.4)	(2.0)
COC$_{t-2}$	−0.001	0.0000	0.001	0.001
	(2.2)	(0.1)	(1.1)	(1.1)
Adjusted R-Squared	0.126	0.164	0.182	0.226

Notes

1. The author thanks Dean Baker, John Caskey, Jerry Epstein, John Keating, and Bruce Petersen for helpful comments and is especially indebted to Andrew Meyer for excellent research assistance.

2. The opportunity cost is the return on funds that firm owners could have earned in the money market if the profits had been paid out as dividends.

3. As of this writing, the growth rate of U.S. real gross domestic product has not exceeded 3 percent for 13 quarters (1989: 2 through 1992: 2) and has exceeded 2 percent only twice in this period. This growth rate averaged only five-tenths of 1 percent over this period. Unemployment has been trending upward from mid-1990 to mid-1992.

4. See Carlson (1991), Figure 6.

5. See, for example, Meyer and Kuh (1957).

6. See Jorgenson's (1971) survey for references.

7. Monetary policy in this framework could also have an indirect impact because of inflation nonneutralities due to nonindexed features of capital income taxation. This point is discussed in the section entitled "Policy Implications."

8. More recently, much empirical work on investment has focused on the estimation of "Euler equations" derived from explicit, dynamic models of firm value maximization. This work is not particularly relevant for the discussion here because the structure of Euler equations usually imposes an important role for the cost of capital rather than testing this impact. Furthermore, the assumptions that underlie the Euler equation approach are usually rejected empirically.

9. This concept goes back at least to Clark (1917).

10. See, for example, Romer and Romer (1990) for an interesting empirical analysis and further references.

11. The primary stabilizing factor is price flexibility. The relevant references are too numerous to include here. See Caskey and Fazzari (1987) and Tobin (1991) for more information.

12. Although the resurgence of interest in this topic is relatively new in the modern economics mainstream, it is prominent in earlier ideas about investment, going back at least to Keynes (1936).

13. For a more extensive discussion of the ideas and results presented here, and for additional references, see Fazzari, Hubbard, and Petersen (1988a).

14. Fazzari, Hubbard, and Petersen (1988a) identify such heterogeneity empirically in the link between investment and internal finance, and a variety of other more recent studies have confirmed this result.

15. See "Wary Lenders: Credit Crunch Appears Likely to Linger on for Years, Some Say," *The Wall Street Journal*, September 30, 1991, p. 1. Bernanke and Lown (1991) provide further discussion of the credit crunch and a detailed empirical analysis.

16. More formally, the point is that the conditions that determine the profit-maximizing interest rate charged by banks, particularly the extent to which rising rates magnify adverse selection and moral hazard problems, are not changed by reduction in the cost of funds. What changes is the optimal quantity of lending for a bank that charges the fixed, profit-maximizing interest rate. In principle, the cost of funds could decline to such a point that rationing would no longer exist because the optimal supply of funds at the profit-maximizing interest rate equals or exceeds demand. There is no guarantee, however, that such a result will occur at a positive cost of funds.

17. Blinder and Stiglitz (1983) reach similar conclusions. They also argue that the impact of tight money through quantity-rationing channels is likely the most severe for firms that do not have access to centralized securities markets (commercial paper, for

example), which may be the firms that produce the majority of output. Bernanke (1983) provides evidence of the importance of the quantity of credit as a determinant of economic activity in the Great Depression.

18. This argument is discussed in detail and supported by empirical evidence in Fazzari and Petersen (1993).

19. Because of the changes in the number of firms tracked over time, the proportion of fixed investment covered by the sample changes. It peaks at 49.2 percent in 1981; the low point is 36.1 percent in 1973.

20. Most accelerator models relate the level of investment to the level or the difference in sales. At the firm level, however, this relation depends on the firm's capital output ratio. This ratio can differ substantially across firms. Therefore, in the research reported here, I use the accelerator theory to motivate a link between the investment capital ratio and sales growth.

21. See Fazzari, Hubbard, and Petersen (1988a and 1988b) and Fazzari and Petersen (1993) for extensive discussion of how to interpret this link. In particular, those works analyze how to distinguish financial effects on investment from the possible role played by cash flow as a proxy for factors that shift investment demand.

22. One must assume a functional form for the regression equation. It is usually linear, which can be viewed as a general approximation to more complicated functions.

23. Another approach to address the Lucas critique uses economic theory to derive specifications for empirical analysis that allow the researcher to estimate parameters that do not vary with policy changes. The particular issues involved are beyond the scope of this chapter. Briefly, to capture the effects of a variety of important issues (the importance of financial constraints or heterogeneity across firms, for example), it would be very difficult, if not impossible, to use an approach that solved the problems of the Lucas critique in all respects. Moreover, attempts to overcome some of the Lucas critique problems in this way would necessarily impose other restrictive assumptions on the analysis.

24. I considered an observation in a high-technology industry if the firm's primary standard industrial classification (SIC) two-digit code was 28 (chemicals), 35 (machinery), 36 (electrical equipment and supply), or 38 (instruments). See Himmelberg and Petersen (1992) for further discussion of these industries and additional references.

25. See the econometric appendix for discussion of the specification used, the lag pattern, and standard errors.

26. The regressions were also run with alternative interest rates, including the federal funds rate and the yields on Treasury securities of different maturities. The results did not change in any material way.

27. For purposes of the calculations in Table 3.4, the depreciation rate was assumed to be 12 percent for all sales growth classes.

28. Again, see Romer and Romer (1990) for a recent interesting discussion and further references.

Bibliography

Auerbach, Alan J. "On the Design and Reform of Capital-Gains Taxation." *American Economic Review*, Vol. 80, May 1992, pp. 263–67.

Bernanke, Ben S. "Nonmonetary Effects of Financial Crisis in the Propogation of the Great Depression." *American Economic Review*, Vol. 73, June 1983, pp. 257–76.

Bernanke, Ben S. and Carla Lown. "The Credit Crunch." *Brookings Papers on Economic Activity*, No. 2, 1991, pp. 205–39.

Blecker, Robert. *Are Americans on a Consumption Binge? The Evidence Reconsidered.* Washington, DC: Economic Policy Institute, 1990.

Blinder, Alan and Joseph Stiglitz. "Money, Credit Constraints, and Economic Activity." *American Economic Review*, Vol. 73, May 1983, pp. 297–302.

Carlson, Keith M. "The Future of Social Security: An Update." *Review*, The Federal Reserve Bank of St. Louis, Vol. 73, January/February 1991, pp. 33–49.

Caskey, John P. and Steven M. Fazzari. "Aggregate Demand Contractions with Nominal Debt Commitments: Is Wage Flexibility Stabilizing?" *Economic Inquiry*, Vol. 25, October 1987, pp. 583–97.

Chirinko, Robert S. "Business Fixed Investment Spending: Modeling Strategies, Empirical Results and Policy Implications." *Journal of Economic Literature* (forthcoming); expanded version available as Federal Reserve Bank of Kansas City, Working Paper, April 1993.

Clark, J. M. "Business Acceleration and the Law of Demand: A Technical Factor in Economic Cycles." *Journal of Political Economy*, Vol. 25, March 1917, pp. 217–35.

DeLong, J. Bradford and Lawrence H. Summers. "Equipment Investment and Economic Growth." *Quarterly Journal of Economics*, Vol. 106, May 1991, pp. 445–502.

Eisner, Robert. "Deficits: Which, How Much, and So What?" *American Economic Review*, Vol. 80, May 1992, pp. 295–98.

Fair, Ray. "History.dat." *FAIRMODEL*, Southborough, MA: MACRO Incorporated, No. 2, 1992.

Fazzari, Steven M. "Tax Reform and Investment: Blessing or Curse." *Review*, The Federal Reserve Bank of St. Louis, Vol. 69, June/July 1987, pp. 23–33.

Fazzari, Steven M., R. Glenn Hubbard, and Bruce C. Petersen. "Investment Financing Decisions and Tax Policy." *American Economic Review*, Vol. 78, May 1988a, pp. 200–205.

Fazzari, Steven M. R. Glenn Hubbard, and Bruce C. Petersen. "Financing Constraints and Corporate Investment." *Brookings Papers on Economic Activity*, No. 2, 1988b, pp. 141–95.

Fazzari, Steven M. and Bruce C. Petersen. "Working Capital and Fixed Investment: New Evidence on Financing Constraints." *Rand Journal of Economics*, forthcoming, 1993.

Freidman, Benjamin M. "U.S. Fiscal Policy in the 1980s: Consequences of Large Budget Deficits at Full Employment." In James M. Rock, ed., *Debt and the Twin Deficits Debate*. Mountain View, CA: Bristlecone Books, 1991.

Hahn, Frank H. "Solowian Growth Models." In Peter Diamond, ed., *Growth/Productivity/Unemployment*. Cambridge, MA: Massachusetts Institute of Technology Press, 1990.

Harris, Ethan S. and Charles Steindel. "The Decline in U.S. Saving and Its Implications for Economic Growth." Federal Reserve Bank of New York, *Quarterly Review*, Vol. 15, Winter 1991, pp. 1–19.

Himmelberg, Charles P. and Bruce C. Petersen. "R&D and Internal Finance: A Panel Study of Small Firms in High-Tech Industries." Working Paper. St. Louis: Washington University Department of Economics, 1992.

Jorgenson, Dale W. "Econometric Studies of Investment Behavior: A Survey." *Journal of Economic Literature*, Vol. 53, December 1971, pp. 1111–47.

Jorgenson, Dale W. and Kim-Young Yun. *Tax Policy and the Cost of Capital*. Discussion Paper Number 1465. Cambridge, MA: Harvard Institute of Economic Research, November 1989.

Keynes, John M. *The General Theory of Employment, Interest, and Money*. London: Macmillan, 1936.

Lindsey, Lawrence B. "The Case for Disinflation." *Economic Commentary*, Federal Reserve Bank of Cleveland, March 15, 1992 (transcription of an address to the Government Bond Club of New England given on March 12, 1992).

Meyer, John and Edwin Kuh. *The Investment Decision*. Cambridge, MA: Harvard University Press, 1957.

Minsky, Hyman P. *John Maynard Keynes*. New York: Columbia University Press, 1975.

Poterba, James M. "Comparing the Cost of Capital in the United States and Japan: A Survey of Methods." Federal Reserve Bank of New York, *Quarterly Review*, Vol. 15, Winter 1991, pp. 20–32.

Romer, Christina D. and David H. Romer. "New Evidence on the Monetary Transmission Mechanism." *Brookings Papers on Economic Activity*, No. 1, 1990, pp. 149–214.

Stiglitz, Joseph and Andrew Weiss. "Credit Rationing in Markets with Imperfect Information." *American Economic Review*, Vol. 71, June 1981, pp. 393–410.

Tobin, James. "Price Flexibility and Output Stability." Cowles Foundation Discussion Paper, No. 994, New Haven, CT: Yale University, 1991.

Youngblood, Dick. "Quick Fix Means Economy Will Be Long-Term Broke." *Minneapolis Star Tribune*, January 27, 1992.

CHAPTER FOUR

Monetary Policy in the 1990s: Overcoming the Barriers to Equity and Growth[1]

GERALD EPSTEIN

CHAPTER SUMMARY

As the long recession of the early 1990s made clear, there is something fundamentally wrong with macroeconomic policy-making in the United States. In the face of enormous economic stress, fiscal policy sat immobilized, leaving to monetary policy the job of fighting the economic slump. The Federal Reserve's policy of repeated but hesitant and small reductions in interest rates, guided by its overriding concern about fighting inflation, has failed to restore robust economic growth.

Monetary policy's failure is only the latest in a series of monetary policies that have failed to restore the U.S. economy to health and, at worst, have been a significant part of the U.S. economy's problems. Since 1979, the Federal Reserve has been conducting a policy biased toward fighting inflation, even at extraordinarily high costs in terms of economic growth, productive investment, and unemployment.

What is required is a new set of goals for monetary policy. Monetary policy should focus more on promoting productive investment and fighting unemployment, giving these goals equal weight with maintaining a stable rate of inflation. To implement the new set of goals, a new policy structure is also required—one in which the Federal Reserve is more accountable to the public, in which monetary policy coordination with fiscal policy is facilitated, and in which policies to improve credit allocation and reduce financial speculation are implemented as needed.

However, there are three major, commonly perceived obstacles to shifting the goals of monetary policy: the costs of inflation itself (the inflation constraint), the constraints imposed by highly integrated international financial markets (the external constraint), and the difficulties of controlling the activities of huge and highly liquid financial markets (the financial market constraint).

In an evaluation of these three constraints, it is crucial to make a distinction between two aspects of each one: economic barriers, which relate to the effects of policies on the size of the economic pie, and political barriers, which involve the effects of policies on the distribution of that pie among different groups. Groups harmed by policies try to put up political barriers to changing them, often by arguing that the policies would have large economic costs.

This chapter argues that the economic constraints to reorienting monetary policy away from a sole concern with inflation fighting, though sometimes important, are not as serious as widely believed; on the other hand, the political barriers can be very strong and therefore must be challenged.

Introduction

As the long, painful recession of the early 1990s has made clear, something is fundamentally wrong with the macroeconomic policy-making apparatus in the United States. In the face of enormous economic stress, fiscal policy sat immobilized for at least two years, leaving to monetary policy the entire job of fighting the unfolding economic slump. This was a bit like asking the fox to guard the henhouse, because it was the Federal Reserve Board (Fed), after all, that had helped to initiate the 1990s recession with its tight monetary policy in the late 1980s and early 1990s. The Fed's subsequent policy of repeated but hesitant and small reductions in interest rates, guided by its overriding concern with fighting inflation, has failed to restore robust economic growth (Galbraith, this volume).

Monetary policy's failure to bring about a much-heralded soft landing is only the latest in a series of monetary policies that, at best, have failed to restore the U.S. economy to health and, at worst, have been a significant part of the U.S. economy's problems. Indeed, since 1979, when Federal Reserve chairman Paul Volcker initiated his watershed tight monetary policy, the Fed has been conducting a policy biased toward fighting inflation, even at extraordinarily high costs in economic growth and unemployment. The result has been historically high real interest rates that have had highly detrimental consequences for the U.S. economy.[2] These problems with monetary policy have achieved enormous importance, because with fiscal policy paralyzed by concerns about the budget deficit, monetary policy has become virtually the only weapon of macroeconomic policy, a situation that has not prevailed in the United States since the 1920s.

In response to these perceived failures, some critics have argued for a restructuring of the monetary policy apparatus. These critics would have the Fed focus less on raising interest rates and fighting inflation and would orient monetary policy more toward increasing productive investment and economic growth (Greider, 1987; Epstein, 1991; Galbraith, Pollin, this volume).

Yet, despite the apparent failures of monetary policy, these advocates of monetary restructuring face enormous skepticism from observers both inside and outside the Washington, D.C., Beltway. These observers believe that, by and large, the Federal Reserve has made the best of a bad situation. The often implicit view is that under modern conditions, the Federal Reserve has relatively little leeway to make policy much different from what it has been. These doubts stem primarily from the perceived evils of inflation and from perceived changes in the nature of both domestic financial markets and the international economy.

More specifically, many argue that the domestic bond markets, combined with internationally integrated financial markets, constrain monetary policy within extremely narrow bounds. According to this view, the Federal Reserve is unable to pursue an aggressively expansionary policy because it would scare the financial markets, both at home and abroad. Worried about future inflation, bond traders will sell bonds, an action that drives down their prices and raises interest rates—thereby undermining the Fed's policy of lower interest rates. In the international markets, any attempt to lower domestic interest rates substantially below those prevailing abroad will lead traders to sell government securities and other dollar-denominated assets to invest in foreign assets. This will cause the dollar to tumble and put upward pressure on interest rates, once again undermining the low-interest-rate policy.

These skeptics believe that the Fed's hands are tied by both domestic and international financial markets; it has done all it can. According to them, considering the great evils of inflation and the financial markets' aversion to inflation, it is essential for the Fed to be using whatever leeway it has to bring down the inflation rate.

In sum, there are three major perceived obstacles to shifting the goals of monetary policy away from a sole concern with inflation fighting and back to a more balanced concern which includes fighting unemployment and promoting productive investment: the inflation constraint, the external constraint, and the financial which includes market constraint. Assessing the importance of these three constraints is central to an adequate assessment of the possibilities for reforming monetary policy along more progressive lines.

In evaluating these three constraints, it is crucial to make a distinction, almost always ignored in policy discussions, between two aspects of each one: economic barriers and political barriers. Economic barriers relate to the effects of policies on the size of the economic pie, namely, the gross domestic product (GDP). Political barriers involve the effects of policies on the distribution of that pie among different groups. Take the inflation constraint, for example. Inflation can affect the economy either by altering the rate of growth of output (GDP) or by redistributing income and wealth, from wealthier creditors to less wealthy debtors. If the first effect is to lower the rate of growth of output, then it can create an economic barrier to policy. The second creates a political barrier, because those who are adversely affected by inflation—in this example, wealthy creditors—will fight against policies that might raise the rate of inflation.[3]

An effective approach in such political battles is for those who are adversely affected to claim that the cost of inflation reduces income for everyone, not just themselves. This attempt to wrap individual harm in the cloak of general welfare is a major reason this distinction between economic barriers and political barriers is rarely made, despite its great importance.

The major objective of this chapter is to evaluate the importance of these three constraints in the making and possible restructuring of U.S. monetary policy. In doing so, I will distinguish carefully between economic and political barriers on monetary policy. I will argue that the economic barriers to reorienting monetary policy away from a sole concern with inflation fighting and toward a more balanced concern with inflation and economic growth, though in many cases important, are not as serious as widely believed. On the other hand, the political barriers can be strong indeed.

In the next section, I assess the extreme case against the possibility of more expansionary monetary policy: the claim that monetary policy has no discernible, long-lasting effect on the economy. I will show that the evidence is clear that, despite the major changes in the domestic and international financial markets, monetary policy can have important effects on the economy. In the third section, I discuss the evidence on the inflation constraint and show that economists have been unable to find large costs from moderate inflation. As a result, within the bounds of moderate inflation, the inflation constraint is primarily a political barrier, not an economic one. Then I discuss the external constraint, arguing that the external constraint is real and binding; but I also argue that how binding it is depends strongly on the particular circumstances. There is no evidence that, in general, U.S. monetary policy is helpless in the wake of international financial integration, as many seem to believe. Here again, as with the inflation constraint, the role of politics should not be underestimated. In the section entitled The Domestic Financial Constraint, I discuss briefly the financial market constraint, arguing that the structure of the financial markets can be a serious constraint on monetary policy but not primarily in the way many believe. The major problem is not that the Fed is powerless to affect long-term real interest rates; even if the Fed has difficulty controlling long-term interest rates, however important they may be, it has considerable leverage over short-term rates, which are also important determinants of macroeconomic activity. The more important problem is this: monetary policy, as it is commonly practiced, may not by itself be sufficiently effective in allocating credit to socially desirable sectors of the economy. In the final section, I describe several paths to monetary reform that attempt to relax the financial market, inflation, and external constraints. However important it is to restructure the financial apparatus to overcome these economic barriers, I suggest that political reform is even more important.

In particular, what is required is a new structure for monetary policy: a new goal and a new institutional structure within which policy will be made. The goals should be more balanced between inflation fighting and promoting productive investment than it currently is. The structure should include more room for policy coordination, accountability, mechanisms of credit allocation, and insulation from international financial speculation. Without these changes, monetary policy will continue to hit up against a real constraint on policy: the underlying stagnation in the productive capacity of the U.S. economy.

Figure 4.1. **Real Interest Rates: Short and Long, Federal Funds and AAA Bonds Minus Inflation, 1955–1992**

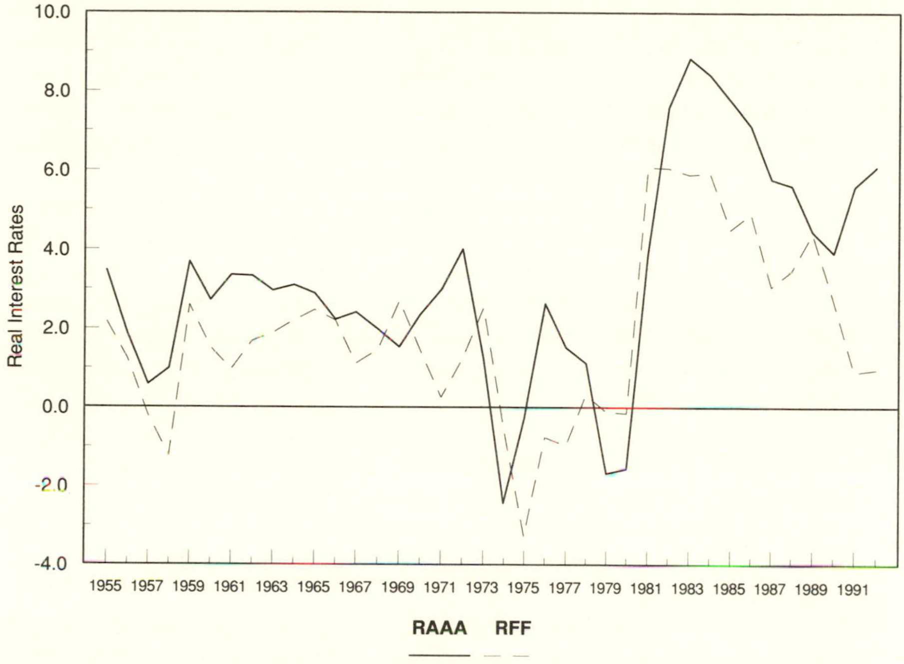

RAAA   RFF

Source: ERP, 1991, B-62, B-71; *Economic Indicators,* July 1992; *The Economist*, August 1992.

The Effectiveness of Monetary Policy

During the past decade and a half, monetary policy has been almost single-mindedly focused on fighting inflation. The result has been a lopsided macroeconomic policy, represented most importantly by historically high real long-term interest rates that have had seriously detrimental effects on the economy. This is just one example of the real effects of monetary policy on the economy.

Critics of recent Federal Reserve policy point to the dramatic increase in real interest rates during the early 1980s, initiated by the Federal Reserve Board under Paul Volcker's chairmanship, and the continued existence of unusually high real rates since that time.[4] More recently, critics have argued that the tight money implemented by Chairman Alan Greenspan's Fed was largely responsible for initiating the recession of the 1990s.

Figure 4.1 charts the recent history of real interest rates in the United States. The figure presents the federal funds rate minus the rate of inflation (short) and the AAA bond rate minus inflation (long). The rates were generally stable at around 2.5 percent for most of the 1960s. They became negative in the early

1970s and then jumped in the early 1980s to 6 percent for short-term rates and more than 7.5 percent for AAA corporate bonds. From 1985 through 1987, real rates fell almost to the levels of the 1960s; then, in 1987–1990, they began to rise again.

The historically high interest rates of the early 1980s have been credited with contributing to many of the ills we face, including the loss of competitiveness in many industries due to the increased value of the dollar at that time, the shift to speculative and risky investments to repay such high rates, the depression in many debtor countries and the consequent decline in demand for products from the United States, the bankruptcy of many farmers who were paying real rates of over 30 percent at this time (Mishkin, 1988), and a worsening of income distribution as creditors' share of income has risen.

Although the dramatic rise in interest rates cannot be denied, the role of monetary policy in generating those rates has been the subject of much dispute. Prime alternative candidates for the rise in real interest rates are the increase in the U.S. budget deficit and the increase in underlying interest rates due to deregulation in financial markets.

On one hand, despite many empirical tests, most evidence suggests that U.S. budget deficits have not raised real interest rates (Evans, 1987; Barro and Martin, 1990). On the other hand, there have been few attempts to test the hypothesis that financial deregulation and speculation have increased real interest rates, so one must remain agnostic on this theory.[5]

However, there is reasonably good evidence that the increase in real rates in the 1980s was due, to a considerable extent, to the change in monetary policy initiated by the Federal Reserve (Huizinga and Mishkin, 1986). Huizinga and Mishkin, for example, estimate the processes determining the real interest rate and find a structural break in the process just at the time when Volcker's Fed tightened policy.[6]

While the effects of the budget deficit on interest rates represent a continuing area of dispute, recent empirical research, using a variety of approaches, has produced abundant evidence that in the United States, monetary policy has important effects on the real economy through its effects on interest rates and bank credit (Huizinga and Mishkin, 1986; Mishkin, 1988; Fair, 1989; Romer and Romer, 1989; Bernanke, 1990; Bernanke and Blinder, 1990; Romer and Romer, 1990).

For example, Bernanke and Blinder find that the federal funds rate—the one interest rate that the Federal Reserve unambiguously controls—is markedly superior to both monetary aggregates and most other interest rates as a forecaster of the economy (Bernanke and Blinder, 1990, pp. 5–16).[7] Moreover, they note that every cyclical peak since 1959 was preceded by a sustained runup in the spread between the federal funds rate and the 10-year Treasury rate (Figure 4.2).[8] Furthermore, only one of the sustained increases in this spread was not followed by a recession. This was the credit crunch of 1966, which was followed by a growth recession.[9]

Such evidence is not definitive. After all, the Federal Reserve does not control

Figure 4.2. **The Federal Funds Rate and Spread, 1955–1991**

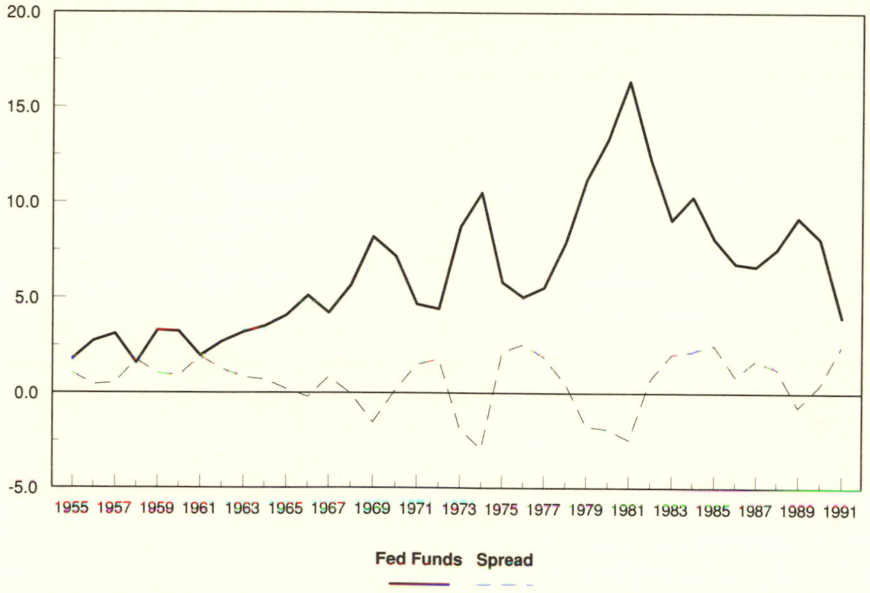

Fed Funds   Spread

Source: ERP, 1991.

the spread between the federal funds rate and the 10-year Treasury bill. That spread is a combination of the federal funds rate, which the Fed controls, and the 10-year Treasury bill, which is controlled by the market.

Moreover, significant recent changes in financial markets might render historically based studies obsolete. Financial deregulation and innovation in the 1970s and 1980s in the United States and elsewhere—which introduced a more flexible exchange-rate system and eliminated international capital controls, interest-rate ceilings, and portfolio restrictions—have brought about profound changes in the domestic and international monetary systems.

Some have argued that these changes have greatly reduced the efficacy of national monetary policy. First, whereas monetary policy used to work by credit rationing and disintermediation brought on by interest rate ceilings, it now must work by affecting interest rates. However—and this is the second point—the ability of the Federal Reserve to alter interest rates is hampered by international financial integration, which reduces the ability of the central bank to set rates different from those in major countries abroad. Moreover, the Fed is hampered by the expectations of the massive bond and stock markets. These markets determine long-term rates on the basis of expectations of future inflation and monetary policy that the Fed might have difficulty controlling. Finally, with vast financial markets to choose from, businesses and consumers are less sensitive to interest rates than before.

Table 4.1

MPS Model Simulation, Effect of One Percentage Point Decline in Federal Funds Rate on Real GNP, by Channel of Transmission
(all figures except in last column are billions of 1982 dollars)

Channel	Quarters After Change				Average, 16 Quarters	
	4	8	12	16	$1982 Billions	Percent of GNP
Cost of capital						
Pre-1980s	15.0	20.5	28.4	41.0	26.2	0.73
1980s	11.6	14.0	14.9	19.6	15.0	0.42
Wealth						
Pre-1980s	2.7	8.4	17.1	23.1	12.8	0.36
1980s	2.7	6.6	10.5	12.2	11.3	0.32
Exchange rate						
Pre-1980s	4.7	13.0	17.1	10.4	11.3	0.32
1980s	8.3	23.2	29.7	17.1	19.6	0.55
All three channels						
Pre-1980s	22.4	41.9	63.2	74.5	50.5	1.41
1980s	22.3	43.8	55.0	48.9	42.5	1.19

Source: Gordon, 1991; adapted from Mauskopf (1990), Table 5, p. 1003. Final column is percent of real GNP in 1985: Q1, the base-line quarter of the simulations.

Recently there has been a great deal of work attempting to assess the effects of monetary policy on the economy in light of recent changes (Chouraqui et al., 1988; Friedman, 1989; Blundell-Wignall et al., 1990; Mauskopf, 1990; Gordon, 1991; Mosser, 1992; Sims, 1992). This work indicates that the channels of monetary policy have changed as a result of domestic and international changes but that monetary policy is still very powerful in its effects on the economy. In particular, monetary policy works less through changes in the direct allocation of credit and changes in long-term interest rates, and more through changes in short-term interest rates and exchange rates.[10] However, while some studies show that U.S. monetary policy is less powerful than it was in the past, it still has a large impact on the U.S. economy.

Table 4.1, adapted from Mauskopf (1990) and taken from Gordon (1991), illustrates these points. The table shows the effects of a one percentage point decline in the federal funds rate on real GNP 4, 8, 12, and 16 quarters later, according to the Federal Reserve's MPS model (used by the Federal Reserve Board to assess the effects of monetary and fiscal policy on the economy). It separates the channels of the effects of monetary policy on the economy into three types. The cost-of-capital channel represents the effects of long-term interest rates on investment in plant and equipment; it also represents the effects of these interest rates on housing investment, both directly through their effects on the costs of mortgages and indirectly through their effects on the availability of mortgage financing.[11] The wealth channel represents the effects of interest rates on the value of household financial portfolios and, therefore, on the amount that households are willing to spend on consumption. The exchange rate channel captures the effects of monetary policy on exchange rates and hence on exports and imports.

The table shows that the cost-of-capital channel, related to disintermediation in the housing sector and long-term interest rates, and the wealth channel of monetary policy, which is closely associated with changes in long-term interest rates, were more powerful before the 1980s than after. The table also shows that the exchange-rate channel, more dependent on short-term interest rates, was less powerful before the 1980s than after. The total effects of policy are about the same after 8 quarters, but by the 16th quarter, the total effect before the 1980s was substantially more—$74.5 billion versus $48.9 billion. However, on average, the decline in effectiveness was small, from 1.41 percent of gross national product (GNP) to 1.19 percent.

According to these results, despite domestic financial deregulation and innovations in the 1980s and despite the decline of capital controls and increased international financial integration, U.S. monetary policy is still powerful.[12] But the channels have changed.

The work by Steven Fazzari (this volume) indicates an additional important channel through which monetary policy operates—through its effects on the availability of credit for investment in plant and equipment. Fazzari emphasizes the importance of investment in the economy for demand stimulus, which he suggests has both short-term and long-run effects, and for supply creation, through the effects of additional capital stock on productivity, capacity, and competitiveness (Fazzari, 1992).

Fazzari notes that new views of capital markets suggest monetary policy affects investment primarily through its effects on the degree of credit rationing by banks and by the overall stimulus to the economy and not chiefly through interest rates and the cost of capital. More stimulus generates more profits and internal cash flow for firms, which provides the funds (at a lower opportunity cost than external funds, according to this view) for more investment.[13] These monetary policy effects are likely to be much more powerful on those firms for which access to external capital markets is most costly: smaller and newer firms, which are likely to be among the fastest growing and those adding significantly to technological advance.

If this channel for monetary policy is important, then Fazzari's analysis suggests that tight monetary policy, by reducing investment of the most technologically advancing firms, should harm productivity growth in the economy. Hence tight money, while reducing demand, might also constrain supply. This fact helps to explain why tight monetary policy fails, fundamentally and once and for all, to slay the dragon of inflation, as Galbraith notes (1992). It may reduce inflation in the short run but usually does so at the cost of worsening the economy's productive capacity.

While it may be that contractionary monetary policy (high interest rates) has strong effects on the economy, does not the experience with expansionary monetary policy in 1991–92 suggest that, however powerful contractionary policy may be, expansionary policy is considerably less powerful? Is not the old adage "You can't push on a string" a true description of the weak effects of expansionary policy in the recession of the early 1990s? Does not the fact that short-term interest rates came down dramatically while long-term rates fell much less indicate that monetary policy is a weak instrument of economic recovery?

The experience with monetary policy in the early 1990s does not show that expansionary monetary policy is ineffective. Rather, it shows that in a serious recession, policy must be more aggressive and determined than at normal times if it is to succeed. The Greenspan Federal Reserve, however, had no such aggressiveness or determination.[14]

As the recession of the early 1990s unfolded, the Federal Reserve acted in a most gradual and incremental manner, dropping the federal funds rate by quarter points, at such a slow speed that their effectiveness probably was greatly reduced. The reason for such slow, incremental policy is clear. As a careful analysis of the record indicates, given the range of forecasts and the uncertainties associated with them, the Federal Reserve's policy was always on the side of caution and restraint. Why? Because at every juncture, faced with choosing between a higher risk of recession and a higher risk that inflation would not continue to fall, the Federal Reserve chose the higher risk of recession.

In short, given all the uncertainties plaguing our economy, Greenspan's Federal Reserve, like any Federal Reserve, made policy to some extent by throwing dice. But—and this is the key point—the Fed chose to play with dice that were loaded against preventing a recession.

The result of this bias toward inflation fighting was a monetary policy that was—in terms of standard measures—at most expansionary to an average degree for postwar recessions.[15] By other measures, however, the policy was less expansionary than average. While short-term interest rates fell more than average, they came down in smaller steps and were spread out over a longer time than in other postwar recessions. Real interest rates remained higher than in most other postwar recessions.[16] And the rate of growth of important monetary aggregates—M2, domestic credit, and bank lending—were extremely low by historical standards. For example, in November 1991, bank lending was only 0.2 percent above the levels of July 1990, whereas it had advanced 11 percent during corresponding periods of previous cycles.[17] M2 remained at the bottom of or below the Federal Reserve's own target range, and after an adjustment for inflation, M2 has declined during most of the recession. Meanwhile, the growth of real credit to nonfederal borrowers fell dramatically during the recession.[18]

While monetary stimulus was painfully tentative, other economic factors called out for a more aggressive policy than usual. Fiscal policy was significantly less expansionary than average. Typically, during postwar recessions, federal fiscal stimulus is almost 1 percent of GDP. During the recession of the early 1990s, however, there was no federal fiscal stimulus.[19] On top of that, most observers agree that the fiscal problems in the state and local sectors generated a significant fiscal drag on the economy. The unusually slow growth in domestic credit described earlier indicates that credit was not expanding as rapidly per unit of monetary policy stimulus as is usually the case. Additional factors suggested the need for more expansionary policy than usual. Consumer confidence was unusually low. Many estimates suggest that 50 percent of the effect of monetary policy comes through increases in exports resulting from a depreciating dollar. And, with our major trading partners experiencing slow growth or recession, the stimulus from this channel of monetary policy was greatly reduced.

As Galbraith (this volume) argues, the large spread between long- and short-term interest rates suggests that the Greenspan Fed had a severe credibility problem that has reduced the effectiveness of the expansionary policy the Fed has undertaken. Because the markets did not believe the Fed would keep interest rates low, they were reluctant to buy long-term bonds. Hence, the spread between long and short rates remained at historically high levels.

In short, recent experience with monetary policy suggests primarily that weak monetary policy, in an environment in which highly aggressive expansionary policy is called for, leads to weak results. However, recent experience does not undercut the argument that expansionary policy, properly conducted, can have powerful effects.

Indeed, one can argue that monetary policy has been effective in preventing the recession from getting worse. Given the fiscal restraint at both the federal and the state and local levels, the recession undoubtedly would have been longer and deeper without the declines in short-term interest rates, hesitant and reluctant as they have been. Moreover, the experience suggests that long-term real interest rates can decline, though perhaps not as quickly and as far as once believed.

Despite this prima facie evidence that monetary policy can have a powerful effect on the economy, skepticism remains. Sure, exchange rate changes can affect the economy, but the potentially powerful effect of exchange rates is a two-edged sword. Given the external constraint, will attempts to use expansionary monetary policy to drive interest rates below those prevailing abroad not lead to a rapid and uncontrolled decline in the dollar that will have disruptive effects on the economy? And, considering that the financial markets know that, will the financial constraint not mean that any attempt to reduce interest rates will be defeated by bond markets worried about a decline in the dollar and about higher inflation? Given all this, isn't the inflation constraint binding? Shouldn't the Federal Reserve focus on fighting inflation and leave it at that?

The Inflation Constraint

The most serious constraints confronting a more expansionary monetary policy are the concerns that such a policy will lead to inflation and that inflation has a strongly negative impact on the economy. The current policy incarnation of this view is the "zero-inflation" target, which some in Congress believe ought to be the goal of the Federal Reserve, and which some in the Fed appear to endorse.

For inflation to be a serious economic barrier to expansionary monetary policy, a number of conditions must obtain. First, there must be a direct link between monetary policy and inflation. Second, inflation must have significant detrimental consequences for the economy. For the so-called zero-inflation option to make sense, yet another condition must be met. The costs of reaching such a target and keeping the economy there must be less than the benefits of achieving zero inflation.

First, the links between monetary policy and inflation are much less clear than many believe. The monetarist view—that increases in the money supply faster than the rate of growth of potential output lead to increases in inflation—is incorrect. As Benjamin Friedman and Kenneth Kuttner (1992) have shown most recently, in the United States in the 1980s, there was virtually no reliable relationship between any measure of the money supply and inflation. As Friedman and Kuttner explain, "Including data from the 1980s sharply weakens the postwar time-series evidence indicating significant relationships between money (however defined) and nominal income, or between money and either real income or prices separately. Focusing on data from 1970 onwards destroys this evidence altogether" (Friedman and Kuttner, 1992, p. 472). The problems with this simple relationship include the enormous financial innovations that have occurred that alter the relationships between money and the economy. Also significant is the fact, important in centuries of debate over monetary policy, that money responds to the state of the economy as much as the other way around.

Yet, as we saw in the previous section, monetary policy can and does affect the economy through its effects on interest rates, credit availability, and the exchange rate. To the extent that monetary policy affects the state of the economy, it can certainly have an indirect effect on inflation. The key issue is, what are these indirect effects?

Again, we are first confronted with a rather simple and extreme theory, the so-called New Classical Macroeconomics. This theory argues that in both the short and the long run, the economy is always at full employment, or the so-called "natural rate of unemployment." If the economy is always at full employment, then any attempt by the central bank to reduce unemployment further, say by lowering interest rates, will simply lead to more inflation without any increase in real output. In more technical terms, according to this view, the economy is characterized by a vertical Phillips Curve (McCallum, 1990, gives a recent survey).[20] It was shown earlier that this view cannot be completely correct, because monetary policy has effects on real output and employment, at least in the short run. Many economists have argued that, while this so-called natural rate of unemployment theory cannot be true in the short run, it is true in the long run. So, in the long run, expansionary monetary policy—say, the lowering of interest rates—can lead only to an increase in inflation, not to an increase in output or employment. This view is the most widely accepted argument against a more activist policy to lower interest rates and revive economic growth.

The "natural rate" view, however, has come under increasing challenge by those who argue that the natural rate is not so natural after all (Blanchard and Summers, 1986; Gordon, 1988). These and other economists argue that macroeconomic policy can have important effects on the prevailing unemployment rate. The implication is that monetary policy can have both long-run and short-run effects on unemployment and the real economy without necessarily leading to runaway inflation.

Much of this reassessment of the so-called natural rate theory was prompted by the effects of the tight monetary policies both in the United Kingdom and in the United States in the 1980s. Why is it that, after the tight monetary policies of the government of British Prime Minister Margaret Thatcher succeeded in reducing inflation, the unemployment rate did not fall back to its previous, "natural" level? Why, in other words, did the so-called natural rate seem to increase in response to tight monetary policy (Blanchard and Summers, 1986)? Gordon (1988) has asked the same question with regard to the United States.

This work suggests a variety of answers to the question, all of which amount to the assessment that monetary policy can have long-run effects on the economy, including the unemployment rate. This important work reassessing the natural rate hypothesis argues that tight monetary policy designed to reduce inflation can be self-defeating. It may lower inflation, at least temporarily, but only at the cost of permanently increasing the unemployment rate and slowing the rate of economic growth. The reasons are the detrimental effects of tight money and high interest rates on investment and productivity growth. As Steven Fazzari suggests (in this volume), tight monetary policy can have serious detrimental effects on investment in the technologically most progressive industries. Tight money reduces bank lending and increases credit rationing by banks. Such credit rationing tends to harm technologically progressive firms because they are relatively small and therefore relatively highly dependent on banks for financing. Through this mechanism, tight money may reduce investment by these firms relatively more than other firms. As a result, tight monetary policy might reduce the level of technological innovation and, as a result, productivity growth. If the rate of productivity growth declines, then an expansion of demand becomes relatively more likely to increase inflation.

A second channel through which tight monetary policy can have long-run detrimental effects on productivity and the rate of inflation for any given unemployment rate is through such a policy's effects on the exchange rate and the trade balance. Many economists now believe the high interest rates that brought about the overvalued dollar in the middle 1980s had long-run negative consequences for U.S. productivity growth and competitiveness because of the great harm it did to sectors subject to international competition.

Among other things, this analysis suggests that an attempt to use tight monetary policy to reach zero inflation is likely to be self-defeating. Raising interest rates to reduce inflation might actually raise the inflation rate at a given rate of unemployment because of its detrimental effects on productivity and economic growth.[21]

The important point that Fazzari makes, and that is seconded by Galbraith, is the following: tight money can be a self-defeating strategy for reducing inflation because of its negative consequences on productivity and the supply side. Conversely, an often-ignored effect of looser monetary policy is its positive consequences for inflation through its positive effects on investment and productivity, holding all else constant.

Even though looser monetary policy and lower interest rates may have these positive effects on productivity growth and inflation there seems little doubt that at times and under certain circumstances, looser monetary policy may lead to higher inflation. This naturally leads to the question of how serious a problem inflation itself is. What are the costs of inflation? How much employment and output should the United States be willing to forgo to reduce the rate of inflation?

In the United States and much of Europe, many policymakers take the answer to be a foregone conclusion: inflation is a prime evil and should be stopped at all costs. Partly because of this widely accepted answer among policymakers, especially central bankers in the United States and Western Europe, we are witnessing some of the most prolonged high levels of unemployment and slow economic growth since World War II.

Given the consensus among central bankers on this topic, it might be surprising that economists have not been able to find large costs of inflation, as long as inflation is below hyperinflation levels of, say, at least 1,000 percent per year (Fischer and Modigliani, 1975; Fischer, 1981; Driffill et al., 1990).[22] The main cost of inflation has been hypothesized to be the reduction in ability of entrepreneurs and consumers to make economic decisions and plans because of difficulty in getting and interpreting information about prices. This reduction in the efficiency of the price system has been hypothesized to result both from an increased variability in the overall rate of inflation and from higher variability in the relative prices of goods as the inflation rate goes up.

Yet despite a number of attempts to discover these relationships, there is little evidence that such effects exist. There have been few cross-country studies of the effects of inflation on measures of economic welfare, so work remains to be done in this area. The one study that has been undertaken, by Robert Barro of Harvard University, concludes that any discernible negative relationship between inflation and economic growth is likely to be due to the negative effect of growth on inflation, rather than the other way around![23] Barro points out that many of the worst-performing economies have relatively low inflation rates.[24]

My previous discussion has been qualified by stating that hyperinflations are probably an exception to the rule that there seem not to be large costs to inflation. But some economists have argued that the distinction I have drawn between moderate inflation and hyperinflation is a false one: that inflations easily get out of control, and so a moderate level of inflation can easily jump to much higher rates. However, hyperinflation is an unusual event. Barro reports that from 1970 to 1985, only 14 of 118 countries in his sample had annual inflation rates that averaged more than 20 percent, and only 7 exceeded 40 percent average inflation. During the 1960–1970 period, there were even fewer in both categories.

Very high and accelerating inflation appears to be a symptom more than a cause: a symptom of serious pathologies within an economy, often associated with war. Such high inflation rates are so rare that there seems to be little evidence that moderate inflations, by themselves, are likely to lead to them. As for the economic costs of moderate inflation, they seem, as I have suggested, to be low to nonexistent.

What, then, can explain the enormous fear and concern about moderate inflation that seem to motivate the policies of many central banks and governments around the world? One possible explanation is that the inflation constraint is really a political barrier. Here the problem is the effect of inflation on income distribution, not on the level or rate of growth of output; in other words, certain groups dislike inflation because of what it does to the distribution of the economic pie, not its size.

Relatively little research has been devoted to the effects of inflation on income and wealth distribution. Most of the research that has been undertaken indicates that, for the United States, inflation is associated with a redistribution of income from those in the higher income brackets to those in the lower income brackets (Wolff, 1979). Hibbs (1987) describes evidence that shows that inflation has reduced the incomes of only the top quintile of the income distribution.[25] The New York Federal Reserve Bank (1986) presents analyses and data that indicate that bank profits go down with an increase in the inflation rate (Mott and Caudle, 1992, give a discussion).

All this evidence suggests that political opposition to moderate inflation rates comes from the relatively wealthy and from banks and other financial institutions. According to this logic, then, the inflation constraint is not an economic constraint at all, but rather is a political barrier. And it is likely to be rather severe, because these groups, at least at certain times, can have considerable political power.

Matters, however, are not quite as simple as this, for Hibbs (1987) and others have also reported that despite the fact that most Americans are not harmed by inflation, the majority of them still oppose even moderately high levels of inflation. Part of the explanation might be that most people confuse inflation, as economists understand the term—a general increase in all prices and wages—with other economic phenomena that often are associated with increases in inflation. Hence, opposition to inflation may really be a result of opposition to other phenomena that have sometimes accompanied inflationary periods.

For example, during the 1970s inflation, there was a substantial increase in the *relative* price of oil, which redistributed a huge amount of wealth from most Americans to the oil producers—in the United States and abroad. This redistribution, resulting from the increase in the relative price of oil, did reduce the standard of living of most people. But the reduction was due to the increase in a price of a particular commodity—oil—not to an increase in all prices, which is what economists mean by inflation. But because the increase in the price of oil was associated with a general increase in inflation, many Americans developed a strong aversion to what policymakers, bankers, and the press referred to as "inflation" *per se.*[26]

So, all else being equal, most people may still prefer to have relatively low levels of inflation, perhaps because of the uncertainty and feelings of insecurity that high levels of inflation bring. But that does not imply that people would prefer to have the high levels of unemployment and slow economic growth that the U.S. economy has experienced in order to bring down the rate of inflation. When the rate of unemployment is high and economic growth slows, polls show that people's main concerns switch from inflation to unemployment (Hibbs, 1987). Given the effects of unemployment versus inflation on most Americans' standard of living, it is doubtful that most Americans would pick the position on the tradeoff apparently chosen by the Federal Reserve *if they were informed of the real choices.*

In the end, then, for moderate rates of inflation, the major constraint is not an economic barrier but rather a political barrier. The political barrier stems primarily from the opposition to inflation by the wealthy and by creditors who stand to lose the most from inflation. But monetary policy cannot ignore opposition by the general population, especially if increases in the rate of inflation are unaccompanied by increases in the standard of living, which was the case in the 1970s.

So far I have discussed the effects of inflation on economic growth. But inflation might indirectly affect the economy and the Federal Reserve's ability to manage it through inflation's interaction with the two other constraints: the external constraint and the financial constraint. Some economists believe that inflation can generate instability in both international and domestic financial markets, an effect that may create serious problems for the financial authorities. So it is important to discuss these two constraints and their interaction with inflation before reaching a final verdict on the true problems posed by moderate rates of inflation.

The External Constraint

It is easy to see why there is a common view that the huge and highly integrated international financial markets might place a serious constraint on monetary policy. The headlines in the newspapers are consistent with people's intuition about the state of the world: "Traders Overwhelm Central Banks" (*International Herald Tribune [IHT]*, September 26, 1992). Mind-boggling numbers seem to confirm the verdict. A recent study reported by the Federal Reserve Bank of New York indicates that global foreign exchange trading has grown by 50 percent over the past three years, to over $1 trillion *each day*, while central bank foreign exchange reserves have grown much more slowly (*IHT*). Yet, the ambiguity of the situation is represented by another headline in the same edition of the same newspaper: "Victories for Central Banks: EMS Stabilization Appears to Be Returning." The two apparently contradictory headlines reflect a reality: international financial markets have become huge and highly integrated. They can pose a serious constraint on the actions of central banks; yet, in the end, central banks of the major industrialized countries, and particularly the United States, Europe, and Japan, are far from powerless against them. In short, the external constraint is real, but it is far from absolute.

What is the effect of this external constraint on monetary policy? First, as with the inflation constraint, it is necessary to distinguish between the economic and the political barriers. Within the economic barrier, it is necessary to distinguish two types. The first is the view implied in the newspaper headline previously quoted: in an internationally integrated world, central banks are simply powerless, ineffective. According to this view, international financial markets are so huge and integrated that the Federal Reserve cannot affect anything; it is simply overwhelmed.

The view that the international economy is a constraint in the sense that it renders policy ineffective has validity only if the government tries to maintain a fixed exchange rate. In this case, the central bank must gear its monetary policies to keeping its currency in line with those of other countries, and its monetary policies might be unable to do anything else.[27] But if the United States is not committed to fixing its exchange rate, then changes in interest rates can be used for domestic purposes.

Here is the rub: changes in interest rates may cause the exchange rate to change. And these changes in exchange rates may have undesirable effects on the economy that constrain the use of monetary policy. This second type of economic barrier concerns the costs of these changes in exchange rates that may result from changes in domestic interest rates relative to those abroad. And here three types of costs have been proposed: inflation, decline in the level of international trade, and economic instability.

Inflation operates as follows: depreciations of the dollar can lead to an increase in the price of imports and import competing goods and therefore an increase in inflation. While that is true in principle, the magnitude of the inflation effects has been exaggerated (Dornbusch and Giovannini, 1990, give a survey). In any case, most of the same issues apply here as in the earlier discussion of the inflation constraint.[28]

A second widely discussed cost of exchange rate changes is that exchange rate variability leads to increased uncertainty and costs of trading and may, therefore, discourage exports and imports. However, few studies have been able to uncover any large effects of this type (see the Dornbusch and Giovannini, 1990, survey).

The third and most important type of potential economic cost stems from the risk that a loose U.S. monetary policy might lead to economic instability. In speculative financial markets, such as the exchange markets, speculation driven by rumor and fancy can cause exchange rates to move far beyond their appropriate level. In the extreme, they can even cause exchange rate changes of such a magnitude that they can disrupt the economy. Because the dollar is the world's major reserve currency, such speculation can disrupt not only the U.S. economy but also the entire international financial system.

These potential economic costs must be distinguished from the political costs of violating the external constraint. In the case of looser monetary policy, the associated decline of the dollar harms some sectors of the economy, perhaps while being beneficial to others. Perhaps most important for monetary policy, the potential inflationary effects of exchange rate depreciation might harm creditors but benefit debtors.[29]

How significant are these economic external constraints on monetary policy? In an effort to answer this question, it will be useful to compare two different periods of loose monetary policy—the late 1970s and the early 1990s—to try to assess the conditions under which monetary policy is constrained economically by the external sector.

In the late 1970s, on one hand, monetary policy is acknowledged to have been severely constrained by the rapid depreciation of the dollar in response to expansionary policy; indeed, it is widely believed that a run on the dollar led both to the appointment of Paul Volcker as chairman of the Federal Reserve Board and to the draconian monetary tightening that followed. In the early 1990s, on the other hand, while the decline in interest rates led to a decline in the value of the dollar against most major currencies, there was nothing even remotely similar to the panic experienced in the 1970s. What can we learn from a comparison of these two experiences?

Figure 4.3 shows the real short-term real interest differential between the United States and Germany and the value of the dollar in terms of deutsche marks. The figure shows a significant difference between the 1976–79 period of monetary expansion and the 1990–1992 period. The former period was accompanied by a large decline in the value of the dollar, whereas the latter period was not.

This difference can be seen more clearly in Figure 4.4, which scales the value of the dollar in 1976 and 1990 to an index value of 100. As the figure shows, the dollar declined by much more over the 1976–79 period than it did during the 1990–92 period despite the fact that the short-term interest rate differential widened by about the same amount (see Figure 4.3).

Part of the explanation may have to do with the different relative inflation

Figure 4.3. **U.S./German Short-Term Interest Differential and Dollar/Deutsche Mark Exchange Rate**

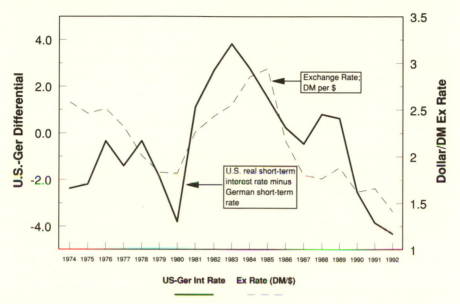

Source: International Monetary Funds.

experiences over the two periods. As Figure 4.5 shows, in the 1976–79 period, U.S. inflation rose relative to German inflation, whereas in the latter period, U.S. inflation fell relative to German inflation. The difference in exchange rate behaviors between the two periods may be attributable to this difference: in the 1976–79 period, a speculative attack was mounted against the dollar because inflation was rising in the United States relative to Germany, apparently out of control and unabated, whereas in the other case, relative inflation rates were moving in the same direction as relative real interest rates. With relative inflation apparently under control, there was little in the structure that would set off a speculative attack against the dollar.

The relative inflation rates prevented an all-out attack on the dollar from materializing, despite very large interest differentials between the United States and Germany. However, in late August and early September 1992, the value of the dollar did begin to decline dramatically relative to the other two major currencies, the German mark and the Japanese yen; indeed, the dollar hit postwar lows against both. Despite these large declines, however, the dollar did not crash. After the speculative attacks against the dollar in late August 1992, the dollar recovered.

Again, the relative inflation experiences of the two periods represent important differences to explain why speculative attacks got out of hand in one period

Figure 4.4. **The Value of the Dollar vs. DM in Two Expansions, 1976–1979 and 1990–1992**

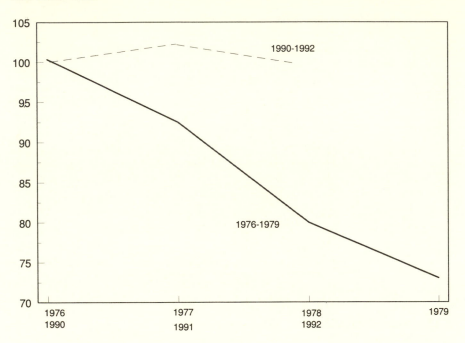

Source: IMF, *International Financial Statistics.*

and not the other. But the role of inflation should not be overestimated, for what is most important is the difference in the two periods in the extent to which the U.S. economy was seen as being out of control in the first period and not in the second. In the 1970s, there seemed to be no end to inflationary processes in the United States. In the current period, Germany was more likely to seem to be in that situation.

Here the inflation constraint plays a role. If inflation is seen to be out of control, then that perception can present a serious constraint on policy through its impact on the external sector. Hence, no economy can ignore inflation.

But that is not the whole story. Apart from relative inflation rates, several other factors also can help to stabilize the dollar. The relative political stability of the United States and the unique military and political power of the United States provide a foundation for the "key currency role of the dollar" (Prem, 1993; Frank, 1992). That role makes the dollar a safe haven in times of political turmoil, which currently characterizes Europe and many other parts of the globe. The safe-haven role can create a demand for the dollar and keep its value up despite declines in interest rates relative to the major foreign currencies.

However, it is important to note that, while this "key currency" role can be a

Figure 4.5. **United States/Germany Inflation Differential, 1974–1992**

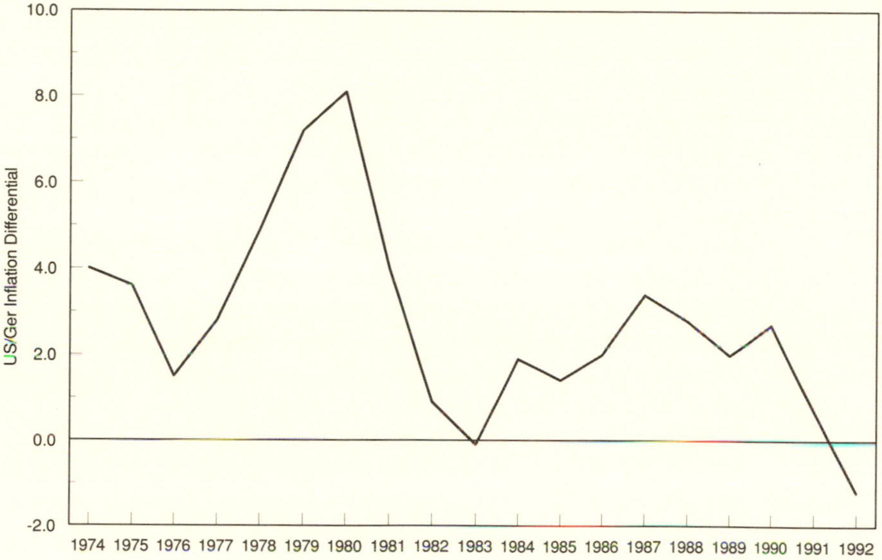

Source: IMF, *International Financial Statistics.*

source of stability at times, it also can be a source of great instability, not only in the United States but in much of the rest of the industrialized world as well. The decline of the dollar to record lows in late August 1992 was followed by the European monetary crisis of September and October of 1992. The two events probably were related. Because of the important role of the dollar, its large decline put enormous pressure on some of the currencies in the European monetary system, whose currencies became very much overvalued. The overvaluation in turn may have helped to precipitate the rash of devaluations that occurred there. The devaluations forced Germany to lower its interest rates and helped to raise the value of the dollar from its record lows. In this case, the key currency role of the dollar helped to stabilize it while destabilizing other countries' currencies. In the 1970s, the key currency role of the dollar had the opposite effect: it helped to destabilize the dollar because once a run on it began, holders all over the globe tried to get out of the dollar (Epstein, 1985).

The differences in these cases indicate that the "external constraint," in the economic costs it imposes, depends on circumstances. This is partly because, given the speculative nature of markets for foreign exchanges, the external constraint depends on expectations and perceptions. These in turn are greatly conditioned by circumstance. It appears that inflationary expectations are an important component of these circumstances. Hence, the external constraint is much less binding if inflation seems under control. This is bolstered by the relative political stability of the U.S. and the concomitant key currency role of the dollar in our unipolar world.

What about the "external political barrier"? This constraint appeared to be important in constraining the Federal Reserve's policy in the early stages of the most recent recession. Records indicate that, initially, the Fed was concerned about the "inflationary effects" of a decline in the value of the dollar associated with a decline in interest rates. I spoke earlier about the degree to which such a concern with inflation, at the levels we have been experiencing, is primarily a political barrier.

The importance of the external economic barrier, especially in terms of potential instability resulting from speculation against the dollar, while it has certainly been exaggerated, should not be dismissed. Depending on the circumstances, interest rates in the major foreign countries do place a constraint on U.S. monetary policy, though recent events suggest they are not as binding as many have thought. What, if anything, can be done about this external constraint?

There are essentially two possible approaches to relaxing the international interest rate constraint. The first is through international coordination of macroeconomic policies; the second is through various forms of capital or exchange controls.[30] A thorough discussion of the possible solutions is beyond the scope of this chapter, but I can say a few words about them here.

The most important solution to the potential problem of external constraint is international policy coordination. In a world recession, for example, a concerted effort by the major central banks to lower interest rates and to revive economic activity would place less stress on exchange rates and financial markets than would an expansionary policy by one country alone. However, coordination appears to be extremely difficult. One major problem seems to be the power of the German Bundesbank and its obsession with fighting inflation. In light of the difficulties with international policy coordination, structural reforms to enhance the autonomy of U.S. monetary policy would be valuable. Perhaps the least controversial of these is Nobel laureate James Tobin's suggestion of a small tax on foreign exchange transactions, called a "Tobin tax." The tax would be small enough not to discourage economically useful foreign exchange transactions but large enough to discourage the highly speculative transactions that drive currencies away from economically viable values and help to undermine expansionary policy.

Indeed, a number of the most economically successfully countries, such as South Korea and Japan, have used much more stringent capital controls to prevent the external constraint from undermining policies (Nembhard, 1992).[31]

The Domestic Financial Constraint

Since other papers in this volume discuss the financial constraint, this section is brief. The financial markets constrain the making of monetary policy in at least three ways. First, high debt levels, the so-called "debt overhang," can reduce the stimulative effect of expansionary policy, as lower interest rates will lead to debt reduction rather than increased investment and home buying. Second, through speculation about the effects of policy on future interest rates and inflation, the financial markets might reduce or even eliminate the Federal Reserve's ability to lower long-term interest rates. If the Federal Reserve reduces short-term rates and the markets expect that reduction to lead to higher inflation, then the markets will fail to reduce—and may even increase—long-term interest rates. Third, even if policy is successful in reducing interest rates, the financial markets may fail to allocate credit to socially productive investment.

All three of these problems are the result of large and highly liquid capital markets in the United States. These markets may be termed highly speculative because speculations about future events, which no one can know with certainty, have a huge effect on the setting of interest rates and financial asset values. Such speculation does not always lead to "efficient" interest-rate and price setting for financial assets (Crotty and Goldstein, this volume). But they have dominant effects nonetheless. The question for us is the extent to which they undermine monetary policy.

The first problem, the debt overhang, is really a function of the third: the fact that in the past, the financial markets have not properly allocated credit; as a result, in the 1980s, private debt reached dangerous levels (Crotty and Goldstein, Pollin, this volume). I will return to this point, but here it is important to note that the debt overhang did not render monetary policy completely powerless in the recession of the early 1990s. The recession was shorter and less severe than it would have been without expansionary monetary policy, halting as it was.

The second problem—the difficulties the Federal Reserve has in lowering long-term interest rates—also was evident in the recession of the early 1990s. U.S. bond markets speculate on the basis of expectations. If they believe that the future holds higher interest rates, or higher inflation rates, the markets will keep long-term interest rates high, even in the face of extremely low short-term interest rates and low inflation. That these bond markets constrain the Federal Reserve's ability to manipulate long-term rates is indisputable. How important the long-term rates are for economic activity is a matter of some debate.

Most evidence on the effectiveness of monetary policy cited earlier stresses the importance of short-term rates and credit allocation. So even if the Federal Reserve cannot manipulate long-term rates as a result of these speculative factors, it can still have an impact through its effects on short-term rates and credit allocation (Fazzari, this volume). Nevertheless, it seems clear that the Federal Reserve's ability to affect the economy, and long-term investment, is enhanced to the extent that it can affect long-term interest rates. In the recession of the early 1990s, long-term rates eventually declined, and they seem to have exerted a powerful influence on home buying. The impact would probably have been even greater had long-term rates come down farther. In sum, it seems clear that bond markets inhibit, even if they do not eradicate, the ability of the Federal Reserve to pursue expansionary policy.

Table 4.2

Constraints on and Barriers to Expansionary Monetary Policy

Constraints and Barriers	Economic	Political
External	Cannot lower real interest below those abroad	Low currency value hurts wealth holders
	Collapse of exchange rates can disrupt economic activity	Unstable values can hurt bank profit
Inflation	Hyperinflations disrupt economic activity	Unanticipated inflation redistributes income from creditors to debtors
Financial	Ability to lower real interest rates constrained by inflation expectations	Low real interest rates harm bank profits
	Markets misallocate credit even at low interest rates	Credit allocations interfere with bank prerogatives

But the biggest financial constraint on monetary policy is that even if the Federal Reserve were able to lower both short- and long-term rates, and even if there were no debt overhang, U.S. financial markets, with their large speculative component, have a history of misallocating credit. The speculative real estate boom of the 1980s and the massive merger wave of the same period have had significant negative effects on the economy (Dymski, Crotty and Goldstein, Wolfson, this volume). Hence, with these markets, a loose monetary policy may not be enough (Pollin, this volume) to overcome the financial constraint on monetary policy. A mechanism to allocate credit away from these speculative uses and toward more productive uses will be important.

But relaxing financial constraints runs into political difficulties. Lowering long-term real interest rates reduces the profits of important financial institutions. Regulating financial markets and engaging in credit allocation circumscribe their prerogatives. In the end, as with the inflation and external constraints, political barriers to socially productive policy are at least as important as economic ones.

Confronting the Political, External, and Financial Constraints on Monetary Policy

Table 4.2 presents a summary of the three constraints on monetary policy—the external, inflation, and financial constraints in forms of the economic and political barriers associated with them. Improving the monetary policy apparatus in the United States will require relaxing some combination of the political barriers and economic constraints.

Table 4.3
Reforms with Alternative Financial and Central Bank Structures

		CENTRAL BANK	
		Independent	Integrated (accountable)
FINANCIAL STRUCTURE	Laissez-faire	United States	Reform I (relaxing the political constraint)
	Allocational	Reform II (relaxing the financial constraint)	Reform III (relaxing both constraints)

To a large degree, relaxing the political barriers will require a political coalition in power in the United States committed to improving the functioning of the financial system so that it serves the needs of the economy, rather than the other way around. This will involve altering the political barrier on policy in the broad sense of that term.

Relaxing the political barrier on monetary policy in a narrower sense may also be required: to get the independent Federal Reserve to make better monetary policy, it may be necessary to make it more accountable to people and communities and less insulated from the democratic process. One way to relax some of the political barriers on policy would be to make Federal Reserve policy more accountable by integrating the independent Federal Reserve into the democratic system, preferably by giving Congress more control. Another possibility would be to implement more direct election of regional Federal Reserve officials and give the regional Federal Reserve banks more power (Epstein, 1991; Pollin, this volume; Galbraith, this volume, gives a general discussion of options for improving the structure of monetary policy).

The financial constraint could be improved substantially both by creating alternative credit allocation institutions that serve unmet needs for socially productive investment and by reducing the incentives for speculative finance: in short, by policies to improve credit allocation (Pollin and other chapters, this volume).

Finally, the external constraint can be relaxed, when necessary, by international coordination of policy or selective capital controls, such as a Tobin tax.

Relaxing the political barrier will go a long way toward relaxing the inflation constraint, since, as I have suggested, the inflation constraint is primarily political. Later, I discuss policies that may be necessary to control inflation in the event it becomes high enough to engender economic difficulties.

Table 4.3 presents some possibilities. Holding the issue of external constraint to one side, the columns refer to the type of central bank structure—independent or integrated. The rows refer to the type of financial structure—laissez-faire or allocational. The United States currently falls into the top left box, with an

Table 4.4
Country Experiences with Alternative Financial Structures

CENTRAL BANK

FINANCIAL STRUCTURE		Independent	Integrated (accountable)
Laissez-faire		*Open* US UK	*Open* Canada
		Managed	*Managed*
Allocational		*Open* Germany	*Open* France Italy
			Japan S. Korea
		Managed	*Managed*

independent central bank and a laissez-faire financial structure. As I have sug-gested, that arrangement maximizes political and financial constraints.

Galbraith (this volume) suggests moving the system to the right—making the central bank more accountable or integrated, keeping interest rates low, and finding another mechanism to control inflation. In this case, it may not be so important to alter the financial constraint, because low interest rates are likely to spur investment. However, given the problems of speculation and misallocation of credit, moving to the bottom right-hand box, as suggested by Pollin (this volume), may be even better!

One can add the third dimension—the degree of control over international capital mobility—by dividing each box in two, with the top segment referring to an open economy, that is, an economy financially integrated into the world economy, and the lower segment referring to one in which that financial integra-tion is managed, say, through capital controls.

Table 4.4 shows where a number of countries are located in terms of these three dimensions. The United Kingdom and the United States occupy the most conservative on all three dimensions; Canada has an integrated central bank, but it can do little good with open international capital markets and a laissez-faire financial system. Most of the industrialized countries that are per-forming well in the world economy have some combination of central bank integration, allocational credit markets, and control over international capital mobility, with South Korea having all three (Nembhard, 1992) and Japan hav-ing all three until recently.

Finally, Table 4.5 presents an integrated view of alternative policy options facing financial reformers. The left-hand column represents a policy of high

Table 4.5

Strategies to Deal with the Inflation, External, and Financial Constraints Under Alternative Policy Regimes

		High Interest Rates	Low Interest Rates
	Laissez-faire	United States (slow growth, low and unproductive investment)	*Inflation constraint:* Price controls
			External constraints: Capital controls International coordination
Financial Structure			*Financial constraint:* Low interest rates
	Allocational	*Inflation constraint:* High interest rates	*Inflation constraint:* Credit allocation
		External constraint: High interest rates	*External constraints:* Capital controls International coordination
		Financial constraint: Credit allocation	*Financial constraint:* Credit allocation

interest rates. The right-hand column represents a monetary policy of low interest rates, perhaps undertaken in a system in which the political barrier on monetary policy has been reduced. The rows refer to the type of financial structure: laissez-faire, as we have in the U.S., and allocational, in which public institutions play a more important role in allocating credit. Within each box, policies required to relax each of the three economic constraints associated with high or low interest rates are indicated.

As a benchmark, observe the top left square. The United States has a laissez-faire financial structure and high interest rates. The result is slow growth and low investment. If the United States were to institute a low-interest-rate policy but maintain a laissez-faire financial structure, then, *if and when the three constraints bind*, it would have to adopt appropriate policies: examples would be price controls to relax the inflation constraint, a Tobin tax or capital controls, or international coordination of policy to manage the external constraint. But with a laissez-faire financial system, the possibilities of constraining financial misallocation and speculation would be limited. Low interest rates would have to be the means of promoting productive investment, but, by themselves, low interest rates may simply lead to wasteful credit allocation of the type we saw with the speculative booms of the 1980s.

If, however, the United States were to adopt credit allocation mechanisms with a low-interest-rate policy, then it could use credit controls as a mechanism both to fight potential inflation and to allocate credit to productive uses. There may still be a need for some form of international coordination or capital controls to prevent capital from fleeing abroad if international interest differentials grew too wide.

Finally, a policy of high interest rates and credit allocation is represented in the bottom left column. This policy structure has the advantage of being able to use high interest rates both to fight inflation and to overcome the external constraint. Subsidized credit would ensure that credit were allocated to productive sectors. The disadvantage of such a policy is that high interest rates can have negative effects on the distribution of income. The policy also creates high incentives for rent seeking—for groups to invest large and wasteful amounts of resources in gaining access to the subsidized credit.

Conclusion

The point of this highly simplified exercise is not to give a blueprint for reform. Rather, it is to suggest that there are alternative packages of reforms that can be used, when necessary to overcome the three constraints. Each of these types of packages, as well as others that can be constructed, has advantages as well as disadvantages.

But, whichever package is promoted, one thing is clear. The current policy package of the United States—an independent central bank obsessed with inflation fighting, and a laissez-faire financial system—has led to a serious impasse: both economic stagnation and severe credit misallocation.

What is needed is a change both in the monetary policy goal and in the monetary policy structure. The goal must be a more balanced approach that gives more importance to promoting productive investment and less to keeping inflation as low as possible at all costs. And the structure must be one that makes monetary policy more accountable to those it affects and that allows for complementary policies of credit allocation and controls on international speculation when necessary.

This long-run change in structure also has implications for short-term monetary policy. When the U.S. economy is mired in a recession, a more aggressive expansionary monetary policy is required. This policy may have to be accompanied by increased tools of credit allocation as well. As this chapter has suggested, the inflation, external, and financial market constraints are unlikely to be the dominant constraint. Above all, the political barrier must be overcome. In the short run, that must mean a closer coordination of monetary policy with the new Administration to obtain a coordinated package of policies that might begin reversing the devastation wrought by the previous 15 years of economic decline.

Notes

1. Associate Professor of Economics, University of Massachusetts, Amherst. This is a revised version of a paper presented to the Economic Policy Institute's Conference on Monetary and Financial Restructuring, June 1992. The author thanks the participants at the conference and especially Gary Dymski, Robert Pollin, and Lance Taylor for many helpful comments on previous drafts.

2. I will discuss later the highly controversial issue of whether the Federal Reserve can affect real (inflation-adjusted) interest rates or not.

3. The distinction between the effects of policy on the level of gross domestic product (GDP) (or its rate of growth), on one hand, and on the distribution of income, on the other, is an artificial distinction, one unlikely to hold in practice in the simple way I have described. For example, an important body of nonmainstream work suggests that changes in income distribution can have important macroeconomic effects. Even in this case, however, the point here is to distinguish the ultimate effects on output from the ultimate effects on distribution and their political ramifications.

4. There have been criticisms of other episodes of Federal Reserve policy from similar perspectives. See, for example, Epstein and Ferguson (1984, 1991) on the Federal Reserve's failure to fight depression in the early 1930s because of, among other reasons, the Fed's concern for bank profits.

5. Note that if there were evidence in favor of this hypothesis, it would strengthen the case for the premise of this book, namely, that monetary and financial restructuring are both necessary to revive our economy.

6. Using the same techniques, Mishkin (1988) identified a change in the real interest rate in the 1920s when the Fed similarly tightened.

7. Their results are for the postwar period until 1979. For a discussion of the effects of monetary policy since 1979, see the section entitled The Inflation Constraint. On evidence that the federal funds rate is under the Fed's control, see Bernanke and Blinder (1990) and Cook and Hahn (1989).

8. Note that the Fed cannot control this spread, *per se*, except insofar as it can control it by controlling the federal funds rate. This inability to control the spread makes this particular piece of evidence about the effects of policy somewhat ambiguous and suggests the need for further evidence, discussed later.

9. See also the evidence in Romer and Romer, 1989, which shows that every time the Federal Reserve decided to increase unemployment to fight inflation, unemployment went up and industrial production went down. Fair (1989) using a structural model, agrees with the direction of the Romers' results but finds that the effects are somewhat reduced. Romer and Romer argue that in the case of 1966, the Fed was not trying to induce a recession. No recession occurred.

10. See, however, the later discussion of Fazzari's work that focuses on credit allocation effects. His work is consistent with the work described here because, first, it stresses the effects of short-term interest rates through their effects on bank lending, and second, it stresses the effects on the allocation of investment among firms, a channel the other models do not include.

11. This indirect effect captures the effects of disintermediation in the face of ceilings on interest rates that savings and loans could charge in the '60s and '70s. When interest rates went up, depositors withdrew funds from savings & loan institutions (S&Ls) to earn higher interest rates elsewhere; S&Ls had to cut back on mortgage lending as a result.

12. On more direct tests of the efficacy of monetary policy in the face of the internationalization of finance, see Radecki and Reinhart (1988) and Kasman and Pigott (1988).

13. For more details, see Fazzari's chapter in this volume and the references cited there.

14. The next several sections are adapted from Dymski et al., 1992. They also are developed in more detail in the chapter by Galbraith (this volume).

15. The Congressional Budget Office (CBO) has made a similar assessment. See *Economic and Budget Outlook*, 1992, chapter 5.

16. CBO, *Economic and Budget Outlook*, 1992, chapter 5.

17. CBO, *Economic and Budget Outlook*, 1992, p. 13.

18. Total bank reserves grew at a rapid pace, but they appear not to have been transformed into rapid growth rates for credit. This discrepancy reflects the financial problems that both banks and borrowers are experiencing, which reduce both the supply and the demand for credit.

19. Ibid.

20. The Phillips Curve measures the relationship between inflation and unemployment. Before the middle 1970s or so, economists commonly believed that this curve was downward sloping, that is, that there is a tradeoff between inflation and unemployment in the long run so that policymakers could choose the level of unemployment and inflation. Since that time, the so-called vertical Phillips Curve argument has gained more acceptance; this view holds that no tradeoff occurs between inflation and unemployment. Rather, any attempt to reduce unemployment below its natural rate will lead only to ever-higher rates of inflation.

21. Furthermore, an increase in interest rates may have a more direct effect on raising inflation. Interest rates are a cost to firms; when they increase, firms may pass along the added costs in the form of higher prices. This action in turn may lead to an increase in inflation. The effect has been dubbed the Patman effect, after Texas congressman Wright Patman, a strong critic of the Federal Reserve who reportedly criticized the use of tight monetary policy on these grounds.

22. There seems not to be a common definition of hyperinflation, though an often used rule of thumb is an inflation rate of more than 1,000 percent a year.

23. One study, by Robert Barro of Harvard University, looked at the relationship between inflation and the rate of growth of gross domestic product for more than 100 countries between the years 1960 and 1985. Using simple correlations, Barro found a very weak negative correlation between various measures of inflation—the average inflation rate, the coefficient of variation in inflation, and the change in inflation—and economic growth. Using multiple regression analysis to look at the effects of inflation on growth rates and holding other factors constant, Barro finds that on average, an increase in the average inflation rate of 10 percentage points is associated with a decline of 0.3 percentage points in per capita economic growth. Barro concludes, "My inference is that real economic performance is significantly and inversely related to an intensification of inflation, although the differences in the behavior of inflation account for only a small fraction of the cross-country variations in growth rates. Moreover, much of the negative relation likely reflects the symptomatic nature of inflation; countries that do badly for other reasons also tend to experience a worsening of inflation" (Barro, 1990, p. 69).

24. There are also so-called shoe-leather costs, when people are hypothesized to go to the bank more often because they do not want to hold money. But with checking accounts earning interest rates that tend to move up with anticipated inflation, these costs are not likely to be large at nonhyperinflation levels of inflation. Indeed, there are reasons to believe that higher inflation, up to a point, would lead to higher levels of output and perhaps higher rates of economic growth. One reason is that higher inflation may redistribute income toward debtors. To the extent that debtors tend to spend a larger fraction of increments to income they receive, higher inflation will lead to more demand and may lead to

higher levels of output. Moreover, higher inflation, to the extent that it lowers real interest rates, may lead to higher investment spending and thereby to higher output and growth.

25. Inflation in the 1970s may have reduced the incomes of the higher income brackets because it pushed people into higher income tax brackets. At that time, the federal income tax structure taxed higher incomes at higher rates, so those pushed into higher brackets paid relatively more in taxes. Those at the middle and bottom, to the extent that they were in debt, however, received other benefits from inflation: since for a substantial period of time, interest rates did not increase with the rate of inflation, the real, inflation-adjusted interest rates they paid fell dramatically. Other features of the 1970s inflation, however, did impose serious costs on many Americans. See the following.

26. In fact, a useful explanation of the 1970s inflation is that it was caused by the decline in incomes that resulted from the oil price increases. According to this view, when people's incomes fell as a result of the increase in oil and other commodity prices, they tried to recoup their losses by raising wages: firms in turn tried to a raise prices to recoup their losses. This led to a wage/price spiral that was "accommodated" by the Federal Reserve's monetary policy. Hence, according to this explanation, the inflation did not cause the decline in incomes but was caused by it (Rowthorn, 1977; Bowles, Gordon, and Weisskopf, 1991).

27. Even here, the central bank of a large country such as the United States can have an impact to the extent that it can affect the world level of interest rates and the policies of central banks abroad.

28. There is the additional issue of changes in the terms of trade and therefore in real incomes available at home as a result of exchange rate changes. I will discuss this later.

29. To the extent that U.S. banks gain competitive advantages vis-à-vis their competitors if the value of the dollar is high and/or stable, a depreciating dollar engenders political opposition from international bankers independent of its effects on inflation. See Epstein (1981, 1985) and Frank (1992) for a discussion of these effects.

30. Note that here I am speaking only about international interest rate constraints on monetary policy. I am not speaking about the broader issues of international constraints on taxation, environmental regulation, and the like.

31. Often these capital controls are accompanied by credit allocation policies that allocate credit to desired firms and sectors. See the section entitled The Domestic Financial Constraint for a discussion of ways these policies might work in combination with capital controls.

Bibliography

Banuri, Tariq and Juliet B. Schor, eds. *Financial Openness and National Autonomy*. Oxford, England: Clarendon Press, 1992.

Barro, Robert. "Comment on 'Extreme Inflation: Dynamics and Stabilization.' " *Brookings Papers on Economic Activity*, No. 2, 1990, pp. 68–75.

Barro, Robert and Xavier Sala i Martin. "World Real Interest Rates." National Bureau of Economic Research Working Paper No. 3317. Cambridge, MA: NBER, 1990.

Bernanke, Ben S. "On the Predictive Power of Interest Rates and Interest Rate Spreads." *New England Economic Review*. Federal Reserve Bank of Boston, November/December 1990, pp. 52–68.

Bernanke, Ben and Alan Blinder. "The Federal Funds Rate and the Channels of Monetary Policy." National Bureau of Economic Research Working Paper No. 3487. Cambridge, MA: NBER, October 1990.

Blanchard, O. and L. Summers. "Hysteresis and European Unemployment." *NBER Macroeconomics Annual*, Vol. 1, 1986, pp. 15–89.

Blundell-Wignall, Adrian and Frank Browne. "Macroeconomic Consequences of Financial Liberalization: A Summary Report." Organization for Cooperation and Development (OECD), Department of Economics and Statistics Working Papers. Paris: OECD, February 1991.

Bowles, Samuel, David M. Gordon, and T. E. Weisskopf. *After the Wasteland.* Armonk, NY: M. E. Sharpe, 1991.

Browne, Frank and Warren Tease. "The Information Content of Interest Rate Spreads Across Financial Systems." Organization for Cooperation and Development (OECD), Economics Department Working Paper No. 109. Paris: OECD, 1992.

Chouraqui, Jean-Claude, Michael Driscoll, and Marc-Olivier Strauss-Kahn. "The Effects of Monetary Policy on the Real Sector: An Overview of Empirical Evidence for Selected OECD Economies." OECD Department of Economics and Statistics Working Paper No. 51, April 1988.

Congressional Budget Office. *The Economic and Budget Outlook: Fiscal Years 1993–1997.* Washington, DC: U.S. Government Printing Office, January 1992.

Cook, Timothy Q. and Thomas Hahn. "The Effect of Changes in the Federal Funds Target on Market Interest Rates in the 1970s." *Journal of Monetary Economics*, Vol. 24, November 1989, pp. 331–51.

Crotty, James. "Keynes on True Uncertainty and Conventional Decision Making." Mimeo. Amherst, MA: University of Massachusetts, Amherst, 1990.

Cunningham, Rosemary and Thomas J. Cunningham. "Recent Views of Viewing the Real Rate of Interest." Federal Reserve Bank of Atlanta, *Economic Review*, July/August, 1990, pp. 28–37.

Dornbusch, Rudiger and Alberto Giovannini. "Monetary Policy in the Open Economy." In Benjamin Friedman and Frank Hahn, eds., *Handbook of Monetary Economics*, Vol. II. Amsterdam: Elsevier Science, 1990, pp. 1231–1303.

Dornbusch, Rudiger, Federico Sturzenegger, and Holger Wolf. "Extreme Inflation: Dynamics and Stabilization." *Brookings Papers on Economic Activity*, No. 2, 1990, pp. 1–84.

Drifill, John, Grayham E. Mizon, and Alistair Ulph. "Costs of Inflation." In Benjamin Friedman and Frank Hahn, eds., *Handbook of Monetary Economics*, Chapter 19, Vol. II. Amsterdam Elsevier Science, 1990, pp. 1013–66.

Dymski, Gary, Gerald Epstein, James K. Galbraith, and Robert Pollin. "A Report Card on the Greenspan Fed." Washington, DC: Economic Policy Institute, February 1992.

Eichenbaum, Martin. "Comment on C. Sims' 'Interpreting the Macroeconomic Time Series Facts: The Effects of Monetary Policy.' " *European Economic Review*, Vol. 36, 1992, pp. 1001–11.

Epstein, Gerald. "Domestic Stagflation and Monetary Policy: The Federal Reserve and the Hidden Election." In Thomas Ferguson and Joel Rogers, eds., *The Hidden Election.* New York: Pantheon, 1981.

Epstein, Gerald. "Monetary Policy, Loan Liquidation and Industrial Conflict: The Federal Reserve and the Open Mrket Operations of 1932." *Journal of Economic History*, Vol. 64, No. 4, 1984, pp. 957–83.

Epstein, Gerald. "The Triple Debt Crisis." *World Policy Journal*, Vol. 2/3, 1985, pp. 625–57.

Epstein, Gerald and Thomas Ferguson. "Answers to Stock Questions." *Journal of Economic History,* March 1991.

Epstein, Gerald. "An Argument for a Democratic Monetary Policy." Mimeo, June 1991.

Epstein, Gerald. "A Political Economy Model of Comparative Central Banking." In Gary Dymski and Robert Pollin eds., *New Perspectives in Monetary Macroeconomics: Explorations in the Tradition of Hyman Minsky.* Ann Arbor: University of Michigan Press, 1993.

Epstein, Gerald and Juliet Schor. "The Political Economy of Central Banking." Working Paper No. 1281. Cambridge, MA: Harvard Institute for Economic Research, 1986.

Epstein, Gerald and Juliet Schor "Corporate Profitability as a Determinant of Restrictive Monetary Policy: Estimates for the Postwar United States." In Thomas Mayer, ed., *The Political Economy of American Monetary Policy*. New York: Cambridge University Press, 1990, pp. 51–63.

Epstein, Gerald and Juliet Schor. "Structural Determinants and Economic Effects of Capital Controls in OECD Countries." In Tariq Banuri and Juliet B. Schor, eds., *Financial Openess and National Autonomy*. Oxford, England: Clarendon Press, 1992, pp. 136–62.

Epstein, Gerald and Juliet Schor."The Federal Reserve-Treasury Accord." *Social Concept*, forthcoming, 1993.

Evans, Paul. "Do Budget Deficits Raise Nominal Interest Rates? Evidence from Six Countries." *Journal of Monetary Economics*, September 1987, pp. 343–67.

Fair, Ray. "Does Monetary Policy Matter: Narrative vs. Structural Approaches." NBER Working Paper No. 3045, 1989.

Fazzari, Steven. "Monetary Policy, Financial Structure and Investment." Paper presented at the 1992 Conference of the Economic Policy Institute's Working Group on Monetary and Financial Restructuring in Washington, DC, June 1992.

Fischer, S. "Towards an Understanding of the Costs of Inflation, II." In K. Brunner and A. Meltzer, eds., *The Costs and Consequences of Inflation*, Vol. 15, Carnegie-Rochester Conference Series on Public Policy. Amsterdam: North-Holland, 1981, pp. 5–41.

Fischer, S. and F. Modigliani. "Towards an Understanding of the Real Effects and Costs of Inflation." *Weltwirtschaftliches Archiv*, Vol. 114, 1975, pp. 810–33.

Frank, Ellen. "Key Currencies, Portfolio Behavior and Exchange Rates." Unpublished paper, University of Massachusetts, Amherst, 1992.

Frankel, Jeffrey. "International Financial Integration, Relations Among Interest Rates and Exchange Rates, and Monetary Indicators." *New York Federal Reserve, 1989*, 1989, pp. 15–49.

Frankel, Jeffrey. "Measuring International Capital Mobility: A Review." *American Economic Review*, Vol. 82, No. 2, May 1992, pp. 197–202.

Friedman, Benjamin M. "The Changing Effects of Monetary Policy on Real Economic Activity." In *Monetary Policy Issues in the 1990s: A Symposium Sponsored by the Federal Reserve Bank of Kansas City*, 1989, pp. 55–111.

Friedman, Benjamin M. and Kenneth N. Kuttner. "Money, Income, Prices and Interest Rates." *American Economic Review*, Vol. 82, No. 3, June 1992, pp. 472–92.

Galbraith, James K. *Monetary Policy in the New World Order*. Washington, DC: Economic Policy Institute, March 1992.

Gordon, David M. "The Un-Natural Rate of Unemployment: An Econometric Critique of the NAIRU Hypothesis." *American Economic Review*, Vol. 78, No. 2, May 1988, pp. 117–23.

Gordon, Robert J. "The Gordon Update." New York: HarperCollins, 1991.

Grabel, Ilene. "Taking Control: An Agenda for a Democratic Financial System." Paper prepared for the Financial Democracy Campaign, 1989.

Grabel, Ilene. "Three Essays on Financial Regulation in Open Economies." Ph.D. dissertation. Amherst, MA: University of Massachusetts, 1992.

Greider, William. *The Secrets of the Temple*. New York: Simon and Schuster, 1987.

Hibbs, Douglas. *The American Political Economy*. Cambridge, MA: Harvard University Press, 1987.

Huizinga, John and Frederic S. Mishkin. "Monetary Policy Regime Shifts and the Unusual Behavior of Real Interest Rates." Carnegie-Rochester Conference Series on Public Policy, Spring 1986, pp. 231–74.

Kasman, Bruce and Charles Pigott. "Interest Rate Divergences Among the Major Industrial Nations." *Quarterly Review*, Federal Reserve Bank of New York, Vol. 13, No. 3, Autumn 1988, pp. 28–44.

Keynes, John Maynard. *The General Theory*. New York: Harcourt Brace Jovanovich, 1946.

Mauskopf, Eileen. "The Transmission Channels of Monetary Policy: How Have They Changed?" *Federal Reserve Bulletin*, December 1990, pp. 985–1008.

McCallum, Bennett. "Inflation: Theory and Evidence." In Benjamin Friedman and Frank Hahn, eds., *Handbook on Monetary Economics*, Vol. 2, Amsterdam: Elsevier Science, 1990, pp. 964–1012.

Mishkin, Frederic S. "Understanding Real Interest Rates." NBER Working Paper No. 2691, August 1988.

Mosser, Patricia C. "Changes in Monetary Policy Effectiveness: Evidence from Large Macroeconometric Models." *Quarterly Review*, Federal Reserve Bank of New York, Spring 1992, pp. 36–51.

Mott, Tracy and Grainger Caudle. "The Role of Rentier in Keynes's and Kalecki's Conceptions of Capitalism." Mimeo. Denver: University of Denver, April 1992.

Nembhard, Jessica. "Capital Controls, Credit Controls and Economic Growth." Ph.D dissertation. Amherst, MA: University of Massachusetts, 1992.

New York Federal Reserve Bank. *Intermediate Targets and Indicators for Monetary Policy; A Critical Survey*. New York: New York Federal Reserve Bank, 1990.

New York Federal Reserve Bank. *International Financial Integration and U.S. Monetary Policy*. New York: New York Federal Reserve Bank, 1989.

New York Federal Reserve Bank. *Recent Trends in Commercial Bank Profitability*. New York: New York, Federal Reserve Bank, 1986.

Palley, Thomas. "The Case for Progressive Monetary and Fiscal Policy: Time to Reassess the Inflation Constraint." Revised version of a paper presented in Washington, DC to a meeting of the Working Group on Monetary and Financial Restructuring of the Economic Policy Institute, June 1992. Mimeo, Graduate Faculty, New School for Social Research, July 1992.

Prem, Roohi. "The Key Currency Issue." Unpublished paper, University of Massachusetts, Amherst, 1993.

Radecki, Lawrence J. and Vincent Reinhart. "The Globalization of Financial Markets and the Effectiveness of Monetary Policy Instruments." *Quarterly Review*, Federal Reserve Bank of New York, Vol. 13, No. 3, Autumn 1988, pp. 18–27.

Romer, Christina and David Romer. "Does Monetary Policy Matter? A New Test in the Spirit of Friedman and Schwartz." NBER Working Paper No. 2966, 1989.

Romer, Christina and David Romer. "New Evidence on the Monetary Transmission Mechanism." *Brookings Papers on Economic Activity*, No. 1, pp. 149–214, 1990.

Rowthorn, R. E. "Conflict, Inflation and Money." *Cambridge Journal of Economics*, Vol. 1, 1977, pp. 215–39.

Sims, Christopher A. "Interpreting the Macroeconomic Time Series Facts; The Effects of Monetary Policy." *European Economic Review*, Vol. 36, 1992, pp. 975–1011.

Wooley, John. *Monetary Politics*. New York: Cambridge University Press, 1984.

Wolff, Edward. "The Distributional Effects of the 1969–75 Inflation on Holdings of Household Wealth in the United States." *Review of Income and Wealth*, Vol. 25, 1979, pp. 195–207.

Zevin, Robert. "Are World Financial Markets More Open? If So, Why and with What Effects?" In Tariq Banuri and Juliet B. Schor, eds., *Financial Openness and National Autonomy*. Oxford, England: Clarendon Press, 1992, pp. 43–84.

PART II
Banking and Financial Regulation

CHAPTER FIVE

How to Rebuild the U.S. Financial Structure: Level the Playing Field and Renew the Social Contract[1]

GARY A. DYMSKI

CHAPTER SUMMARY

This chapter argues that the role of the U.S. financial structure is to perform three functions: fostering of productive investment, enhancement of economic opportunity, and maintenance of a stable economic environment. But this structure's recent performance has been wanting in all three areas. Simply eliminating remaining barriers to market entry will not achieve the three functions, because financial relations are replete with spillover effects and informational problems that must be factored into any regulatory and institutional design for a fully functional financial structure.

First, the chapter develops a perspective on the design of the U.S. financial structure and on why it has become dysfunctional. That perspective, common to all of the chapters in this section, is contrasted with both the free market and narrow-banking perspectives on financial reform.

Then the chapter proposes broad reforms for the U.S. financial structure, which incorporate the proposals set out in greater detail later in this section. These proposals call, first of all, for leveling the financial playing field, as do the free market and narrow-banking proposals:

- Deposit insurance should be restricted in focus;
- Interstate and product line expansion for intermediaries should be allowed;
- Strict capital adequacy and oversight guidelines should be affirmed and applied for all financial intermediaries;
- The too-big-to-fail doctrine should be repealed, but the lender-of-last-resort principle should be affirmed.

But the proposals made here then go beyond the free market and narrow-banking perspectives by arguing for additional measures designed specifically to foster economic opportunity and productive investment while discouraging

101

redlining, discrimination, and speculation. These impositions into "pure" market outcomes are needed in order to renew the social contract between financial intermediaries and the firms and households for whom access to credit for productive purposes is problematic in autonomous markets. The proposals for "renewing the social contract" encompass five points.

• All financial intermediaries should comply with the D'Arista-Schlesinger licensing proposal;
• All financial intermediaries, not only banks and thrifts, should meet minimum performance requirements under the Community Reinvestment Act (CRA);
• Regulatory monitoring of CRA performance should not be held hostage to prudential regulation for intermediary safety and soundness;
• Innovative programs and institutions should be encouraged for depressed areas, and these alone should receive institutional subsidies and guarantees;
• Infusions of public funds into intermediaries in the course of lender-of-last-resort interventions should be treated as an ownership interest, and the intermediaries in question should orient their activities toward accomplishing public purposes.

The Plight of the Commercial Banks and the Unmet Need for Reform

The Bush administration made banking reform one part of its six-point program for economic recovery. Its Treasury plan sought to make banks sound by deregulating them and establishing an early warning system that identifies weak institutions. However, a year-long administration effort to achieve passage of this plan in 1991 fell short. The Federal Deposit Insurance Corporation Improvement Act (FDICIA), approved by Congress in November 1991, provided $70 billion in borrowing for the bank insurance fund. In addition, FDICIA imposed new capital adequacy standards and strengthened supervision by installing a regulatory early warning system.[2] But FDICIA changed none of the major existing restrictions on bank activities and ownership.

Bankers have complained that FDICIA actually worsened their plight: regulators, their resolve stiffened by the Salem-witch-trial attitude of Congress (Independent Bankers Association to U.S. Secretary of the Treasury Brady, in Rosenblatt, 1992), have become tougher and chilled banks' lending. This excuse was offered for the persistence of the credit crunch on small and medium-sized businesses despite the Federal Reserve System's (Fed's) determined (if belated) effort to reduce the cost of bank funds and spur bank lending.

But if a 3 percent federal funds rate did not boost bank lending, it did lead to record industry profits of $30 billion in 1992. This earnings surge reduced the prospects for a protracted taxpayer bailout akin to that for thrifts and gave regulators the breathing space to risk-adjust banks' deposit insurance premiums.[3]

Nonetheless, the U.S. commercial banking industry remains in dire straits. During 1992, many banks added substantially to their reserves against prospective losses in commercial and residential real estate. This undoubtedly represents just the first installment against losses from financing the 1980s' speculative office-building binge.

The implementation of FDICIA's capital adequacy requirements in December 1992 also highlighted the banks' continuing weaknesses. *American Banker* reported in December 1991 that 41 operating banks and 82 thrifts fell below the 1991 Act's 2 percent core capital rules (Atkinson, 1991).[4] The actual implementation of the capital adequacy requirement was a nonevent largely because of regulatory forbearance and the effects of record profits on banks' core capital. But during 1992, many banks (and especially large banks) went through wrenching staff cuts and asset sales, submitted to merger, or both. More staff cuts and mergers lie ahead.

Beyond Bank Deregulation: Financial Reform

So after the respite offered by the 1992 election year, broad-based banking reform remains prominently on the table. The reform debate has centered on just how much product market and geographic deregulation of commercial banks should be approved. But as the following discussion makes clear, restricting the scope of reform debate in this way assumes that the remaining portions of the U.S. financial structure are performing their allocation functions reasonably well, and that no other important aspects of bank behavior will be significantly affected by these deregulatory steps, and hence that none of these need be drawn into the debate.

But the common analytical thread of the chapters in this section makes it clear that those assumptions are not warranted. It might be useful to clarify this analytical thread via a quick tour through the four other chapters in this section.

Wolfson suggests that the U.S. financial structure was rebuilt in the 1930s on two principles: restrictions on competition, so that different intermediaries carried out different roles, and government protections. These two features ensured financial stability through the early post-war years. But once macroeconomic conditions changed, these very features triggered innovations that cut the ground out from under commercial banks and thrifts. The presumed solution of easing some barriers on competition has, ironically, put more pressure on the remaining barriers to competition without enhancing banks' profitability; in turn, this has forced the government to extend its protections ever further. This drift is untenable and unsustainable. Either the system must be completely deregulated and all control over the economic functions it performs and over the social goals it fulfills surrendered, or an alternative organizing principle for regulating the system must be articulated and developed.

D'Arista argues that a useful first step in articulating such an alternative would involve shifting deposit insurance back to its original mission of guaranteeing individuals' and smaller businesses' accounts and renouncing its acquired characteristic of underwriting the solvency of financial institutions in the name of ensuring financial stability. Here D'Arista articulates an important principle—that public support must be reserved for public purposes. This shift, she argues, is necessary at present because insured institutions, handicapped in their competitive struggle with unregulated intermediaries, have been failing in unprecedented numbers. As insured intermediaries have lost market share, they have looked for new money-making opportunities. In particular, they have extended lines of credit and guaranteed access to financing facilities for third parties whose riskiness is not overseen by regulators. So banks have rescued a role for themselves, in part, by insuring credit extensions in the least responsible section of the credit market.

Campen too worries that CRA advocates have won the battle—the right to systematically collect powerful data about these institutions—only to lose the war. The portions of the system whose social accountability has been recognized—thrifts and commercial banks, in the main—have been the least profitable and the slowest growing.

D'Arista and Schlesinger then enter in with their analysis of the parallel banking system. Alongside the "regulated" banking structure has grown a parallel one, with some significant differences: its credit risks are not systematically evaluated by regulators, nor are its credit composition and banking activity made socially accountable.

In sum, deregulating banking will not solve the system's problems. This structure has required increasingly large subsidies and protections, even as the political backlash from ever-larger public outlays for an ever-more dysfunctional financial structure has grown apace. The notion that deregulation will end this vicious cycle is, at best, wishful and naive. Banks, flushed out of a portion of their "preferred habitat," will not suddenly win back their previous market shares and become superprofitable; nor will banks' new competitors benignly serve public purposes and generate more stable profit streams over the long haul just because of deregulation.

These chapters challenge the conventional analysis at its root. The pace of change has altered the U.S. financial structure profoundly; mundane assurances that all will be for the best in the best of all free market worlds should not be accepted at face value. We must go back both to some basic considerations about the goals of the financial structure itself and to the role of financial institutions.

The Components and Functions of the Financial Structure

A *financial structure*, broadly defined, is a set of institutional arrangements allowing economic agents to make transactions and to either expand the scale of their operations or enhance the value of their wealth holdings, through the creation and circulation of financial claims. *Financial firms* earn income primarily through either providing means of payment for transactions or intermediating in credit markets between wealth owners and borrowers. *Banks* are firms that do both and have federally insured deposits.[5]

The financial behaviors actually observed result from the dynamic combination of an economy's institutional configuration, its firms' and households' market behaviors, and its regulators' conduct in enforcing its fixed (statutory) rules. Credit flows, the heart of any financial structure, depend on lenders' assessments of potential borrowers' capacity or willingness to repay. When borrowers' net worth is large relative to their credit demand, then repayment is virtually guaranteed as long as borrowers are willing to pledge their net worth as collateral. When a borrower has (or pledges) less net worth than the borrower wishes to borrow, other factors come into play: the borrower's track record and reputation, signals of the borrower's creditworthiness, and the lender's ability and willingness to monitor the borrower's behavior after extending credit to the borrower.

Two types of credit market linkages may occur: direct credit, wherein households and firms with excess savings make credit arrangements directly with borrowers, and intermediated credit, wherein a financial intermediary smooths the friction between these two parties. Intermediated credit dominates when borrowers' net worth is less than their credit amount, because intermediaries can exploit economies of scale in assessing creditworthiness and monitoring borrowers' behavior.

What Are the Functions of the Financial Structure?

The foregoing definitions describe what *any* financial structure does; but its degree of success and in turn any assessment of what about it requires fixing depend on whether it is working well or badly. When resources are allocated in competitive markets without spillover effects, an extra-market assessment of performance is unnecessary. But this is not so when, as argued later, market transactions do have spillover effects; then market outcomes *per se* provide no indication of social optimality. To determine how well this structure is performing, we must specify its functions.[6]

The financial structure provides three broad functions for the economy as a whole:[7]

• providing finance and other requisites—such as transaction outlets—for productive investment and consumption;
• fostering economic opportunity by channeling financial resources to neglected, but potentially viable, areas and individuals within the economy;
• maintaining a stable financial environment.

The first function turns on the distinction between productive and unproductive, or speculative, finance. This distinction is difficult to make categorically; broadly speaking, finance is speculative when it increases any firm's net financial obligations without significantly increasing its net output or its output potential.

The second function recognizes that a financial structure should transfer savings efficiently to those who have the capacity to produce or innovate but lack the wealth required to initiate their plans.

The third function, stability, is crucial because financial instability destroys the confidence of both borrowers and lenders. Confidence is crucial, in turn, because the success of financial transactions depends not just on purchase and sale volumes in any period but also on buyers' willingness to *hold* portfolios of their purchases over extended periods. To a large extent, success in meeting the first two functions—avoiding speculative investments and finding able borrowers—guarantees the third.

From a different angle, a financial structure's function is to maximize financing linkages while keeping risks within bounds that do not trigger financial instability. Units that create credit or supply means of payment or both take on several types of risk. The most well-known is the *default risk* that credit will not be repaid. But lenders take on *liquidity risk* when they make asset commitments that will not be repaid before the lender's liabilities may be called in. Lenders are also exposed to *rate risk* when they support lending at a fixed rate with borrowing at a variable rate.

Managing risk is difficult because information is incomplete in financial markets. To minimize default risk, the lender must seek out information about the borrower's "type" and then monitor the borrower's activities after credit has been extended. To minimize liquidity risk, the lender should match the maturities of its asset and liability instruments so that assets mature when liabilities do. To minimize rate risk, the lender should match not only maturities but also fixed and flexible instruments. Banks' dual activities of credit creation and transactions supply routinely expose them to all three types of risk. Although minimizing risk is one goal of banks, that goal must compete against banks' other goals of making profits and maximizing market share. Given incomplete information about risk, competitive pressures may push lenders into overlending without due caution because of "herd behavior."

A dysfunctional financial system that does not achieve these goals imposes social and private costs. Failing to finance productive investment leads to lower growth rates, as does failing to efficiently identify opportunities for lending among those now shut out of the credit market. Financing speculative activities may quicken financial instability by increasing firms' cash flow obligations without proportionately enhancing their income flows.

Indeed, unsatisfactory performance of any one financial function may well lead to deteriorating performance of the other two functions. For example, the financing of speculative projects may lead to "shock" events, which in turn force economic units to make decisions in turbulent environments, leading to behavioral and market fluctuations and to greater turbulence. A reduction in lending capacity, due to lenders' failure or to their greater conservatism, may result from these events. If so, then financing opportunities for minority entrepreneurs and other deserving borrowers are pinched. In effect, these financial functions are connected by positive feedback effects that will amplify the effect of any deviations from a prior level of performance.

The Design and Decline of the Old U.S. Financial Structure

An extensive set of public regulations and guarantees was built into the U.S. financial structure in the 1930s; these interventions aimed at ensuring its performance of the first and third of the functions listed earlier. Commercial banking and wholesale banking (underwriting and securities selling) were institutionally separated to guard against speculative and insider loans and to ensure an adequate credit supply for firms' working capital needs. Banks' markets were separated and their deposit rates regulated to obviate ruinous competition and to encourage banks to finance productive investment spending within their local market habitats. Deposit insurance and lender-of-last-resort powers minimized the threat of destabilizing bank runs and market crashes.

This redesigned U.S. financial structure was predicated on the dominance of commercial banks and thrifts in providing particular kinds of credit, specifically, short-term business working capital (commercial banks) and home mortgages (thrifts). The regulatory separation of markets and product lines ensured this by giving these institutions near monopolies in those lending markets. The dominance of banks was also ensured because banks' demand deposits were the only alternative to cash as a payment vehicle. There was no practical difference between the government's rules and guarantees to accomplish particular public purposes and its rules and guarantees for banks and thrifts. Deposit insurance evolved, in practice, into a limited form of bank solvency insurance; to the lender-of-last-resort principle was added the too-big-to-fail doctrine.

Banking and the Social Contract

These public interventions into financial arrangements involved an implicit social contract: in exchange for government underwriting and competitive protection, financial markets provided financial stability, and banks provided a reliable credit channel for business and homeownership opportunity.

This arrangement facilitated relatively stable U.S. economic growth between World War II and the early 1970s. At the same time, the potential cost of public guarantees and hence the true scope of the social contract went untested *because* the macroeconomic environment remained stable. As Wolfson noted, the 1930s banking structure rested on low nominal interest rates and steady economic growth.

Thus far, we have mentioned the first and third functions of the financial structure but not the second—fostering economic opportunity. This second function was historically a latecomer. It was recognized formally only with the passage of the Civil Rights and Equal Credit Opportunity Acts in the 1960s and the CRA in 1975. The social movements of the 1960s and 1970s succeeded in exposing bank decisionmaking and bank credit flows as color sensitive. The CRA also affirmed banks' responsibility to take affirmative steps to overcome the cumulative effects of subpar credit flows and financial services in impacted communities. As discussed later, this requirement makes sense if the existence of significant spillover effects in lending is recognized.

The Decline of the Old Financial Structure

Wolfson's chapter shows how deteriorating macroeconomic conditions since the 1970s caused the insured depository system to malfunction. Three other broad forces have undercut the effectiveness of the bank-centered financial structure constructed in the 1930s:

Technological change: The development of credit cards, automated teller machines, wire services, and point-of-sale transfers are revolutionizing monetary transactions. Insured financial intermediaries no longer uniquely provide monetary transactions services. And technological advances have created important economies of scale in the information gathering and processing activities at the heart of the credit decision. Only the largest financial firms will be able to invest in these new technologies and exploit these economies of scale.

The proliferation of *new suppliers in money and credit markets*, including the emergence of secondary markets based on credit contracts: Insured intermediaries no longer uniquely provide short-term credit for other economic units. New financial suppliers have increased the competition for borrowers and for loanable funds. This has squeezed the interest margin at both ends.

Internationalization of financial markets: The global trend toward financial liberalization has challenged government's efforts to carve out more restrictive financial standards than the governments of their international competitors are willing to impose domestically.

All these forces have attacked the centrality of banks in the U.S. financial structure. Insured intermediaries have lost their monopoly in supplying means of payment. Many firms that previously obtained credit from banks now obtain it directly from wealth-holding units or indirectly from nonbank financial firms. Further, the new financial suppliers have broken the loan process into its constituent parts of origination, financing, servicing, and holding. As a result, banks no longer necessarily carry out the entire loan process; instead, the different parts of the loan process are shared among several banking and nonbanking institutions. So the default, liquidity, and rate risks associated with the loan process are parceled throughout the entire financial system—insured and uninsured. Banks have reacted to the loss of some of their better borrowers by seeking out new borrowing markets: in the

1970s and 1980s, these new markets included less developed countries (LDCs), commercial real estate, and highly leveraged transactions. Overlending due to "herd behavior" has resulted in all these cases, often with disastrous consequences.

The only portions of the deposit and credit markets left unaffected by the assaults of other financial market players on banks' turf are the less wealthy households and the less-well-established or smaller firms. And even among these market segments, ironically, fringe banking institutions that offer financial services at very steep prices have begun to proliferate.

The special regulatory attention paid to banks—market segmentation and guarantees--before these changes occurred was justified by banks' special role in the financing (and payments) chain. But deep questions about regulation must be asked in the wake of the structural changes in the credit and transactions markets. Is the current pattern of public guarantees and subsidies still appropriate, given the shifts of significant risks to nonbank institutions? Are banks special in the financial structure any longer? And if they are not, is the financial structure still functional (see The Components and Functions of the Financial Structure)?

This question is especially urgent because the efforts of regulators and of banks themselves to protect banks as operational entities have often, ironically, accelerated the financial system's drift into dysfunctionality. In effect, the failure of one of the financial system functions set out earlier has often triggered reactions that cause other functions to break down. Consider regulators' reaction to banks' (especially large banks') distress: the extension of guarantees and subsidies from depositors alone to the uninsured bond holders of failed banks, and even to past and/or prospective owners. This is justified because of the need to avoid financial instability. But paying liability holders off rather than risking market failure simply demonstrates to market players that there is little or no downside risk from failure. This leads to excessive risk taking and to more bank failures.

Now consider banks' reactions to their balance-sheet distress. Banks have reduced staff, closed branches, and centralized and quantified loan-making decisions, and instead of holding to term the loans they make, as they did before, for some loan categories they now originate loans with the intention of selling them off in the secondary market. These reactions, whatever their effect on the balance sheet, may well reduce banks' fostering of economic opportunity. As Campen (1993) documents, branches are disproportionately closed in lower-income, high-minority areas. Relying on arm's-length assessments of creditworthiness results in less lending for firms and individuals in economically impacted communities; secondary market criteria especially have been inhospitable for loans made in lower-income areas. So the bank activity sought under the CRA, already affected because the proportion of lending by CRA-regulated institutions has been falling, may decline still more.

The Free Market Approach to Bank Regulation and Financial Reform

Debate about bank reform has been dominated by two perspectives, which are described in this section and in the next. This section sets out the free market view that informed the Bush administration's Treasury plan of 1991.

The free market perspective begins with the premise that financial markets represent a close, real-world approximation of the model of perfect competition enshrined in economic theory, which says that financial markets are efficient: when opportunities exist for earning profit from offering monetary transactions or supplying credit, firms will quickly exploit them. This idea has two corollaries: (1) if no firms provide a given financial service in a given area, then that service is not economically viable there, and (2) governments cannot—directly or by mandates—identify areas in which financial services are socially needed better than can private markets. Financial markets are driven by considerations of self-interest to maximally efficient outcomes. If government policies seek social efficiency, they must accommodate financial market forces and not stand against them.

The factors cited in the section on the old financial structure—technological advances, nonbank competitors, and internationalization—may have created temporary problems for banks. But more important, they bring financial markets in the real world ever closer to the perfect-competition ideal. With information now instantaneously available, risks can be assessed more accurately than in the past. With many credit suppliers, even exceptional risks can be priced and underwritten. So truly creditworthy borrowers are never rationed.

This view of financial markets and their evolution toward ever-greater efficiency has powerful implications for the role of banks:

• Banks differ from any other credit market participants only because of their government guarantees and the government restrictions on and oversight of their activities.

• The revolution in information technologies creates economies of scale in the acquisition, processing, and use of information; so in information-intensive industries such as banking, larger firms have inherent advantages over smaller ones.

By implication, dismantling government banking restrictions and rules will lead to more efficient market outcomes. With innovators ceaselessly exploiting profit-making opportunities in financial markets, commercial banks are no longer an essential vehicle in providing either transaction services or credit. Further, the commercial banking industry will remain viable only if the number of banks shrinks while the average size of surviving banks grows. Bigger is better.

In this view, all three of the financial functions enumerated in the section entitled The Components and Functions of the Financial Structure are accomplished best in free markets. Credit suppliers will deploy their lending power in order to finance productive investments with the highest return in the course of pursuing their own self-interest. Potential borrowers lacking net worth can use signaling mechanisms set up by utility-maximizing intermediaries to indicate their creditworthiness; so special measures (like CRA) to "channel" credit are unnecessary and inefficient. And market instability due to bank runs or panics should be understood as evidence not of market failure but of market forces working very rapidly to adjust prices and portfolio positions in light of new information about the underlying value of deposit or equity shares.

In its extreme version, the free market view seeks a banking system with no federal deposit insurance or safety net, no restrictions on bank activities, timely and realistic accounting information, and an automatic, solvency-based closure rule. "Market discipline" should largely replace regulatory oversight: equity owners and depositors will discipline overly risky or incompetent banking firms while potential market entrants will prevent banking firms from earning monopoly rents.

Government intervention into banking markets should be reduced dramatically, in this view. And because there is nothing special about banks or thrifts, their survival or extinction is unimportant. Thomson writes, "[I]t is the restrictions on organizational form, where they can do business, and what businesses they can be in, coupled with access to federal deposit guarantees . . . that make depository institutions special" (1990, p. 32). Bank failures do not have a high social cost. In Thomson's view, new lenders will move into the viable credit and transactions market niches left unserved by bank failures.

Deposit insurance takes the edge off this Darwinian mechanism because it reduces depositors' vigilance over bank asset quality and encourages bank managers to take excessive risks. Public efforts to channel credit according to social purposes will fail and will be burdensome to banks, and regulations inconsistent with bank profit maximization will simply spur innovations that contravene regulators' intentions. If rules for credit market institutions are administered impartially, the benefits of market discipline will be undone by regulators and legislators. As the influential Shadow Financial Regulatory Committee[8] put it:

> *Deregulation* does not mean no regulation at all. It implies a change from government regulation to market regulation. . . . But for market regulation to work effectively, market discipline must be permitted to function. This includes penalties for poor performance. However, . . . policy makers were generally reluctant to permit some forms of market discipline to be applied, in particular, the liquidation or reorganization of institutions that had . . . become economically insolvent. Thus, the reduction in government discipline from deregulation was not matched by a corresponding increase in market discipline. (Kaufman, 1990, p. 63)

The Treasury Plan

The Bush administration's financial reform plan, set forth in the massive 1991 Treasury report, embodied this free market perspective on financial reform. The bulk of the report documented the problems in the banking system and traced them to two roots.

The first root consisted of restrictions on banking competition: "Old laws designed to 'protect' banks from competition have become barriers that impede banks from adapting to changed market conditions. The result has been financial fragility and losses" (U.S. Department of the Treasury, 1991, p. 5). Restrictions on product line entry have denied banks the benefits of "synergies" between their traditional activities and new areas such as insurance and securities. Restrictions on ownership of banks by nonfinancial firms have denied the banking industry some sorely needed capital and made banking riskier. Restrictions on interstate branching have both limited the size of banks' markets and imposed additional costs, because banks operating in more than one state had to maintain separate boards of directors and operating systems. Eliminating these restrictions would allow stronger banks to increase their market share, would diversify banks' asset portfolios, and would inject new capital into the banking system. Having larger banks would, in turn, restore U.S. international competitiveness in banking.[9]

The second root of banks' problems was deposit insurance, which encourages unsound loan making. Regulators have compensated for this by imposing burdensome restrictions on banks, but the cost of those restrictions exceeds banks' benefits from public guarantees.

Together, these two root problems put banks at a disadvantage on an uneven playing field: unregulated lenders are able to offer any service that commercial banks can, but at lower cost. The value of a banking franchise consequently declines, encouraging the emergence of even more nonbank lenders.[10]

In sum, market segmentation and excessive regulation explain banks' decline. But less regulation would not simply make banks more competitively viable; it would also enhance the performance efficiency of the financial system as a whole.

The Treasury proposal itself did not seek to deregulate banking completely but contained most elements of the free market view. It called for increased bank capital, with the degree of regulatory supervision geared to banks' capital/asset ratio. It sought interstate branching and would have allowed well-capitalized banks to hold financial affiliates in securities, mutual fund, and insurance activities. Deposit insurance would have been reduced for individuals and removed for brokered deposits. Banks' uninsured liability holders would be covered under deposit insurance only when necessitated by considerations of systemic risk. State-chartered banks would have been barred from direct investment and other activities not allowed to federally chartered banks.[11]

"Narrow Banking" and the Structural Reduction of Risk

Several broadly similar reform proposals that differ from the free market view have also been proposed. These proposals, usually termed "narrow banking," partially accept the free market view but are skeptical about the capacity of financial markets to absorb risk.

The discussion in The Plight of the Commercial Banks and the Unmet Need for Reform introduced the three types of risks in financial markets. Free market advocates are confident both that liquidity risk is increasingly irrelevant because of the continual deepening and broadening of financial markets and that rate risk can be eliminated through the widespread adoption of floating-rate instruments. In the free market view, the maturation of a financial system—which encompasses the elimination of all barriers to originating or holding any instrument by any intermediary—will effectively eliminate all but default risks; these must be borne.

But what if liquidity and rate risks do not disappear with financial market evolution?[12] What if modern financial markets remain susceptible to overlending manias? Actual occurrences of default might still lead to rapid portfolio shifts among different instruments; tightened monetary policy may drive up borrowing rates; and overlending manias such as those that plagued U.S. banks in the 1980s may recur. Unfettering financial institutions provides no safeguard against such events. That *some* institutions may have foreseen the risk of (say) tightened borrowing markets and matched their maturities does not mean that *all* will do so. In the real world of banking, to ignore the possibility of contagion or of overlending manias is almost certainly to invite it.[13]

Evidence from banks' experience in financial markets supports this respect for the endurance of risk. To take just one example, consider the testimony of Michael DeStefano of Standard & Poor's before the Senate Banking Committee (1990, p. 2).

> [T]he systematic nature of credit problems . . . points not just to lax underwriting standards but to a deeper problem: aggressive overlending to growth sectors of the economy and in risk categories of loans . . . .This trend toward greater asset risk reflects the need to maintain profitability in the face of competitive pressure on margins for lower risk business. (1990, p. 2)

It is certainly true that banks have used innovative instruments to reduce their risk exposure and increase cash flows. Secondary markets for debt instruments allow banks to reduce liquidity risk; variable-rate debt instruments allow them to shift interest rate risk onto borrowers; and off-balance-sheet and pass-through credit arrangements allow them to earn fixed fees up front. But these adjustments may ultimately increase banks' risk exposure. For one thing, credit risk may be higher when loan origination and holding are separated. Banks may be less concerned with default likelihood when the borrower's paper does not remain on their books, and they will know less about the creditworthiness character of paper they buy from others. And if securitized assets should go into arrears, how much recourse is possessed by asset holders against those assets' originators (commercial banks) is unclear.[14]

So authors such as Litan (1986), Bryan (1991), and Pierce (1991) have argued that bank reform should create institutional structures minimizing the potential for interaction among the risks to which financial systems are prone (including contagion effects). These authors agree that banks have become uncompetitive because of a mismatch between the conditions underlying banking in the 1930s and those prevailing today.

Their solution is to erase this mismatch by segmenting the various functions of banking (deposit taking, loan making) into independent economic units. Bryan, for example, would separate banks into three new entities. "Core banks" would take deposits and lend to small enterprises; these "safe" activities would be federally insured. More hazardous activities would occur in two uninsured entities: money market investment banks and finance companies making real estate and other risky loans. The companion plans suggested by Litan and Pierce differ in that their core banks would not make any loans; this converts them into narrow banks. Bryan sees the core banks as eventually consisting of 10–20 large, multiregional institutions, with assets ranging from $50 to $200 billion or more; these would result from mergers of the top 120 bank holding companies. He believes that small, independent core banks would survive by the thousand, and he anticipates only a handful of large money market investment banks and finance companies.

Litan's view is close to that of Bryan, who thinks that narrow banking should be made voluntary, not mandatory, and that it will be most attractive to money center banks. He too envisions a large number of smaller niche institutions surviving in the future.

Pierce has a viewpoint closer to the free market perspective set out earlier. He writes:

> Fundamentally, banking and the government programs that condition the industry are becoming incompatible with the integrated, high-technology financial world in which we live. This fact is central to banking's future success. (1991, pp. 3–4)

Pierce calls for a dual banking system, with corporate unity but with assurances that losses or capital can be shifted from one part of the dual banking organization to the other. He argues that banking in the traditional sense is dead: he observes, by way of proof, that only 62 percent of commercial banks' assets are in loans (as of year-end 1989) and that just 30 percent of loans were to commercial and industrial customers (1991, p. 80).

Litan, Bryan, and Pierce correctly acknowledge both the risks inherent in financial activities and banks' susceptibility to those risks. But their solution is too timid, because it concedes too much to the free market perspective. The narrow banking idea focuses on designing some intrafirm structural safeguards within an otherwise deregulated financial environment so that the financial system will accomplish the third of its three functions—stability. Stability will result from the structural separation of the means of payment and credit facilities of the narrow banks. Stability will also result from this proposal's broad-based deregulation, which allows larger banks to grow. This conclusion is rooted in the assumption that larger and more technologically adept firms will be best able to exploit the emerging economies of scale in financial activities: thus, as they grow, their income-earning capacity should expand; and with more profitable institutions dominating the banking market, that market will be more stable. So the advantages of size will outweigh the vicissitudes of manias and panics.

But narrow banking is also too timid in that it disregards the first two functions of the financial structure in its focus on the third. The narrow banking plans follow the free market view in assuming that the first two functions—promoting productive investment and economic opportunity—will be largely accomplished in a deregulated financial marketplace. There is some concern that integrated, securitized financial markets may leave some credit need unmet, especially for the marginal participants in the credit market. But the social contract that underlay the 1930s financial restructuring cannot be renewed.

Consider the work by Pierce. The most market oriented of the three, Pierce argues that banks now merely duplicate much of what other players do. The sole exception is

> in furnishing loans to businesses too small to use securities markets. Banks have special expertise in assessing and monitoring such projects. One would not want this service to disappear, but it is probably less than 10% of what the banking industry does. Is it really necessary to protect and regulate the other 90% of bank activities to assure provision of this credit? (pp. 81–82)

The answer to this well-posed question is perhaps not the clear-cut negative Pierce anticipates. *For isn't this "10 percent" of what banks do precisely their unique economic function in today's economy?* Pierce also envisions a world of increasing securitization, in which some loans—idiosyncratic loans, especially those for small business—will not participate. These loans—again, his "10 percent"—must be carried on the balance sheets of his envisioned financial service companies, while they sell off most other credits to other financial firms.

Narrow banking surrenders the first two functions of the financial structure to accomplish the third. But should a large and contentious financial restructuring be undertaken that results in only a partially functional result? Will the financial functions left out of this plan be adequately served if not explicitly considered in this restructuring?

Holes in the Free Market Logic: A Deeper Critique

This section argues with the root assumption of the deregulation and narrow banking views that bank consolidation will stabilize the financial markets and bring about a set of efficient financial markets to serve the real economy. There is no denying the impact on banking of technological change, new nonbank credit suppliers, and internationalization. But we argue three points.

• Simply having bigger banks will not enhance performance efficiency and profits in the banking system;

• There is no clear connection between larger U.S. banks and increased U.S. international competitiveness;

• Even the efficient financial markets of the present day leave large gaps in credit availability due to underappreciated spillover effects in credit markets.

Another spillover from having more and more large banks is also explored—the potential for larger financial disturbances when banking firms get into trouble. The implications of these criticisms for plans to reform the financial structure are discussed in the Conclusion.

Bigger Banks with More Activities
May Not Be More Successful Banks

The free market/deregulation perspective interprets market and firm expansion as natural: restoring the banking franchise requires bank expansion across state lines and into new product lines. At the heart of this plan are two ideas: if banks become bigger (through interstate branching), they will become more profitable due to economies of scale; if banks can branch out into nonbanking activities, their incomes will rise or at least become more stable. The evidence on these two assertions, however, is weak at best.

Consolidation—a decrease in the number of banks combined with an increase in their average size (Boyd and Graham, 1991)—is occurring throughout the commercial banking industry. There were 14,500 banks in 1984 and only about 12,300 in 1990. And the banks that remain are larger, on average. Rhoades (1985) shows that between 1960 and 1983, consolidation occurred via acquisitions of smaller banks by larger banks. Since 1983, of course, the weak performance and insolvency of many banking firms, combined with the laissez-faire approach of the Reagan/Bush Department of Justice, have offered unparalleled opportunities for large banking firms to acquire weak mid- and even giant-size banks.

But are bigger banks more efficient? There are reasons to be skeptical on this point. The formal empirical literature on economies of scale in banking is complex and inconclusive. Economies of scale appear to be slim for traditional banking activities (loan making and deposit taking) but may be significant in other activities in which linked automated networks and superior processing capacity can affect costs.

An informal test of the link between market efficiency and firm size is offered by the actual profitability experience of banks of different sizes. Brumbaugh and Litan (1990) summarize their comprehensive study of commercial banks' balance sheets in the 1980s.[15] These authors found that commercial banks' financial condition began to bifurcate sometime in 1987. Most banks were financially healthy, but the number of insolvent banks grew dramatically in that year, and industrywide net income fell dramatically in 1987 "due almost entirely to money center bank additions to reserves for losses on loans to LDCs" (p. 4). Bigger banks, after all, are able to make worse overlending mistakes, and they may be more prone to "herd behavior" because of their greater concern with protecting their market share in lending areas.

And as with thrifts in the early 1980s, weak banks have infected the commercial banking system as a whole. The asset size of banks with negative net income between 1986 and 1989 grew by 17 percent in the 1986–89 period; most of these banks made dividends payments, and this group suffered an overall decline in its average capital/asset ratio, which fell from 7.4 to 3.4 percent. In consequence, the capital/asset ratios of *all* commercial banks declined in this period. So while operational advantages of size may exist to some extent, they are readily squandered.

How are banking and banks' balance sheets likely to be affected by expanding into financial activities outside commercial banking proper? Benston (1990) argues that significant advantages will accrue from universal banking, including more consumer choice, greater financial stability (due to risk-to-return benefits of diversification), and enhanced economic development (because a fuller range of services will be offered to commercial and industrial customers). Benston discounts the dangers arising from concentration of power or self-dealing, given antitrust protections and strictly enforced capital adequacy standards.

At the heart of this positive assessment is the assertion that financial economies of scope exist. Interestingly, Benston's review of the literature on economies of scope in banking views the formal studies on economies of scope as "suggestive. Perhaps the only conclusion we should draw is that total risk . . . is unlikely to decline if commercial and investment banking were combined, while total return might increase" (p. 156). Rose (1987) too reviewed the literature on how nonbank activities in the 1960s through the 1980s have affected bank profits and drew even more cautious conclusions:

> Overall, the research evidence supporting the wisdom of conglomerate expansion by bank holding companies is not especially convincing. Few, if any, concrete benefits—such as more services, greater convenience, improved efficiency, greater safety, or lower prices—seem to accrue to the public. . . . Nor can it be argued convincingly, on the basis of the research to date, that affiliated nonbank businesses outperform other firms in their own industries. Rather, nonfinancial objectives—especially achieving geographic penetration of new financial service markets—appear to have been the key motivators of conglomerate expansion by bank holding companies. (Rose, 1987, pp. 296–97)

An early skeptic of the virtues of commercial bank penetration of nonbank financial services was Edmister (1982), who considered bank conglomerate expansion a "strategic error." The markets for traditional banking services are substantially larger than the markets for nonbank services, and

> depository institutions are already engaged in [these] fastest growing financial markets. . . . banking advances in transactions, credit, currency exchange, and other services are significant in capturing market share. Therefore, maintaining dominance in these areas would appear to be of greater importance than entering the slower growing insurance and broker/dealer markets. (Edmister, 1982, p. 12)

In fact, government actions have already helped banks to expand across state lines and into new activities. Most obviously, large injections of deposit insurance funds and federal tax writeoffs have facilitated the cross-border takeover of weak and failed banks and thrifts by stronger competitors. But the Fed itself has been chipping away at legislative barriers for years. A loophole in the 1956 Bank Holding Company Act (BHCA) allowed one-bank holding companies (OBHCs) to engage in activities defined as illegal for banking firms *per se*. OBHCs accounted for one-third of commercial bank assets by 1970. Most OBHCs ventured into finance, insurance, and real estate. But 1970 amendments to the BHCA closed this loophole, requiring that future acquisitions of nonbank firms entail "public benefits" and be "so closely related to banking or to managing or controlling banks as to be a proper incident thereto." The Fed, as administrator of the BHCA, has permitted a substantial increase in bank holding companies' nonbank financial operations, many across state lines, particularly in investment advisory services, mortgage and industrial banking, leasing, and trust companies.

Larger U.S. Banks Will Not Augment U.S. Competitiveness

Next, consider the argument that the largest U.S. banks must become substantially larger to restore U.S. competitiveness in financial services. That is, whereas U.S. banks once figured among the world's largest, now their asset sizes make them strictly secondary players. But in the international competitiveness game, why does it matter that large U.S. banks win foreign market share and fees? If large U.S. banks do not operate abroad, will foreign banks refuse to serve the needs of U.S. firms engaged in foreign trade and production? And couldn't poor performance by large banks cast a pall over the economies of their headquarters states?

Recent developments suggest two flaws in this argument. First, some of the money center banks that once held high the American presence internationally are now much sadder and wiser organizations. Even within the United States, money center banks are losing their preeminence in the face of the emerging superregional banks.

Second, many of the banks against which U.S. banks are negatively compared have themselves experienced financial distress. Most recently, events have turned against Japanese banks. The slow-motion crash of the Tokyo stock exchange revealed that many of these banks had made unwise loans to brokers and investors; for example, *The Economist* reported that the Industrial Bank of Japan had lent $1.8 billion to a stock market speculator whose debts later came to more than $4 billion. The stock market crash also damaged banks through ripple effects on asset prices in Japan (including real estate values). The nonbank financial institutions on the fringes of the Japanese system, which use loans from large Japanese banks to take substantial risks, also became deeply troubled. All this domestic financial chaos affected Japanese banks' overseas prominence: the Japanese share of overseas banking business fell from over 40 percent in 1989 to less than a third in 1991.

Credit Markets Have Public Good
Characteristics (Spillover Effects)

For autonomous markets to coordinate resources well, the goods they allocate must have no important spillover effects. If they do, market processes will misallocate resources because prices will not represent accurate assessments of the social costs associated with the public goods generating the spillovers. The free market perspective implicitly assumes spillovers are unimportant in banking markets.

One banking spillover has occupied center stage in reform debates: public insurance of bank deposits. This deposit insurance reduces the risk of bank runs by guaranteeing depositors' funds *ex ante,* regardless of the financial condition of the banks themselves. A "commons" problem accompanies this guarantee: with depositors who are indifferent to their banks' individual financial soundness, bank managers or owners have incentives to take excessive risks. Excessive bank risk taking then spills over into taxpayers' pockets.

But other areas of banking in which privately assessed and social costs might diverge have not been recognized. Banking consolidation itself may have a spillover effect. When numerous small banks serve deposit and loan markets, the failure or financial distress of any individual bank—due to bad luck or bad judgment—will have little effect on market credit flows. But as the number of firms supplying deposits and credit shrinks, the failure or financial distress of one bank can seriously compromise the vitality of the entire credit market. Only the large banks that remain can quickly replace the services previously offered by a large, failed bank. So consolidation becomes irreversible. In turn, larger banks can take larger risks than can the smaller ones, leading in the event of larger banks' failure to market gaps that none of the remaining market institutions are strong enough to fill.

A second spillover effect is associated with banks' performance in providing financial transactions and credit. The deregulation perspective assumes that financial markets are efficient and banks redundant. That is, any creditworthy borrower can readily attract credit from those with excess savings—either individual wealth owners or financial intermediaries.

But this assumption is flawed. Borrowers' creditworthiness is not necessarily transparent; small economic units' resources and capabilities cannot be determined at arm's length. So most households and firms can attract credit only if they can establish relationships with financial intermediaries willing and able to assess and monitor their creditworthiness. Borrowers' creditworthiness depends on their income flows and the value of their assets. Less wealthy households' and small businesses' economic vitality depends on the vitality of the communities in which they live.

This is where spillover effects enter in. The availability of jobs and the value of homes and businesses depend on whether bank credit is available there for residents and firm owners. The return that any bank can expect from lending to a borrower in any community depends on how much lending other banks have done there. So loans in communities have spillover effects on jobs and asset values there, and hence on creditworthiness for the economic units located there.

There is clearly an unstable dynamic component to these spillover effects. Over time, units in communities receiving lower credit flows will become less creditworthy through spillover effects. Some communities become sites for extensive bank branch networks and credit flows and in turn job and business opportunities, while others languish and fall behind. In some neighborhoods, property titles change hands when households move out; in other neighborhoods, only the names of the renters change. Households in communities with robust credit flows and asset resale markets can build up equity in their homes; households in neighborhoods lacking resale markets never have this opportunity. Because of these unstable dynamics, what may initially be perceptual differences between areas based on racial perceptions or on unequal bank branch networks will eventually rigidify into material differences. Social costs then rise in the communities that become economically backward: income transfers are required, crime and socially aberrant behavior increase, and so on.

So private market decisions concerning credit flows will not fully reflect their attendant social costs and benefits. Banking markets, left entirely to their own devices, will produce a dynamically unstable checkerboard pattern of prosperity and depression.

Conclusion: Level the Playing Field
and Renew the Social Contract

Financial reforms like those advocated by the Bush administration will not make the financial structure fully functional again. The Bush administration argued that deregulation would allow the largest banking firms to take advantage of economies of scope and scale, eliminating most smaller banks and thus much of the industry's excess capacity and overcoming the exhaustion of the banking franchise. The difference between a functional and a dysfunctional financial structure consisted of excessive regulation and restraints on competition. A competing plan, narrow banking, differs from this perspective primarily in insisting on a structural separation between payments and credit activities so as to reduce some risks.

This chapter has argued that the free market approach is profoundly misguided and that the narrow banking approach is too timid in its criticism of the free market view. The argument has centered on three points. First, banking and credit markets are replete with risks whose true magnitude is much easier to determine after the fact. Because of evolution in markets and internationalization, risks cannot be bounded (as in the past) by simple categorical rules on admissible bank activities. Instead, firm but fair prudential oversight for *all* lenders like that imposed under FDICIA is needed to ensure that the market works.

Second, the advantages of size should not be counted on to salvage bank profitability. The empirical evidence on economies of scale and scope in banking gives little reason to believe that geographic and product line expansion will increase the profitability of large banks. The banking franchise may have little value for money center banks seeking a niche among multi-billion-dollar brokers and traders in international markets. But this franchise is not exhausted for all banks. Indeed, the superregional banks, which now have more core capital and a larger deposit base than money center banks, have succeeded largely by staying with the bread-and-butter banking activities of deposit taking and loan making.

Third, to accomplish the second and third functions of the financial structure, there must be explicit recognition that financial markets have spillover effects apart from those associated with deposit insurance. The most important of these are the spillovers from credit flows for homes and businesses to the value of homes and businesses in their surrounding communities. These lending spillovers will cause prosperous areas that receive substantial credit flows to become more prosperous while speeding the decline of underdeveloped areas. In communities without a large number of wealthy households or well-established businesses, credit markets may not even open, despite an evident need. The credit markets uniquely served by banks in their roles as information specialists and performance monitors are socially made, not presocially given.

An Alternative Approach to Financial Reform

The remainder of this chapter spells out an alternative approach to banking reform. One should note, however, that the banks' recovery depends on restoring a robust macroeconomy. A robust banking sector is inconsistent with a sick economy consisting of anemic job growth and debt-ridden firms and households. The combination of healthy banks and unhealthy communities is unstable. Bank profits are the root of bank equity; these profits depend on realized interest margins that, in turn, depend on the capacity of nonfinancial firms and households to handle and productively deploy debt. The Federal Reserve combined low nominal interest rates with a steep yield curve to generate record commercial bank profits in 1992 despite a stagnant macroeconomy and low bank lending. The episode simply showed that the banking industry can earn profits even if it is not fulfilling its social function. That said, we turn to the proposals, which build both on the other chapters in this section and on the arguments made above. These proposals are aimed at achieving a financial structure that is fully functional.

Changes in banking law must take account of technological advances and of new financial instruments and markets. Banks can no longer be universally protected from competition and guaranteed a positive lending margin. Public guarantees must be reformulated and targeted so that they achieve public purposes that might otherwise go unserved in financial markets. Public subsidies should be reserved for the accomplishment of publicly valued outcomes that will go unmet in autonomously functioning financial markets subject to dynamically unstable spillover effects.

Level the Playing Field

The playing field for banks and nonbank financial intermediaries must be leveled. Those commercial banks that want to compete in world markets with foreign banks and securities firms are free to do so, but they must meet rigorously enforced capital adequacy criteria, and their liability holders must be prepared for the possibility of failure. Ironically, leveling the playing field by expanding the powers of banks implies that whatever regulations and rules apply now to insured intermediaries—commercial banks and thrifts—must be extended to all financial intermediaries.

The proposals set out here try to level the playing field in a way that does not jeopardize the third financial function—maintaining stability in financial markets.

1. *Deposit insurance should be narrowed so that it is again a safeguard against runs and no longer an operational subsidy for a special class of financial intermediaries.*

Deposit insurance has been stretched too much. Its present status, as a program for holding harmless all liability holders of banks except equity owners *and* for financing the cost of reconstituting failed banking firms, is untenable. Deposit insurance should simply insure the holdings of all households up to some maximum amount (perhaps $40,000), with the express purpose of avoiding runs at the "micro" (banking firm or regional) level. D'Arista's chapter in this volume suggests that this can be done most expeditiously by insuring individuals, not institutions. This position has been controversial.[16] The question is whether the absence of deposit insurance for institutions will lead to ebbs and flows of funds that either effectively discipline financial intermediaries or, instead, spread financial instability more quickly (forcing more Fed lender-of-last-resort interventions). This unsettled question cannot be settled here, but it deserves further exploration. If deposit insurance does remain with accounts of particular kinds, all financial intermediaries willing to abide by regulatory rules on accounts of this type should be able to take advantage of it.

2. *Banks' safeguards against ruinous competition should be removed. Let banks expand across state borders and into new asset-side activities, and let banks fail.*

This expansion of bank powers must be carried out on the explicit understanding that bankruptcy proceedings are the price of insolvency. The deposit insurance fund must no longer be used as a residual insurance fund for a special class of financial intermediaries. One issue that deserves special attention concerns the treatment of financial intermediaries that are corporate subsidiaries of larger entities. When such intermediaries approach insolvency, should their parent corporations be allowed to assist them with upstream injections of capital? If yes, then such intermediaries would have a tremendous competitive advantage. The interests of fair competition would seem best served if all intermediaries had the same recourse to capital. This complex issue has not been treated here; it clearly must be addressed to ensure the principle of a truly level playing field.

3. *All entities functioning as financial intermediaries in credit markets should be held to the strict oversight and capital adequacy guidelines established under FDICIA.*

Since there will no longer be insured financial intermediaries, leveling the financial market playing field means that all financial intermediaries, that is, all entities that connect borrowers and lenders, will be held to FDICIA's oversight standards. The banking system's outcry that FDICIA's guidelines are too strict should not guide regulatory policy. The guidelines on capital adequacy embodied in FDICIA are derived from a 1988 international agreement, the Basel Accord. The accord established strict capital standards that banks in all the advanced industrial countries had to meet by the end of 1992. Given the performance of the banking industry during the 1980s, there is no compelling argument for reducing capital standards and hence intermediaries' prudential cushion against loss. Given the need to manage an increasingly internationalized financial system, the Basel Accord should be upheld—and, if anything, extended.[17]

4. *Prudential oversight responsibilities should be consolidated and systematized. Intermediaries should not be able to go shopping for regulators offering the most lenient standards. State regulations should give way to federal regulations when the latter are tougher.*

Public oversight will be facilitated if it pertains inclusively to all financial institutions in the economy. The new rules for home mortgage disclosure (instituted under FIRREA) represent a step in the right direction: until 1990, home mortgage originations were reported only by insured financial intermediaries;

from 1990 onward, mortgage companies—though uninsured—must file detailed reports on their home mortgage originations. And oversight should be not only broadened but also unified. The tangled regulatory treatment of nonbank banks in the 1980s offers a case example by negation: self-interested firms will use overlapping regulatory and statutory jurisdictions with different standards and objectives, when these exist, to achieve the outcomes that least constrain them.[18]

5. *The Federal Reserve should maintain its role as the lender of last resort, but the too-big-to-fail doctrine should be retired.*

The Fed's lender-of-last-resort role remains crucial, especially given a more restrictive form of deposit insurance (as previously proposed). But eliminating the too-big-to-fail doctrine—a key step in leveling the playing field—will be feasible only if regulators and elected officials take firm and creative steps to deal with credit market crises as they arise.

The Bush administration's workout policy on failed banks was to make good on the bad assets of sufficiently large banks. When Fleet/Norstar took over the failed Bank of New England, the government offered Fleet both the right to send any unwanted assets to the Bank Insurance Fund and $2.5 billion to seal the deal. Meanwhile, smaller bank failures were treated harshly, as in the well-known case of Harlem-based Freedom National Bank.

We have emphasized that credit relations entail serious risk. The too-big-to-fail doctrine can be eliminated safely only if credit market crises are handled with due diligence and in a creative way. An example is offered by the regulatory response to the LDC debt crisis of the 1980s. Congress tried to rein in the danger to banks by passing the International Lending Supervision Act of 1983. Still in effect, this act requires special reserves against impaired assets, sets capital adequacy standards for banks involved in international lending, and mandates public disclosure of concentrations of overseas lending. The Foreign Debt Reserving Act of 1989 was then passed to help remove LDC loan losses from large banks' balance sheets. This act (Wells, 1990) mandates a regulatory review of reserves held against the loans of the 17 most highly indebted developing countries; it exempts banks from increased reserve requirements if they participate in Brady plan deals.[19] Thus far, four Brady plan deals have been negotiated. Leaving aside whether this legislative response was as humane or just as it could have been for residents in indebted countries, these acts, together with other regulatory responses, allowed the banking industry to defuse a time bomb that could have bankrupted more of the banking firms involved.

Renew the Social Contract

The first five points aimed at implanting the third financial function (stability) by affirming the need for effective oversight by extending financial regulations to all intermediaries. The next five points argue that public subsidies, when extended, should be used to achieve purposes that "free" banking markets might overlook due to spillover effects. They also redefine the social responsibility of financial intermediaries in light of the structural changes suggested in the first five points. The overriding purpose of these points is to ensure that the financial structure fulfills its first and second functions.[20]

6. *All financial intermediaries should be licensed per the licensing proposal set out by D'Arista and Schlesinger in this volume.*

7. *All financial intermediaries, including those that are foreign owned, should be required to meet minimum performance standards under broadened CRA guidelines. (Campen's essay in this volume discusses how CRA goals can be set and met.)*

These complementary points aim at the same goal. Clearly, if the distinction between "insured" and "uninsured" financial intermediaries is effectively eliminated, and if special subsidies and guarantees are no longer extended to privileged subsets of intermediaries, then all intermediaries must bear responsibility for financing productive investment and fostering economic opportunity.

Point 6 needs little elaboration, in view of the careful treatment by the authors of this proposal. Suffice it to simply note that licensing provisions, although aimed primarily at the first two financial functions, may also make the financial system more stable (the third function) by establishing competency hurdle rates.

Point 7 is a direct implication of the "leveling" proposals made earlier. The CRA cannot be restricted to banks and thrifts when these entities are no longer the recipients of special guarantees and market protections. Instead, all financial firms must take some responsibility for accomplishing CRA's goals. Financial intermediaries that offer credit to borrowers must offer credit, either directly or indirectly, to underserved areas and customers. Financial intermediaries that provide monetary transactions must contribute toward building up the financial infrastructure in underserved areas.

8. *Both prudential supervision of intermediaries and hard-headed supervisory assessment of intermediaries' CRA performance are crucial for a fully functional financial structure. Neither oversight responsibility should be held hostage so as to accomplish the other.*

CRA performance assessments have often been merely perfunctory, with "satisfactory" ratings being given too generously. The cost of such generosity is a partially dysfunctional financial structure that does not foster economic opportunity. And as Campen documents in this volume, recent supervisory efforts to toughen CRA assessments have been misguided in that they have emphasized form over substance. Performing well under CRA should not be treated by intermediaries and regulators alike as an onerous bureaucratic burden, but rather as a vital substantive challenge. This point also addresses a regulatory conflict of interest that has emerged during the banking crisis of the past several years. The Federal Reserve has been charged with both resolving intermediaries' problems in a least-cost fashion and, at the same time, assessing intermediaries' performance under CRA. Its response has often been to set aside its latter obligation so as to pursue the former. The assumption is that CRA compliance is costly and hence counterproductive given the Fed's greater concern with bank solvency. This regulatory response is, perhaps, understandable given the rigid bureaucratic interpretation of CRA and given the Bush and Reagan administrations' overarching hostility to what Wolfson terms "public regulation." But given the importance of the second financial function and given the pervasiveness of spillover effects (not to mention dynamically unstable spillovers) in credit markets, regulators must take their CRA responsibilities as a serious substantive charge if the U.S. financial structure is to be fully functional again.

It is not clear how best to accomplish effective prudential regulation *and* hard-headed CRA monitoring. One approach would be to have separate regulatory agencies handle these two oversight responsibilities. The drawback of such a scheme is that the CRA monitoring agency might lose its clout by being isolated from the prudential regulation process. At the same time, leaving the two functions under one regulatory roof risks devaluing CRA monitoring. An alternative might be to have separate regulatory facilities (either within one agency, such as the Federal Reserve, or in different agencies), with the CRA monitoring arms playing a limited strategic role in the prudential regulation process. An example of this "strategic role" is the requirement under current law that banks wishing to merge or expand their branch networks must prove, subject to public review, that their CRA performance is adequate.

9. *Innovative programs and institutions—community-based credit unions, community loan funds, and other microcredit vehicles—should be encouraged under programs designed to spur economic activity in depressed areas. The range of these institutions' activities will be carefully circumscribed to socially productive purposes. These special categories of institutions alone should benefit from institutional subsidies and guarantees.*

Some have argued that nationwide bank branching and bank expansion into nonbanking financial activities might worsen the neglect of lower-income and high-minority communities, or even of disfavored regions, by banking firms. Whether this fear is justified depends on the strength of regulators' and legislators' commitment to supplying credit and banking services in underserved areas. At present, despite banks' complaints about the cost of complying with CRA criteria, most banks evidently are doing little about underserved areas' credit and banking needs other than shuffling paper for Fed regulators. Banks' attitudes about CRA efforts would, perhaps, change if it were appreciated that areas become viable or unviable from a credit risk perspective due to the operation of dynamically unstable spillover effects. The way to overcome these spillover effects is to target resources. The efforts of more than one institution may well be needed.

No one model appears to offer an obviously superior means of getting credit to communities in need and accomplishing the second financial function. It might be best to encourage intermediaries to adopt a range of approaches to banking in neglected communities. Some banks might operate branch operations directly in impacted neighborhoods: others might be more effective at working through subsidiary community banks or community development corporations.[21]

It would be a mistake to think that development banking in impacted communities can necessarily be a money-making proposition. To the contrary, some programs may require subsidies to continue. The Grameen Bank of Bangladesh is often cited as a success story about a bank that works exclusively with poor depositors and borrowers. This is true. It is also true that Grameen's success in achieving near immaculate repayment rates by borrowers and in changing poor people's lives does not yield them a profit. At present, Grameen's banking operations are about one-quarter subsidized. These operating subsidies allow Grameen to have a low borrower/supervisor ratio, which in turn helps to account for its success. To require this bank to turn a profit might well lead it to dismantle the very policies that have made it a success.

The experience to date with models that seek to foster economic opportunity through financial intermediation is preliminary and incomplete. This should be recognized, with efforts in this area characterized by a spirit of openness and experimentation. There is a tendency to seize on models that have worked in particular places for particular reasons—such as the Grameen Bank of Bangladesh or the South Shore Bank of Chicago. But it is too soon to lionize any one model, and, most likely, no one model can be best for the needs of all underserved individuals and areas.

10. *If financial intermediaries receive transfusions of public funds under the lender-of-last-resort doctrine, these funds should be understood as constituting a public ownership interest. Institutions receiving these funds should take exemplary steps to fulfill financial functions that might be left underserved by autonomous market forces.*

The Continental Illinois experience, wherein public funds were used to stabilize and recapitalize a major banking firm, may well be repeated. There is a fine line in practice between the lender-of-last-resort doctrine and the too-big-to-fail principle. Eliminating the too-big-to-fail doctrine, in practice, means not using public funds—that is, revenues collected through statutory provisions on individuals or firms—to recapitalize only those entities that are sufficiently big. Long-term investments of public funds must be restricted per point 9. But the temporary or short-term use of public funds to rescue financial intermediaries cannot be ruled out; again, the Continental Illinois experience makes clear that it is difficult in practice to distinguish what "temporary" means in this context.

Leaving these vagaries aside, a principle related to using public funds to accomplish the lender-of-last-resort purpose can be clearly enunciated. Intermediaries that receive short-term public funds should provide some quid pro quo. These funds are effectively an ownership interest, so the intermediaries in question should tilt their activities toward accomplishing social purposes—financing affordable housing, funding small business credit programs, opening branches in underserved areas, and so on—that might be poorly met in autonomously functioning private markets.

Parting Words

These 10 points are offered as part of the alternative vision of financial restructuring that the chapters in this section offer. The points are aimed at reconstituting the U.S. system of financial intermediation in such a way that it bows to the forces of modernization and internationalization while accomplishing the functions that a healthy financial structure must provide for the economy it serves. What is crucial about these points is that they affirm the financial structure's functions of facilitating productive investment and fostering economic opportunity, rather than discarding these functions as antiquated.

For accomplishing this purpose there may be a more elegant or effective formulation than these specific points. Others have offered related plans that also recognize the need to renew the social contract.[22] The important thing is to broaden debate so that the three functions of a productive financial system are understood as mutually reinforcing, not contradictory.

In sum, insisting that banks live up to a social contract without providing them the means of competitive survival is shortsighted. But providing a level playing field without insisting that the reconfigured system of financial intermediation fulfill public purposes is foolish. It is best simultaneously to level the playing field and renew the social contract.

Notes

1. The author wishes to acknowledge the comments of Jim Campen, Jane D'Arista, Jerry Epstein, Sherry Ettleson, George Kaufman, Robert Litan, Bob Pollin, Jean Wells, and an anonymous referee on an earlier draft of this paper. Remaining errors and omissions are his own.

2. FDICIA's regulatory oversight provisions call for more frequent and tougher inspections of commercial banks and thrifts. The law places institutions into five risk classes based on their capital adequacy; an institution's risk class then determines the severity of regulatory oversight and the extent of the institution's powers. The deposit insurance fee, which before 1991 was $.19 per $100 of deposits, was raised to $.237 in May 1992.

3. As of January 1, 1993, well-capitalized banks about which supervisors have no concern pay $.23 per $100 in deposits, as all banks did before that date. But rates have risen to $.29 for undercapitalized banks meriting no supervisory concern, $.29 for well-capitalized banks meriting substantial supervisory concern, and $.31 for undercapitalized banks meriting substantial supervisory concern.

4. When the FDIC released rules for risk-based deposit insurance premiums in mid-September 1992, some 266 banks were classified as undercapitalized, and while bank regulators predictably expressed supervisorial concern for 93.2 percent of undercapitalized banks, 17.5 percent of well-capitalized banks were also placed in the "supervisorial concern" category.

5. Nonfinancial firms too routinely create credit by offering and accepting trade credit

(accounts receivable) and by selling instruments in financial markets. The distinction between financial and nonfinancial firms is based on whether the credit supply function is a means of enhancing the volume of the firm's other activities or is its institutional raison d'être. D'Arista and Schlesinger point out that this distinction is a muddy one for some of the largest nonbank finance companies attached to integrated manufacturing firms (for example, GMAC and GM).

6. The success of any economic subsector is normally not measured by how well it meets some specified goals for the economy as a whole. The test of success is typically how robust its income flows are over time; goals are simply the objectives pursued by individual decisionmaking units. But because the financial system and its institutions deal completely with intangible goods, whose value in use (taken on its own) is nil, in some sense resources not needed for these intangible manipulations are freed up for use elsewhere. A smaller financial system is not necessarily better, as Gurley and Shaw (1960) recognized long ago: having more financial intermediaries can expand the set of investment possibilities by providing more channels for financing productive activity.

7. These goals appear in no formal legislative declaration such as the declarations of the Full Employment Act of 1946 or the Humphrey-Hawkins Act of 1978 about the government's full-employment goals. The author offers these goals primarily to suggest that it might be useful, in thinking about what should be done *with* the financial sector, to begin by thinking about what is expected *of* it. The distance between such functional performance goals and the actual tenor of banking policy debate is illustrated dramatically by the atmosphere surrounding the passage of FDICIA. The defeat of the Treasury plan in November 1991 was due largely to financial lobbyists' inability to agree on a mutually acceptable compromise. After the defeat of a conference committee bill that he and Senator Riegle had concocted, Rep. Henry Gonzalez told *The New York Times*, "Lobbyists worked this bill day and night like nothing that I've ever seen in my 30 years in Congress." This article chronicled some of the lobbyists involved in this defeat, including the National Association of Realtors, which had contributed $3.09 million to 1990 campaigns; insurance lobbyists, $2.86 million; the American Bankers Association, $1.47 million; credit unions, $0.51 million; and J. P. Morgan, $0.4 million.

8. For example, this group's Statement No. 41, "A Program for Deposit Insurance and Regulatory Reform" (reproduced in Kaufman, 1990, pp. 163–68), which predates the passage of FDICIA by more than two years, anticipates the capital adequacy and regulatory monitoring sections of FDICIA in almost every detail. The common denominator of this "self-appointed group of 12 experts," which was founded on the model of the Shadow Open Market Committee, is its members' "public recognition as experts on the industry, and their preferences for market solutions to problems and the minimum degree of government regulation consistent with efficiency and safety" (Kaufman, 1990, pp. 2, 150). The group has met quarterly since February 1986.

9. This view was perhaps expressed most forcefully by Gerald Corrigan in his 1990 testimony before the House Banking Committee.

10. The chapter by D'Arista and Schlesinger in this volume documents the rising importance of nonbank lenders in U.S. credit markets.

11. As discussed the section entitled The Plight of the Commercial Banks, the only provisions of this plan incorporated into FDICIA were those concerning bank capital levels and regulatory supervision. Given the hue and cry raised by the banking industry about these provisions in the latter part of 1992, it is interesting to note that these appeared in FDICIA almost exactly as proposed by the Administration.

12. In this regard, consider the secondary mortgage market, perhaps the most illustrious example of the reapportionment of default risk. The raw material for most of the instruments sold in this market is the fixed-rate mortgage. The institutions that made these

mortgages took on rate risk. They disposed of that rate risk by selling off their fixed-rate mortgages, but the risk does not thereby disappear, even though it may take on a different appearance for the ultimate holder of the mortgage instrument.

13. Consider the crash of the California residential and commercial real estate markets less than 10 years after the same markets collapsed in Texas, Oklahoma, and Louisiana.

14. Hull (1989) shows that the choice of whether to securitize credit or not, for commercial banks, has been driven largely by legal definitions and tax treatments of the contracts involved. In practice, that is, the only distinction between securitized and non-securitized bank debt involves the transfer of ownership over its payment stream. There is too little case law for precedents on recourse to be well established. A prime example of upstream credit risk is offered by the failure of Continental Illinois, most of whose defaulted loans were originated and sold to its portfolio by Penn Square Bank of Oklahoma.

15. These authors' results are developed further and discussed at greater length in Barth, Brumbaugh, and Litan (1992).

16. Wolfson's proposal, for example, seeks to retain "needed public protection for financial institutions," which could encompass deposit insurance for institutions, continuance of the Fed's lender-of-last-resort role, and/or continued recourse to the too-big-to-fail doctrine when needed to retain financial stability. The need for a Fed lender-of-last-resort role is universally agreed on. D'Arista's proposal suggests removing deposit insurance for institutions, and this chapter suggests eliminating the too-big-to-fail doctrine. The latter two positions, of course, assume there will not be severe consequences in terms of financial instability. Again, the matters deserve further study.

17. This agreement was so named because it was promulgated by the Basel-based Bank for International Settlements (BIS), a consortium of OECD bank regulators. According to the Basel Accord, all banks must hold common equity totaling 4 percent and overall capital totaling 8 percent of their risk-adjusted assets. The impetus for approval of these capital standards was international regulatory concern that financial innovations—which were increasing direct credit flows and off-balance-sheet bank credit commitments and leading to new derivative credit instruments—were increasing credit risk due to "more distant business relationships between debtor and creditor" (BIS, 1986, p. 67). On taking the BIS chair, Gerald Corrigan of the New York Fed has indicated he will write new rules for such innovative instruments (*The Economist*, Oct. 26, 1991, and see endnote 15).

18. To regain some control over the pace of innovation in financial markets and to provide banks with some relief from non-banks' competitive heat, Congress passed the Competitive Equality in Banking Act (CEBA) in 1987. CEBA extended the Glass-Steagall prohibitions on interlocking directorates and shared officers between member banks and securities operations, which had previously applied only to state member banks and national banks and to nonmember insured banks; it also established a moratorium on new bank or securities activities. So, through CEBA, Congress temporarily prevented the creation of new nonbank banks, both by banks and by nonfinancial firms. In so doing, it blocked banks from using their prevailing method for avoiding geographic restrictions, that is, acquiring (partial-service) finance companies, mortgage banks, leasing firms, and the like.

Commercial banks overcame Congress's intent through a variety of creative steps. Commercial banks accomplished geographic expansion by branching under state laws. And banks exploited court interpretations of the Glass-Steagall and Bank Holding Company acts to expand the scope of their activities. The leading Supreme Court ruling, in 1971, interpreted legislative intent as seeking to avoid the "subtle hazards" that might arise when commercial banks engage in proscribed securities activities, including "promotional and other pressures." The Court opened the way for the Office of the Comptroller of the Currency to approve services that could pass the "subtle hazards" test.

19. The "Brady Plan" is the name given to a Bush administration initiative aimed at providing relief for overindebted developing countries and the U.S. banks that had made loans to them. A variety of creative means were made available to reduce the outstanding balance of debt. In the case of Mexico, which received the lion's share of Brady Plan benefits, debt was converted into securities and sold off into financial markets; it was converted into equity claims; its maturity and terms were restructured; and so on.

20. It should be noted that proposals made in the public investment section of this volume will also augment the goal of financing productive investment either by establishing further inducements for socially productive investment or by imposing costs on speculative investments.

21. Consider two stories of reinvestment success. The first is that of South Shore Bank in Chicago, which has operated as a profit-making institution while making loans in neglected areas. The AmeriTrust Development Bank of Cleveland, a state-chartered subsidiary of AmeriTrust Corporation of Cleveland, offers another model. This bank has Cleveland corporations as depositors and lends funds for housing and commercial development in Cleveland's neighborhoods. Its president, John Kolesar, told the Senate Banking Committee (100th Congress, 2nd session, 1988, on CRA) that its success is due to higher quality and volume of loans, not to profit margins (positive but lower than industry averages).

22. One example is the plan offered by the Greenlining Coalition, published in *The New York Times* of December 10, 1992 (p. A17).

Bibliography

Atkinson, Bill. "New Capital Rule Hits 200 Banks and Thrifts." *American Banker*, December 9, 1991, pp. 1, 6, 7.

Bank for International Settlements. "Recent Innovations in International Banking." Report by Study Group established by the Central Banks of the Group of Ten Countries, 1986.

Barth, James, R. Dan Brumbaugh, Jr., and Robert E. Litan. *The Future of American Banking.* Armonk, NY: M. E. Sharpe, 1992.

Benston, George. *The Separation of Commercial and Investment Banking.* Oxford, England: Oxford University Press, 1990.

Boyd, John H. and Stanley L. Graham. "Investigating the Banking Consolidation Trend." Federal Reserve Bank of Minnesota. *Quarterly Review*, Spring 1991, pp. 3–15.

Brumbaugh, Dan and Robert E. Litan. "A Critique of the Financial Institutions Recovery, Reform, and Enforcement Act of 1989 and the Financial Strength of Commercial Banks." Mimeo. Washington, DC: March 18, 1990.

Bryan, Lowell L. *Bankrupt: Restoring the Health and Profitability of Our Banking System.* New York: HarperBusiness, 1991.

DeStefano, Michael. Statement to the U.S. Senate Banking Committee. Washington, DC, September 12, 1990.

Edmister, Robert. "Commercial Bank Market Share of the Financial Services Industry: A Value Added Approach." Paper presented at the Conference on Bank Structure and Competition. Federal Reserve Bank of Chicago, 1982.

Hull, Everette. "The Complete Story on Securitization of Bank Assets." Parts 1 and 2. *Journal of Commercial Bank Lending*, November and December 1989.

Kaufman, George G., ed. *Restructuring the American Financial System.* Boston: Kluwer Academic Publishers, 1990.

Litan, Robert. *What Should Banks Do?* Washington, DC: The Brookings Institution, 1986.

Pierce, James L. *The Future of Banking*. The 20th Century Fund. New Haven, CT: Yale University Press, 1991.

Rhoades, Stephen A. "Mergers and Acquisitions by Commercial Banks, 1960–83." *Staff Study* 142. Board of Governors of the Federal Reserve System. Washington, DC: January 1985.

Rose, Peter S. *The Changing Structure of American Banking*. New York: Columbia University Press, 1987.

Rosenblatt, Robert A. "Bankers Say Fed Rules Make Them Afraid to Lend." *Los Angeles Times*, September 22, 1992, pp. D2 and D5.

Thomson, James B. "Using Market Incentives to Reform Bank Regulation and Federal Deposit Insurance." *Economic Review*, Federal Reserve Bank of Cleveland, 1990.

U.S. Department of the Treasury. *Modernizing the Financial System: Recommendations for Safer, More Competitive Banks*. Washington, DC: U.S. Government Printing Office, February 1991.

U.S. General Accounting Office. *Bank Insurance Fund: Additional Reserves and Reforms Needed to Strengthen the Fund*. Washington, DC: U.S. Government Printing Office, September 1990.

U.S. General Accounting Office. *Deposit Insurance: Analysis of Reform Proposals*. Staff Study. Washington, DC: U.S. Government Printing Office, September 30, 1986.

U.S. Senate. Committee on Banking, Housing, and Urban Affairs. Hearings on Community Reinvestment Act Held March 22–23 and September 8–9, 1988.

Wells, F. Jean. "Banks and Thrifts: Restructuring and Solvency 1990." Congressional Research Service Congress, Library of Congress. Washington, DC: August 6, 1990.

Wells, F. Jean. "Banks and Thrifts in Transition." CRS Report for Congress, CRS. Washington, DC: Library of Congress, July 9, 1991.

CHAPTER SIX

The Evolution of the Financial System and the Possibilities for Reform[1]

Martin H. Wolfson

CHAPTER SUMMARY

Significant reform of the institutional structure of the financial system is "on the agenda." To understand the possibilities for reform, it is necessary to understand the concrete conditions created by the historical evolution of the financial system.

The system of financial regulation in the United States was constructed in the 1930s. It was based upon two principles: (1) restriction of competition among financial institutions and (2) government protection, including federal insurance of deposits and a federal commitment to prevent financial panics. Its structure was designed for the economic conditions of the times—an environment of low inflation and interest rates, high liquidity, and low debt levels. Because those conditions also characterized the early post–World War II period, the system of financial regulation promoted stability.

But as economic conditions began to change, banks and thrifts (primarily savings and loan associations [S&Ls]) experienced increasing difficulties. Financial innovation and technological change have made possible a partial dismantling of the barriers to competition that previously protected banks and thrifts. Government protection has expanded dramatically in response to these intermediaries' problems, for example, protection of banks "too big to fail" and the S&L bailout.

Therefore proposals for reform need to take account of the following concrete conditions: (1) the continuing need for government protection in light of financial intermediaries' present difficulties and the environment of high debt levels, (2) the difficulty of "rolling back the clock" to a regulatory structure no longer compatible with current economic conditions, and thus (3) the need for mechanisms to promote stability in place of restricted competition.

Reform proposals based on free market principles alone eliminate the old regulatory structure but provide no new mechanism to promote stability. They run the risk of either financial crises or further taxpayer bailouts of financial institutions. An alternative approach would introduce a framework of public regulation to incorporate public policy goals explicitly into financial institutions' behavior. The issues then become (1) how to formulate this public regulation so it benefits the broad majority and (2) how to carry it out democratically.

Introduction

Significant reform of the U.S. financial system is "on the agenda." Reform proposals must be based not only on appropriate public policy goals but also on the concrete condition of the financial system. Therefore, to understand the possibilities for reform, it is necessary first to understand the historical evolution of the financial system.

This chapter proposes that significant changes are required in the institutional structure of the financial system because of the breakdown of the old regulatory framework. In particular, increased public regulation is needed to restore stability to the financial system. The nature of that public regulation will depend upon what public policy goals are sought.

The next two sections of this chapter examine the old institutional structure of the financial system—why it has succeeded and why it is now experiencing difficulties. The fourth section then considers the efforts to restructure this system; the fifth summarizes its current condition. The next section contrasts two competing frameworks for reform—the free market and public regulation approaches. The final two sections explore the public regulation approach in more detail.

The Post-war Financial System

The institutional structure of the U.S. financial system was reconstructed in the wake of the financial turmoil of the 1930s. Stability was restored for the nation's troubled financial system via legislative and regulatory changes based on two principles: government protection for special classes of financial institutions and restrictions on financial competition. Measures implementing these principles sharply differentiated depository and nondepository financial institutions and provided each of the institutions with insured deposits with a degree of monopoly in its asset and liability markets.

Government Protection

The most important form of government protection was the introduction of federal deposit insurance, based on the creation of the Federal Deposit Insurance Corporation (FDIC) in 1933 and of the Federal Savings and Loan Insurance Corporation in 1934. Following the banking crises and widespread bank runs of

1931–33, the federal insurance of deposits was instrumental in restoring confidence in the banking system. Deposit insurance effectively created two categories of financial intermediaries: those whose deposit liabilities were insured and those whose liabilities were uninsured. The "depository institutions" in the former category, collectively termed the "banking system," consisted largely of commercial banks, thrifts (S&Ls and mutual savings banks), and credit unions. In addition, the creation of the FDIC enhanced the safety and stability of the banking system by expanding government's regulatory and supervisory role.

Government support of the banking system was further enhanced by an expansion in the powers of the Federal Reserve system. Power was centralized in the Federal Reserve Board, and control over open market operations was consolidated. The collateral acceptable for discount-window lending was liberalized, lending to nonmember banks was permitted, and, in general, the Federal Reserve's ability to act as a lender of last resort was strengthened.

Restriction of Competition

The restriction of competition took several forms. The Federal Reserve under Regulation Q established ceiling rates for banking system deposits to preclude further episodes of what were perceived as banks' destructive bidding wars for liabilities in the 1920s. Maximum interest rates were set for savings deposits, and the payment of interest on demand deposits prohibited altogether.

The 1930s' legislation also restricted competition by extending the "compartmentalization" of financial institutions. Commercial and investment banking were separated under the Glass-Steagall Act. This demarcation reinforced existing delineations among depository intermediaries' assets: thrifts specialized in home mortgages, commercial banks in business lending, and credit unions in consumer finance. Competition was also restricted on intermediaries' liabilities. Only commercial banks were allowed to offer checking accounts; thrift institutions concentrated primarily on savings deposits. Other financial institutions such as investment banks and insurance companies were not allowed to offer deposit accounts, and their liabilities were not subject to federal deposit insurance.

Prohibition of interstate banking constituted a third restriction on competition. Banks were not allowed to establish branches in states other than those in which they were chartered; in addition, many "unit-banking" states prohibited banks from having more than one branch.

The Importance of Initial Conditions

The institutional structure created in the 1930s was remarkably successful for much of the early post–World War II period. Its institutional configuration conformed with conditions in credit markets and in the economy as a whole during that era.

During the Depression, many firms failed and their debt obligations were repudiated. Economic activity was stagnant. As a result, prices fell, and the demand for credit to finance new business and consumer spending was minimal. The economy revived with the coming of World War II. But private debt creation was limited, and the government's borrowing for its war effort, which dominated financial markets, was financed at interest rates pegged by the Federal Reserve (a policy continued until the Federal Reserve–Treasury Accord of 1951). As a result of these special conditions, interest rates remained extraordinarily low. The prevailing rate on prime commercial paper of four to six months' maturity remained at 1 percent or less from June 1934 through August 1947 (Board of Governors, 1943, p. 451; 1976, p. 674).

Government securities came to dominate the portfolios of both banks and nonfinancial companies. Because of their broad market and unquestioned credit quality, these securities could easily be sold for cash with little variation in price. The financial system's liquidity was thus greatly increased.

The stability of depository institutions and of the financial system as a whole was enhanced by these economic and financial conditions. The liquidity of financial institutions, the low levels of private debt, and the restrained demand for credit kept interest rates low and stable. This interest rate environment, in turn, reduced depositories' uncertainty about the cost of funds and facilitated their lending at fixed rates. This helped to restore depository institutions' profitability, as did the barriers to entry enforced by "compartmentalization" and by the ban on interstate banking (which especially benefited smaller banks), the subsidy implicit in federal deposit insurance,[2] and the positive spread between long-term and short-term interest rates. This profitability, in turn, justified the renewed public confidence in banks after the implementation of deposit insurance, and this confidence stabilized banks' deposit base and further augmented their earnings.

The stability of the interest rate spread encouraged the development of the 30-year amortized mortgage; before the 1930s, the most common form of the mortgage loan was a shorter-term balloon involving a large repayment of principal when the loan matured. But in an environment of stable interest rates, thrift institutions in particular could make guaranteed profits simply by financing long-term mortgage loans with short-term deposits. This arrangement also contributed to the growth of home ownership and the housing industry in the postwar period.

The new financial structure, with a stable and profitable banking system at its center, contributed to a prolonged period of economic growth.[3] But that growth eventually led to changes in the conditions on which the institutional structure of the financial system was premised. Under those changed conditions, the institutional arrangements that had previously supported stability for depository intermediaries eventually became obstacles to continued stability.

Increasing Difficulties in the Post-war Financial System

Changing Conditions and Increasing Problems

Economic growth in the post-war period gradually changed the unusual debt and liquidity conditions that had existed at the end of World War II. As more investment and consumption opportunities were exploited and the pace of expansion quickened, the level of outstanding private debt rose. Without continued, large government financing of war debt, the relative importance of government securities in the portfolios of financial institutions began to fall. Increasing debt and declining liquidity moved the U.S. financial system away from the uniquely robust condition it had enjoyed in the early postwar period. The first postwar financial crisis took place in 1966; crises have occurred with increasing frequency and severity since then (Minsky, 1986; Wolfson, 1986, 1990).

In the late 1960s, inflation and interest rates began to rise, undermining two other preconditions of the U.S. financial structure. With higher interest rates, the restriction of competition—which had helped to bring about stability in the early post-war period—now limited depository intermediaries' ability to adapt. Instability and financial difficulties resulted.

Interest-rate ceilings became a particular problem for depositories. While interest rates remained low, rate ceilings had promoted stability by curbing the deposit rates offered by aggressive institutions. But under high and rising interest rates, interest rate ceilings led to *disintermediation*—that is, the shift of financial holdings from intermediary deposits to the money market, where higher rates could be earned.

Financial innovation and technological change increased the severity of disintermediation in the mid-1970s. Previously, the extent of disintermediation had been limited because only depositors with large amounts on account could take advantage of market interest rates (for example, $10,000 was required for investment in Treasury bills). But as interest rates rose in the 1970s, the interest foregone for depositors due to rate ceilings increased. This encouraged the growth of money market mutual funds (MMMFs). MMMFs provided market rates of return to a larger number of people by pooling their funds and investing these in money market instruments.

The Erosion of Restricted Competition

MMMFs challenged depository institutions' monopoly on deposit accounts. Technically, MMMF liabilities were not deposits. They were not protected by deposit insurance, so investors were not assured of full repayment of principal. However, MMMF liabilities closely resembled deposits; they could be withdrawn easily, they were relatively safe, and some even offered limited check-writing capabilities. One of the barriers to competition, built into the financial system in the 1930s, had been effectively breached.

The threat of disintermediation and the challenge of MMMFs affected commercial banks and thrifts differently. For thrifts and small banks, the threat was a loss of deposits. But large banks had been issuing large, negotiable certificates of deposit (CDs) at market rates since 1961. Indeed, MMMFs were investing a significant proportion of their funds in the large CDs of large commercial banks.

Large banks were threatened not so much by a loss of funds as by the need to pay higher rates for their deposits. And a new threat to banks accompanied that from increased competition for liabilities: increased competitive pressure on their asset portfolios due to the loss of their traditional monopoly on lending to business.

Finance companies, often owned by large, nonfinancial corporations, have taken advantage of the growth of MMMFs to fund their lending activities by issuing commercial paper, especially to MMMFs. Their loans to business compete directly with those made by commercial banks.[4] Large corporate borrowers have used their high-credit-quality rating to issue commercial paper directly, without the use of intermediaries such as banks and finance companies. Smaller companies with a greater credit risk, and corporate raiders and other participants in the market for corporate control, have also dispensed with intermediaries and issued securities directly; with the assistance of investment banks, they have financed their activities with high-yield (junk) bonds.

In general, many borrowers have shifted away from credit extension by depository intermediaries and toward the direct use of securities markets. This general process of *securitization* has been accelerated by the specific process of dedicating the interest and principal payments from specific pools of loans to support the issuance of securities. The most commonly securitized loans thus far have been residential mortgages; government agencies such as Ginnie Mae (the Government National Mortgage Association) have helped to create an active secondary market for these mortgage-backed securities. And the securitization of other types of loans, such as credit card and business loans, has been increasing.

The increasing use of securities markets for the extension of credit has been helped by the late post-war period growth of large institutional investors such as life insurance companies and pension funds. Households have increasingly used these institutions as savings vehicles. As a result, life insurance companies and pension funds have encroached on depository intermediaries' roles as the repository of household savings and the ultimate holder of borrowers' credit obligations.

The increasing globalization of the financial system also has played a role in challenging commercial banks' traditional monopoly on business lending. Foreign banks operating in the United States have challenged domestic banks in some of their domestic credit markets, especially including lending to nonfinancial corporate borrowers.

Thus banks have faced increasing pressures from nonbank competitors. In addition, because the restricted competition for their deposits has also been eroded, banks' lending margin has been squeezed from both ends.

Attempts to Restructure the Post-war Financial System

This section investigates responses by legislators, regulators, and depository institutions themselves to these threats. These attempts to restructure the old financial system have emphasized relaxing the system's principle of restrictions on competition. This section then considers the consequences of the breakup of the old system for the second principle of the old system: government protection. The net result has been a *partial* dismantling of the barriers to competition and *increasing* government protection.

Partial Dismantling of Barriers to Competition

When the old institutional structure was no longer promoting stability, depositories attempted to restructure their activities in various ways. The response of legislators and regulators, especially in the case of the S&Ls, was to remove those barriers to competition that now appeared to be the source of the instability. The experiences of thrifts and commercial banks are considered here in turn.

Thrift Institutions

In an effort to eliminate the problem of disintermediation, Congress passed the Depository Institutions Deregulation and Monetary Control Act in 1980. This legislation phased in the elimination of all interest-rate ceilings on deposits. However, in the high interest-rate environment of the early 1980s, this development was disastrous for the thrifts, and especially so for S&Ls.

Under compartmentalization, S&Ls had specialized in making long-term mortgage loans. Because of their long maturity, many of the mortgage loans on S&L books had been made when interest rates were much lower.[5] With interest-rate ceilings eliminated, S&Ls were paying more interest for deposits than they were receiving on their mortgage loans. (Prior to the 1980s, S&Ls were not allowed to offer adjustable-rate mortgages.) Also, thrifts' asset portfolios, weighed down with older, lower-interest-rate loans, suffered larger losses in market values than did the asset portfolios of commercial banks or other intermediaries.[6] In the early 1980s, many S&Ls were not only running operating losses; they were also insolvent on a market-value basis.

So the old institutional structure, which had worked well under earlier economic conditions, began to cause problems when those conditions changed. The attempt to eliminate the problem by removing one restriction on competition (interest-rate ceilings) only served to expose S&Ls to another problem—losses from a maturity mismatch (funding long-term mortgages with short-term liabilities). But these losses were, in turn, due to another feature of the old structure that was designed to restrict competition—S&Ls' specialization in holding long-term residential mortgages. In effect, instability in the thrift industry was due now not to interest-rate ceilings but to the role assigned thrifts under the compartmentalization scheme of the old system.

These barriers to competition were soon removed as well. The Garn–St. Germain Act of 1982 gave S&Ls more latitude in the types of loans they could make. Some state legislatures and regulators (most notably in California) went further, allowing state-chartered S&Ls almost unlimited freedom in their choice of assets. It was hoped that thrifts could use portfolio diversification to reduce their vulnerability to the maturity mismatch problem in an environment of high interest rates.

Unfortunately, this further attempt at easing the restrictions on competition again created difficulties. S&Ls had little or no experience in new areas such as commercial real estate, real estate development, and junk bonds. Under the free market ideology dominant at the time, the regulatory agencies paid little attention to these new areas' safety. Many S&Ls suffered losses, especially in commercial real estate. Thus, the deregulation of the asset side of the S&Ls' balance sheet substituted a credit-quality problem for an interest-rate risk problem.[7]

Commercial Banks

The response of the banks, especially the large banks, to the erosion of restricted competition involved three strategies. First, they have turned to fees and trading income for a larger proportion of their income. This has generated revenue in the short run. But such increasingly common activities as foreign-exchange speculation and interest-rate swaps carry increased risks.

Second, they have sought out new areas for loan growth. Faced with pressure on their profit margins, they have moved to seek greater loan revenue from lending to finance less developed countries (LDCs), the oil industry, commercial real estate, and merger and acquisition (M&A) activity.

But banks' borrowers in these credit areas have had more difficulty repaying loans, in part due to the higher debt burdens in the post-war period. Defaults by borrowers in each of the areas of lending previously mentioned have produced well-publicized problems: LDCs, the deduction of $3 billion in profits by Citicorp in 1987 to establish reserves for losses on LDC loans; oil, the failures of Penn Square Bank in 1982, Continental Illinois in 1984, and the large Texas banks in the mid- to late-1980s; and commercial real estate, the failure of the Bank of New England in 1991.[8] The end of problems from commercial real estate overlending in the 1980s has not yet been seen, and the threat of losses from banks' lending in order to finance M&As and other "highly leveraged transactions" remains.

Third, banks have made partially successful attempts to remove barriers to competition directly. Some large banks have tried to expand into some activities proscribed under the Glass-Steagall Act. The banks' argument is that other financial institutions have encroached upon banks' product areas, so banks should be allowed to expand reciprocally into such areas as investment banking, insurance underwriting, and real estate investment. For example, investment banking companies using their own MMMFs have competed with banks for deposits; so banks have argued that they should be able to compete with investment banks by underwriting corporate securities. Banks such as J. P. Morgan and Citicorp have had some success in petitioning the Federal Reserve to allow them limited underwriting powers. Full-fledged forays into such activities, however, await a congressional decision about the fate of the 1930s' barriers to competition.

Larger banks also have tried to remove barriers to competition in interstate banking. Their efforts have been more successful, but only at the state level. Some states have liberalized regulations regarding intrastate banking by allowing more statewide branching. Also, some regional compacts have been developed, e.g., in New England. These typically allow bank holding companies from state A to operate banks in state B if state A grants similar permission to state B.

Attempts at the federal level to allow full interstate banking have thus far been unsuccessful. They have been opposed by small banks fearful that interstate banking would threaten their viability.

Increasing Government Protection

The increasing financial difficulties have necessitated an expansion in the level of government protection. The federal government has expanded its protective role in the financial system in three major areas: the lender of last resort, deposit insurance, and bailouts of failing and failed institutions.

Lender of Last Resort

As financial crises and failures of financial institutions increasingly began to threaten the stability of the financial system, the federal government, in particular the Federal Reserve, has been forced to intervene as a lender of last resort. Originally, the role of lender of last resort meant literally lending to financial institutions that were having temporary liquidity problems. However, in the late post-war period in the United States, the Federal Reserve has interpreted the role of lender of last resort as a more general responsibility for attempting to stabilize the financial system as a whole.

As the problems of the financial system have increased, the Federal Reserve has gradually expanded the activities encompassed by the lender of last resort. When Franklin National Bank encountered financial difficulties in 1974, fear of the repercussions of its failure led the Federal Reserve to keep Franklin alive through discount-window loans for several months until another bank was found to take it over. Unfortunately Franklin had been actively involved in the Eurodollar market and the foreign exchange market. So in the process of keeping Franklin alive through the discount window, the Federal Reserve effectively replaced Eurodollar deposits lost by Franklin's branch in London. The Federal Reserve Bank of New York also acquired $725 million of Franklin's foreign-exchange liabilities. The Federal Reserve's actions in rescuing Franklin were unprecedented in that the lender-of-last-resort role was used for the first time to protect financial markets overseas.

The concept of a lender of last resort was expanded again when Continental Illinois National Bank was on the verge of failure in 1984. In that case, federal regulators determined that Continental was too big to fail, or more precisely, the possibility of loss for Continental's institutional investors was too threatening to overall financial stability. As a consequence, regulators took the unprecedented step of guaranteeing all holders of Continental's liabilities against loss. Even such a step, however, was insufficient to stop completely the run on Continental's liabilities. Because a merger partner could not be found to take over such a large bank, the Federal Deposit Insurance Corporation (FDIC) wound up taking control of Continental. The bank was effectively nationalized.

Deposit Insurance

The protection afforded by deposit insurance has been expanded in two ways. First, the extent of coverage has been gradually expanded from the original limit of $2,500 in 1933. In 1980, as is generally known, deposit insurance coverage was increased to $100,000 per deposit. Second, and perhaps more significantly, there has been a change in the de facto coverage of deposit insurance.

In both of the previous examples involving the lender of last resort, the original concept of deposit insurance was significantly expanded. In 1974, Franklin National Bank's Eurodollar deposits were protected. This was an expansion of deposit insurance coverage to include foreign deposits, since banks pay deposit insurance only on domestic deposits. In 1984, with the concept of the bank too big to fail, there was an expansion of the concept of deposit insurance to include not only deposits over the limit of $100,000, but also *all* of Continental's liabilities.

Government Bailouts

In addition to the bailout of Continental, perhaps the most obvious example of increasing government protection of financial institutions was the public guarantee and rescue of the federal deposit insurance fund for the S&Ls. The fund had been drained by S&L failures. The Financial Institutions Reform, Recovery, and

Enforcement Act of 1989 established the principle that the federal government would guarantee insured deposits regardless of the condition of the fund. It also created a new organization, the Resolution Trust Corporation (RTC), to close insolvent thrifts, and began the long process of requesting public money from the Congress to carry out the job.

The Bank Insurance Fund of the FDIC, which insures deposits at commercial banks, also has been drained of funds by bank failures. It is possible that the eventual bailout of the banks' insurance fund will rival that of the S&Ls.

Current Conditions in the Banking System

It may be useful to summarize the argument thus far. The basic problem faced by the U.S. banking system is that its defining characteristics—restrictions on competition and government protection—succeeded under economic and financial conditions that no longer exist. For example, ceiling rates on deposits and long-term amortized mortgages were profitable for S&Ls in an environment of low and stable interest rates. The monopoly power due to compartmentalization also boosted profitability as long as barriers to entry weren't capable of being breached. Deposit insurance was most successful when there were no banks too big to fail. These factors, combined with low debt loads and high liquidity throughout the economy, contributed to a relatively steady economic expansion and provided for the success of the intermediaries whose liabilities were federally insured.

But the strong growth that the old institutional structure facilitated eventually undermined the conditions that had made this structure successful: debt burdens increased, liquidity declined, and inflation and interest rates rose. Under these changed conditions, the old institutional structure no longer led to profits and stability but led instead to financial crises, insolvencies, and depository failures.[9]

An effort to remedy the situation by dismantling barriers to competition within the banking system was undertaken. But this partial deregulation merely shifted the locus of instability without diminishing its magnitude. The continued instability, in turn, called forth more and more government protection and interventions.

Continuing Financial Difficulties

The increased government protection that has been required in the late post-war period has been relatively effective in two respects. First, increasing Federal Reserve intervention as a lender of last resort has prevented a repetition of the panics and the sharp crashes that regularly plagued the financial system in the 19th and early 20th centuries. Second, expanded deposit insurance coverage and government bailouts have maintained confidence in the banking system, if only because of government's willingness to become a "payer of last resort" when the deposit insurance funds stand empty.

Unfortunately, the government's success has not been unqualified. Interventions to prevent financial panics have had the side effect of increasing long-term financial fragility (Wojnilower, 1980; Minsky, 1982, 1986). When the Federal Reserve allows innovative financial practices and protects troubled financial institutions, those practices and institutions often continue to expand credit into the future.

Moreover, expanding government protection has not solved the basic problems of banks and thrifts: their failure rates have continued to rise while the condition of many more remains precarious. Further, in contrast to the 1930s, when many insolvent banks were forced to close, many insolvent banks and thrifts today have been allowed to stay open because of the bankruptcy of the deposit insurance funds. The ultimate cost of "resolving" these institutions has thus often been magnified.

The loosening of barriers to competition, which was inevitable given changing economic conditions, has threatened many institutions with extinction. The geographical and product-line protection that once sheltered banks and thrifts, especially the smaller ones, has been gradually swept away. Mergers and failures, together with the Federal Reserve's too-big-to-fail doctrine, have led to continuing consolidation within the industry.

The continuing financial difficulties of banks and thrifts have led to a further problem. To improve their declining fortunes, many banks and thrifts took on increasing levels of risk in the 1980s. The increase in risk incurred by thrift institutions is by now a familiar story: seeking a way out of their financial difficulties, and relatively unrestrained by regulators, they lent money on weak or nonexistent collateral and financed projects with inadequate cash flow (Mayer, 1990; White, 1991). In particular, they were caught up in speculative lending in the area of commercial real estate.

The commercial banks also lent heavily to finance commercial real estate. They also financed other relatively risky and speculative activities, such as hostile takeovers, leveraged buyouts, and other types of "highly leveraged transactions."

Economic Conditions

In contrast to its condition in the early post-war period, the financial system is relatively fragile. Debt levels are higher and liquidity is lower.

Currently, inflationary pressure is subdued and interest rates have fallen. However, this situation exists not because the financial system is robust, as in the early post-war period, but rather because the U.S. economy is stagnant. High debt levels and financial system fragility have, in turn, contributed to the slow economic growth.

Given these changes in economic conditions and their effect on the financial system, it is unlikely that the old institutional structure can be reintroduced. It no longer conforms with economic conditions.

Frameworks for Reform

What new institutional configuration will restore stability to the financial system? We now examine two frameworks for reform that answer this question differently: the free market approach and the public regulation approach.

The Free Market Approach

There are several varieties of the free market approach. Their unifying principle is that the source of instability plaguing the financial system consists of the restrictions on competition left over from the 1930s' legislation. Therefore the policy recommendations of such approaches emphasize eliminating these remaining restrictions: the intensified competition that ensues will, it is asserted, restore profitability and stability to the financial system.

One variant of the free market approach was presented by the Bush Administration (U.S. Treasury, 1991). Although this specific proposal expired, it is likely to reappear again in a similar form. Bush's Treasury proposal called for eliminating most remaining barriers to competition in the banking system: it would have permitted interstate banking, the entry of commercial banks into investment banking, and some insurance powers for banks. It also would have eliminated the wall between banks and nonfinancial companies and allowed nonfinancial companies to own banks.

While committed to free market principles, the Treasury Department proposal nevertheless retained the expanded levels of government protection that have become necessary in the late post-war period. After earlier indications that deposit insurance coverage would be reduced to promote "market discipline," the Treasury bill suggested few changes in deposit insurance and provided for a bailout of the commercial banks' deposit insurance fund. The too-big-to-fail doctrine was explicitly recognized in a provision calling for the Federal Reserve and FDIC to rescue banks whose failure could threaten financial stability.

Another variant of the free market approach is the "narrow bank" approach (Litan, 1987). Under this proposal, any bank wanting federal insurance for its deposits would be required to invest those deposits in safe assets such as government securities. This "narrow" bank could remain part of a holding company also including an affiliate bank with substantial freedom in its choice of assets. The 1930s' restrictions would be removed for the affiliated bank: it could engage in both commercial and investment banking, participate in real estate and insurance, and branch across state lines. However, the affiliate's liabilities would not qualify for federal deposit insurance. This proposal tries for the best of both worlds: a deposit insurance option for risk-averse customers combined with the greater flexibility sought by the large banks.

One useful way to analyze these approaches is to view them in terms of the two principles of the old institutional structure: government protection and the restriction of permissible activities for financial institutions. Both the Treasury proposal and the narrow bank idea would finish the process of eliminating the barriers to competition under the old institutional framework. But neither of them would replace the outdated restrictions with any significant new limitations on financial institutions' activities. This is consistent with the free market philosophy that unregulated competition by itself is capable of restoring stability.

Lessons from the S&L Debacle

Because of the current conditions in the financial system, the free market strategy runs the risk of serious financial instability. There is a basic problem that the free market proposals do not confront. The problem is that the 1930s' restrictions on competition allowed many more financial institutions to survive than would have under less-protected conditions. Thus, eliminating these 1930s' restrictions on competition, given 1990s' conditions, implies that many financial institutions no longer will be viable.

Moreover, eliminating the remaining barriers to competition when many financial institutions are experiencing continuing difficulties would only increase the problem of overcapacity. Letting overcapacity develop in this context, guided only by the "free market," would likely result in two consequences: (1) increasing losses for many financial institutions, accompanied by increased risk-taking, escalating failure rates, and continuing financial instability, and, ultimately, (2) a decrease in competition, as the winners of the competitive struggle consolidated their economic and political power.

The experience of S&Ls in the 1980s is a perfect example of how not to handle the process of deregulation. As noted above, the elimination of restrictions on S&Ls' activities was accompanied by the simultaneous elimination of any significant regulatory presence by federal and state officials. S&Ls were left to survive as best they could in the new competitive environment. Unsure of their new powers, many took on excessive risks, suffered outsized losses, and depleted the federal deposit insurance fund (White, 1991).

The Treasury plan, perhaps recognizing the potential for turmoil in eliminating competitive restrictions, maintained existing levels of government protection for financial institutions. At the same time, the plan eliminated barriers to a free market in banks' activities. This plan included language to the effect that early warning signals would be used to ensure that corrective action would be taken before the public's bailout costs mounted. But it was unclear whether, in practice, early warnings of bank troubles would prevent banks from experimenting at public expense.

On the other hand, the narrow bank proposal would restrict the scope of deposit insurance, and it would eliminate explicit government liability for bank failures. But it would do little to protect society against the risks of unacceptable financial instability.

Thus one variant of the free market approach (the Treasury proposal) would risk a larger taxpayer bailout of the banking industry. The other (the narrow bank proposal) would risk a major financial crisis. The basic problem with both proposals is that they do not reestablish the proper balance between public protection and public regulation.

The old institutional structure had struck a balance between public protection—the government safety net of deposit insurance and lender of last resort—and public regulation—the restriction of competition to promote stability and profitability. As economic conditions changed, public regulation was reduced as public protection was expanded. The Treasury bill would only exacerbate this unhealthy and unbalanced trend. The narrow bank proposal aims for a new balance by reducing both public regulation and public protection to minimal levels. But this new balance would most likely be unstable; if implemented, the narrow banking proposal would have to make the same concession to reality as the Treasury bill. That is, the federal safety net would be extended to cover the activities of "unregulated" banks. [10]

Therefore, relying on the free market under current conditions will lead to either financial instability and an increase in the concentration of power or an expanded taxpayer bailout (or both). The key to avoiding both of these unacceptable alternatives is to restore the proper balance between public protection and public regulation.

The Public Regulation Approach

The public regulation approach would retain the government protection that financial institutions require in the late post-war period; at the same time, it would remove many of the barriers to competition under the old institutional structure. However, it would also impose some public regulation over financial institutions' activities. [11] How broadly this public regulation would be applied and the timing of its introduction are matters to be determined in specific proposals embodying this approach. The aim of the discussion that follows here is to set out the broad principles of this alternative approach to financial structure. [12]

The general principle asserts that government protection for financial institutions and liberalization of restrictions on the number of activities in which they could engage would go hand in hand with greater public regulation over the content of those activities. As long as the public provides a safety net under the banking system, then greater freedom of activity implies greater accountability in the use of that freedom.

The public regulation approach would attempt to find ways to encourage the use of financial institution powers both to promote productive investment and to discourage speculation and other activities that would only increase the financial fragility of the system.

Table 6.1

Institutional Frameworks for the Banking System

Institutional Framework	Government Protection	Public Regulation
1930s reforms	Yes	Yes (restriction of competition)
Free market (Treasury)	Yes	No
Free market (narrow bank)	No	No
Public regulation	Yes	Yes (public policy goals)

Unlike the narrow bank approach, the public regulation approach would retain needed public protection for financial institutions. Like both the narrow bank and the Treasury Department proposals, the public regulation approach would remove some outdated restrictions on competition. However, unlike either, it would replace those restrictions with new mechanisms of public regulation. Table 6.1 makes explicit the differences between the three approaches along these lines.[13]

Broadly interpreted, the public regulation approach *explicitly recognizes the public interest in the activities of private financial institutions and takes the steps necessary for the financial system to achieve specified public policy goals.* In practice, this is not a new idea. Historically, bank regulation has channeled bank activities into socially productive avenues (or restricted their scope for engaging in potentially destructive or destabilizing activities). Because banks have been "special" in providing society's means of payment and supplying many of its credit needs and because bank failures have had such disastrous consequences, public policy has accepted the idea that banks should be regulated in the public interest. In other words, their behavior should not simply be formed according to their private criterion of profitability. Society's needs have to be respected and banks' behavior has to be adjusted accordingly.

Public interest motives have *implicitly* informed bank regulation from the 1930s onward. These motives were, in a sense, invisible in the old regulatory structure because they were built into the walls separating different segments of the banking industry by the Depression-era legislation. If those walls tumble, the assertion of the public interest in banking through public regulation of substantive bank activities cannot but be explicit.

Allowing interstate banking, investment powers for commercial banks, and so on might be appropriate, but such measures should be accompanied by changes in the scope of public regulation in order to ensure that the financial system and its institutions achieve public policy goals. For example, if the public allows banks to underwrite corporate securities, then the public can legitimately ask whether the securities underwritten will support speculation or productive investment.

This raises the crucial question for this approach: what goals would be sought under public regulation? This question is addressed in the following section.

The Goals of Public Regulation

What should the public policy goals underlying public regulation be? The above discussion points toward financial stability as an important public policy goal for the financial system. The public regulation approach seeks ways of reorienting the banking system away from behavior that produces speculation, financial fragility, and instability, and toward behavior that promotes productive investment.

Moving the financial system toward stability could involve three broad steps. (Mechanisms to accomplish these objectives are discussed in the next section.) First, reduce the level of risk undertaken by financial institutions. Second, reorient the lending and investment policies of financial institutions to promote stability—for example, by reducing their financing of hostile takeovers and speculative commercial real estate ventures. Increase financing of productive investment to build up our communities, improve productivity, and increase our standard of living. Third, invest public resources in financial institutions that will promote financial stability and productive investment.

Using Public Regulation to Achieve Narrow Goals

Enhancing stability is clearly a priority. In light of recent events, it might be seen as the sole objective of financial policy reform. However, an examination of past examples of public regulation indicates that additional public policy goals are needed if public regulation is to be a tool for the interests of more than a handful of the members of society.

One example is the bailout of New York City in 1975. Since this involved rescuing a bankrupt institution, it resembles the current situation in the financial system. In that case, New York received state and federal aid under the conditions that New York cut public spending, reduce the wages of public employees, and generally cut expenses to restore profitability. In exchange for public protection (loans), New York was required to submit to public regulation (orders to cut spending and reduce wages).

These actions resemble those of corporate raiders in the aftermath of hostile takeovers. To improve short-term cash flows and meet debt obligations incurred in the takeover, raiders have cut workers' wages, closed plants, and terminated pension plans. If public interventions into troubled banks aimed solely at restoring their stability by increasing their profitability, then similar measures—wage reductions and layoffs for bank employees, branch closings, tightened creditworthiness criteria excluding all but large businesses and the wealthy—might be taken in the name of the "public" (taxpayers') interest, without regard for the deleterious consequences of these actions on the communities served by the banks in question.

Another example is the public regulation exerted by the International Monetary Fund (IMF) over Third World countries. In an effort to restore the "profitability" of individual Third World countries (in this case, their foreign exchange balances), the IMF held up its "seal of approval" and hence loan flows until the borrower countries agreed to specific changes in their economies. The IMF conditions included measures to lower aggregate demand, slow public spending, and reduce workers' wages—that is, measures strongly resembling those applied in the New York City bailout and in corporate takeovers.

A Broader Agenda

In effect, public regulation has often been used by a government-bank-corporate partnership to boost profitability and balance-sheet stability at the expense of other social interests. The interests of workers, consumers, small business, communities, and others outside the "insider loop" of wealth and power have often been ignored. Ironically, the increase in profitability may be transitory; longer-term profitability could suffer, along with increased stability and growth for society as a whole.

Is it possible to base public regulation on a broader agenda? Some additional public policy goals are suggested as follows.

Promoting Equal Opportunity

During the 1980s, large commercial banks financed vacant office buildings and junk-bond-backed hostile takeovers while local economic development and minority housing needs went unfulfilled (Campen, 1993). Public regulation could play a role in reversing the long-run decline of lower-income communities by enforcing equitable access to credit by all, regardless of race, and by lending more in neglected communities.

It may be argued that this practice would subvert the purely economic goals of banks and other financial institutions—that is, their ability to maximize profits. But it is not clear that banks' credit flows to those who appear most likely to repay on a purely "economic" basis have been wildly profitable. It was, after all, the unrestrained pursuit of profits that produced the office-space overhang and the LDC crisis.

So ignoring equal opportunity and awarding credit on a business-as-usual basis—to those who need it the least, as the adage puts it—has been no guarantee of success. Indeed, public guidelines would most likely have led to fewer resources being used to build vacant office buildings in the 1980s, less redlining of minority communities, less discrimination in lending, and more resources to fund affordable housing and community development.

Maintaining Workers' Rights

Public regulation could be used to protect the rights of workers, especially given the wave of mergers and acquisitions afflicting banks and other financial institutions. Increasing banks' profits should not be accomplished by cutting the wages and worsening the working conditions of bank employees.

Large banks perceive that a large share of the gains from merging lie in closing redundant branches and in laying off redundant workers. Public regulation could protect workers' rights in mergers, ensuring that adequate provisions for retraining and alternative employment for laid-off workers have been arranged. Moreover, community input into the process could determine if closing branches would cut off certain classes of borrowers from access to credit.

Limiting Excessive Concentration

While the current overcapacity of the banking industry suggests that some additional concentration is probable, public regulation should ensure that such concentration is not excessive. Small banks that serve a useful purpose by offering access to credit to those who otherwise would lack it should be allowed to survive. New financial institutions like grass roots banks that promote community development and productive investment should be encouraged (Schlesinger, 1992).

The Mechanisms of Public Regulation

The guidelines in the previous section suggest the goals that public regulation might pursue. But what are the mechanisms of public regulation that could reduce risk, reorient lending, and invest resources to promote financial stability, equal opportunity, worker rights, and limited concentration? This concluding section points to three general mechanisms: safety and soundness regulation, asset regulation, and public investment.

Safety and Soundness Regulation

It is generally recognized that the regulatory agencies should increase their scrutiny of bank activities to promote safety and soundness. Public opinion has been critical of the lax attitude of regulators and of political interference with regulatory action, especially in the case of the S&L industry. Increased supervision of depository institutions, including more frequent on-site examinations, is clearly a priority.

In addition, higher capital requirements are clearly needed. Bank regulators have been moving in this direction throughout the 1980s, and thrift regulators are now recognizing the importance of increased capital. This need for greater capital has now been recognized by the international banking community (in the Basel Accords) and in banking legislation passed in November 1991 in the United States (Dymski, 1993).

Asset Regulation

Public regulation could also work by indirectly influencing financial intermediaries' choice of assets. This approach has already been put into effect in the Basle Accords. This international agreement on risk-based capital requirements, which was signed by the U.S. with an effective date (under complementary U.S. legislation) of December 19, 1992, combines both safety and soundness regulation and asset regulation. Under these new standards, banks' required capital levels increase in proportion to the riskiness of their assets. Thus banks would have an incentive to invest in less risky assets. A distinction between loans to promote speculation and loans to promote productive investment, while not now a part of these standards, would represent a natural extension of this risk-reduction mechanism.

A similar approach to regulating bank assets is to establish supplemental reserve requirements on bank assets. This proposal, first made by former Federal Reserve Board Governor Andrew Brimmer, would require banking institutions to put aside a variable amount of additional reserves according to the type of asset category.[14] Like the risk-based capital requirements, this approach would discourage banks from making speculative loans by making these loans more expensive.[15]

Public Investment

On the basis of an ownership interest, public authorities can influence bank activities to promote public policy goals. The opportunity to take an ownership interest is amply provided by the many insolvent institutions that have been or will be seeking government/deposit insurance fund "assistance."[16]

The idea of public investment in financial institutions is not without precedent in U.S. history. During the Depression, the Reconstruction Finance Corporation (RFC) used public funds to invest in private corporations, both financial and nonfinancial. The investment was in the form of preferred stock, which carried voting rights. Moreover, the RFC influenced bank behavior by encouraging greater business lending (Keeton, 1992).

In 1984, the effective failure of Continental Illinois National Bank required a government bailout that essentially amounted to a nationalization of the bank by the FDIC. More recently, Congress passed in 1991 the FDIC Improvement Act, which called for early government investment in troubled banks that could be saved from failure.

In all these examples, the principle of public investment in troubled financial institutions has been firmly established. Given the overcapacity and troubled condition of financial institutions today, an extensive area of public investment certainly could be established once such a policy were agreed on.

The Need for Democracy

Public priorities are more likely to be addressed if the people most directly affected have a say in the priorities' formulation and implementation. It will be necessary to promote local democracy by electing local community representatives to the boards of directors of financial institutions, by formulating community investment needs to which financial institutions must pay attention, and by monitoring compliance with existing laws such as the Community Reinvestment Act. Such steps could empower those whose interests have traditionally been secondary in financial institution decisionmaking: consumers, workers, and community representatives.

Because the financial institutions that are responsible for the allocation of credit and whose actions influence financial markets often are active on both national and multinational levels, democratic input that remains only at the community level will be insufficient. Also, because the role of depository intermediaries is shrinking in the overall financial system, a focus solely on banks and thrifts will likewise be insufficient.

It will not be easy to design a democratic system of public regulation that takes account of the international and integrated nature of the modern financial system. It will not be easy to adapt that program continually to take account of changing conditions and the continual conflict between private profitability and public goals. It will not be easy to counter the undue influence of economic power on the political process. But no other way will suffice if the goals are financial stability and productive investment on the basis of equity, equality of opportunity, and democracy.

Notes

1. The author would like to thank Paul Burkett and Gary Dymski for helpful comments.
2. By reducing the risk that depositors face, federal deposit insurance allows financial institutions to pay less to attract deposits.
3. See Wolfson (1993) for elaboration of this thesis and for a discussion of institutional developments in the international financial system. It might be argued that the institutional configuration of the financial system was irrelevant to the restoration of stability and profitability: the emergence of a robust financial system (high liquidity, low debt, stable interest rates, etc.) was all that was needed. In other words, robustness was both necessary and sufficient for stability and profitability. But that argument overlooks the direct contributions made by the new institutional arrangements (such as restricted competition) and by the ways these arrangements took advantage of robust conditions (for example, the thrifts). In the U.S. environment, which relies primarily on the free market,

robustness may be necessary, but it is not always sufficient. Moreover, in a more controlled financial system like Japan's, in which the government has used debt to regulate economic activity, robustness may not even be necessary.

4. For a discussion of this "parallel banking system," see D'Arista and Schlesinger (1993).

5. The maturity of a loan is the stated period of time after which the principal is due to be repaid. For home mortgage loans, the maturity is typically 30 years. Actually, since many mortgage loans are repaid early, the effective maturity is less than 30 years (although clearly still longer than the effective maturity of deposits).

6. The market value of an asset is affected by the present value of the future receipts that the asset is expected to generate. To calculate this present value, it is necessary to discount the future receipts by the relevant interest rate. The farther into the future these receipts are, that is, the longer the maturity of the asset, the more the present value of the asset will fall with an increase in interest rates.

7. Congress in 1989 decided that the dismantling of this barrier to competition was a mistake. Under the Financial Institutions Reform, Recovery, and Enforcement Act (FIRREA), savings and loan associations had to increase the share of their assets in housing-related investments to 70 percent.

8. Losses on commercial real estate also contributed to the failure of the Texas banks.

9. This is not to imply that other influences apart from the institutional structure of the financial system were not important determinants of growth in the early postwar period. Similarly, the problems created by that structure amid new economic conditions were not the sole cause of economic instability later on. See Minsky (1986) and Wolfson (1990) for a more complete analysis.

10. This development would be a continuation of the process that has been ongoing for the past two decades: the expansion of the Federal Reserve's role as a lender of last resort to cover an expanding array of financial instruments and markets far beyond the narrow payments mechanism as traditionally defined (see Wojnilower, 1980; Minsky, 1986; Brimmer, 1989).

11. For an approach along similar lines, see Grabel (1989).

12. This public regulation would be aimed initially at the activities of large banks, since they are the ones whose activities would be most immediately liberalized. However, given the narrowing market share of commercial banks and the growing interdependence of the financial system, it would most likely be necessary at some point, and also more equitable, to apply public regulation more widely to all financial institutions. Moreover, to avoid destabilizing shifts of capital, a more uniform regulatory approach would be needed.

13. The entries in the table for the narrow bank proposal refer to the affiliates of the narrow bank. The entry in the table under government protection for the narrow bank proposal is "no" because technically the federal safety net would not protect affiliates of a narrow bank. In practice, however, federal authorities might find it necessary to do so in order to prevent instability.

14. For a more detailed discussion of this policy, see Pollin (1993).

15. Because banks do not receive interest on reserves held at Federal Reserve banks, requiring them to hold additional reserves for speculative loans would cost them the interest income they could have received had they invested the reserves.

16. The potential problem of overcapacity in the banking industry can be turned to advantage if the resources being released by the competitive process are used, through public investment, to promote innovative alternatives like the grass roots banks described by Tom Schlesinger (1992). Such banks have shunned risky speculative lending in favor of investments in their local communities.

Bibliography

Board of Governors of the Federal Reserve System. *Banking and Monetary Statistics: 1914–1941*. Washington, DC: Federal Reserve, 1943.

Board of Governors of the Federal Reserve System. *Banking and Monetary Statistics: 1941–1970*. Washington, DC: Federal Reserve, 1976.

Brimmer, Andrew F. "Distinguished Lecture on Economics in Government: Central Banking and Systemic Risks in Capital Markets." *Journal of Economic Perspectives*, Vol. 3, No. 2, 1989, pp. 3–16.

Campen, James T. "Banks, Communities, and Public Policy." This volume, 1993.

D'Arista, Jane W. and Tom Schlesinger. "The Parallel Banking System." This volume, 1993.

Dymski, Gary Arthur. "How to Rebuild the U.S. Financial Structure: Level the Playing Field and Renew the Social Contract." This volume, 1993.

Grabel, Ilene. "Taking Control: An Agenda for a Democratic Financial System." *Dollars and Sense*, November 1989, pp. 15–18.

Isenberg, Dorene and Gary Dymski. "Financing Affordable Housing in the 1990s: A Progressive Approach." Mimeo, Drew University and University of California, Riverside, 1993.

Keeton, William R. "The Reconstruction Finance Corporation: Would It Work Today?" *Federal Reserve Bank of Kansas City Economic Review*, Vol. 77, No. 1, 1992, pp. 33–54.

Litan, Robert E. *What Should Banks Do?* Washington, DC: The Brookings Institution, 1987.

Mayer, Martin. *The Greatest-Ever Bank Robbery: The Collapse of the Savings and Loan Industry*. New York: Charles Scribner's Sons, 1990.

Minsky, Hyman P. *Can "It" Happen Again?* Armonk, NY: M. E. Sharpe, Inc., 1982.

Minsky, Hyman P. *Stabilizing an Unstable Economy*. New Haven, CT: Yale University Press, 1986.

Pollin, Robert. "Public Credit Allocation through the Federal Reserve: Why It Is Needed; How It Should Be Done." This volume, 1993.

Schlesinger, Tom. "Grassroots Banks Could Be Right Answer for Cities." *Greensboro News and Record*, May 31, 1992.

U.S. Treasury. *Modernizing the Financial System: Recommendations for Safer, More Competitive Banks*. Washington, DC, 1991.

White, Lawrence J. *The S&L Debacle: Public Policy Lessons for Banks and Thrift Regulation*. New York: Oxford University Press, 1991.

Wojnilower, Albert M. "The Central Role of Credit Crunches in Recent Financial History." *Brookings Papers on Economic Activity*, Vol. 2, No. 2, 1980, pp. 277–326.

Wojnilower, Albert M. "Financial Change in the United States." Paper presented at the Conference on the Origins and Diffusion of Financial Innovation at the European University Institute, Florence, Italy, October 7–9, 1985.

Wolfson, Martin H. *Financial Crises: Understanding the Post-war U.S. Experience*. Armonk, NY: M. E. Sharpe, Inc., 1986.

Wolfson, Martin H. "The Causes of Financial Instability." *Journal of Post Keynesian Economics*, Vol. 12, No. 3, 1990, pp. 333–55.

Wolfson, Martin H. "The Financial System and the Social Structure of Accumulation." In David Kotz, Terry McDonough, and Michael Reich, eds., *Social Structures of Accumulation: The Political Economy of Growth and Crisis*. Cambridge, England: Cambridge University Press, 1993.

CHAPTER SEVEN

The Parallel Banking System[1]

JANE W. D'ARISTA AND TOM SCHLESINGER

CHAPTER SUMMARY

This chapter presents an analysis of the U.S. financial system and a detailed proposal for achieving greater regulatory equality in it. The major elements of the proposal include the following:

• establishment of intracompany firewalls both to separate entities performing financial functions from their financial and nonfinancial parents and affiliates and to effectively prohibit tying and other forms of anticompetitive interaffiliate transactions;

• licensing financial intermediaries on a renewable basis;

• systemwide compliance with the Community Reinvestment Act and other federal fair-lending statutes;

• uniform application of comparable reserve, capital, and liquidity requirements; comparable risk diversification standards and risk-weighting techniques; limits on concentration and prohibitions against conflicts of interest and self-dealing;

• greater systemwide transparency through the regular public disclosure of Uniform Performance Reports;

• greater harmonization of the methods and costs of supervision and examination on both domestic and international bases;

• enhanced self-regulation and consolidation of duplicative regulatory functions.

Introduction

The problem: Between 1985 and 1990, more than 1,000 banks failed, including major institutions in many parts of the country. As recession expanded the volume of banks' nonperforming assets, the Bank Insurance Fund of the Federal Deposit Insurance Corporation became deeply insolvent, to the point of operating on $70 billion of borrowed money.

Following on the heels of a savings and loan collapse that may cost taxpayers half a trillion dollars, the commercial banking crisis has severely eroded the public confidence essential to all financial activity. In September 1991, an

NBC/*Wall Street Journal* poll found that 62 percent of all respondents were concerned about the soundness of the banking system and that 11 percent had withdrawn funds because of that concern (Hart and Teeter, 1991, pp. 22–29).

Banks' problems and the erosion of consumer confidence reflect profound changes in the U.S. financial system. During the past two decades, that system has been reshaped by the spread of multifunctional financial conglomerates and the emergence of an unregulated parallel banking system. Along with other powerful trends like securitization, these events have broken down the carefully compartmentalized credit and capital marketplace established by New Deal legislation 60 years ago.

Today, a variety of unregulated financial intermediaries operate on the fringes of the financial system. Check-cashing and pawn shops offer expensive services to consumers bypassed by mainstream financial firms. Mortgage companies, less regulated than their thrift competitors, constitute a parallel housing finance system. Similarly, finance companies anchor the lending side of a parallel banking system. The finance companies obtain their funds from banks as well as from the money market mutual funds (MMMFs) and other institutional investors who buy their notes, bonds, and commercial paper.

Measured in terms of their aggregate assets and the size of individual companies, finance companies rank as the largest single group of unregulated intermediaries. Because of their size and their ability to lend to business as well as household borrowers, finance companies affect credit markets more than do other types of unregulated intermediaries. Finance companies are the most important "nonbank" intermediaries because they function like banks with virtually no regulatory costs.[2]

Finance companies make the same kinds of loans as do banks. Like banks, they fund their loans by issuing liabilities held directly as investments by households and businesses or by other intermediaries that accept funds from those sources. Unlike banks, finance companies need not comply with capital and reserve requirements, limits on loans to single or related borrowers, or limits on transactions with parents and affiliates. They are not bound by community investment demands under the Community Reinvestment Act or the restrictions of the Glass-Steagall Act. They can operate anywhere, nationwide. As a result, finance companies enjoy major advantages over banks in terms of their cost of funds, pricing of loans, and opportunities for growth and profitability.

The exploitation of these advantages—along with other factors such as increased, uneven competition from foreign-based banks[3]—has eroded the role of U.S. banks in financial intermediation. In 1980, the outstanding assets of domestic finance companies ($242.8 billion) amounted to 15.8 percent of the outstanding assets of domestically chartered commercial banks ($1,537.9 billion). By midyear 1992, finance company assets ($790.4 billion) had risen to 26.1 percent of banks' assets ($3,033.9 billion).

During the same period, commercial paper issued by finance companies tripled as a percentage of banks' time and savings deposits, jumping from 8 percent to 24.2 percent. The slower growth in bank assets and liabilities relative to those of finance companies is reflected by the decline in banks' share in credit flows. Banks held 39.1 percent of total credit market debt owed by nonfinancial borrowers in 1980. Twelve years later, their share had fallen to a low of 26.5 percent. Even more significant, finance companies' once-modest share of total credit extensions to business had grown rapidly, to reach two-thirds of the share held by banks at midyear 1992 (FRB, *Flow of Funds*).

Some analysts welcome the rise of a parallel banking system. An economist at the Federal Reserve Bank of Kansas City recently enthused, " . . . the development of money market funds has made deposit rates more responsive to capital market rates. As a result, household savings flow more readily to the best investment opportunities, improving the efficiency of the intermediation process" (Sellon, 1992, p. 67). In an October 1991 article entitled "Lending When Bankers Won't," *The New York Times* suggested that commercial finance companies had revived small and middle-market businesses drained by a bank credit crunch. "The longer the squeeze continues, the more companies like us will grow to fill the gap," a finance company executive told the *Times*. "It may be hard for the larger banks to come back after they have burned so many people" (Quint, 1991, p. C1).

In fact, despite its many built-in competitive advantages, the parallel banking system has mismanaged many "investment opportunities," as proven by the events of November 1992. Weaknesses in the loan portfolios of many companies suggest that the parallel system has developed in a manner that ultimately may undermine, not strengthen, U.S. credit markets and the nation's underlying economy. Ironically, banks have increased this prospect by issuing billions of dollars of financial guarantees that nurtured the growth of their unregulated rivals while increasing their own exposure to risk.

The growth of the parallel system raises a number of new public policy concerns. The ownership of large finance companies by major nonfinancial corporations makes markets more susceptible to concentration and anticompetitive practices. A shift in lending from banks to the parallel system distorts the distribution of credit. Financial fragility increases as banks' declining market share weakens their portfolios and exposes the deposit insurance fund to additional risk.

Most disturbing, the rise of a parallel system affects the primary role of banks in transmitting monetary policy and deploying central bank liquidity to smooth out volatility, prevent disruptions, and manage crises. As banks' role in credit markets shrinks, so does the Federal Reserve's leverage.

The failure of policymakers so far to address these concerns is epitomized by the Bush administration's 1991 proposal for financial restructuring. Focused primarily on the banking industry, it recommended loosening restrictions on banks to increase their profitability. Ignoring the structural problems posed by the parallel banking system, President Bush's program sought to incorporate these fringe credit institutions formally into the financial system by offering their commercial owners expanded opportunities to own banks.

That model for restructuring will not work. By applying soundness regulation to banks but not to their major competitors, the Bush proposal offered finance company owners insufficient incentives to forgo their largely unregulated status. Indeed, the plan would have perpetuated the existence of a parallel banking system, operating with the public's money outside the norms of financial regulation and reducing banks' share of total credit extensions, profitability, and soundness.[4]

The solution: Any serious effort to reconstitute the U.S. financial system must begin by defining its current structure—not the structure outlined in law and regulation, but the actual framework in practice in the marketplace. All indicators confirm that banks no longer maintain a dominant place in that system. Others, obviously, have assumed their functions. Since soundness regulation clearly is needed for banks, it should be extended as well to institutions that have assumed many of the functions of banks.

It is widely agreed that the current regulatory and supervisory framework for the U.S. financial system is obsolete. But banks—meaning the functions and obligations of a banking system—certainly are not. No other set of institutions fulfills the unique and vital combination of roles—financial intermediation, money creation, and payment system operation—provided by the banking system. If that combination of roles is allowed to fade away, as some observers have suggested, banks would simply have to be reinvented.

Rather than allowing a repetition of the piecemeal deregulation experiments of the past decade, new strategies must be forged to restore the soundness of the U.S. financial system. The financial playing field must be leveled by raising—not lowering—standards of prudential supervision and public obligation. In other words, all financial institutions should be treated the same way.

To achieve this goal, we propose the establishment of a Financial Industry Licensing Act requiring all financial firms to be licensed and to comply with the same major regulations with respect to soundness. Uniform licensing requirements should be applied to any entity that

• directly accepts funds from the public for investment;
• makes loans to the public or buys loans or securities using funds other than its own equity capital and retained earnings; or
• sells loans or third-party securities to financial institutions or investors.

A detailed proposal for achieving greater regulatory equality is presented in the concluding section of this chapter.

Restoring soundness will require that federal regulations cover any institution operating in any form in more than one state. The nationwide operations of finance, insurance, and mortgage companies cannot be monitored with adequate attention to their overall soundness by state regulators whose ability to coordinate regulatory policy and enforcement is significantly inhibited by differences in state laws. Inefficient and insufficient regulation of large, important financial industry groups constitutes a serious threat to soundness because of such groups' potential for initiating crises that could spread to other institutional and market segments.

Within the framework proposed in this paper, it will be possible to apply uniform standards or definitions governing expected losses or nonperforming assets; comparable regulations would govern the establishment of reserves against problem assets.

Such a framework should encourage an ongoing evolution, innovation, and experimentation in institutional structures and products. It will also eliminate the regulatory distortions that have made the credit markets less responsive to monetary policy and less capable of promoting sustainable growth.

Although the ongoing integration of financial industry activities makes it increasingly difficult to separate banking and securities operations meaningfully, this chapter does not incorporate a recommendation for repealing the Glass-Steagall Act. As most recently demonstrated in the October 1987 market crash, the separation of banking and securities functions represents a proven, least-cost method of preventing the problems of one financial sector from spilling over into the other.

However, a system of uniform licensing and regulation will readily accommodate our proposal for a new financial products holding company charter. A major feature of the new charter would require firewalls legally separating the operations of multifunctional bank and nonbank financial conglomerates (i.e., firms owning affiliates that include finance companies, mutual funds, insurance companies, securities firms, mortgage banks, etc.).

Any proposal to extend consistent prudential supervision throughout the entire financial market naturally raises questions about the uneven application of public guarantees to different segments of the financial industry. Several major components of the industry—depositories, private insurers, securities firms, and pension funds—participate in financial guarantee programs. These include the deposit insurance funds, state guaranty associations, the Securities Investor Protection Corporation, and the Pension Benefit Guaranty Corporation. If entities such as mutual funds that accept money from the public are subjected to banklike soundness regulation, should they also receive the benefit of direct public guarantees? If those same prudential standards cover finance company affiliates of industrial parent firms, will the parents gain access to an already overburdened public safety net?

In fact, the parallel banking system already benefits indirectly from that safety net. Our answer to these questions is to insure the aggregate savings of individuals up to a given amount, regardless of where they are placed, rather than insuring single accounts or entire financial firms. In addition to reducing taxpayer exposure to financial industry failures, this method will also provide stability, including protection of the payment system. The chapter called "No More Bank Bailouts" (D'Arista, this volume) presents a complete description of the public guaranty reforms that would complement the proposal made here.

The analysis in this chapter focuses on finance companies as the sector that best explains the need to license all financial institutions and subject them to uniform soundness requirements. Even though other cases abound throughout the financial market, the banklike activities of finance companies offer the clearest case of regulatory inequality because they compete with the most regulated segment of the industry.

The Development of a Parallel Banking System

A parallel banking system emerged during the 1970s with the introduction of MMMFs. These funds helped to expand the commercial paper market and offered finance companies cheaper and more plentiful funds by purchasing their paper. The parallel system divided intermediation between two separate entities, each of which dealt directly with the public through only one side of the balance sheet.

Finance companies come in a variety of shapes (consumer, commercial, acceptance, independent, captive), sizes, and geographic arrangements.[5] Most take funds indirectly, rather than directly, from the public.[6] Some smaller finance companies rely on borrowings from banks to fund their operations. Larger firms raise funds by issuing bonds, notes, and commercial paper. They sell the bulk of their commercial paper to MMMFs.

Although finance companies lend directly to many of the same household and business customers sought by banks, they are not subject to legal prohibitions on links between banking and commerce. Some of the major finance companies are owned by industrial corporations (General Motors, General Electric, Chrysler, Ford, Xerox, ITT, Westinghouse, IBM, AT&T, Whirlpool, and Textron). Many have affiliates engaged in securities and insurance activities (see Table 7.1).

Several of the top finance companies (GE Capital Corp., Sears Roebuck Acceptance Corp., Transamerica Finance Group, and American Express Credit Corp.) belong to the major nonbank, multifunctional financial conglomerates that have helped to reshape the U.S. financial landscape. Indeed, finance companies have become the conglomerates' in-house banks, providing funds for other financial and nonfinancial members of the group.

Unlike finance companies, MMMFs compete with banks in attracting funds directly from the public. But, unlike banks, MMMFs do not lend directly to households and businesses. Instead, they invest in short-term, tradable instruments—predominantly bank certificates of deposit, commercial paper, and government obligations (Table 7.2).

Linking the two halves of the parallel banking system is the commercial paper market. Commercial paper is a form of uncollateralized borrowing—a promissory note issued directly by borrowers or indirectly through brokers. Because commercial paper is sold only in large denominations, financial regulators have assumed that it will be bought by "sophisticated" investors. As a result, the instrument is not defined as a security under the Securities Act of 1933. With commercial paper issuers exempt from the act's disclosure provisions, MMMFs and other institutional investors must rely on private rating agencies for information on the issuers.

Table 7.1

Regulated Affiliates of Selected Finance Companies (millions of dollars)

Company	Insured Deposits at 12–31–91		Insurance Company	Securities/ Investment Firm
	Commercial Bank	S&L or Savings Bank		
Associates First Capital Corp.	S ($15.9)	• (see Ford)	S	
Ford Motor Credit Corporation	• (see Associates)	S($14,051.9)	•	
American Express Credit Corp.	• (1,465.1)		•	•
Beneficial Corp.	S (284.7)	S(75.2)	S	
GE Capital Corp.	S (20.7)		•	•
Household Financial Corp.*	• (86.5)	• (6,542.9)	•	•
ITT Financial Corp.		S (581.8)	•	
Sears Roebuck Acceptance Corp.	• (5,033.1)	•(3,684.6)	•	•
Total insured deposits	(6,907)	(24,936.4)		

Sources: Annual reports; 10-Ks; *Thomson Savings Directory* (July-December 1992); *Thomson Bank Directory* (July-December 1992).

*Household International reported an additional $1.6 billion in foreign deposits at year-end 1991.

Note: S = subsidiary

　　• = affiliate within holding company

During the 1980s, finance companies and MMMFs fed one another's soaring asset growth and boosted their share of total outstanding credit market debt (Table 7.3). Measured as a percentage of banks' assets, the assets of finance companies rose steadily from 15.8 percent in 1980 to 26.1 percent at midyear 1992 (Table 7.4). Meanwhile, outstanding commercial paper issued by finance companies climbed from 8 percent to 24.2 percent of banks' outstanding savings and time deposits (Table 7.5).

While money market funds themselves compete with banks for funds, they also invest a significant share of their funds in banks' liabilities (Table 7.2). However, in every year after 1982, MMMFs' holdings of bank deposits fell below their holdings of commercial paper.

Predictably, the symbiotic growth of MMMFs and finance companies set off a surge in the commercial paper market. As Table 7.6 shows, finance companies now reign as the primary issuers in this market. Direct borrowing by nonfinancial companies accounted for less than 27 percent of outstanding commercial paper issues in every year after 1981.

The spread of the parallel banking system is rooted in regulatory inequalities. Long after the removal of Regulation Q's formal rate restrictions, MMMFs

Table 7.2
Assets of Money Market Mutual Funds (billions of dollars and percent)

	1980	1981	1982	1983	1984	1985	1986	1987	1988	1989	1990	1991	1992:Q2
Total assets[a]	$76.4	$186.2	$219.8	$179.4	$233.6	$243.8	$316.1	$292.1	$338.0	$428.5	$498.4	$539.6	$557.7
Time deposits and other bank-related Instruments:[b]													
Amount	$33.6	$76.7	$81.1	$58.6	$66.4	$62.1	$94.2	$73.5	$104.9	$122.6	$118.5	$122.6	$126.6
Percent of total	44.0%	41.2%	36.9%	32.7%	28.4%	25.5%	29.8%	25.2%	31.0%	28.6%	23.8%	22.7%	22.7%
U.S Treasury, federal agency and tax-exempt Securities:													
Amount	$9.2	$36.1	$67.8	$53.0	$66.2	$79.0	$102.9	$106.9	$95.7	$105.6	$166.0	$210.8	$216.7
Percent of total	12.0%	19.4%	30.8%	29.5%	28.3%	32.4%	32.3%	36.6%	28.3%	24.6%	33.3%	39.1%	38.9%
Commercial paper:													
Amount	$31.6	$70.4	$69.1	$66.2	$98.0	$99.1	$111.3	$105.3	$129.1	$186.5	$206.7	$191.9	$196.9
Percent of total	41.4%	37.8%	31.4%	36.9%	41.9%	40.6%	35.2%	36.0%	38.2%	43.5%	41.5%	35.6%	35.3%
Money market mutual funds' holdings of commercial paper as a percentage of total commercial paper outstanding[c]	26.0%	43.7%	42.7%	36.1%	42.2%	33.7%	34.1%	28.2%	28.6%	35.7%	37.1%	36.3%	36.1%

Source: Federal Reserve System, *Flow of Funds Accounts: Flows and Outstandings, Second Quarter 1992*, September 28, 1992.
Notes:
[a] The liabilities of money market mutual funds are their shares.
[b] Includes checkable deposits, large time deposits, federal funds, security repurchase agreements, and deposits abroad.
[c] See Table 7.6 for source.

Table 7.3

Total Assets of Selected Financial Intermediaries as a Percentage of Outstanding Credit Market Debt Owed by Domestic Nonfinancial Sectors

	1980	1981	1982	1983	1984	1985	1986	1987	1988	1989	1990	1991	1992:Q2
Commercial banks	39.1%	38.0%	38.2%	37.0%	34.9%	33.4%	33.0%	30.3%	29.5%	28.9%	28.0%	27.4%	26.5%
Finance companies	6.2	6.3	6.2	6.2	6.2	6.3	6.8	6.8	6.9	7.1	7.2	7.2	6.9
Money market mutual funds	1.9	4.3	4.7	3.4	3.9	3.5	4.0	3.4	3.6	4.2	4.6	4.8	4.9

Sources: Federal Reserve System, *Flow of Funds*, September 28, 1992; *Federal Reserve Bulletin*, various issues, Table 1.25; *Annual Statistical Digest*, 1980–1989.

Table 7.4

Outstanding Assets of Domestically Chartered Commercial Banks and Finance Companies (billions of dollars)

	1980	1981	1982	1983	1984	1985	1986	1987	1988	1989	1990	1991	1992:Q2
Commercial bank assets	$1537.9	$1639.2	$1800.4	$1948.7	$2107.7	$2314.2	$2581.0	$2593.0	$2751.0	$2913.6	$3010.3	$3072.0	$3033.9
Finance company assets	242.8	273.2	292.3	326.5	371.3	440.2	530.6	583.9	645.5	719.3	772.1	803.7	790.4
Finance company assets as a percentage of commercial bank assets	15.8%	16.7%	16.2%	16.8%	17.6%	19.0%	20.6%	22.5%	23.5%	24.7%	25.6%	26.1%	26.1%

Sources: Federal Reserve System, *Flow of Funds; Federal Reserve Bulletin,* various issues Table 1.25; *Annual Statistical Digest, 1980–1989.*

Table 7.5

Changes in Outstanding Commercial Paper Issued by Domestic Finance Companies and Outstanding Savings and Time Deposits of Domestically Chartered Commercial Banks (billions of dollars and percent)

	1980	1981	1982	1983	1984	1985	1986	1987	1988	1989	1990	1991	1992:Q2
Banks' savings and time deposits	$753.9	$872.0	$988.5	$1099.6	$1107.3	$1195.9	$1276.1	$1333.3	$1441.1	$1554.7	$1657.4	$1372.7	$1371.7
Outstanding commercial paper issued by finance companies	60.1	74.1	74.2	86.7	100.7	140.7	181.7	212.6	270.5	301.7	335.0	322.8	332.1
Commercial paper issued by finance companies as a percentage of banks' savings and time deposits	8.0%	8.5%	7.5%	7.9%	9.1%	11.8%	14.2%	15.9%	18.8%	19.4%	20.2%	23.5%	24.2%

Sources: Federal Reserve System, *Flow of Funds*; *Federal Reserve Bulletin*, various issues, Table 1.25; *Annual Statistical Digest*, 1980–1989.

Table 7.6

Amount of Outstanding Commercial Paper (billions of dollars and percent)

	1980	1981	1982	1983	1984	1985	1986	1987	1988	1989	1990	1991	1992:Q2
A. Amounts outstanding (billions of dollars at year end)													
All issuers	$121.6	$161.1	$161.8	$183.5	$231.7	$293.9	$326.1	$373.6	$451.8	$521.9	$557.8	$528.1	$544.7
Financial companies	86.6	107.6	109.2	125.2	145.5	187.8	225.9	258.6	316.1	351.7	365.6	347.9	355.5
Bank related	25.9	33.0	34.6	38.0	44.1	46.4	43.1	44.6	44.4	48.8	30.1	24.3	22.5
Finance companies	60.1	74.1	74.2	86.8	100.8	140.7	181.7	212.6	270.5	301.7	335.0	322.8	332.1
Nonfinancial companies	28.0	42.7	37.6	36.8	58.5	72.2	62.9	73.8	85.7	107.1	116.9	98.5	111.7
B. Shares of total outstanding (in percent)													
All issuers	100%	100%	100%	100%	100%	100%	100%	100%	100%	100%	100%	100%	100%
Financial companies	71.2	66.8	67.5	68.2	62.8	63.9	69.3	69.2	70.0	67.4	65.5	65.9	65.3
Bank related	21.3	20.5	21.4	20.7	19.0	15.8	13.2	11.9	9.8	9.4	5.4	4.6	4.1
Finance companies	49.4	46.0	45.9	47.3	43.5	47.9	55.7	56.9	59.9	57.8	60.1	61.1	61.0
Nonfinancial companies	23.0	26.5	23.2	20.1	25.2	24.6	19.3	19.8	19.0	20.5	21.0	18.7	20.5

Source: Federal Reserve System, Flow of Funds.

continue to enjoy regulatory advantages over banks in competing for funds from households and businesses. The freedom from reserve requirements on demand deposits gives MMMFs their principal edge.

With their monopoly on interest-free, third-party-transferable demand deposits, banks can attract substantial amounts of low-cost funding. But this capacity does not advantage banks in terms of pricing loans or maximizing spreads between the cost of and return on funds. Because reserve requirements "sterilize" $10 ($12 before February 1992) of every $100 of demand deposits, only $90 ($88 previously) can be invested in interest-earning assets. Because MMMFs can place all their funds in interest-bearing investments, their return on total assets is higher. Thus, they can offer savers a higher yield on their liabilities.

MMMFs avoid other significant costs faced by commercial banks, too. MMMFs do not pay deposit insurance premiums. Nor do they pay for developing specific information about their assets or maintaining offices and automated teller machines that provide services for less-affluent and less-sophisticated depositors and borrowers.[7] The absence of these costs to MMMFs also provides a price advantage that can be passed on to their customers.

Like MMMF retail customers, finance companies also benefit from these price advantages. Over the past decade, finance companies reduced their borrowings from banks and increased their outstanding issues of commercial paper as a share of total liabilities (Table 7.7). Their other major source of funds—longer-term notes and bonds—also declined relative to outstanding commercial paper. In other words, finance companies grew as a sector by accessing the expanding supply of lower-cost household savings drawn to MMMFs.

The decline in finance companies' cost of funds enhanced their profitability as well as their ability to compete with banks. In earlier decades, finance companies lent mostly to consumers: In 1965, more than 55 percent of their loans went to consumers, 30 percent to businesses, and 10 percent for mortgages. By 1975, consumer lending had dropped to 45 percent, while business lending jumped to 41 percent of the industry's total assets (Federal Reserve System, *Flow of Funds*).

As Tables 7.7 and 7.8 demonstrate, these trends accelerated in the 1980s. They also changed somewhat in composition. Business loan growth in the 1970s tended to reflect expanded lending by "captive" finance companies to affiliates and customers of their parent companies. However, the steady climb in business lending during the 1980s was fueled by noncaptive finance companies' providing credit for an assortment of nonaffiliated borrowers.

By the end of the 1980s, finance companies had made deep inroads into the core business of commercial banks. Between 1980 and midyear 1992, the share of outstanding business debt owed to finance companies rose from 6.0 percent to 8.2 percent. During the same period, the share owed to banks dropped from 19.1 percent to 12.4 percent (Table 7.8). With one-quarter the total assets of banks, finance companies now claim more than two-thirds the business loans held by banks.

Table 7.7

Selected Components of Outstanding Assets and Liabilities of Domestic Finance Companies (billions of dollars and percent)

	1980	1981	1982	1983	1984	1985	1986	1987	1988	1989	1990	1991	1992:Q2
Assets													
Total assets (billions of dollars)	$242.8	$273.2	$292.3	$326.5	$371.3	$440.2	$530.6	$583.9	$645.5	$719.3	$772.1	$803.7	$790.4
Percentages which are credits extended to:													
Consumers	32.5%	32.1%	31.9%	31.8%	30.1%	30.1%	28.5%	26.4%	24.1%	20.1%	18.0%	15.8%	15.3%
Businesses	36.5	36.4	34.3	34.8	37.1	36.1	33.4	36.6	38.0	37.6	38.0	36.4	37.2
Mortgages	21.3	21.6	23.4	23.4	24.0	23.5	27.1	24.4	24.6	28.1	29.3	28.2	28.7
Liabilities													
Total liabilities (billions of dollars)	$216.6	$245.1	$262.2	$293.4	$336.3	$404.7	$491.5	$551.4	$601.5	$664.0	$708.4	$738.9	$723.3
Percentages which are:													
Bank loans	11.3%	10.2%	10.1%	8.9%	8.0%	7.3%	6.8%	5.7%	4.7%	4.8%	4.7%	5.1%	5.3%
Commercial paper	27.7	30.2	28.3	29.6	30.0	34.8	37.0	38.6	45.0	45.4	47.3	43.7	45.9
Corporate bonds	42.5	40.8	42.9	42.5	43.3	37.0	38.1	30.7	24.3	25.7	24.2	26.7	23.7

Source: Federal Reserve System, Flow of Funds.

Table 7.8

Outstanding U.S. Credit Market Debt Owed by Households and Nonfinancial Businesses (billions of dollars and percent)

	1980	1981	1982	1983	1984	1985	1986	1987	1988	1989	1990	1991	1992:Q2
Total credit market debt owed by:													
Households	$1405.8	$1521.7	$1600.3	$1766.0	$1993.3	$2271.0	$2584.0	$2861.3	$3177.3	$3508.2	$3780.6	$3938.6	$4010.8
Nonfinancial businesses[a]	1484.3	1650.0	1775.4	1946.2	2249.5	2512.2	2806.3	3034.6	3281.6	3512.0	3618.0	3593.2	3602.3
Outstanding finance company credit to consumers													
Amount	$78.9	$87.8	$93.2	$103.7	$111.7	$132.4	$151.0	$154.0	$155.3	$144.6	$138.7	$126.7	$120.8
Percentage of total debt owed by households	5.6%	5.8%	5.8%	5.9%	5.6%	5.8%	5.8%	5.4%	4.9%	3.8%	3.7%	3.2%	3.0%
Outstanding finance company credit to businesses													
Amount	$88.7	$99.4	$100.4	$113.4	$137.8	$158.7	$177.2	$213.8	$245.3	$270.2	$293.5	$292.6	$293.7
Percentage of total debt owed by non-financial businesses	6.0%	6.0%	5.7%	5.8%	6.1%	6.3%	6.3%	7.0%	7.5%	7.7%	8.1%	8.1%	8.2%
Outstanding bank loans to individuals													
Amount	$181.2	$186.1	$191.6	$217.4	$258.4	$299.5	$321.5	$334.3	$361.5	$382.3	$384.7	$369.6	$358.8
Percentage of total debt owed by households	12.9%	12.2%	12.6%	12.3%	13.0%	13.2%	12.4%	11.7%	11.4%	10.9%	10.2%	9.4%	8.9%
Outstanding commercial and industrial loans of banks													
Amount	$282.9	$317.9	$355.5	$381.3	$430.0	$446.6	$487.8	$481.9	$501.1	$517.7	$512.7	$464.5	$446.3
Percentage of total debt owed by non-financial businesses	19.1%	19.33%	20.0%	19.6%	19.1%	17.8%	17.4%	15.9%	15.3%	14.7%	14.2%	12.9%	12.4%

Source: Federal Reserve System, *Federal Reserve Bulletin,* various issues, Table 1.25 (Assets and Liabilities of Commercial Banking Institutions), *Flow of Funds.*
a Includes farm, nonfarm noncorporate sectors.

Banks' Role in Promoting the Parallel System

Perhaps the greatest irony associated with the parallel banking boom is the degree to which it has been aided by commercial banks' provision of additional stability and liquidity for their unregulated competitors. Given its reliance on the commercial paper market as a source and use of funds, the parallel banking system is not inherently stable. Each component of the system shares the banking industry's susceptibility to runs. A failure in any one segment could spread rapidly to other financial and nonfinancial companies that issue or hold commercial paper. The absence of soundness standards and supervision increases the potential for surprise events that could trigger a breakdown.

But historically, major losses and even defaults by commercial paper issuers have not resulted in runs. The reason is backup credit lines, provided by federally insured commercial banks for a variety of commercial paper issuers, including finance companies. Banks began to offer guarantees to issuers two decades ago, when the commercial paper market foundered in the aftermath of Penn Central Railroad's 1970 default on $83 million of maturing paper. The introduction of these guarantees expressed the banks' own self-interest. Banks themselves relied on the fragile market because the 1970 Bank Holding Company Act amendments imposed limits on their lending to parent companies and nonbank affiliates. Thus, commercial paper became the main vehicle for funding bank holding companies' nonbank activities. By offering guarantees to other issuers, banks could help restore confidence in a market crucial to their parents' funding needs. They could also create a new source of fee income in the process.

During the 1980s, bank issuances of commercial paper diminished as bank guarantees for commercial paper skyrocketed (Tables 7.6, 7.9, and 7.10). Gradually, those credit lines emerged as the major link between banks and finance companies. Although the guarantees funneled fee income into the banks' coffers, they also cut the cost of liabilities for finance companies, since investors accept a lower return because of the guarantee. During the 1980s, the lower cost of funds enabled some finance companies to diversify away from their captive role and become third-party lenders to a wider assortment of borrowers.

By 1990, the amount of commercial paper issued by the 15 largest finance companies ($131 billion), 77 percent of which was backed by banks, was larger than the entire commercial paper market had been just one decade earlier ($122 billion). As Table 7.9 shows, bank guarantees for finance company commercial paper have expanded in absolute terms and as a percentage of outstanding paper. Between 1989 and year-end 1991, bank credit lines backing up paper issuances by the 15 largest nonbank finance companies rose 28 percent, from $87.2 billion to $111.5 billion. Measured as a portion of outstanding paper, combined bank guarantees to the 15 firms soared from 65.9 percent to 90.8 percent.

A series of developments in the 1980s—securitization, foreign bank lending in the U.S. market, and the growth of finance companies—worked together to undermine banks' asset quality. At the same time, banks' off-balance-sheet commitments to commercial paper issuers intensified their portfolio risk. If the rating on an issuer's paper is downgraded and its cost rises above the cost of the loan commitment made by a bank, the issuer will borrow from the bank. This is what General Motors Acceptance Corporation did in early 1991 after its parent reported a loss for 1990. A finance subsidiary that loses access to the market altogether, as Chrysler Financial Corporation did in 1990, also will borrow from banks.

These developments, described more fully later, suggest that bank portfolios will become more risky if the parallel system falters. But they also became more risky because of a thriving parallel system. Clearly, the parallel system as presently constituted threatens the soundness of commercial banks—and the continued viability of the intermediation function itself.

At the same time, the entire panoply of bank guarantees has become something of a parallel system in itself—an immense volume of contingent liabilities rivaling the actual volume of loans on the books of the largest banks.[8] Although this system purports to substitute private guarantees for public support, it actually creates an explicit channel through which all issuers in the commercial paper market gain access to the public-sector lender of last resort.

The development of a thickly tangled web of bank guarantees ensures that a future confidence-shaking crisis involving a major issuer would precipitate systemic consequences. Such an eventuality would require massive lending by the Federal Reserve to provide the real backup for banks' backup credit lines. Capping this chain of ironies is the modest nature of banks' short-term rewards. Typically, bank fees for providing credit liens range from only 25 to 75 basis points. In return for furnishing $6 billion in guarantees to the Westinghouse Credit Corporation (WCC) in 1992, 49 major banking organizations will split the grand total of $13 million in fees from WCC and $91 million in origination fees from the parent company.

Structure and Operations of Finance Companies

Enriched by their ties to powerful industrial and commercial parents, large finance companies have risen to the top of the financial market. But while they enjoy important advantages over banks, finance companies also face serious weaknesses. The structure, operations, and specific problems of major finance company types—as well as the best-known individual firms—are described below.

Finance companies are characterized by a considerable degree of diversity in their ownership, structure, and operations. Most of the largest companies are owned by parent corporations engaged in manufacturing or retail operations (Table 7.1). Some (American Express Credit Corp., Transamerica Finance Group) are subsidiaries of nonbank finance conglomerates: others are subsidiaries of domestic banks (Norwest Financial Services) or foreign banks (Heller Financial, CIT Group Holdings).[9] The sixth and eleventh largest, Household

Table 7.9

Commercial Paper Issuances by Leading Finance Companies

Company (12-31-91 Assets, billion dollars)	1991 Commercial Paper			1991 Bank Guarantees		1990 Commercial Paper			1990 Bank Guarantees		1989 Commercial Paper			1989 Bank Guarantees	
	Amount (billion dollars)	Percent of Company Liabilities	Percent of Total Outstanding Commercial Paper	Amount (billion dollars)	Percent of Commercial Paper	Amount (billion dollars)	Percent of Company Liabilities	Percent of Total Outstanding Commercial Paper	Amount (billion dollars)	Percent of Commercial Paper	Amount (billion dollars)	Percent of Company Liabilities	Percent of Total Outstanding Commercial Paper	Amount (billion dollars)	Percent of Commercial Paper
General Motors Acceptance Corp. ($102.9)	$27.5	29.2%	5.2%	$25.4	92.4%	$30.3	32.1%	5.4%	$20.6	68.0%	$33.8	35.3%	6.5%	$17.3	51.2%
GE Capital Corp. ($80.5)	36.9	50.8	7.0	19.7	53.4	33.6	52.9	6.0	18.4	54.8	28.9	54.4	5.5	14.7	50.9
Ford Motor Credit Company ($56.9)	18.0	34.8	3.4	10.6	58.9	22.8	42.1	4.1	9.4	41.2	18.2	36.0	3.5	9.4	51.6
Associates First Capital Corp. ($21.6)	8.0	40.6	1.5	6.0	75.0	6.0	38.7	1.1	4.4	73.3	5.3	39.3	1.0	1.3	24.5
Chrysler Financial Corp. ($21.3)	0.3	1.9	0.1	8.1	2700.0	1.1	4.5	0.2	8.8	800.0	10.1	37.0	1.9	8.5	84.2
Household Financial Corp. ($17.3)	2.4	15.2	0.5	4.0	6.7	3.3	21.4	0.6	3.8	115.2	3.6	26.1	0.7	3.2	88.9
Sears Roebuck Acceptance Corp. ($14.7)	5.3	45.3	1.0	11.8	222.6	6.9	55.2	1.2	10.8	156.5	9.9	84.6	1.9	10.8	109.1

Table 7.9 *continued*

Company															
American Express Credit Corp. ($14.1)	7.5	61.5	1.4	3.9	52.0	7.3	58.4	1.3	3.8	52.1	5.2	46.8	1.0	3.5	67.3
ITT Financial Corp. ($12.6)	3.7	33.0	0.7	3.3	89.2	4.4	42.7	0.8	3.5	79.5	4.1	43.6	0.8	3.2	78.0
IMB Credit Corp. ($11.3)	2.2	21.6	0.4	0.2	9.1	2.0	19.6	0.4	—	—	1.2	13.9	0.2	0.6	50.0
Beneficial Corp. ($10.0)	1.6	21.8	0.4	2.1	110.5	2.1	25.3	0.4	2.1	100.0	1.8	25.6	0.3	2.0	111.1
Westinghouse Credit Corp. ($8.6)	2.2	29.3	0.4	6.0	272.7	3.7	40.7	0.7	5.3	143.2	4.0	49.2	0.8	3.8	95.0
TransAmerica Finance Group ($7.3)	2.6	35.6	0.5	4.0	153.8	2.7	38.0	0.5	3.6	133.3	3.0	40.5	0.6	4.0	133.3
Commerical Credit Corp. ($6.7)	2.3	34.3	0.4	2.6	113.0	2.7	43.5	0.5	3.0	111.1	1.4	32.3	0.3	1.9	135.7
American General Finance Corp. ($5.4)	2.0	37.0	0.4	3.8	190.0	2.0	41.7	0.4	3.8	190.0	1.8	38.3	0.3	3.0	166.7
Totals*	$122.8	34.7%	23.5%	$111.5	90.8%	$130.9	37.9%	23.5%	$101.3	77.4%	$132.3	40.5%	25.3%	$87.2	65.9%

*May not add up due to rounding.
Sources: Annual reports of companies.

Table 7.10
Bank Guarantees to Selected Finance Companies

Guarantor	J.C. Penney Funding Corporation • $500M Lines of Credit •• $750M Revolving Credit Facility	Sears Roebuck Acceptance Corporation • 4.2B Revolving Credit Facility •• $275M Revolving Credit Facility ••• $450M Revolving Credit Facility •••• $700M Revolving Credit Facility	Westinghouse Credit Corporation $6B Credit Facility	ITT Financial Corporation (Line of Credit Per Bank (million dollars)
Bank America	•	•• (coagent)	•	$175 (incl. Security Pacific)
Citibank	•	•	•	$50
Chemical Bank	•	•• (coagent)	•	$175 (incl. MHT)
Morgan Guaranty	•	••• (lead agent)	•	$60
NationsBank	•		•	$60
First Interstate	•	• (lead manager)	•	$36
NBD Bank	••	•	•	$20
First Chicago	•	• (lead manager)	•	$70
Crédit Lyonnais	••	••• (coagent)	•	$55
Fuji Bank	•	••••	•	$35
Banca Nazionale del Lavoro	•	•• (lead manager)		$25
Sumitomo Bank		•••••	•	$47.5

Sources: Annual reports.

Financial Corporation and Beneficial Corporation, respectively, are independent companies connected to an array of regulated and unregulated financial affiliates. Most other independents are smaller, regional firms.

The industry's operations can be visualized along a spectrum bounded at one end by "captive" companies and at the other by independent firms such as Beneficial and Household. Generally, the business of captives is limited to purchasing parent companies' customer receivable balances (if the parent is a retailer) or providing loans, leases, or inventory finance for parent company customers if the parent is a manufacturer. Some captives also provide financing for the parent's primary activities by acquiring the parent's short-term notes.

By contrast, independent finance companies make consumer and/or commercial loans to third parties and are unaffiliated with any industrial or retail parent. At the midpoint of this spectrum stand a number of diversified finance companies engaged in a mix of activities related and unrelated to their parents' principal lines of business. The biggest and most familiar residents of this spectrum are the automobile finance companies and General Electric Capital Corporation.

At year-end 1991, General Motors Acceptance Corporation (GMAC), Ford Motor Credit Company (FMCC), and Chrysler Financial Corporation (CFC) ranked first, third, and fifth, respectively, among U.S. finance companies (Table 7.11). While engaged primarily in promoting the sale of parent company products, the Big Three's finance companies also are linked to affiliates conducting an array of activities.

For example, GMAC subsidiaries include a captive automobile insurance company, an industrial loan subsidiary, GMAC Mortgage Corporation (one of the largest U.S. mortgage bankers), and Electronic Data Systems (EDS)—which owns an additional layer of subsidiaries engaged in finance (*Moody's Bank and Finance Manual*, 1990, p. 5447; 1991, p. 5455).

FMCC started diversifying into nonauto consumer lending as early as 1966. FMCC is part of a group of finance subsidiaries that also includes First Nationwide Financial Corp., the country's fifth-largest savings and loan, and the Associates Corporation of North America, the fourth- largest U.S. finance company.[10] Ford acquired the Associates from Paramount Communications in 1989 to make financial services a larger part of its earnings stream and to "counterbalance . . . the cyclical nature of the automotive industry." Two years later, the Associates helped accomplish this goal (though not, perhaps, as originally envisioned) by purchasing $2.2 billion of receivables from FMCC (*Moody's Bank and Finance Manual*, 1991, p. 3039; FMCC 1991 Annual Report, p. 21).

At year-end 1991, GMAC remained the largest consumer finance operation in the nation. But its share of the market and that of the other two automobile finance companies had declined. In 1988, the assets of the three automobile finance units accounted for 28.4 percent of total finance company assets. By 1991, their share had fallen to 22.6 percent as slumping auto sales slowed the growth in receivables (Table 7.11).

Table 7.11

Top 12 Nonbank Finance Companies Ranked by Assets

	1991		1990		1989	
	Amount (billions of dollars)	Percent of total for all Finance Companies	Amount (billions of dollars)	Percent of Total for all Finance Companies	Amount (billions of dollars)	Percent of Total for all Finance Companies
General Motors Acceptance Corp.	$102.9	12.8%	$105.2	13.6%	$103.6	14.4%
General Electric Capital Corp.	80.5	10.0	70.4	9.1	58.7	8.2
Ford Motor Credit Company	56.9	7.1	59.0	7.6	54.9	7.6
Associates Corp. of North America*	21.6	2.7	16.9	2.2	14.8	2.1
Chrysler Finance Corp.	21.3	2.7	24.7	3.2	30.1	4.2
Household Financial Corp.	17.3	2.2	16.9	2.2	15.1	2.1
Sears Roebuck Acceptance Corp.	14.7	1.8	15.4	2.0	14.4	2.0
American Express Credit Corp.	14.1	1.8	14.2	1.8	12.6	1.8
ITT Financial Corp.	12.6	1.6	11.7	1.5	10.6	1.5
IBM Credit Corp.	11.3	1.4	11.1	1.4	9.7	1.3
Westinghouse Credit Corp.	8.6	1.1	10.3	1.3	9.3	1.3
Beneficial Corp.	10.0	1.2	9.3	1.2	7.9	1.1
Total	$371.8	46.4	$365.1	47.1	$341.7	47.6

Sources: Moody's Bank & Finance Manual; American Banker, November 8, 1990, p. 14; December 11, 1991, p. 11.
*A subsidiary of Ford Motor Company.

As the carmaker finance units lost market shares, GE Capital Corporation (GECC) gained. The company's parent is one of the largest and most diversified industrial corporations in the world; it operates approximately 182 manufacturing plants in 35 states and Puerto Rico, plus 79 manufacturing plants in 19 other countries. During a major expansion and diversification drive in the 1980s, GE acquired RCA, Montgomery Ward, and other firms, broadening its already imposing assortment of industry segments.

GE also expanded the range and volume of its financial services in the 1980s when it formed General Electric Financial Services, Inc. (GEFS), to acquire Employers Reinsurance Corp. from Texaco, Inc., for $1.1 billion. GEFS was then given 100 percent interest in GE Credit Corporation; subsequently, GE acquired the securities firm Kidder Peabody. GEFS now operates in all major segments of the industry: securities, insurance, lending, leasing, and other activities closely related to banking.

GECC is the core company in this diversified financial conglomerate. It operates primarily as a finance company engaged in a full range of leasing, loan, and asset management services; it also engages in insurance activities. These various business lines are conducted through 53 consolidated subsidiaries and joint ventures with Caterpillar Tractor Co. and BMW of North America. GECC's consolidated subsidiaries include the captive finance company of Montgomery Ward—a GE affiliate.[11]

GECC competes with other major finance companies in automobile leasing and finance, mortgage credit, and consumer loans. The company's growing portfolio of business and commercial real estate loans reflects wider industry trends and illustrates the extent to which GECC and other aggressively expanding finance companies have become major competitors of banks.

While the outstanding assets of all finance companies grew rapidly in the 1980s, GECC grew at an even faster rate. Between 1983 and year-end 1991, GECC's total assets rose more than 400 percent, from $15.7 billion to $80.5 billion. During that span, GECC's assets jumped from 6.3 percent to 10 percent of total finance company assets. In 1983, GECC accounted for more than 3 percent of all outstanding issues of commercial paper and for 7 percent of paper issued by finance companies. By 1991, those proportions had risen to 7 percent and 11.4 percent, respectively (Table 7.12).

Problems Confronting Finance Companies

Despite their substantial advantages, many of the biggest and best-known finance companies stumbled at the turn of the decade. Some managed to fall into the same asset-quality traps that snared regulated lenders. Others were hammered by economic forces and management failures afflicting their parent companies and the sectors in which they operated. According to the Federal Reserve Bank of New York, loan loss rates at finance companies jumped from 1.95 percent of

Table 7.12

General Electric Capital Corporation: Selected Components, Consolidated Balance Sheet (millions of dollars and percent)

	1983	1984	1985	1986	1987	1988	1989	1990	1991
Total assets/liabilities	$15,719	$18,467	$22,469	$27,970	$36,644	$47,766	$58,696	$70,385	$80,528
Liabilities									
Bank loans	53	72	37	3	3	15	2	13	41
Commercial paper	6,156	7,216	9,204	12,654	15,901	22,568	28,898	33,614	36,932
as percentage of total liabilities	39.2%	39.1%	41.0%	45.2%	43.4%	47.2%	49.2%	52.9%	50.8%
Stockholders equity as percentage of year-end assets	9.8	8.5	8.7	9.0	8.9	9.6	9.5	9.8	9.8
Selected comparative ratios									
GECC's assets as percentage of assets of all domestic finance companies	6.3%	6.5%	6.4%	6.8%	8.1%	9.8%	11.3%	11.0%	10.0%
GECC's outstanding commercial paper									
As percentage of total outstanding commercial paper	3.2	3.0	3.1	3.8	4.4	4.9	5.4	6.0	7.0
As percentage of total outstanding commercial paper issued by domestic finance companies	7.0	7.1	6.5	7.0	7.5	8.4	9.6	10.0	11.4

Source: Moody's Bank & Finance Manual, 1990, Vol. 2, p. 3375; 1991 Annual Report, pp. 17 and 25; see also Tables 7.4 and 7.6 in this chapter.

net receivables in 1988 to 2.55 percent in 1991, outstripping loss rates at banks, which hovered around 1.45 percent of total loans in 1991 (Frydl, 1991, p. 21).

In late fall 1992, finance companies suffered a stunning "November Night-mare." In the space of six days, three of the nation's biggest finance companies announced moves that revealed acute problems. Wracked by huge losses at its credit affiliate, Westinghouse Electric Company decided to liquidate or sell WCC. Buffeted by credit rating downgrades, Chrysler Corporation sold its lucra-tive Chrysler First consumer finance subsidiary to NationsBank. With its access to the commercial paper market reduced, GMAC was forced to drop its profit-able, $6-billion portfolio of loans to non-GM customers and dealerships.

For the auto finance companies, these developments marked the latest in a series of recession-related reversals. Lower credit ratings for both the parent and its finance unit began to severely limit CFC's access to funding in 1990; losses at General Motors and Ford in 1990 resulted in lower ratings for GMAC, FMCC, and their parent companies in early 1991. All three finance units cut their issu-ance of commercial paper and drew on more expensive bank credit lines.

The changing composition of short-term liabilities at Chrysler Financial dra-matically illustrates what can happen to the availability and cost of funds for finance companies when their parents' fortunes decline (Table 7.13). Steeper funding costs contributed significantly to a $5.4-billion decline in CFC assets in 1990 and an additional $3.4 billion drop in 1991. As cheaper funding sources dried up, CFC increasingly relied on securitization of receivables to finance Chrysler products. In 1990 and 1991, it sold $15.9 billion of receivables. But it could no longer engage in promotional, below-cost financing to increase car sales. As its borrowing from banks rose, CFC lost its advantage over banks in financing car loans and dealer inventories.

With its parent company debt downgraded below investment grade, Chrysler Financial acknowledged "significant liquidity problems" and attempted to re-place and restructure its bank lending facilities. The pressure of rising funding costs and constricting bank credit forced both GMAC and FMCC to follow Chrysler's lead in securitizing more of their receivables.[12] As their assets dwindled, Ford and GMAC saw their share of outstanding commercial paper issues shrink from 9.6 percent ($53.7 billion) in 1990 to 8.6 percent ($45.6 billion) in 1991.

Compared to the automobile finance units, GE Capital appears healthy. The company's assets have climbed steadily, with 14 percent growth in 1991. Com-mercial paper outstandings expanded as well, jumping from $33.6 billion in 1990 to $36.9 billion in 1991. However, in 1990 and 1991, rising levels of nonearning loans and losses demonstrated the firm's vulnerability to changes in the economy.

GE Capital's commercial real estate (CRE) portfolio was heavily concen-trated in apartment and office buildings (which accounted for 65 percent of total CRE loans) and showed signs of quick deterioration. Nonperforming CRE loans nearly quintupled between 1989 and 1991, soaring from $104 million to $512 million. Even though credit losses on CRE loans ballooned (from $62 million in

Table 7.13

Chrysler Financial Corporation: Short-Term Liabilities (millions of dollars, at year-end)

Funding Sources	1989	1990	1991
Commercial paper	$10,061	$1,114	$339
United States	9,233	957	271
Canada	828	157	68
Bank borrowings	—	6,241	6,633
United States	—	5,824	6,272
Canada	—	417	361
Total short-term liabilities	10,061	7,355	6,972

Sources: Annual reports; *Moody's Bank and Finance Manual*, Vol. 2, 1991, p. 3055.

1990 to $210 million in 1991), they were outpaced by commercial and industrial loan losses.

Most of the commercial and industrial loan losses—$323 million in 1991, up from $56 million in 1989—were on loans classified as highly leveraged transactions (HLTs).[13] GE Capital's HLT portfolio amounted to $6.5 billion—60.2 percent of its total commercial loans and 8.1 percent of its total assets. Moreover, its HLT portfolio was significantly concentrated in the communications industry (41 percent), with 22 percent of the total lent to cable television companies (the competitors—and potential acquirees—of its sister affiliate, NBC), 10 percent to media firms, and 9 percent to "broadcasting and other companies" (GECC, 1991, p. 12).[14]

GE's long-time rival Westinghouse was beset by a credit-unit portfolio that made GECC's appear prudent by contrast. Leveraged buy-out loans accounted for 45 percent, and commercial real estate loans 35 percent of Westinghouse Credit Corporation's $10.3 billion of assets when the company took a $1.48 billion third-quarter loss in 1991. WCC lost $975 million in 1990 (*The Wall Street Journal*, 1991, p. A1), with a single industry segment accounting for 30 percent of its leveraged buy-out loans and a single borrower accounting for 7 percent of its CRE loans.

The flamboyant failures financed by WCC ranged from hotel complexes in Coral Gables and Atlantic City to a renovated 19th-century office building in Pittsburgh. Westinghouse's fate now rests mainly in the hands of banks that provided WCC's backup credit lines. They include Mellon, NationsBank, Citibank, First Fidelity, Crédit Lyonnais, and Fuji Bank (see complete listing in Table 7.14).

Table 7.14

Banks Extending $6 Billion Guarantee to Westinghouse Credit Corporation

HAWAII
  Bank of Hawaii

ILLINOIS
  The Bank of Nova Scotia
  Bayerishe Vereinsbank AG
  Continental Bank, N.A.
  The First National Bank of Chicago
  The Toronto-Dominion Bank

MARYLAND
  The First National Bank of Maryland

NEW JERSEY
  First Fidelity Bank, N.A.

NEW YORK
  Arab Banking Corporation
  Bank of Ireland
  Bank of Montreal
  The Bank of Tokyo Trust Company
  Banque Nationale de Paris
  Barclays Bank PLC
  Bayerishe Landesbank Girozentrale
  BBL Bank Brussels Lambert
  Casa di Risparmio delle Provincie Lombarde (CARIPLO)
  Chemical Bank
  Citibank, N.A.
  Credito Italiano
  Crédit Lyonnais
  Crédit Suisse
  The Dai Ichi Kangyo Bank, Ltd.
  Deutsche Bank AG
  Dresdner Bank AG
  First Interstate Bank of Japan, Limited
  The Fuji Bank, Limited
  The Hokuriku Bank, Ltd.
  The Industrial Bank of Japan, Limited
  Instituto Bancario San Paolo di Torino
  Long-Term Credit Bank Trust Company
  The Mitsubishi Bank, Limited
  The Mitsubishi Trust & Banking Corporation
  The Mitsui Trust Bank (U.S.A.)
  Morgan Guaranty Trust Company of New York
  The Sanwa Bank, Limited
  Société Générale
  The Sumitomo Bank, Limited
  The Sumitomo Trust & Banking Company, Limited
  The Tokai Bank, Limited
  Union Bank of Switzerland
  Westdeutsche Landesbank Girozentrale
  Westpac Banking Corporation
  Yasuda Bank and Trust Company (U.S.A.)

NORTH CAROLINA
  NCNB National Bank of North Carolina (NationsBank)

PENNSYLVANIA
  ABN AMO Bank, N.V.
  Mellon Bank, N.A.
  Pittsburgh National Bank
  The Royal Bank of Canada

Source: Westinghouse Credit Corporation Annual Report.

Although it became the industry's most dramatic recent failure, Westinghouse is not the only large, diversified finance company to experience losses and lowered credit ratings. In 1991, Moody's downgraded Household Financial Corporation's commercial paper rating along with the long-term debt rating of HFC's parent company. Despite its name and reputation as a consumer finance firm, Household is a diversified holding company engaged in both consumer and commercial lending as well as insurance underwriting (Table 7.1). During 1991, HFC's nonperforming commercial loans and foreclosed real estate more than doubled, to $688 million.

Like the auto finance companies, HFC was forced to step up its securitization and sales of receivables ($6.6 billion in 1990 and 1991) while paring back its commercial paper issues (reduced by a third during 1991). Like GE and Westinghouse, Household's portfolio exhibited signs of unhealthy concentration. At year-end 1991, fully 22 percent of its domestic receivables were in California, the site of a real estate collapse that jeopardized a number of major finance companies. For example, 67 percent of ITT Financial's CRE receivables were located in California (up from 66 percent in 1990). At Beneficial Corporation—one of the few financial firms to receive a debt rating upgrade in 1991—California loans accounted for 23 percent of total receivables at year-end 1991. Real estate secured 90 percent of Beneficial's California portfolio—but only 58 percent of the company's total receivables (BC, 1991, p. 48, note 23).

Public Policy Concerns

Any effort to modernize financial regulation must address the inequalities that have helped to create the parallel banking system. The following discussion outlines some of the key issues in accomplishing this modernization.

Implementing Monetary Policy and Performing
the Lender-of-Last-Resort Function

The most troubling consequences of a parallel banking system affect the Federal Reserve System. The parallel system not only stretches the central bank's lender-of-last-resort function but also may compromise its ability to implement monetary policy.

The immense volume of bank guarantees to the parallel banking system has placed banks in a no-win situation in which they are both weakened by the support they provide already-advantaged competitors and faced with greater risks if the parallel system falters. Clearly the risk to the banks creates risk for the lender of last resort. The symbiotic relationship between commercial banks and their rivals in the parallel banking system leaves the Federal Reserve with much less room for discretion in exercising that role.

By blanketing the parallel banking system with fee-generating guarantees, the banks have exposed the central bank to a contingent liability domino effect of major proportions and complexity. In the event of a parallel banking system crisis, the Federal Reserve may not have the option to choose the institutions or markets to which banks will channel the liquidity it makes available. Banks have already made those choices by issuing guarantees. The Fed will have to endorse those guarantees to protect the banks.

While this lender-of-last-resort scenario may affect the Fed only in the uncertain future, America's parallel banking system is affecting monetary policy even now. To appreciate that impact, it is useful to revisit the role of reserve requirements in intramural financial industry competition as well as in monetary decisionmaking.

Complying with reserve requirements represents a cost. Combined with other regulatory requirements, that cost has hampered banks' ability to compete with a growing assortment of parallel lenders. Thus the banking industry and its supporters have proposed "fixing" the problem by requiring that the Federal Reserve pay interest on reserves. Some have suggested the more radical step of abolishing reserve requirements entirely and leaving open market operations as the Federal Reserve's sole tool for implementing monetary policy. This action would require the Fed to restructure its balance sheet and to remove bank reserves as liabilities that expand or contract in response to purchases and sales of government securities.

While relaxing or removing reserve requirements might slow the decline in banks' share of credit extensions, it would beg a far more important issue. Reserve requirements can be an effective policy tool—but only if they affect a critical mass of institutions that hold the liquid funds of households, businesses, and other relevant economic sectors. The immense growth in MMMFs, credit card usage, and other parallel lending phenomena has narrowed the institutional mass that made this tool so effective in the past. After a brief experiment with special deposit requirements on nondepository institutions in 1980 (discussed later), the Fed returned to its focus on banks as the channel for policy, thus accommodating the slump in banks' credit market share that reduced the Fed's own leverage in implementing monetary policy.

In the meantime, the effectiveness of open market operations was also eroded by the size of foreign flows into and out of U.S. financial markets. The lag in obtaining information on these flows puts the Fed in the position of playing blind man's bluff in gauging the appropriate response to changes in the market. As a result of these developments, the monetary authority finds itself less able to operate by taking small, gradual steps toward its targets. The more forceful actions that it now must take to change monetary aggregates render the implementation of monetary policy less a factor in stabilizing financial markets than a component of instability.

Accountability and Investor Protection

The disclosure provisions of the Securities Act of 1933—the foundation stone of U.S. investor protection law—provide the primary oversight of finance companies. These disclosure provisions also apply to other corporate entities within the financial system, including bank and thrift holding companies. However, soundness regulation, supervision, and examination augment disclosure as part of an oversight package for deposit-taking institutions.

Moreover, the information disclosed by commercial and industrial parents of finance companies is seldom comparable to that available for other financial sectors. Indeed, very little uniformity exists within the closed universe of finance company disclosure itself. Parent firms may report in detail on a finance subsidiary's loan portfolio only when it contains the significant adverse information required for investor protection under the securities laws.

This regulatory scheme does not offer sufficient protection to institutions that supply funding for finance companies owned by a commercial or industrial parent. Short-term lenders may be protected from losses by their ability to not renew funding when finance companies release adverse information. But long-term debt and equity holders may be less fortunate.

Bank guarantees will protect them in the short run, providing an alternative source of funds if the company cannot sell commercial paper. But the resort to bank guarantees will raise the finance company's cost of funding, generating additional balance sheet pressures and jeopardizing the value of long-term holdings in the firm. Most finance companies simply do not disclose adequate portfolio composition data until it's too late to help investors.

Private ratings agencies constitute the sole independent source of investor information on finance companies. To some extent, their ratings of notes, bonds, and commercial paper reflect the performance of the parent rather than the financial affiliate that is the issuer, even when the finance company is lending to outside borrowers rather than its parent's customers. The ratings assigned to finance companies owned by nonfinancial firms also reflect an assumption that the parent will provide substantial support to offset any difficulties that might be experienced by its subsidiary.

The problem with rating services using this implicit source-of-strength doctrine is that losses by finance subsidiaries can also contaminate the credit rating of the parent company—as the experience of Westinghouse demonstrated. In addition to raising the parent corporation's cost of capital, those losses inhibit growth in other, more immediate ways by absorbing funds needed for ongoing operations. Over time, these contagion effects will erode the value of investments in the parent company, substantial portions of which are held by pension funds that pool the savings of workers who can least afford losses on investments.

The growing links between nonfinancial firms and financial product providers require a reassessment of the kind, scope, and uniformity of disclosure that these conglomerates should provide to ensure investors adequate information. Greater transparency alone, however, will not solve the problems of regulatory inequality or market instability.

The Absence of Firewalls

During the early evolutionary stages of America's multifunctional financial conglomerates, most nonfinancial parent firms entered the financial market through
their captive finance companies. In many cases, the finance company became a
diversified, even quasi-independent, lender as the parent expanded into other
financial services.

Now that finance companies have become major players in intermediation,
their unregulated status carries increasingly important implications for their relationships to and transactions with other financial service firms within the conglomerate. Regulators have few, if any, tools to prevent the problems of the
parent or its finance company subsidiary from spilling over into and absorbing
the resources of regulated financial affiliates such as securities firms, insurance
companies, and insured depositories.

As the resources of such regulated affiliates expand, so do the potential problems associated with missing firewalls. As Table 7.1 shows, a handful of the
largest finance companies control banks and thrifts that already hold more
than $30 billion in deposits. First Nationwide (the Ford subsidiary), Sears
Savings Bank, and Household Bank FSB rank among the nation's top 25
insured thrifts.

The absence of firewalls may prove problematic even when the parent corporation is an independently owned finance company. For example, the condition
of Household International does not suggest it is a source of strength for Household Finance Corporation's national bank or savings bank. In 1990, the parent's
equity-to-assets ratio fell below the standard required for commercial banks.

Equally important, consolidated capital reported by Household International
at year-end 1991 failed to match the capital levels reported separately for the
firm's regulated and unregulated subsidiaries.[15] It is not clear whether or what
regulatory leverage exists to require that Household International maintain and
accurately report the resources needed to ensure the viability of its insured depository institutions.

The apparent ease of intracorporate transfers also raises questions about
regulators' ability to prevent finance companies from selling poorer-quality assets to affiliated depository institutions or insurance companies. Similarly, if a
conglomerate uses its securities subsidiary to underwrite instruments for a troubled borrower of its finance company, Securities and Exchange Commission
enforcement of disclosure and due diligence requirements may not guarantee the
same careful scrutiny that occurs in an arms-length transaction. Only the most
inquisitive, sophisticated outside investors may recognize the issuer's problems
and the conflict of interest inherent in a transaction involving affiliates.

Finally, even if the problems of the parent or an unregulated finance subsidiary do not directly undermine their condition, a general loss of confidence can
raise funding costs for regulated financial affiliates.

Portfolio Diversification

The meager information disclosed by finance companies suggests that America's parallel banking system does not maintain a diversified asset portfolio. By definition, captive firms concentrate their loans to a single sector and, in some cases, single borrowers (i.e., the parent companies). But there are also cases in which companies that used bank guarantees to escape captive status then made themselves captives to undiversified lending.

Large concentrations of loans in individual sectors appear common among finance companies that specialize in financing or leasing certain kinds of equipment. For example, John Deere Capital Corp., one of the 20 largest finance companies, acknowledged in its 1991 annual report (p. 13) "significant concentrations of credit risk" with 60 percent of its receivables in the farm sector and another 22 percent in the recreation sector. However, some companies with a virtually unlimited third-party clientele have achieved much the same result. The ill-fated WCC, for example, filled as much as 80 percent of its portfolio with leveraged buy-out and CRE loans.

What constitutes a reasonable pattern of diversification in this industry may vary in relation to a company's business objectives and expertise. But the kind and degree of concentration exhibited by the portfolios of John Deere Capital and Westinghouse Credit show a blatant disregard for prudential standards and common sense.

Concentration and Anticompetitive Practices

In 1991, the 12 largest nonbank finance companies accounted for 46 percent of the total assets held by all finance companies (Table 7.11). The five largest companies held nearly 35 percent of this sector's assets and accounted for 17 percent of total outstanding issues in the entire commercial paper market (Table 7.9). This high degree of concentration is neither unusual nor new in the financial industry. At year-end 1984, for example, less than 1 percent of the total number of commercial banks, securities firms, and life and health insurers held more than 50 percent of the assets and/or capital of their respective industries (U.S. Congress, 1986, p. 226). Compared with other countries, however, the U.S. system appears extraordinarily diverse because of the immense number of small institutions that operate in local markets and hold a small percentage of the system's total assets.

Despite this apparent diversity at the bottom, rising levels of concentration at the top challenge the efficiency of an American system that depends to a unique degree on private-sector competition to preserve the openness and fairness of markets. The economies of most other industrial countries function under some form of industrial policy, the most obvious being the unquestioned agreement of their public and private sectors on the need to cooperate in promoting exports.

This particular priority means that concentration is not viewed as a problem for the financial systems in those countries. Indeed, a greater number of decisionmakers with different points of view would be counterproductive. Rather than asking their domestic financial system to do the job, most export-dependent industrial nations let the global market for tradable goods select sectoral winners and losers. Funding the winners becomes the task of the financial institutions of these countries.

In the United States, national objectives have not played as forceful a role in shaping credit decisions. Instead, credit markets have been organized around the assumptions that profit opportunities motivate financial institutions and that maximizing profits will result in credit decisions that increase the common wealth. Among other things, however, these assumptions fail to reckon with the effects of increasing capital mobility. Propelled by technological advances, the scale of international capital flows now dwarfs underlying economic activity and enlarges the difficulties faced by national authorities in promoting sustainable growth. In the U.S., global capital mobility has exacerbated disinvestment in bypassed economic sectors, communities, and regions of the country. The results lead to a slowdown in economic activity that further shrinks the supply of funds for investment. In short, lending decisions motivated by short-term returns have undermined, not promoted, the common wealth.

In the United States, continued reliance on private markets to make credit decisions requires a renewed role for government in ensuring that markets remain open, fair, and undominated by a few large market makers. The bipartisan consensus that ignored growing levels of financial industry concentration over the past two decades has contributed to some of the weaknesses in the U.S. economy.

The regal position and market power of a few large institutions in each financial sector have contributed to unusually destructive, lemminglike behavior in all sectors. During the 1980s, financial product providers of all sizes and types—banks, securities firms, insurance companies, and finance companies—followed the fads that expanded credit flows for mergers and acquisitions, leveraged buyouts, and CRE speculation. Coping with the consequences of their own excesses has undermined the ability of those same firms to fuel productive growth.

The same patterns also hindered economic restructuring in the United States. Rising levels of institutional concentration made it harder for the financial system to assist the development of small, innovative companies and processes that will mature in time to ease the disruptions caused by declining older firms and methods. Large institutions with large pools of funds deemed it unprofitable to finance small firms and lacked motivation to provide venture capital.

The lack of capital and credit for smaller enterprises stems not only from growing institutional concentration but also from shrinking levels of competition in local lending markets that ostensibly feature a large number of flourishing smaller lenders. This decline is particularly troubling because local markets continue to be the primary avenue for small businesses to access credit and other financial services. Despite the boom in debt issuances of all kinds by nonbanks, research by the Federal Reserve staff clearly shows that only commercial banks provide borrowers the "cluster of banking services" they usually seek (Elliehausen and Wolken, FRB, 1990).

Competition for this "cluster" and for primary banking services to middle market companies is rapidly receding due to a number of factors that include rising, government-encouraged merger activity in the private market and government-assisted consolidation carried out by the Federal Deposit Insurance Corporation and Resolution Trust Corporation in resolving insolvent depositories. Given the repeatedly demonstrated effects of the concentration in price relationship, the nation's economy is clearly a loser if its chief sources of new jobs— small and medium-sized businesses—find themselves increasingly underserved by financial concentration.[16]

In this context, the growing role of the parallel banking system creates an additional concern. Given the absence of disclosure and oversight for finance company loan portfolios, there can be no assurances that the parallel banking system is not replicating the kind of closed linkages that characterize the Japanese *keiretsu*. Finance subsidiaries of commercial corporations exercise considerably more market power than do independent finance companies, banks, securities firms, or insurance companies. One consequence is a growing potential for anticompetitive practices such as self-dealing or tying, namely, requiring that parent firm suppliers obtain funding from the parent's financial subsidiaries as a condition for access to the parent as a customer.

The operations of automobile finance companies demonstrate the hazards of enhanced market power. The Big Three have been able to offer car loans at below-market rates—indeed, rates below their own cost of funds—because they could make up the difference by boosting the price of the car. Bereft of any similar opportunity, the independent lender cannot compete. The results are reflected in the dramatic expansion in finance company credit market share during the 1980s. The opportunity to promote parent and affiliate products and services will continue to drive this growth as long as regulatory guidelines and supervisory practices mandate a standard of economic neutrality for some financial sectors but not others.

In the American system, economic diversity and innovation are likely to suffer when an expanding share of credit decisions is channeled through in-house intermediaries whose chief aim is augmenting their parents' profits. Over time, financial stability may suffer as well. The need to attract or support suppliers or customers for the parent firm—or customers for sister financial affiliates inside the conglomerate—can distort lending judgments.

The hallmark of the American intermediary system has been a set of dispersed, independent lenders whose prosperity depended solely on the success of their borrowers. However, the comfort of a potential bailout—whether from government or parental coffers—weakens the imperative to link credit decisions to the borrower's prospects for growth; it may also encourage short-term financial speculation by investors and lenders.

Meanwhile, the ability of major manufacturers and retailers to provide secure in-house financing in order to market their products and services has promoted complacency at the expense of competitiveness. U.S. automobile manufacturers, for example, emphasized the competitiveness of the finance rates they could offer car buyers at a time when many of their products were not competitive with foreign autos in terms of quality. Clearly, this paper-oriented approach to competition makes losers of consumers and the domestic economy when it results in higher prices, lower quality, and industrial decline.

The Need for Uniform Regulation

Regulatory equality is the answer to much of the inefficiency, unresponsiveness, and myopia that characterize the U.S. financial system—as long as it levels the playing field by raising standards for all players. Subjecting the system to another dose of 1980s-style laissez-faire medicine—by relaxing the rules for regulated lenders or permitting them to become niche players in the credit market—would further hamper the ability of monetary policy and private-sector competition to promote greater financial stability and improve national economic performance. More deregulation would detonate, rather than defuse, the land mines that have developed in the symbiotic relationship between the regulated banking system and its shadow, parallel competitor.

Although the imposition of additional rules on less-regulated lenders likely would raise their costs and those of their customers in the short term, the broader impacts would serve to steady financial markets and benefit the real economy over the long haul. In practical terms, establishing a prudential floor-underneath-lender behavior is the only alternative to the ad hoc, industry-driven downward spiral of deregulation that characterized federal policy during the 1980s.

One measure of the failings of that policy is its lack of public support and its corrosive effect on public confidence as evidenced in recent polls. Financial reform should not be driven solely by poll results. However, it should respond to clear and repeated expressions of concern by the public whose participation, confidence, and full faith and credit are essential to any financial system. Recasting the balance of regulatory and market forces in any industry requires a judicious hand. Recasting them in an industry that is unique, crucial, and fragile requires special attention to the kinds of public perceptions and democratic preferences voiced by poll respondents witnessing the deterioration of their financial infrastructure.[17]

A Proposal for Licensing Parallel Banking Institutions

Accordingly, we propose a Financial Industry Licensing Act that would apply prudential standards to firms such as finance companies, mortgage firms, and private insurers not currently regulated for soundness at the federal level and would supersede, when necessary, the relevant sections of existing statutes, including (but not limited to) the Bank Holding Company Act, the Investment Company Act, the Securities Acts, and the McCarran-Ferguson Act.

While this proposal departs from the direction of most recent policy debates and initiatives, it does draw on a precedent from the not-so-distant past. In 1980, responding to a presidential directive issued under the Credit Control Act, the Federal Reserve System implemented a credit restraint program that went beyond the banking system and the usual boundaries of its scope of action.

The Federal Reserve program included a special deposit requirement of 15 percent on all extensions of consumer credit through credit cards, check-credit overdraft plans, unsecured personal loans, and secured loans except those issued to finance the purchase of the collateral. This deposit requirement applied to all consumer lenders, not just depository institutions, and it was extended to MMMFs as well. In addition, the Federal Reserve brought all finance companies, as well as depository institutions, under a domestic voluntary credit restraint program designed to limit the growth of credit to the industrial and commercial sectors.[18]

The Fed's program illuminated the parallel, partially regulated, banking system, but only in the most brief and incomplete fashion. And it did so at a moment of spiraling inflation, soaring nominal interest rates, and great geopolitical turmoil—hardly an ideal laboratory for monetary experiments. Since that experiment, the role of the parallel system in U.S. credit markets has been ignored.

Today, it is time to end a decade of disorder in credit markets. The Financial Industry Licensing Act would achieve that goal by placing all lenders within the same regulatory ambit while maintaining the fundamental barriers between borrowers and creditors that are necessary for the effective, economically neutral functioning of the financial system. A broad outline of the act follows.

Who Should Be Licensed?

To promote economic growth, a stable financial system, and regulatory equality, comparable soundness requirements and prohibitions against unfair competition or excessive concentration should be applied to any entity that
 • directly accepts funds from the public for investment;
 • makes loans to the public or buys loans or securities using funds other than its own equity capital and retained earnings; or,
 • sells loans or third-party securities to financial institutions or investors.

To ensure the impartiality of credit decisions and to further promote financial market stability, a series of protective requirements should separate entities performing the aforementioned functions from their financial and nonfinancial parents and affiliates. These safeguards should include the following requirements:
 • All parent companies of entities performing the aforementioned functions should be chartered as Financial Product Holding Companies (FPHCs) and meet

the same licensing and regulatory requirements as their financial affiliates. However, nonfinancial FPHCs should be barred from engaging directly in any activities permitted their financial affiliates.

• Each licensed entity affiliated with an FPHC should be separately capitalized, incorporated, and managed (by independent officers and directors);

• Management interlock prohibitions included in the Depository Institution Management Interlock Act should be applied to all licensed entities, including FPHCs;

• Each FPHC and its licensed affiliates should meet antitying restrictions and comply with prohibitions on affiliate transactions modeled after the restrictions included in Sections 23A and 23B of the Federal Reserve Act and the firewall provisions in the Securities Regulatory Equality Act proposed in 1991.[19]

What Form Should Licensing Take?

Any entity engaged in the business lines described should apply for a renewable charter that constitutes its license to access or use funds. To receive its initial license, an applicant should demonstrate the financial and managerial resources needed for safe and sound operations.

To maintain its license, an entity should seek renewal on a regular, periodic basis. Renewal should be predicated on the applicant's ability to meet specific public obligations as well as to comply fully with soundness guidelines (discussed later).

Additionally, each salaried officer of the licensed financial firm should obtain a practitioner's license as a condition of employment. This certificate—also renewable at regular intervals—should indicate the individual's familiarity with laws, regulations, and business practices required for sound lending and investment.

The administration (awarding, monitoring, suspension, revocation, reinstatement, etc.) of the practitioner's license should be the responsibility of self-regulating trade groups, just as the National Association of Securities Dealers administers its broker-dealer license. The primary federal regulator for each industry segment should oversee these self-regulatory organizations.

What Public Obligations Should the License Include?

As a minimum condition of its license, each entity should comply fully with the standards set forth in the Community Reinvestment Act, Home Mortgage Disclosure Act, Truth in Lending Act, Equal Credit Opportunity Act, Fair Credit Reporting Act, and other federal statutes related to fair lending.

Which Soundness Regulations Should the Licensing Arrangement Cover?

Licensed entities should be held to comparable reserve, capital, and liquidity requirements when applicable. Finance companies and other lenders that do not take funds directly from the public should be subject to special deposit requirements modeled on those imposed by the Federal Reserve in 1980. These deposit requirements should apply to all lending activity, not only consumer lending. The requirements need be no more than a nominal percentage of outstanding credit under current conditions. Implementing them now will permit the kinks to be worked out in advance so they can be increased gradually at later stages in the business cycle, if and when they are needed.

In addition, assets and off-balance-sheet items should be risk-weighted in uniform fashion for all regulatory determinations of the capital adequacy of licensed entities. Similarly, all licensees should meet comparable risk diversification standards, such as limits on loans to a single borrower and restrictions on real estate lending or other sectoral concentrations.

To achieve greater systemwide transparency, each licensed entity should complete and publicly disclose at regular intervals (e.g., quarterly or annually) a Uniform Performance Report providing detailed information on its income, expenses, assets, and liabilities. The Uniform Performance Report should require licensees to report in as much detail as practically feasible the geographic and sectoral distribution of its assets and/or underwritings.[20]

The maintenance of vigorous market competition is critical for effective soundness regulation. In addition to complying with prohibitions against conflicts of interest and self-dealing, licensees also should operate in an environment free from excessive concentrations of market power and inequitable or inconsistent applications of antitrust law.

Unfair, market-distorting exemptions to the antitrust laws, such as the McCarran-Ferguson Act, should be repealed and replaced by new antitrust guidelines and enforcement practices rooted in the principle of uniformity and structured by actual market conditions. The needs of vulnerable borrowers, such as small, middle-market, rural, and inner-city businesses, should play a key role in determining new guidelines and practices. As long as such firms continue to require a "cluster of banking services" and lack access to national capital markets, antitrust enforcement should focus on local and regional lending markets. Additionally, state attorneys general and the U.S. Department of Justice should assume primary responsibility for enforcement, a role they currently share with banking regulators.

To further promote regulatory equality, the use of examination procedures, enforcement actions, and penalties should be harmonized across all forms of licensed activity. In other words, standards should be developed for each industry segment in order to provide equivalent supervision and examination at reasonably equivalent cost.

As part of a commitment to effective and fair national treatment of internationally active firms, U.S. financial regulators and trade negotiators should seek the adoption of similar standards on a multinational basis—a global strategy of regulatory floor-setting that encourages the pursuit of distinctive national economic priorities.

Who Will Do the Licensing and Regulating?

The approach outlined here would go a long way toward eliminating the traditional competition in laxity that has haunted domestic and international financial regulation. If that competition disappears or substantially diminishes, so will much of the imperative to rearrange the furniture of financial regulation.

To effectively modernize soundness regulation, all licensees that operate in more than one state or above a designated size threshold (e.g., more than $1 billion in combined assets) must be subject to federal oversight. With the advent of federal regulation for these firms, the traditional benefits of the dual system, such as innovation and flexibility, can more properly be focused on the development of smaller institutions serving state and local needs.

The recommended approach to regulatory equality could be administered by a single regulator, multiple regulators, regulators whose mission is defined by industry segments, or regulators whose mission is defined by function.

Clearly, some modicum of functional regulation will result because of the concentrations of regulatory expertise over certain segments of the financial markets. And clearly some umbrella oversight must be exercised over entities engaged in more than one financial function. Those elements of the licensing and regulatory process most liable to multiagency duplication (e.g., disclosure) could be entrusted to a new federal Financial Licensing Office created out of overlapping departments in the existing agencies.

Enhanced self-regulation should become a vital part of any movement toward regulatory equality. Financial firms deal with one another constantly. Their own ability to detect problems or wrongdoing outstrips the ability of any outside party. The obligation to self-regulate should supplement—not substitute for—the supervisory power of independent regulators. The most meritorious and time-tested elements of the securities industry's self-regulating organizations could provide a model for marketwide self-regulation.

To build on that tradition, the licensing agency(ies) should charge financial organizations with formal responsibility for reporting unlawful or anticompetitive activities to their self-regulating trade associations. Those trade groups would then bear a statutory responsibility for evaluating the information and passing on their findings to the appropriate federal regulator.

Finally, we believe the Federal Reserve should maintain a substantial role in the overall regulation of financial entities so as to ensure the effectiveness of monetary policy decisions. Its unique economic responsibilities compel the Federal Reserve to monitor constantly the impact of financial regulation on economic activity; its unique institutional capacity provides the Fed the necessary tools to evaluate and, if necessary, shape the impact.

We believe as well that monetary policy must be publicly accountable so that it enhances public confidence in financial markets and the nation's economy. A number of mechanisms ranging from prompt and complete disclosure of FOMC transcripts to broader representation on the Federal Advisory Council and reserve district bank boards could expedite this movement toward increased accountability. If the nation's economic welfare is too important to be left to the parallel banking system, it is also too important to leave to the private financiers who today shape the policies of America's central bank.

Notes

1. The authors wish to thank Izabel Carsalade and Jessica Chia-Chen Lee, graduates of the LL.M. program in International Banking Law Studies at Boston University School of Law, and Marty Leary, Phil Cargile, and Carol Mason Howle, of the Southern Finance Project, for their contributions to the research for this paper. In addition, the authors are grateful to Konrad Alt and Sheldon Friedman for their helpful comments.

2. The Federal Trade Commission (FTC) is charged with regulating finance companies for compliance with federal consumer credit protection statutes such as the Equal Credit Opportunity Act and the Fair Credit Reporting Act. Under Section 5 of the FTC Act, the agency also has the authority to seek permanent injunctions and consumer redress in the event it uncovers fraudulent practices by consumer loan companies. With the exception of these consumer protection statutes, no other forms of federal financial regulation are applied to finance companies (Noonan, Buffon, and Le Fevre, 1991, pp. 1093–97).

3. For additional details on foreign bank lending in the U.S. market, see McCauley and Seth (1992, pp. 52–65).

4. Indeed the Administration proposal amounted to a "heads I win, tails you lose" invitation to financial instability. Had the Bush plan somehow succeeded in inducing commercial firms to expand their direct ownership positions in banks, the resulting combinations would have jeopardized further the impartiality of credit decisions. The sizable risk posed by such combinations is reflected in the fact that no major industrialized nation currently permits commercial firms to control banks having access to a safety net of public insurance.

5. See SNL Securities (1992, pp. 3–21) for a useful description of finance company types and the environments in which they operate.

6. Two notable exceptions are American Express, which offers savings plans to charge card customers, and IBM Credit Corporation, which takes funds directly from uninsured money market deposits for its commercial lending (Zuckerman, 1991, p. 6).

7. As Table 7.2 shows, money market mutual funds invest in liabilities of banks, governments, government agencies, and commercial paper issuers. These assets are rated by rating agencies, and the cost of information is minuscule compared with the information costs involved in lending to households and businesses.

8. Bank lines of credit to commercial paper issuers constitute only a fraction of total off-balance-sheet activity by banks. Total commitments and contingent liabilities for domestic banks could range from $1.4 trillion to $5.6 trillion. The larger estimate, based on data submitted to the U.S. Senate Banking Committee by federal financial regulators, includes interest rate and foreign exchange swaps omitted from the smaller estimate.

9. As part of its effort to stave off collapse, Manufacturers Hanover Trust sold CIT to Dai-Ichi Kangyo Bank in 1989. Heller Financial and its parent company, Heller International Corp., are wholly owned subsidiaries of Fuji Bank.

10. First Nationwide's expansion has been financed in part by taxpayers. According to Resolution Trust Corporation estimates, the Federal Home Loan Bank Board committed $4 billion in promissory notes, capital loss and yield maintenance agreements, and other

payments when it transferred four thrifts with $8.6 billion in combined assets to First Nationwide in December 1988 (RTC, 1990).

11. According to GE, "Virtually all products financed by GE Capital are manufactured by companies other than GE" (GEC, 1990, p. 65). In fact, the parent company makes direct loans to purchasers of its aircraft engines and finances those loans with borrowings in the commercial paper market that are separate from those of its finance subsidiaries. At the same time, GECC lends to the commercial airline industry, indirectly supporting the parent's commercial and manufacturing activities.

12. In 1990, finance companies began to feel the impact of the imposition of capital adequacy requirements on commercial banks in both the cost and availability of bank credit lines and the number of banks willing to provide backup lines for finance companies' commercial paper (Kramer and Neihengen, 1991, p. 55).

13. HLTs are loans for leveraged corporate restructuring, management buy-outs, and recapitalizations.

14. NBC lobbied vigorously to remove barriers prohibiting cross-ownership of cable systems and television networks. Those efforts paid off when, on June 18, 1992, the Federal Communications Commission eliminated the ban. As a result, NBC is now positioned to acquire some of the cable companies financed by GECC. The implications may be troubling, according to accounts of GE's interventions in NBC's journalistic practices. Ben H. Bagdikian (1992, p. 51) writes that "Lawrence Grossman, former head of NBC News, revealed recently that following the stock market crash of 1987, Jack Welch, CEO of NBC's owner, General Electric, called to say that he did not want the network's newscasts to use language that might depress GE stock."

15. According to year-end 1991 data reported in the Thomson Bank Directory, Thomson Savings Directory, Best's Insurance Reports, and Household Financial Corporation's annual report, the aggregate equity capital and paid-in surplus of Household International's four main subsidiaries totaled $2.64 billion. The parent company's annual report disclosed consolidated capital of $2.03 billion.

16. Elliehausen and Wolken (1990) confirm the local nature of lending markets for small business and the continuing relevance of the "cluster of banking services" in measuring competition levels in those markets. Dunham (1986) points out the dilemma of middle-market borrowers that depend on an already small universe of lending institutions and lack access to national capital markets. The Southern Finance Project (1991) found that, as a result of the huge BankAmerica–Security Pacific merger, nearly two-thirds of all primary banking relationships with middle-market firms in the Puget Sound area would be controlled by a single lender. Hannan (1991) reviews the concentration price relationship.

17. In a September 1991 NBC/Wall Street Journal poll, 51 percent of all respondents said banking regulation was too lax; 52 percent felt the same way about insurance industry regulation. Only a small percentage thought regulation was "too strict" (6 percent for banks, 9 percent for insurers) (Hart and Teeter, 1991, pp. 26–29). In 1991, only 15 percent of the respondents to the Gallup Organization's 1991 Consumer Survey for American Banker said they had "a great deal of confidence in the safety and security of the U.S. banking and financial system." For the first time in Gallup's polling for American Banker, more people said they had "little or no confidence" in the system than said they had "a great deal of confidence." The results of Gallup's 1992 survey were virtually unchanged from the previous year (American Banker, 1991 and 1992 surveys).

18. For additional discussion, see Wolfson (1986, pp. 79–80).

19. Sponsored by the bipartisan leadership of the U.S. House of Representatives Committee on Energy and Commerce, the Securities Regulatory Equality Act addresses such issues as independent directors and borrowing from affiliated banks.

20. This would require reporting by zip code and three- or four- digit SIC code.

Bibliography

American Banker. "1991 Consumer Survey," 1991a.

American Banker. "Top Finance Companies in the U.S." December 11, 1991b, p. 8.

American Banker. "1992 Consumer Survey," 1992.

American Express Credit Corporation Annual Report. Wilmington, DE: American Express Company, 1991.

American General Finance Corporation Annual Report. Evansville, IN: American General Corporation, 1991.

Associates First Capital Corporation Annual Report. Dallas: Associates First Capital Corporation, 1991.

Bagdikian, Ben H. "Journalism of Joy." *Mother Jones,* May-June 1992, pp. 48–51.

Beneficial Corporation Annual Report. Wilmington, DE: Beneficial Corporation, 1991.

Chrysler Financial Corporation Annual Report. Southfield, MI: Chrysler Corporation, 1991.

Commerce Clearing House. "Consumer Credit Guide," July 18, 1991, pp. 1083–98.

Commercial Credit Corporation Annual Report. Baltimore: Commercial Credit Corporation, 1991.

D'Arista, Jane. *The Evolution of U.S. Finance, Vol. II: Restructuring Institutions and Markets.* Armonk, NY: M. E. Sharpe, Inc., forthcoming 1993.

Dunham, Constance. "Regional Banking Competition." *New England Economic Review,* July-August 1986, pp. 3–19.

Elliehausen, Gregory and John Wolken. "Banking Markets and the Use of Financial Services by Small and Medium-Sized Companies." Federal Reserve Board Staff Study. Washington, DC: Federal Reserve Board, September 1990.

Federal Reserve System. *Annual Statistical Digest: 1980–1989.* Washington, DC: Federal Reserve Board, 1991.

Federal Reserve System. *Federal Reserve Bulletin.* Table 1.25, Flow of Funds. Washington, DC: Federal Reserve Board, various dates.

Federal Reserve System. *Flow of Funds Accounts: Flows and Outstandings, Second Quarter 1992.* Washington, DC: Federal Reserve Board, September 28, 1992.

Ford Motor Credit Corporation Annual Report. Dearborn, MI: Ford Motor Company, 1991.

Frydl, Edward J. "Overhangs and Hangovers: Coping with the Imbalances of the 1980s." *Federal Reserve Bank of New York Annual Report* 1991. New York: Federal Reserve Bank of New York, 1991.

General Electric Credit Corporation Annual Report. Stamford, CT: General Electric Corporation, 1991.

General Motors Acceptance Corporation Annual Report. Detroit, MI: General Motors Corporation, 1991.

Hannan, Timothy. "Bank Commercial Loan Markets and the Role of Market Structure." *Journal of Banking and Finance,* No. 15, 1991, pp. 133–49.

Hart, Peter and Robert Teeter. "Poll on Bank and Insurance Industries." NBC/WSJ Poll, September 20–24, 1991, pp. 22–29.

Household Financial Corporation Annual Report. Prospect Heights, IL: Household Financial Corporation, 1991.

International Business Machines Credit Corporation Annual Report. Stamford, CT: International Business Machines Corporation, 1991.

International Telephone & Telegraph Credit Corporation Annual Report. St. Louis: International Telephone & Telegraph Incorporated, 1991.

John Deere Capital Corporation Annual Report. Reno, NV: John Deere Corporation, 1991.

Kramer, Mark C. and Raymond M. Neihengen Jr. "Analysis of Finance Company Ratios in 1990." *Journal of Commercial Bank Lending*, September 1991, pp. 54–61.

McCauley, Robert H. and Rama Seth. "Foreign Bank Credit to U.S. Corporations: The Implications of Offshore Loans." *Quarterly Review*, Federal Reserve Bank of New York, Spring 1992, pp. 52–65.

Moody's Banks and Finance Manual, Vol. 2, 1990; Vol. 2, 1991; Vol. 2, 1992.

Noonan, Jean, Kathleen Buffon, and John Le Fevre. "Federal Trade Commission Developments in Consumer Financial Services." *Business Lawyer*, May 1991, pp. 1093–97.

Quint, Michael. "Lending When Bankers Won't." *New York Times*, October 7, 1991, p. C1.

Resolution Trust Corporation. *Report to the Oversight Board of the RTC and the Congress on the 1988/1989 FSLIC Assistance Agreements.* Washington, DC: U.S. Government Printing Office, September 1990.

Sears Roebuck Acceptance Corporation Annual Report. Wilmington, DE: Sears Roebuck Corporation, 1991.

Sellon, Gordon H. "Changes in Financial Intermediation: the Role of Pension Funds and Mutual Funds." *Economic Review*, Federal Reserve Bank of Kansas City, 1992, pp. 53–70.

SNL Securities. *The Directory of Financial Services Companies: 1992.* Charlottesville, VA: SNL Securities, 1992.

Southern Finance Project. "The Bigger They Come." Charlotte, NC: Southern Finance Project, September 1991.

TransAmerica Finance Group Annual Report. Los Angeles: TransAmerica Corporation, 1991.

U.S. Congress, House Committee on Energy and Commerce, Subcommittee on Telecommunications, Consumer Protection and Finance. *Restructuring Financial Markets: The Major Policy Issues.* Washington, DC: U.S. Government Printing Office, 1986.

The Wall Street Journal. "In-House Lenders," October 8, 1991, p. A1.

Westinghouse Credit Corporation Annual Report. Pittsburgh: Westinghouse Corporation, 1991.

Wolfson, Martin H. *Financial Crises: Understanding the Postwar U.S. Experience.* Armonk, NY: M. E. Sharpe, Inc., 1986.

Zuckerman, Sam. "As Washington Dithers, Nonbanks Advance." *American Banker*, March 15, 1991, p. 6.

CHAPTER EIGHT

No More Bank Bailouts: A Proposal for Deposit Insurance Reform[1]

Jane W. D'Arista

CHAPTER SUMMARY

By the end of the 1980s, it had become apparent that the U.S. government's role as a financial guarantor posed an unprecedented threat to the taxpayer. President George Bush's 1991 budget proposal acknowledged that *all* deposits held in U.S. banks, thrifts, and credit unions—approximately $3 trillion—are a contingent liability of the federal government. With this admission, the Administration registered both its concern about the escalating costs of financial failures and its ignorance about how to stop the rising numbers of bailouts.[2] According to the U.S. General Accounting Office (GAO), taxpayer exposure may be as high as $5 trillion if other financial guarantee and credit programs are taken into account.[3]

Financial guarantee programs were originally designed to pay off depositors of failed institutions. But in the 1980s, they took on a different function: financing the buy-out of failed or failing banks. Mixing these two functions vastly escalated the government's potential liability.

This chapter proposes a new system for providing financial guarantees—one that both insures individual savers and protects the capacity of financial institutions to support the transactions essential for economic stability and growth. A new system is needed for the obvious reason that the size of the government's liability has gotten out of hand; whatever gains may accrue to individuals in their role as savers may well be lost when they are required, as taxpayers, to foot the bill. But there are other reasons as well: to separate the different purposes that government guarantees serve in protecting consumers/savers, communities, and the economy as a whole; to ensure that financial guarantees enhance, rather than impede, the role of the financial system in promoting economic growth; and to clear the way for revitalizing the government's function as a guarantor and regulator in a new and different financial environment.

In the case of financial guarantee programs intended to protect savings, this chapter argues that coverage should be based on the aggregate holdings of individual savers rather than on individual accounts or institutions. Individuals would be protected from loss of a set amount, independent of whether their assets are confined to one institution or spread throughout a variety of accounts in federally regulated institutions: bank, thrift, or credit union deposits; mutual funds; or pension plans governed by the Employee Retirement Income Security Act (ERISA).

Providing equal coverage for different types of savings instruments held in federally regulated institutions means that all institutions must be regulated with equal attention to soundness and stability. That will require a corollary agenda for reform—an overhaul of the regulatory framework that revitalizes the tools of regulation to reflect current needs and practices.

In the case of protecting the funds needed for current transactions (e.g., payrolls, purchases, bills, and other payments that support ongoing economic activity), this chapter argues that limiting insurance for these accounts is unrealistic. For example, if even the smallest institution fails, the current $100,000 in coverage will not ensure that local payrolls are met. The subsequent interruption in payments down the line will result in a widening circle of losses.

Thus, all transactions accounts must be 100 percent insured. Insured transactions balances must be held in the form of non-interest-bearing demand deposits, in a federally regulated depository institution, and invested in a portfolio of loans and liquid assets that meets accepted standards of diversification in terms of economic sectors and maturity. Depository institutions will be allowed to deduct a reasonable amount from earnings on their investments for profits and to cover the cost of reserves that are held in the Federal Reserve banks. The remainder—the interest forgone by depositors—will be paid into the insurance fund.

To make the case for this new approach to federal financial guarantee programs, this chapter first outlines the history and purposes of financial guarantees and describes the structural changes that have undermined a system that worked so well in the past. It then presents detailed proposals for reforming federal insurance of savings and transactions deposits.

An Overview of Federal Financial Guarantee Programs

Federal deposit insurance for commercial banks and thrift institutions was authorized in the 1930s after decades of debate and experimentation in state programs. The success of these federal insurance programs in restoring confidence in depository institutions after the wave of bank failures in the early years of the Depression was seen by economists, including Milton Friedman and Anna Schwartz, as the "most important structural change in the banking system" and a fundamental contribution to U.S. monetary and financial stability (1963, p. 434). The growing perception of deposit insurance as a cornerstone of financial stability and its record in providing protection at minimal cost led to the creation, in 1970, of insurance funds for securities firms, credit unions, and, in 1974, pension funds.

Meanwhile, some states also administered funds that insured the depository institutions they chartered. In the period between 1969 and 1972, most states set up guarantee funds for the insurance industry, which is the only segment of the financial services industry that is regulated solely by states. All these guarantee funds were introduced for the same purpose as federal programs: to protect customers and to provide liquidity in the event of failures.

The deposit insurance funds for commercial banks, thrifts, and credit unions insure individual deposits up to $100,000. They generate income by charging insured institutions premiums based on their total domestic deposits and from interest received by investing these premiums in U.S. government securities. Federal deposit insurance funds have always had the authority to borrow from the U.S. Treasury, and that authority was significantly expanded in 1989.[4]

The deposit insurance funds were originally intended for use in paying off depositors of failed insured institutions. In 1935, they were granted additional authority to undertake preventive actions, and the form of assistance gradually changed. Since 1960, the funds have been used more often to lend to presumably stronger institutions for the purpose of acquiring banks that are failing or about to fail. Such operations are known as "supervisory mergers" or "purchase and assumption" transactions.

Unlike the deposit insurance agencies, the Securities Investor Protection Corporation (SIPC) is not a government agency. It is a private membership corporation whose members are securities brokers who handle cash and securities of U.S. resident customers. Its authority is more limited than is that of the deposit insurance funds in that its reserves cannot be used to assist mergers or to make loans to troubled broker-dealers; the reserves can be used only to pay off customers in the event of insolvency. Moreover, SIPC protection extends only to the return of cash and securities to the customers of the failed firm, not to market losses affecting the value of the securities.[5]

The Pension Benefit Guaranty Corporation (PBGC) was established under the ERISA of 1974, to insure basic benefits in cases where pension plans terminate without adequate funds to pay vested beneficiaries. The PBGC is government owned and covers all qualified private-sector plans with benefits defined and guaranteed by the employer. Defined contribution plans—those that are constituted by contributions from both the employee and the employer, that are not guaranteed by the employer, and that do not specify the ultimate amount of benefits—are not covered. The PBGC is financed primarily by premiums paid by covered plans, but it also derives income from selling the assets of terminated plans, from investment income, and from charges levied on employers who terminate plans. It, too, is authorized to borrow (up to $100 million) from the U.S. Treasury.

In the mid-1980s, the PBGC was the guarantor for the pension benefits of approximately 38 million American workers who were covered by more than 112,000 plans. It was faced by a gap of liabilities over assets of more than $1.3

billion. Despite increases in premiums, the PBGC's negative net worth rose to $1.8 billion in September 1990. At that time, its cash flow was positive and funds were adequate to meet current obligations. But the PBGC's exposure to possible losses from underfunded plans of financially troubled employers totaled $8 billion, or about 10 times its annual premium income (*The Wall Street Journal*, 1991, p. 2).

Another segment of the public's savings—that held by insurance companies—is also protected by guarantee funds administered by individual states. In most states, surviving companies are charged premiums to pay for claims against insurers that have been declared insolvent. Because there is no preexisting pool on which to draw, policyholders and annuitants face uncertainty and lengthy delays before receiving benefits. Although no retirement benefits were lost in the 1983 collapse of Baldwin-United, the GAO has warned that benefits may not now be secure for the 3–4 million retirees with insurance annuities. The recent insolvency of Executive Life increased awareness of both the fragility of the industry and the limited resources available to prevent losses to customers (U.S. GAO, 1991).[6]

The growing number of individuals whose retirement funds are invested in annuities and guaranteed investment contracts sold by insurance companies and the immense growth in mutual funds over the past two decades make it clear that the original rationale for differences in the various systems of protection has eroded. If the objective is still to protect small savers, the focus on depository institutions is misplaced. The bulk of the funds of small savers are held in tax-deferred retirement plans and invested in or by institutions—banks, mutual funds, and insurance companies—across the whole spectrum of the financial services industry. Moreover, if the intention to "protect communities, states or the Nation against the economic consequences of bank failure"[7] remains valid, then the focus on deposit insurance for small savers as the primary federal program for providing protection is also misplaced.

The exclusion of securities and insurance companies from the original proposals for federal financial guarantee insurance programs is not surprising. In the 1930s, the savings and transactions accounts of households and small businesses were held primarily in banks. As the cycle of business failures and bank closures gained momentum, the public lost confidence in banks and withdrew deposits. At that point, the failure of banks was itself the cause of economic dislocation. Losses of demand deposits were more immediately disruptive than losses of savings. The inability of individuals and businesses to meet payment schedules—salaries, rent, supplies, and the like—slowed or even halted economic activity in many regions of the country. Hence, the emphasis was placed on insuring the institutions themselves rather than the customers.

In the six decades that have followed the enactment of deposit insurance, changes in the financial system have altered the ways in which savings are channeled into investments. As noted, the majority of small savings are now managed by private pension plans, and another sizable portion—the savings of public school teachers, policemen, firemen, and other state and local government workers—are held in state and local pension plans that are not federally insured.[8]

Insurance companies also have become more directly involved with consumers over the years as life, health, disability, homeowner, and automobile insurance have become increasingly indispensable for the financial security of households. Securities firms, too, have become more involved in managing the savings of households, competing successfully with banks and insurance companies to manage pension funds and individual retirement accounts (IRAs). And mutual funds now manage a significant portion of the nation's transactions balances held in money market funds. Thus, insurance companies and securities firms meet more of the financial needs of American families now than in the past, and they reach as broad a spectrum of savers and investors as depository institutions.

The average American family views its expanded and rechanneled use of financial services as essential to its economic stability. The proliferation of financial guarantee programs reflects this public perception. The result has been a dramatic escalation in federal (and state) liability for financial guarantee programs. As former Securities and Exchange Commission (SEC) Commissioner Bevis Longstreth observed, it has become more difficult to "draw the circle" around those financial transactions and assets that should be protected to achieve the original objectives of the various financial guarantee programs (U.S. Congress, 1983). It has also become increasingly clear that these various programs cannot cope with the mounting problems in the financial system. The pools of guarantee funds are too small and the burden of higher premiums on institutions struggling for survival is too great. And if these programs cannot cope with the current situation, they will be counterproductive. Existing guarantee programs will undermine, not promote, stability and confidence in the financial system.

Recent Proposals for Reform

It is ironic that many who have been eager to restructure the U.S. financial system in truly radical ways—by allowing the formation of multifunctional financial conglomerates that include depository institutions and by permitting them to be owned by commercial and industrial firms—have been unwilling to confront the implications of the unknown level of risk posed by the government's huge credit and financial guarantee programs. The Bush administration's proposal for modernizing the financial system dealt with the issue of financial guarantees in ways that were both narrow and conventional.[9] It focused only on depository institutions, ignoring the role of pension funds in channeling savings. The amount of coverage proposed failed to distinguish between the differences in protection needed for transactions balances as opposed to savings vehicles. Further, it would have perpetuated the system of insuring institutions instead of individuals and thus encouraged continuing, costly government intervention to prevent the failure of large banks.

The main thrust of the Bush administration's proposal was to end the institutional segmentation that, even now, functions to moderate the spread of problems from one financial sector to another. In encouraging the proliferation of financial conglomerates without a coherent program for reforming the financial guarantee system, the proposal appeared to advocate ever-freer financial markets with ever-growing government protection and liability. The rationale for marrying such contradictory notions was expediency—finding a quick source of new capital for banks and enhancing banks' ability to compete with other financial service providers in national and global markets.

Concern about the adequacy of banks' capital arose in large part because the banking sector, along with other components of the financial system, has been expanding steadily into the business of offering financial guarantees. New and innovative concepts, based on such traditional instruments as letters of credit and acceptances, had swollen the off-balance-sheet liabilities of banks to levels that finally persuaded regulators to take steps to limit their growth. Capital adequacy standards will eventually cover contingent liabilities and require capital backing for these guarantees. But in the meantime, banks' guarantees to their customers (for a fee) that bank credit will be forthcoming, if other credit sources dry up, and their guarantees that direct investors will be paid if borrowers default could lead to still more bank failures and increase the likelihood of a systemic crisis. And if a systemic crisis should occur, the intertwining of private and public financial guarantees would undercut the government's ability to halt the slide.

The Bush administration's proposal and others like it also failed because they did not recognize that financial crises and the diminishing role of banks are due to macroeconomic policy more than to excessive (or insufficient) regulation or institutional segmentation. Rampaging inflation in the 1970s ravaged the stock and bond markets but opened the way for the creation of money market mutual funds by securities firms. These funds, in turn, grew rapidly at the expense of the banking sector's deposit base.

Confronted by unstable economic and financial conditions, U.S. financial institutions necessarily engaged in a quest for new markets to stabilize profits. In particular, the largest U.S. banks expanded abroad. But their success in the global arena was undercut by domestic economic mismanagement.

U.S. banks dominated the ranks of the largest banks worldwide when the United States was the world's largest creditor nation. But when the United States became the largest debtor, its banks were necessarily at a disadvantage compared with those in creditor nations. A low U.S. saving rate coupled with budget and trade deficits left U.S. banks without surplus funds to channel into markets at home and abroad, unlike their more successful foreign competitors. And the falling dollar, which improved the trade balance, added to U.S. banks' competitiveness woes by lowering banks' asset and capital values relative to those of banks in countries with strong currencies, thus making it even harder to attract capital.

The remedies prescribed in the proposals of the Bush administration and of others—more powers and products for banks, infusions of capital from nontraditional sources, and regulatory relaxations—were further manifestations of the focus on protecting international capital. Lost in this perspective was concern for what could happen to more vulnerable participants in the financial system—in particular, community banks and their customers—and to the average taxpayer, who remained liable for excessive losses. Moreover, these prescriptions would not have overcome the major competitive disadvantages faced by the larger banks. Putting U.S. banks on a level playing field with their foreign competitors will require putting the U.S. economy on a managerial par with other developed economies.

More important, failure to address our macroeconomic problems will further weaken the U.S. financial system as a whole. No system—whatever its institutional and regulatory structure—can remain sound and protect its customers by promoting growth while operating in an unstable macroeconomic environment. Thus, the thrust of recent proposals for institutional and regulatory restructuring is more likely to perpetuate instability than to address the narrow issue of banks' competitiveness on which they have been focused.

In general, most reforms that have been proposed, enacted, or implemented by regulators have given priority to higher capital standards, linking banks' deposit insurance premiums and their ability to expand to their capital-to-asset ratios. As one observer has noted, emphasizing the primacy of capital for soundness could lead to the neglect of equally important measures such as asset quality, management ability, liquidity, and earnings stability (Friessen, 1991, p. 13A). Moreover, higher capital standards offer little protection if institutions fail to diversify assets.

In the case of banks, satisfying diversification requirements has meant limiting loans to a single borrower in relation to capital. The inadequacy of this standard was used to support proposals for interstate branching that would, presumably, improve diversification by preventing the concentration of a depository institution's loans in a limited geographic region (U.S. Department of the Treasury, 1991, pp. 49–50; Woodward, 1990, p. 15). Although experience shows that economic weakness can be concentrated in specific regions while others are unaffected, this was not the only kind of weakness that plagued the banking system in recent years.

Concern for diversification has not yet included the problems that emerge because of sectoral concentrations outside the context of geography. While many small banks failed in the farm belt, many large banks—some with worldwide branch networks—were weakened by overlending to specific types of borrowers: real estate investment companies, operators of tankers, and less developed countries in the 1970s and commercial real estate developers, borrowers for highly leveraged corporate acquisitions, and leveraged management buyouts in the

1980s. When the ratio of a bank's loans to one sector or type of borrower rises significantly relative to total loans, concentrations develop that are as detrimental to soundness as are more traditional violations of diversification standards. Guidelines must be revised to prevent sectoral concentration and to improve the ways in which diversification requirements are applied and implemented in the context of the current financial and economic environment.

The escalating failures of depository institutions generated attempts to find the equivalent of a magic bullet—a single strategy, such as capital standards or the "safe" bank—that would inoculate the system against unsoundness. Such narrow approaches ignore the extensive body of law and regulation governing the financial system, the wealth of strategies it contains to implement the many different objectives of financial regulation, and the continued validity of its unifying theme: recognition of the special nature of the financial system and its role in transforming financial capital into economic activity and growth.[10] Regulatory strategies designed to prevent institutional concentrations and conflicts of interest (and to ensure access to credit) were bypassed as the trend toward deregulation gained momentum in the wake of financial instability. But the link between soundness regulation and protection is such that the regulatory issues cannot be ignored in any proposal for reforming the mechanisms for protection. The need for new strategies is imperative.

Reforming deposit insurance or, as this chapter argues, the financial guarantee system as a whole will not solve the basic problems of instability that confront the financial system. But such reform is a needed response to the proliferating costs that accompany instability. No one argues that reform is not needed. In fact, the public debate about deposit insurance reform has reflected the necessary sense of urgency. But most proposals for changing the system of deposit insurance have failed to come to grips with the real scope of the problems that must be addressed; many could actually exacerbate the problems they were intended to solve.

Meanwhile, the Federal Deposit Insurance Corporation's (FDIC's) administrative response to the mounting crisis—raising insurance premium assessments—can be characterized as too little too late. Despite losses amounting to 70 percent of gross assessments in 1981–82—compared with losses averaging 9 percent of assessments in the period 1934–1980—the FDIC failed to raise premiums until rising bank failures and declining insurance reserves reached levels that threatened confidence in the insurance fund. In 1984, even as the list of problem banks rose to more than 800 institutions, the FDIC continued to rebate that portion of assessments not used to cover expenses and relied primarily on earnings from investments for reserve growth (U.S. Congress, 1986, pp. 345, 352).[11] Rebating assessments during periods of earnings growth and raising premiums during periods of difficulty have a procyclical effect, putting additional pressure on banks during a period of economic weakness and declining profits. Moreover, the sharp increase in premiums from 12 cents to 19.5 cents per $100 of deposits in January 1991, and then again to 23 cents in midyear 1992, fell most heavily on community and regional banks without access to noninsured foreign deposits. Thus, they posed a greater threat to insured consumer deposits while lowering the relative cost of large Eurodollar deposits. The growing perception that higher premiums could prove counterproductive, and the shift toward making premiums "risk based," may limit further overall premium increases.

Pressure for higher U.S. capital standards began in the early 1980s;[12] the need for uniform capital adequacy standards has been recognized by all the major industrial countries. This is a constructive response, widely advocated by academics, regulators, and members of Congress, that cushions the effects of losses and reduces the insurance coverage needed to protect depositors.[13] But this reform has been difficult to implement in a period of economic weakness and is unlikely to add significant protection for depositors in the near term.[14]

Also unlikely to add near-term protection for depositors are several other recent steps to prevent catastrophic bank losses—the FDIC's adoption of variable insurance premiums based on capital-to-asset ratios, and the 1991 banking law's requirement that there be prompt regulatory intervention into institutions threatened with bankruptcy. These are constructive proposals if the current system of insuring institutions remains unchanged. But these steps could and should have been implemented earlier to be effective as preventive measures.

It is beyond the scope of this chapter to enumerate and critique all the mechanisms associated with reform proposals that would continue to insure depository institutions.[15] Moreover, most witnesses before congressional committees and most members of Congress tended to favor more than one proposed mechanism (Riegle, 1990, footnote 14, S13826). Few of the current proposals have attempted to sort out the differences in protection needed for savings and for transactions accounts. One that has—Robert Litan's 1986 proposal for a "safe" or "narrow" bank that is required to invest all deposits in U.S. Treasury obligations (1987, pp. 164–89)—points up the limitations of attempts to perpetuate a system of insuring institutions. The Litan proposal ignores one of the key functions of a private banking system: intermediation. The objective of a system that moves private savings into productive private investment is to enhance economic activity both in the local community, as underscored by the Community Reinvestment Act, and in the nation as a whole. The opportunity to invest individual savings in government securities already exists. It can be done directly by buying marketable bonds or savings bonds or by investing in a government bond mutual fund. If there is a need to expand these opportunities—to provide that demand as well as savings deposits be invested in government securities—it might be better to propose the reestablishment of a postal savings system than to divert commercial banks from more useful purposes in supplying the credit needs of households, businesses, and communities.

Overall, the irrelevance of most recent proposals for reform is the outcome of a failure both to identify appropriate goals for financial guarantee programs in the current financial and economic environment and to evaluate the effectiveness of existing programs. The conceptual poverty of these proposals is implicit in their thrust—to shore up and perpetuate current mechanisms.

The Need to Reframe Reform Proposals

The savings and loan (S&L) crisis tended to focus reform efforts on protecting savings and minimizing government (i.e., taxpayer) liability. The heretofore vague and seemingly contingent relationship between the protected saver and the liable taxpayer has been made clear. Certainly minimizing the taxpayer's liability is a worthy objective but, in reality—across the entire spectrum of financial guarantees for pensions, annuities, and savings deposits—the saver and the taxpayer are one and the same. However, sorting out the fairness in paying the bill does require shaping the system to better fit the needs and appropriate responsibilities of individuals.

Constructing a system that will minimize taxpayer liability in the context of current and future financial and economic instability—the likely context for at least the first half of the 1990s—requires shifting insurance coverage and its cost from institutions to individuals. Posing a choice as to who pays the premiums for deposit insurance clarifies the issue of who gets protection. If the financial institution pays the premium, it is insured. It is the client of the insurance agency, and its depositors are relegated to the role of nominal beneficiaries. This has tended to encourage a save-the-institution mentality on the part of the insurance agency and its congressional watchdogs. Of course, depositors too are protected in this process. But only up to a point—the point at which the losses of institutions exceed the pool of funds their premiums have created. At that point, the depositors lose—*because the benefit of their protection will be taxed away*.

The system of insuring institutions has led to distortions in regulatory emphasis as well. Regulatory objectives have tended to move in the direction of fostering institutional profitability. Profitability is certainly an important measure of the soundness of institutions and, in the normal course of events, constitutes an additional umbrella of protection for depositors. But insuring institutions in periods of financial and economic instability or weakness means that institutional profitability is the only assurance of protection, short of the taxpayer, because profitability determines the viability of the insurance fund itself. Insuring institutions gives priority to the entrepreneurial activities of depository institutions in pursuit of profits at the expense of their prudential obligations. And the depositor has been assumed to have primarily entrepreneurial objectives as well—to be more concerned with interest earnings than with the safety of principal or the possible consequences of failure for tax liability.

The search for stable profits in an unstable financial and economic environment necessarily requires an unending game of innovation. Financial institutions and their regulators have focused on guessing what new products, powers, or markets are most likely to ensure continued profitability. The problem is that financial innovation, whatever else it has done, has made no positive contributions to economic stability and may have had negative effects. In any event, innovation is no guarantee of profitability for financial institutions in the face of economic weakness.

Finally, the system of insuring depository institutions rather than their depositors does not work anymore. It has already broken down in the case of the S&L crisis and has resulted in a level of costs that will retard economic growth for years to come. The enormity of this outcome is only now beginning to be recognized. As recognition develops, the weaknesses of proposals that tinker at the margins of the current system will become clearer and the search for more radical solutions will intensify.

It is in that context that the following alternative proposals are offered. They propose a different option—insuring individual savers and the transactions balances of businesses and other economic sectors rather than institutions—and attempt to sketch out how such a system might work. The overall objectives of these two proposals are to provide sufficient protection for the saver/taxpayer at a known and affordable cost, to avert the economic dislocation that results when banks fail, and to preserve the role of depository institutions in financial intermediation. These proposals will not solve all the problems confronting the financial system, but they provide a more realistic framework for dealing with those problems than do the proposals they replace.

An Alternative Proposal for Protecting Savings

Constructing a fair and rational system for protecting savings in the 1990s would include the following key elements as described.

• All individuals and households would be required to purchase financial guarantee insurance to cover savings up to a given amount. They would do this by accepting a lower rate of interest on insured assets than could be earned on uninsured assets. The lower rate would reflect the deduction for the insurance premium. A compulsory system is necessary to ensure that all savers are covered, that reserves are adequate, and that liability for losses is fairly distributed.

• Covered assets could be held in a variety of accounts in federally regulated institutions: bank, thrift, or credit union deposits; mutual funds; or pension plans governed by ERISA. A financial guarantee program must focus on all channels for savings if it is to offer adequate protection for the average saver whose primary savings are deferred income that may be invested in pools or other vehicles chosen by employers.

• Premiums would be collected from the interest or gains on covered savings assets, offset by a full tax deduction. The amount of the premium would be deducted by the institution and paid directly into the insurance fund before the accrued interest or gains are credited to the saver's account. Statements on premiums paid would be added to reports on earnings and filed with the individual's tax form as a deductible item. A compulsory system involving individuals will work only if paying premiums is relatively automatic and painless; that is, if it does not involve earned income.

• The amount of savings in the various accounts of individuals will be reported to the Internal Revenue Service by financial institutions, and records of aggregate savings of individuals and households will be maintained by the insurance fund. This requires modifying the current reporting system to include all principal amounts in addition to interest income and the fair market value of IRA accounts that are currently reported for individual Social Security numbers.

• Although financial institutions would be exempted from paying premiums, they also would lose their special tax status, including tax deductions on loan loss reserves in the case of depository institutions. A neutral tax system for financial institutions will ensure that they share equally with individuals and households in any tax increases needed to offset losses by the insurance fund and enhance their stake in soundness.

• Strategies for soundness regulation would be revitalized to reflect changes in institutional structure; to reflect the need to regulate all institutions that handle the core savings of individuals and families with equal regard for soundness and stability; and to enhance the efficiency of the financial system in accomplishing the goals of its role as an intermediary between savers and borrowers.

• Insurance reserves would be invested in U.S. government obligations as they are now. Continuing this practice under a regime in which individuals pay premiums clarifies the relationship between the individual's role as saver/taxpayer. Because the assets of the fund are those for which savers/taxpayers are already liable, savers' premiums will reduce their tax liability if failures are contained. If failures exceed acceptable levels and seriously deplete reserves, the impetus for action to address problems will be enhanced by a tax liability that kicks in earlier in the slide.

This basic framework could be elaborated or modified in a number of respects. For example, it could better reflect the needs of savers by doubling the amount of coverage for a given Social Security number if the aggregate accounts were held in the names of two people (husband and wife, parent and child, etc.) or by expanding coverage for households on the basis of the number of dependents. Thus, individuals might be insured up to a maximum of $100,000 and couples up to $200,000; families could be granted an additional $25,000 for each dependent. These figures are arbitrary—coverage could be lower or higher depending on the evolution of information about the value of the average family's total savings—but they suggest the potential for adding flexibility to the framework that would address the needs of individuals and households rather than those of institutions.

Obviously, the savings of individuals and households will grow over time and may exceed the maximum amount covered by insurance. At that point, the effect of limiting coverage will introduce an element of coinsurance for older or more affluent households. This does not detract from the advantages of limiting coverage since all savers will be assured that a basic portion of their funds is safe, while the remainder, exempt from premiums, will earn the higher rate that is the reward for risk. But the amount of coverage should be reviewed at periodic intervals to maintain its adequacy in relation to changes in the rate of inflation. Increased coverage on that basis will automatically increase the flow of premiums into the insurance fund and maintain the needed ratio of reserves to liabilities.

Small savers could be given additional advantages such as a waiver of premium payments on aggregate accounts under $10,000 (again, a hypothetical figure), or on a sliding scale for premiums based on gross income. To emphasize the protection of pension benefits, all pooled savings in either defined benefit or defined contribution plans of individuals over age 50 (hypothetically) with a gross income below a given level could be covered if coverage of other savings accounts were reduced by an appropriate amount. Coverage should be extended to state and local government pension plans. The fact that state and local government pension plans are no less vulnerable to economic weakness than are private plans (as demonstrated in the New York City crisis in the mid-1970s) suggests that including them in a national financial guarantee program would be desirable. Moreover, these funds are very large and cover primary savings for millions of moderate-income Americans whose work is vital to society and the economy.

Proposing that state and local pension plans be covered raises difficult political issues in the context of this proposal's recommendation that covered assets be held in federally regulated institutions or pension plans regulated under ERISA. Combining both recommendations would require either that all pension fund regulation be turned over to the U.S. Department of Labor or that all states be required to adopt ERISA guidelines in administering plans. The latter would appear to be the more feasible solution, and, in fact, many states do follow ERISA guidelines. However, some oversight responsibility by the Department of Labor could be authorized to monitor compliance with the guidelines.

Requiring federal regulation also leaves an obvious and important gap in coverage of assets held by insurance companies. But that is only one reason for advocating that insurance be regulated at the federal level. The major reason is that insurance cmpanies now manage one-third of the nation's pension assets, offer other savings vehicles for small savers, and serve as the primary providers for the nation's health insurance system. Other reasons include differences in the quality of regulation from state to state, the questionable effectiveness of state guarantee funds for this industry, and the fact that the industry is dominated by a number of large companies that operate nationwide and cannot be effectively supervised by individual states.

Finally, questions about the effectiveness of financial regulation must be addressed. This means more than simply rearranging the responsibilities of regulatory agencies. What is required is a thorough reexamination of the objectives and tools of regulation no matter what reforms are undertaken.

Protecting Transactions Balances

Before considering a financial guarantee program that protects funds needed for current transactions, one must accept a fundamental premise: it is unrealistic to limit insurance coverage for accounts that are necessary to sustain economic activity. The current $100,000 limit on coverage is clearly inadequate in the case of employers, whether it be for large or small businesses, farmers, nonprofit organizations, or state and local governments. If payrolls are not met, the interruption of payments down the line will result in a widening circle of losses. In the case of regional or money center banks that have large customers and hold clearing balances for other financial institutions, inadequate coverage of transactions balances can result in even broader repercussions, causing dislocations to any number of communities or even to the nation as a whole.

Because these repercussions are too destructive, the too-big-to-fail approach has become a reality under the current system. But it is a reality that encompasses small as well as large banks, that involves any account, of whatever size, that can precipitate a chain of events that results in economic dislocation. A small community bank that holds the demand deposits of the local hospital is too big to fail because its failure means that all salaries will not be paid, all supplies cannot be purchased, and care cannot be provided for all patients. In this context, the FDIC's inclination to prevent failure and thus cover uninsured deposits may be justified. But the current system fails to take into account the differences in protection needed for savings and transactions balances. Thus the criterion for too big to fail is the size of the institution, not the size or function of the deposit.

A more effective and affordable means for safeguarding transactions balances requires the following key elements as described.

• Coverage must be unlimited. The transactions accounts of General Motors or IBM, like those of the local hospital or municipal government, must be protected regardless of the multimillions of dollars involved. Clearing balances of other financial institutions also must be covered, and unlimited coverage also would extend to individuals.

• Insured transactions balances must be clearly defined as non-interest-bearing demand deposits in federally regulated depository institutions that are payable at par with no limit on the number of withdrawals. Foreign deposits—which are interest-bearing time deposits, not demand deposits—are excluded. Funds held in money market mutual funds or money market funds in depository institutions also are excluded from this form of coverage but would be covered as part of an individual's aggregate savings accounts.

• The interest that depositors forgo will be assumed to be equivalent to the interest on Treasury bills. Depository institutions will be allowed to deduct a reasonable profit from earnings on the loans and other assets in which transactions balances are invested, deduct the cost of holding reserves against these balances with Federal Reserve banks, and pay the remainder of the earnings into the insurance fund at short, periodic intervals.[16] Like the fund for savings, premiums will be invested in U.S. government securities.

• Transactions balances must be invested in a segregated pool of loans and investments that will receive special attention from regulators. These assets must meet accepted standards with respect to liquidity, maturity, and diversification in loans to individual borrowers, and economic sectors, and in loan characteristics. If a depository institution's portfolio meets those standards, it will be permitted to advertise that its transactions balances are insured.

• If the assets held by a depository institution as backing for insured transactions balances fail to meet accepted standards, the institution will be required to set aside loan loss reserves equal to 100 percent of substandard assets within a given time and to write off nonperforming loans against reserves as needed to maintain sufficient earnings on assets to pay insurance premiums. Transferring bad loans from a pool that backs transactions balances into one that backs time deposits will be prohibited.

• In cases in which institutions fail to take the necessary steps to improve the quality of assets or appear unlikely to be able to do so, permission to advertise that transactions accounts are insured will be withdrawn and institutions will be required to advertise that funds deposited in both transactions and savings accounts after a certain date will not be insured. While this will certainly create runs on individual institutions and result in failures, funds will move to other depository institutions that offer insured transactions balances. Thus, a generalized loss of confidence in depository institutions will be avoided by an explicit assurance that institutions that are permitted to accept insured deposits will remain sound.

Two of the elements in this proposal require additional explanation. One is the emphasis on soundness regulation that appears unavoidable given the instability in the current financial and economic environment. The other is the requirement that insured transactions balances in depository institutions be non-interest-bearing. The non-interest-bearing feature has obvious practical value in providing sufficient funds to build up and maintain adequate reserves in the insurance fund. Moreover, it will restore the ability of depository institutions to attract funds at a cost that is significantly below the return on the asset paying the lowest amount of interest in their portfolio (i.e., the Treasury bill) and enable them to pass on lower costs to borrowers. This occurs because unlimited insurance coverage will encourage depositors to hold the funds they need for transactions in banks. But the fact that they are non-interest-bearing will discourage the use of transactions balances as investment assets and thus will limit the insurance fund's aggregate exposure.[17]

The context for this proposal also requires additional emphasis. Transactions balances are a very specialized instrument. Until the 1970s, commercial banks had a monopoly on their issuance and, since 1933, banks have been prohibited from paying interest on demand deposits. The fact that funds could be withdrawn at par whenever the depositor needed them was thought to be a sufficiently attractive feature to warrant withholding interest payments as a way of compensating banks for the risk involved in guaranteeing their return on those conditions. However, as the macroeconomic environment became less stable, resulting in historically high rates of inflation in the 1970s and early 1980s, the old rationale governing the handling of checkable deposits was undermined. The development of money market mutual funds forced banks to offer interest on demand deposits through repurchase agreements and sweep accounts, and the clamor for fairness between large and small customers of banks led to the authorization of limited transactions features for interest-bearing savings accounts in all depository institutions. Even though inflation *per se* offers no justification for interest earnings on short-term balances used for immediate payments, the inflationary environment contributed to a pervasive focus on higher returns that ignored the possibility that a higher return could jeopardize the possibility of getting any return at all.

Unlimited insurance coverage on non-interest-bearing demand deposits will increase the volume of these deposits and reduce banks' cost of funds. This will improve the profitability of banks without the necessity for higher-risk loans. The present $100,000 limit on insurance coverage has encouraged depositors to hold a significant portion of their transactions balances outside depository institutions. At the same time, the cost of the banks' role as intermediaries between depositors and borrowers has risen as a result of the deregulation of interest rates on time deposits and the shift of transactions deposits into interest-bearing accounts. To maintain profitability, banks must translate these higher costs of attracting deposits into higher interest rates on the loans they make, and hence into higher costs for borrowers. As a result, banks have lost prime customers to the commercial paper market, where highly rated commercial firms can now borrow more cheaply. The banks are left with weaker loan portfolios and greater incentives than in the past to make the higher-risk loans that increase profits. And their weaknesses as intermediaries between depositors and borrowers have increased the risk to the payments system.

The risk to the payments system posed by the systemic weakness of depository institutions is a major issue in the debate on reform. The fact is that no other institutions can serve as efficient intermediaries in transferring payments under the current structure for clearing transactions balances. Only depository institutions have access to the clearing arrangements used to transfer payments between third parties. A money market mutual fund can offer the customer only the opportunity to write a check against the fund's account in a bank. Money market mutual funds have access to the payments system only through banks, and they cannot—and are not required to—permit withdrawals of funds at par. Access to the Federal Reserve's discount window might improve their ability to return funds at par, but moving money market mutual funds from a peripheral to a central position in offering transactions balances would require reinventing the banking system so that such funds would function as banks do now.

Recognition of this dilemma is responsible for much of the support for the "safe" bank proposal. But the "safe" bank enhances the soundness of its role in the payments system by abandoning its role as an intermediary between depositors and borrowers. However, both functions are necessary in a system that uses the lending activities of private depository institutions as the fulcrum for money creation. This proposal differs from "safe" bank proposals in that it seeks to preserve a structure in which deposits are invested in private loans that fuel productive investment.

No strategy for protecting customers of financial institutions will succeed if the system fails to function as a dynamic catalyst in promoting economic growth. Financial guarantee programs can bolster confidence and mitigate the effects of financial failures, and soundness regulation can prevent the excesses that result in nonperforming loans and insolvencies. But they are not sufficient to promote growth by themselves. Further proposals for reforming the structure and regulation of the financial system must be forthcoming to ensure that financial institutions perform their economic function. This proposal for reform of financial guarantee programs represents only the first step in that process.

Notes

1. This article is based on an earlier proposal written by the author in *Restructuring Financial Markets: The Major Policy Issues,* a Report from the Chairman of the Subcommittee on Telecommunications, Consumer Protection, and Finance of the U.S. House of Representatives Committee on Energy and Commerce, July 1986. The author thanks Jeff Faux, Eileen Appelbaum, and Michael Mandler for their helpful comments.

2. In February 1991, the Federal Deposit Insurance Corporation (FDIC) announced that it expected 180 banks to fail in 1991 and 160 in 1992. Insurance reserves were expected to fall to $4 billion in 1991 and to $2.4 billion in 1992. These figures were based on the assumption that the recession would end in six months. If that were not the case, bank failures would be higher (230 in 1991, 210 in 1992) and reserves lower (zero in 1991, minus $5 billion in 1992). Based on these estimates, the FDIC raised premiums from 19.5 cents per $100 of deposits (up from 12 cents in January 1991) to 23 cents at midyear 1992 and made plans to borrow $10 billion from the Federal Financing Bank (Rehm, 1991, pp. 1 and 12).

3. Aside from the enormity of this figure, the GAO pointed out that programs have been badly managed, that little (and largely inaccurate) information is available on current losses, and that these programs pose an unknown level of risk (1989, p. 2).

4. Before the enactment of the Financial Institutions Reform, Recovery, and Enforcement Act of 1989 (FIRREA), authority to borrow from the Treasury was limited to $3 billion for the Federal Deposit Insurance Corporation, $750 million for the Federal Savings and Loan Insurance Corporation, and $100 million for the National Credit Union Association. Under FIRREA, administration of the fund for savings institutions was shifted to the FDIC and provisions made for its recapitalization. These provisions in-

cluded payments into the fund, now called the Savings Association Insurance Fund (SAIF), by the Treasury, of amounts sufficient to bring the fund up to $2 billion in each fiscal year during the period 1992–99. The FDIC's limit for direct borrowing from the Treasury for the Bank Insurance Fund (BIF) was raised from $3 billion to $5 billion. In addition, the FDIC was authorized to issue notes or incur obligations backed by the full faith and credit of the United States for either BIF or SAIF up to 90 percent of the fund's gross assets (maintaining net worth equal to 10 percent of gross assets) and also to borrow up to $5 billion more than net worth from other entities (such as the Federal Financing Bank) if it reduces its borrowing from the Treasury.

5. SIPC has no direct authority to borrow from the U.S. Treasury. However, it is subject to oversight by the Securities and Exchange Commission (SEC) and the U.S. Congress, and it has legislative authority to borrow up to $1 billion from the U.S. Treasury through and with the approval of the SEC.

6. Losses in the Executive Life insolvency involved defined contribution pension plans that are not insured by the PBGC.

7. *Deposit Insurance in a Changing Environment,* a study of the current system of deposit insurance pursuant to Section 712 of the Garn–St. Germain Depository Institutions Act of 1982, submitted to the U.S. Congress by the Federal Deposit Insurance Corporation (FDIC, 1983, p. vii).

8. Total holdings in private and public pension plans are approximately $3 trillion. The Pension Benefit Guaranty Corporation's (PBGC) liability—limited to qualified, private, defined benefit plans—was $700 billion at year-end 1988 (U.S. General Accounting Office, 1989, Appendix IV, p. 40). While banks manage about one-third of the assets held by these plans, the assets are generally held in trust, not as bank deposits. Moreover, about one-third of the assets in pension funds are managed by insurance companies.

9. With respect to deposit insurance, the 1991 Treasury bill proposed reducing the "overextended scope of deposit insurance" on multiple insured accounts by limiting individual coverage to $100,000 per institution, with a separate $100,000 coverage for retirement savings held in depository institutions. It also recommended setting a goal for limiting coverage to $100,000 across all depository institutions after the submission of an 18-month FDIC feasibility study. Other recommendations include eliminating pass-through coverage for pension funds, eliminating the coverage of brokered deposits and nondeposit creditors, and limiting coverage of uninsured depositors (U.S. Department of the Treasury, "Conclusions and Recommendations," 1991, p. 16).

10. For a more extensive discussion of these strategies, see U.S. Congress (1986).

11. See also Rehm, 1991.

12. An earlier warning about the need to address the erosion in banks' capital/deposit ratios was given by Donald D. Hester of the University of Wisconsin (1976).

13. G. Thomas Woodward, specialist in macroeconomics at the Congressional Research Service, notes that recommendations "for tough capital standards and quick intervention are nearly universal" (1990, p. 13, footnote 12). Among those testifying before the Senate Committee on Banking, Housing, and Urban Affairs in April, May, June, and July 1990 who supported these recommendations were Kenneth Scott (Stanford University), George Kaufman (Shadow Financial Regulatory Committee), James Barth (Auburn University), and Federal Reserve Board Chairman Alan Greenspan (Woodward, 1990). See also the statement of Senator Donald W. Riegle Jr., chairman, Committee on Banking, Housing, and Urban Affairs, United States Senate, on introducing S. 3103, the Comprehensive Deposit Insurance Reform and Taxpayer Protection Act of 1990, which contains provisions for strengthening capital standards and prompt intervention (Riegle, 1990).

14. Even the commercial and industrial firms that some proposals envision as sources for recapitalizing banks would find it difficult to divert resources for this purpose in a

recession. Raising capital standards for banks above current levels—or even maintaining current standards—could make banks less attractive acquisitions for these companies than other financial firms. Consumer and commercial finance companies are likely to continue to be more attractive as affiliates of commercial and industrial firms because of their lower capital standards and the fact that they are not regulated as financial institutions and not subject to restrictions on intracompany transactions.

15. Among the other reform plans that have been discussed are proposals that would reduce the maximum for deposit insurance coverage below $100,000, drop coverage for interbank deposits, implement a mutual deposit guarantee plan, restrict brokered deposits, develop a reinsurance scheme that would have the FDIC purchase private insurance to reduce its risk and/or improve its ability to assess risk in setting risk-based premiums, and enforce a coinsurance structure that would provide coverage for only a given percentage of deposits.

A useful summary and analysis of these proposals is provided in Woodward (1990), together with a list of witnesses at the April-July 1990 Senate hearings who supported or opposed these or similar proposals. Also see the chapter by Dymski in this volume, which reviews the bank reform debate of recent years.

16. Hyman P. Minsky suggests that banks be allowed to charge fees for handling insured transactions accounts, thus making the function a profit center for banks, as are vendor discounts on credit cards and currency exchanges. By relieving pressure on the interest rate differential needed to cover the costs of information and confidentiality, these fees would help to preserve access to borrowing by smaller, nonpublic companies.

17. Michael Mandler of Harvard University agrees that prohibiting interest payments on transactions balances will limit the insurance fund's aggregate exposure. But, he argues, this may defeat the proposal's objective of expanding coverage beyond $100,000. He believes that the absence of interest will force depositors out of the system, that they will therefore lose the government guarantee, and that this could undermine the goal of providing security for the entire system.

Bibliography

Federal Deposit Insurance Corporation. *Deposit Insurance in a Changing Environment: A Study Submitted to the U.S. Congress.* Washington, DC: U.S. Government Printing Office, 1983.

Friedman, Milton and Anna Jacobson Schwartz. *A Monetary History of the United States 1867–1960.* Princeton, NJ: Princeton University Press, 1963.

Friessen, Connie M. "International Competitive Consequences of Capital Guidelines." *American Banker,* February 26, 1991.

Hester, Donald D. "Opportunity and Responsibility in a Financial Institution." *Financial Institutions and the Nation's Economy,* Book I, Compendium of Papers Prepared for the FINE Study, Committee on Banking, Currency, and Housing, U.S. House of Representatives. Washington, DC: U.S. Government Printing Office, June 1976, pp. 182–89.

Litan, Robert. *What Should Banks Do?* Washington, DC: The Brookings Institution, 1987.

Rehm, Barbara A. "FDIC Plans to Raise Premium to 23 Cents." *American Banker,* February 26, 1991.

Riegle, U.S. Senator Donald W. "Comprehensive Deposit Insurance Reform and Taxpayer Protection Act of 1990." *Congressional Record,* September 26, 1990.

U.S. Congress. House Committee on Banking, Currency, and Housing. *Financial Institutions and the Nation's Economy,* Book I, Compendium of Papers Prepared for the

Committee on Banking, Currency, and Housing. Washington, DC: U.S. Government Printing Office, 1976.

U.S. Congress. House Committee on Energy and Commerce. *FDIC Securities Proposal and Related Issues.* Hearings before the Subcommittee on Telecommunications, Consumer Protection, and Finance of the Committee on Energy and Commerce. Washington, DC: U.S. Government Printing Office, June 16, 1983.

U.S. Congress. House Committee on Energy and Commerce. *Restructuring Financial Markets: The Major Policy Issues.* Report from the Chairman of the Subcommittee on Telecommunications, Consumer Protection, and Finance of the Committee on Energy and Commerce. Washington, DC: U.S. Government Printing Office, 1986.

U.S. Department of the Treasury. *Modernizing the Financial System: Recommendations for Safer, More Competitive Banks.* Washington, DC: U.S. Government Printing Office, 1991.

U.S. General Accounting Office. *Federal Credit and Insurance: Programs May Require Increased Federal Assistance in the Future.* Report to the Chairman of the Subcommittee on Oversight and Investigation of the House Committee on Energy and Commerce. Washington, DC: U.S. Government Printing Office, 1989.

U.S. General Accounting Office. *Private Pensions: Millions of Workers Lose Federal Benefit Protection at Retirement.* Washington, DC: U.S. Government Printing Office, 1991.

Wall Street Journal. "Pension Guarantee Agency Reports a Net Loss for 1990." February 28, 1991, p. 2.

Woodward, G. Thomas. *Deposit Insurance Reform: Evaluating the Proposals.* U.S. Library of Congress, Congressional Research Service Report No. 90–403E. Washington, DC: U.S. Government Printing Office, 1990.

CHAPTER NINE

Banks, Communities, and Public Policy[1]

James T. Campen

CHAPTER SUMMARY

The Community Reinvestment Act (CRA), passed in 1977 in response to a nationwide grass roots movement against bank redlining of low- and moderate-income neighborhoods, formally established banks' "affirmative obligation to help meet the credit needs of the local communities in which they are chartered." Twelve years later, reactivated by mounting evidence that neither banks nor their federal regulators were taking their obligations under the law seriously, a resurgent community reinvestment movement helped to obtain amendments to the CRA—and to its companion, the Home Mortgage Disclosure Act (HMDA)—that required increased public disclosure of information on bank performance.

This increased information has led to greater awareness of the inadequate performance of banks and their regulators. The industry has pursued an aggressive campaign to weaken the CRA and cut back on HMDA reporting requirements. Instead, the new Congress and new Administration should adopt revised policies that strengthen community reinvestment performance standards, enhance regulatory enforcement, and expand disclosure of lending data.

Both banks' performance and public policy proposals should be evaluated in relationship to appropriate public policy goals: (1) ending racial discrimination by banks, (2) guaranteeing the availability of low-cost basic banking services for low-income individuals, (3) ensuring that the credit needs of low-income and minority communities and individuals are served as aggressively and creatively as those of other segments of society, and (4) providing public accountability for both banks and their regulators.

A mounting body of research documents the continuing failure of banks to adequately meet the credit and banking services needs of low-income and minority people and communities. There are disproportionately few mortgage loans for homes located in minority neighborhoods and disproportionately many denials of loan requests from minority applicants. Residents of low-income and minority communities find few banking offices in their own neighborhoods and too few banks anywhere offering affordable basic banking accounts. Small businesses, especially those in inner-city or rural areas and those owned by minorities, have difficulty obtaining adequate credit.

Why have banks done so poorly in this area? The primary reasons include failure to exploit profitable business opportunities in low-income and minority communities, racial discrimination in the provision of credit, ineffective performance by federal bank regulators; removal of legal barriers to geographic expansion and consolidation within the banking industry; and external factors that prevent socially desirable community reinvestment activities from being profitable for individual banks.

Public policy proposals to improve needed flows of credit and financial services to low-income and minority individuals and neighborhoods should include extending community reinvestment obligations to nonbank financial institutions, including government-sponsored enterprises such as Fannie Mae, and establishing community-oriented not-for-profit banks. Nevertheless, there is no substitute for substantially improved performance by banks themselves. At least five types of changes in federal policy toward the banks could help to bring this about:

- enhanced enforcement of laws prohibiting racial discrimination;
- mandated provision of affordable basic banking services;
- improvements in the CRA examination and evaluation process;
- material incentives for improved bank performance;
- increased disclosure of information on CRA-related lending.

Introduction

Popular distrust of banks and government banking policies has been a feature of American life since the founding of the nation. The struggles over the 1791 establishment of the Bank of the United States as our first central bank (culminating in its charter nonrenewal 20 years later) were based on a still-continuing sense that banks tend to serve the wealthy and powerful at the expense of ordinary people, local communities, and small businesses. The past two centuries have witnessed periodic popular (sometimes Populist) movements centered on financial issues (Greider, 1987, ch. 8).

The most recent manifestation of this phenomenon—the community reinvestment movement—originated in the 1970s. It linked urban neighborhood deterioration with the systematic abandonment of these areas by banks and insurance companies (redlining). This grass roots movement was instrumental in the passage of two important pieces of federal legislation: the Home Mortgage Disclosure Act (HMDA) of 1975 and the Community Reinvestment Act (CRA) of 1977. HMDA mandates public disclosure of the geographic location of each bank's mrtgage loans, thus facilitating investigations of whether banks reinvest funds in the communities from which they draw deposits. The CRA established banks' "affirmative obligation to help meet the credit needs of the local communities in which they are chartered" and required federal bank supervisors to assess each bank's "record of meeting the credit needs of its entire community, including low- and moderate-income neighborhoods," especially when considering bank applications to open new branch offices or to merge.[2]

The reinvestment movement has subsequently expanded its range of concern to struggles over how well banks are meeting credit and financial service needs in rural *and* urban low-income and minority communities, locally and nationally. The CRA and HMDA have provided the solid foundation for these struggles: the CRA established the legal requirement that banks respond to community needs; HMDA data have constituted the lion's share of information about actual bank lending practices.[3]

In the late 1980s, a resurgent reinvestment movement, aroused by the failure of banks and regulators to meet their obligations during the decade following enactment of the CRA, won important amendments that strengthened public disclosure under both the CRA (requiring for the first time that performance evaluations for individual banks be made public) and HMDA (requiring disclosure of the race, sex, and income level of mortgage loan applicants, instead of information merely on how many loans were made by census tract).[4]

Because of the existence of the CRA and of HMDA data, community groups in more than 150 cities and rural areas have prevailed on banks to commit to increased lending of at least $7.5 billion in low-income and minority neighborhoods. In addition, major banks facing regulatory review of proposed mergers have announced more than $23 billion of unilateral commitments for such targeted lending (Goldberg, 1992, p. 181).

Nevertheless, 15 years after passage of the CRA, the banking system is still failing to meet the needs of low-income and minority people and communities. The expanded HMDA data for 1990 and 1991 lending decisions, mandated by the 1989 amendments, provided well-publicized evidence of dramatic racial disparities in mortgage rejection rates. In October 1992, a study by the Federal Reserve Bank of Boston provided the first rigorous statistical evidence that racial discrimination by banks was one cause of these lending disparities. Meanwhile, the new requirement for public scrutiny of bank performance evaluations has led bank examiners to give poor ratings for the first time to a significant number of banks. This newly available evidence on mortgage lending disparities and on banks' poor CRA performance, in combination with concern over the costs of the S&L cleanup, commercial bank insolvencies, and deepening poverty and income inequality, has increased public pressure for a more responsive banking system.

The banking industry has responded to this popular pressure with an aggressive attempt to weaken the CRA and to cut back on HMDA reporting requirements. The CRA and HMDA have been portrayed as examples of the burdensome overregulation that has diverted bankers' energies from the business of banking—and meeting credit needs—to government-mandated paperwork tasks. Even though bankers' complaints about implementation of the CRA have some merit, the thrust of their proposals is in precisely the wrong direction.

Indeed, mounting evidence of the extent of banks' inadequate performance in low-income and minority communities indicates that CRA requirements should be strengthened, not eviscerated. Continuing failures by bank regulators to carry out their responsibilities effectively indicate the need for enhanced, not weakened, regulatory oversight. And lack of information about bank performance in areas other than mortgage lending indicates the need for expanded, not reduced, disclosure of lending data.

Policymakers thus face a choice between these two distinct responses to the current system of monitoring and assessing banks' performance in the communities they serve. This chapter presents a case for choosing strengthened community reinvestment performance standards, enhanced regulatory enforcement, and expanded data disclosure. The first section suggests an appropriate set of public policy goals for community reinvestment. The following section surveys the evidence on ways banks have failed to meet the needs of low-income and minority communities. The third section explores the mechanisms that lie behind poor bank performance in this area. The final section, An Agenda for Community Reinvestment Policy, outlines a set of progressive public policy proposals in response to the problems identified.

Objectives for Community Reinvestment Policy

Public policy for community reinvestment should be directed toward four major goals, each of which is discussed below:

 • ending racial discrimination by banks;
 • guaranteeing the availability of low-cost basic banking services for low-income individuals;
 • ensuring that the credit needs of low-income and minority communities and individuals are served as aggressively and creatively as those of other segments of society; and
 • providing public accountability for both banks and their regulators.

The first goal, eliminating racial discrimination in the provision of credit and banking services, is so broadly shared as to be almost uncontroversial. Discrimination against individuals is illegal under the Fair Housing Act (1968) and the Equal Credit Opportunity Act (1974).[5] These fair lending laws, concerned with equal treatment of individuals, are distinct from the CRA itself, whose language emphasizes the credit needs of "low- and moderate-income neighborhoods."

The second goal addresses the importance of providing all citizens with ways to store their money safely, to convert other financial assets into cash conveniently, and to have access to checks as a way of paying bills. Lack of access to basic banking services—such as savings accounts, checking accounts with limited check-writing and ATM transaction provisions, and the ability to cash government checks, with appropriate identification, at any bank—subjects low-income people to the risk and inconvenience associated with using only cash and the unnecessary expense of relying on check-cashing establishments. It also removes the opportunity to develop knowledge and skills needed for full participation in the economic life of the wider society. Federal banking regulators currently encourage, but do not require, banks to make such basic bank accounts available (Canner and Maland, 1987); they consider provision of basic banking services in determining a bank's CRA rating.

The third goal derives from the CRA's injunction that each bank serve "the credit needs of its entire community, including low- and moderate-income neighborhoods, consistent with the safe and sound operation" of the bank. Serving credit needs involves more than simply responding in a fair and nondiscriminatory manner to loan applications received. It requires affirmative and imaginative efforts to determine latent credit needs, to develop appropriate credit products, and to market these products effectively to potential borrowers. Meeting community needs for sustained flows of capital and credit is vitally important if a community is to break the cycle of stagnation and decay.

The fourth and final goal for public policy in the area of community reinvestment promotes the achievement of the other three. It requires the availability of accessible and affordable data about what banks are doing to fulfill their community reinvestment obligations, so that interested parties can evaluate bank performance—and that of the regulatory agencies—in an informed manner and can respond appropriately.

The central goal of meeting community credit needs is often misunderstood in several respects. On one hand, increased credit flows into poor and minority communities are not always a good thing. The type of credit matters as well as the amount; what is especially important is whether borrowers in low-income and minority communities have the opportunity to take on "productive" credit that will allow them to own and maintain homes or to run and expand businesses.

Further, larger credit flows are not beneficial if they involve excessive indebtedness, as when heavy borrowing by some Third World countries has led to harsh austerity programs imposed by the International Monetary Fund. Nor is increased credit desirable if it leads to repayment burdens that cannot be met, as when federally insured home mortgage loans were pushed on underqualified minority families in connection with exploitative campaigns to promote and profit from racial change.[6] Furthermore, larger credit flows into a neighborhood are not beneficial if they are used to finance gentrification, which displaces neighborhood residents by eliminating affordable housing. In short, simply maximizing credit flows into low-income and minority communities is a poorly specified goal, because excessive indebtedness, credit of an inappropriate kind, or loans with overly burdensome terms can be destructive.

On the other hand, the numerous problems facing minority and poor people and communities in this society have multiple causes and deep roots, and it would clearly be unreasonable to call upon banks to solve all of them. The public policy goal of having banks meet community credit needs does not entail any expectation that banks should provide subsidies to make up for the massive gaps created by falling incomes, soaring home prices, and cutbacks in public-sector support for housing and community development. It is, however, entirely reasonable to expect that banks should contribute to the solution of these problems within a broader framework of public and private initiatives; they should be willing partners in efforts in this area that involve private financing in connection with public or private grants.

In sum, banks must operate in a way that, at a minimum, does not exacerbate the problems of the poor and minorities and, when possible, helps to facilitate steps toward progress in eliminating poverty and racial injustice. An appropriate goal for public policy is to make banks' behavior, on balance, a force tending to increase rather than to decrease opportunity and justice.

Bank Performance in Meeting Community Needs

During the past 20 years, research ranging from sophisticated econometric studies by social science researchers to simple data displays by community organizations has documented the failure of U.S. banks to adequately meet the credit and banking services needs of low-income and minority people and communities. The banking system's community reinvestment performance is particularly appalling because it has coexisted with the provision of excessive credit for speculative real estate development, high-risk corporate takeovers, and other ill-advised ventures that resulted in the S&L debacle and the solvency crisis in commercial banking.

This section summarizes the available evidence on bank performance in meeting community banking needs, under three headings: residential mortgage lending, provision of basic banking services, and lending to minority and community-based small businesses. The causal factors and mechanisms that may account for the low level of bank performance are examined in the next section.

Mortgage Lending

The *Atlanta Journal and Atlanta Constitution*'s publication in May 1988 of its Pulitzer Prize-winning series "The Color of Money" brought the problem of dramatic racial disparities in residential mortgage lending to the nation's attention.[7] The study compared stable, middle-income neighborhoods that were at least 80 percent white or 80 percent nonwhite. It found that between 1984 and 1986, Atlanta banks and S&Ls made over 4.5 times as many loans per 1,000 single-family structures in white neighborhoods as in comparable black neighborhoods (Dedman, 1988).

In city after city, subsequent studies documented similarly dramatic racial disparities in mortgage lending.[8] In Boston between 1981 and 1987, banks made 2.9 times as many mortgage loans per 1,000 housing units in low-income white neighborhoods as in black neighborhoods with similar incomes (Finn, 1989). In Detroit between 1981 and 1986, the seven largest lenders got 13 percent of their total metropolitan area deposits from residential neighborhoods within the city proper but made only 5.6 percent of their metropolitan area mortgage loans within the city. The ratio of the mortgage lending rate (loans per 1,000 homes) in middle-income white neighborhoods to that in middle-income black neighborhoods rose every year of the study period, reaching 3.14:1 in 1986 (Blossom, Everett, and Gallagher, 1988). Similar results were found in a 14-city study by the Center for Community Change (1989), as well as for such cities as Chicago (Shlay, 1988), Los Angeles (Dymski, Veitch, and White, 1991), Milwaukee (Squires and Velez, 1987), and New York (Williams, Brown, and Simmons, 1988).

Most of the studies were based on pre-1990 Home Mortgage Disclosure Act (HMDA) data, which provide information about loans by census tract[9] but give no information about the individuals receiving loans. These pre-1990 HMDA data can be combined with decennial census information to examine loan flows into neighborhoods with different racial compositions and income levels.

The first major study that investigated lending imbalances based on the race of loan *applicants* (instead of the racial composition of *neighborhoods*) examined the more than 10 million housing loan applications received by all of the nation's 3,100 S&Ls and savings banks between 1983 and 1988.[10] The study found that rejection rates for blacks were more than twice as high as for whites (23.7 percent vs. 11.1 percent); that in many areas, the rejection rates for high-income blacks were greater than those for low-income whites (in 85 of the 100 largest metropolitan areas, this was true in at least one year); and that racial disparity in loan decisions was worsening rather than improving over time in 13 of 17 cities for which comparable data were available (Dedman, 1989).

The 1989 amendments to HMDA require that mortgage lenders report more comprehensive information about all loan applications—including applicants' race, sex, and income, and the application's disposition—as well as the previously required loan flows by census tract. Analyses of these richer data for 1990 (such as Canner and Smith, 1991; Thomas, 1992a) have emphasized the striking differentials in denial rates for black and white applicants—overall, 34 percent of black applications for conventional home mortgages were rejected, compared to a 14 percent rejection rate for white applicants. (Hispanics were rejected at a 21 percent rate; rejection rates for Asians were slightly lower than for whites.) Large differentials persisted even when comparisons were limited to applicants in the same income categories.

In the ensuing months, banks, industry groups, and regulatory agencies all professed concern and resolved to change the practices that had resulted in less lending to minorities. Nevertheless, when the 1991 HMDA data were released in late October 1992, they revealed racial disparities in denial rates almost identical to those of the previous year (Canner and Smith, 1992).

Banking Services

For people at the lowest income levels, lack of access to affordable basic banking services is a greater concern than difficulty in obtaining credit.[11] People with somewhat higher incomes who aspire to home or business ownership may find it more difficult to obtain credit if they lack a history of managing a bank account. Furthermore, the physical presence of a branch office in a community provides a bank with information useful in evaluating credit applications at the same time as it provides community residents with a visible symbol of credit availability. So banks' branch office locations, their offerings of basic banking services, and adequate credit flows are mutually reinforcing in low-income and minority communities.

Surveys in a number of cities have found that low-income and minority neighborhoods are underserved by banking offices. In Boston, a 1989 survey found that "Boston's 12 largest lending institutions have five times more offices in white areas than in areas [with the same total population] that are predominantly black or Hispanic" (Hanafin, 1989); another investigation revealed that between 1978 and 1988, banks closed 40 percent of their branch offices in minority areas while increasing the number of branches in mainly white neighborhoods by over 30 percent (Community Investment Coalition, 1989). A comprehensive study of bank office location in the low-income and minority neighborhoods of six major cities found that "communities with large concentrations of low-income or black residents are only about half as likely to have a bank as other communities" (Caskey, 1992).

Low-income households often cannot obtain basic banking services at an affordable price. A study by the General Accounting Office found that approximately 17 percent of U.S. families (over half of whom had incomes below $10,000) did not have bank accounts in 1985; the most common reasons for lacking accounts were high costs, high minimum balance requirements, and inconvenient locations and hours of bank offices (U.S. General Accounting Office, 1988). A 1985 American Bankers Association survey indicated that only 21 percent of all commercial banks offered basic bank accounts (Canner and Maland, 1987). In addition, only a small minority of banks would cash government checks for non–account holders.

The number of banks offering basic bank accounts and allowing government check cashing has certainly grown in recent years. But the strength of industry resistance to legislative proposals for mandatory basic bank accounts, the prominence of provisions for basic banking services in recent community reinvestment agreements between community advocates and banks, and the rapid recent growth of what John Caskey has called "fringe banking"—check-cashing stores and pawn shops serving a primarily low-income clientele—indicate that banks themselves are leaving many needs for basic financial services unfilled (Caskey, 1991a and 1991b).

Economic and Community Development Lending

The problem of inadequate bank financing of small and minority-owned businesses, particularly those located in low-income areas, is in some ways the most serious of the three major problems addressed here. Economic development is essential to providing the jobs and incomes that are necessary for community vitality. All types of businesses require credit to support both ongoing operations and expansion. However, large firms may have direct access to credit markets or be able to obtain funds from other kinds of financial companies, while smaller businesses are almost exclusively dependent on banks themselves. A recent Federal Reserve study found that "Overwhelmingly, the single most important financial institution for nearly every financial product and service used by small and medium-sized businesses is a local commercial bank" (Elliehausen and Wolken, 1990, pp. 31–32).

In spite of the importance of small business lending, however, there is almost no systematic data that would allow documentation of the extent of the problem in this area. A recent study on poverty, race, and credit in Los Angeles noted that "Perhaps the outstanding finding concerning economic development lending is that very little is known in this area" (Dymski, Veitch, and White, 1991, p. 11). One community advocate put the matter more forcefully in recent congressional testimony: "There is an alarming lack of statistical data on the availability of credit for inner-city and minority-owned small businesses . . . [and] an urgent public policy need for systematic data collection in order to measure the dimensions of the problem" (Bhargava, 1992, p. 3).

While systematic data are lacking, at least one careful statistical study of the financing obtained by over 7,000 new small businesses (almost 40 percent of which were black-owned) concluded that "Commercial banks, the largest single source of debt for business start-ups, extend generally smaller loan amounts to blacks. . . . black-owned firms, according to the econometric findings, received smaller loan amounts than white-owned firms possessing identical measured characteristics" (Bates, 1991, pp. 65, 79). Moreover, there is no lack of anecdotal evidence on the difficulties that minority-owned and other small businesses, particularly those in low-income areas, have in obtaining credit.[12]

Furthermore, the previously noted shortage of bank branches in low-income and minority neighborhoods is consistent with reports about the difficulties that small businesses located in those neighborhoods have in obtaining both credit and routine banking services. In any case, there is little dispute about the absence of adequate bank lending in this area; regulators have joined community advocates in calling on banks to do better. For example, Federal Reserve Board

Governor Lawrence Lindsey called, in a May 1992 speech to the California Bankers' Association, for a "much more active role in lending to small business, particularly minority small businesses" (U.S. Senate Banking Committee, 1992b, Vol. 2, p. 482).

Banks are also failing to meet the credit needs of community-based nonprofit organizations. Even though there are even fewer data in this area than for small business lending, anecdotal evidence suggests that community institutions such as child care centers and mental health clinics have tremendous difficulties in obtaining credit. For example, mental health centers that operate on Medicaid reimbursements often cannot get lines of credit to bridge the gaps between their expenditures and their reimbursements from state governments.

Information Disclosure and Data Availability

The body of evidence cited here has been developed in the face of almost 20 years of federal regulatory resistance to making data available to community and academically based researchers. The general pattern, which has been accurately characterized as a "long history of opposing disclosure before it has been enacted and minimizing disclosure after," (Bradford, 1992a, p. 161) can be illustrated by several examples.

I have already mentioned the case of the Federal Home Loan Bank Board's failure to put to any use the rich data on mortgage applications and race that it was compelled to gather under the terms of a 1979 civil rights suit settlement (see note 9).

Second, continuing obstacles have been placed in the way of those who want to obtain and use HMDA data (for details, see Bradford, 1992b). For example, anyone wishing to use 1990 HMDA data for independent analysis, even for a single bank or a single city, must purchase four computer tapes at a price of $500.[13]

Third, regulators have consistently opposed providing meaningful public information about the results of their examinations of banks' CRA performance. The agencies' 1978 regulations implementing the CRA required that all information about these examinations, including the information used and ratings awarded, be kept confidential.[14]

When the 1989 amendments to the CRA required public performance evaluations, the agencies initially adopted procedures that made it very difficult for community advocates even to learn when ratings for individual banks were available (more reasonable procedures were adopted only in response to intense community-based protests and strong congressional pressure). Furthermore, the evaluations made public thus far have provided little actual data about bank performance (U.S. Senate, 1992b, pp. 48–50).

A final example is provided by the regulators' implementation of the provisions of the Federal Deposit Insurance Corporation Improvement Act of 1991 (FDICIA) in which Congress took a modest initial step toward providing data on small business lending. The law mandated that each bank's quarterly call report (a public document) include data on the number of loans to small businesses and small farmers, including the number of loans to minority-owned firms and to start-up businesses. However, the final regulations issued in November 1992 required only that banks report the total number of businesses of any size receiving "small" loans (of $1 million or less); reportage on small, minority-owned, and start-up businesses *per se* was simply eliminated from the final regulations.

Understanding Poor Performance: Its Causes and Mechanisms

Banks' performance in meeting low-income and minority communities' credit and basic banking needs, despite the barriers to data disclosure, is a matter of record. The facts of racial disparities in mortgage lending patterns, of too few bank branches in poor and minority neighborhoods, and of the substantial unmet credit needs of small inner-city and rural businesses are generally acknowledged. But the *reasons* for the existence and persistence of this unresponsive record are controversial. This section reviews the underlying causes and mechanisms that have been suggested and debated. In doing so, it seeks to provide a systematic basis for developing appropriate public policy proposals for community reinvestment, such as those outlined in the following section.

The causes and mechanisms underlying banks' poor performance in meeting community banking needs are grouped under five headings: bank failures to exploit profitable business opportunities, racial discrimination, ineffective regulatory performance, financial restructuring and deregulation, and external factors that make socially desirable community reinvestment activities unprofitable for individual banks.

Failure to Exploit Profitable Business Opportunities

For almost 20 years, the community reinvestment movement has argued that banks have been passing up profitable lending opportunities within low-income and minority neighborhoods. This is inconsistent, of course, with the abstract model of profit maximization that appears in economics textbooks. Nevertheless, it is entirely understandable if bank behavior is more realistically portrayed as shaped by bank managers who act, and set incentives for their staffs, in accordance with their own attitudes and perceptions. Profit-maximizing opportunities would then be readily missed due to bank executives' mistaken perceptions and lack of information about low-income and minority individuals and communities. This is entirely plausible given the racial composition and socioeconomic backgrounds of bank executives and managers.

Bankers most frequently justify their lack of greater CRA lending with one or both of the following two claims: that the low level of lending reflects low demand for loans and that these types of loans entail too much risk. Neither of the claims is able to withstand careful scrutiny.

Low demand fails as an explanation for low lending volumes for two reasons. First, when adequate data have been available to test this claim statistically (particularly for mortgage lending), high denial rates have been a significant determinant of low lending levels. Second, "demand" is not a fixed entity to which businesses respond, especially in the 1990s; successful businesses view demand as created and expanded by tailoring products for specific potential markets and then employing aggressive marketing. This is why the drafters of the CRA charged banks with an "affirmative obligation" to meet the credit needs of their local communities. Lack of bank activity may as readily be a cause of low levels of observed demand as an effect. That banks do not seek out loan customers in minority and low-income neighborhoods as aggressively and imaginatively as they do in other areas reflects their preconceptions and attitudes as much as any hard-headed analysis of potential profitability.

High risk as an explanation for low lending volumes fails for at least three reasons, even though the CRA explicitly restricts banks to activities "consistent with [their] safe and sound operation." First, in contrast to commonly expressed beliefs, mortgage loans in low-income and minority communities may be *less* risky than other lending, even residential lending. Even though no systematic study has been done on this issue, substantial anecdotal evidence suggests that CRA-oriented lending programs typically have very low default rates.[15]

Second, because a bank's credit risk is generally reduced by diversification, it follows that expanding the share of CRA-related loans in bank loan portfolios where they are currently underrepresented would tend to *reduce* overall credit risk. Third, in any case, arguments based on banking prudence lack even minimal credibility after the experiences of the 1980s; an industry that has lost hundreds of billions of dollars making dubious loans in the Third World, to the energy industry, for leveraged buyouts, and to highly speculative developers of luxury condominiums, shopping centers, and office towers can hardly claim that excessive risk was really the factor that kept them from more active lending in poor and minority communities.

What happened is that the commercial credit and securities markets matured, costing banks many of their traditional blue-chip customers as they were pushed out of many of the credit markets they formerly dominated (Wolfson, Dymski, this volume). Banks then looked elsewhere for profitable lending niches. Indeed, they looked precisely to commercial real estate, Third World loans, and the other forenamed areas responsible for massive losses in the 1980s and early 1990s. In the wake of innovations in credit markets and of banks' loan losses, their niche now consists of areas in which they have informational advantages and in which their potential customers cannot access credit markets directly. So, as *Business Week* recently observed, "Although they may have been dragged into the business kicking and screaming, many banks admit they've stumbled upon a new— and modestly profitable—niche in tailoring traditional services to meet the needs of low-income residents" (Foust, 1992).

Racial Discrimination

Press coverage of community reinvestment often leaves the impression that the single community reinvestment issue with any salience is whether or not banks engage in racial discrimination against individuals seeking loans. In fact, the concerns of the community reinvestment movement both encompass racial discrimination and, at the same time, extend well beyond this issue. Nevertheless, the legacy of American history leaves little doubt that racial discrimination is a major civil rights problem, and to the extent that it biases credit market outcomes, it is a major impediment to healthy community development as well.

The existence of discrimination in credit markets is still not universally considered proven. As recently as May 1992, two authoritative papers presented at a Fannie Mae–sponsored conference on discrimination in the housing and mortgage markets found insufficient evidence to conclude that banks discriminate in the mortgage market, according to the standards of statistical significance applied in social science research (Galster, 1992b; Wienk, 1992). They acknowledged that many studies (such as those reviewed in the previous section) had found substantial racial *disparities* in the loan flows into neighborhoods and in the rejection rates for mortgage loan applicants. But they maintained that available data did not provide a sufficient basis for concluding that these disparities resulted from *discrimination* by banks; for example, the dramatically higher rejection rates for black mortgage applicants could have resulted from lower wealth, worse credit histories, or other factors relevant to creditworthiness that are excluded from the HMDA data. These authors called for obtaining and using data sets that include detailed information that is generally available only in banks' individual loan files.

Less than six months later, researchers at the Federal Reserve Bank of Boston reported the results of a large multivariate statistical analysis designed very much along the lines identified by Galster and Wienk as necessary and sufficient to demonstrate compellingly the existence of discrimination (Munnell et al., 1992). This study examined detailed data from the loan files for all mortgage loan applications by blacks or Hispanics at all of the 131 mortgage lenders in the Boston metropolitan area that had received 25 or more total mortgage applications, together with a carefully selected random sample of comparable mortgage applications from whites. The authors gathered data on 39 variables from the application forms, from credit reports, and from lenders' worksheets, including information on credit history, wealth, debt burdens, loan-to-value ratios, and other variables whose absence has been most often cited as making it impossible to infer the existence of discrimination from HMDA data alone. Even after all these other variables had been incorporated into the econometric analysis, the denial rate for black and Hispanic applicants was 60 percent higher than that for white mortgage applicants (17 percent vs. 11 percent). One high-ranking official of the Massachusetts Bankers Association described this as finally providing the "smoking gun" that established the existence of racial discrimination in mortgage lending beyond a reasonable doubt. Federal regulators and banking industry leaders seem in rare agreement that, indeed, the findings of the Boston Fed study are convincing.

In fact, there had long existed several bodies of evidence that, while they fell short of the statistical standards of proof required in social science, provided an adequate basis for reasonable people to conclude that banks discriminate. To begin with, the pervasiveness of discrimination in the United States in general, and its well-documented presence in the housing market in particular, made it implausible on its face to maintain that discrimination is absent from the banking industry. Historical research has thoroughly demonstrated that "race is a factor that has long been explicitly identified and overtly utilized in all aspects of the housing industry and in public regulation of that industry" (Squires, 1992b, p. 3). Even when explicit policies have changed, it is difficult to believe that no legacy remains from these now-disavowed past practices, which were current when today's senior banking officials were trained.

Further, the disproportionately small number of blacks and other minorities among bank managers and loan officers—as well as the disproportionately few banking offices located in minority neighborhoods—makes it highly improbable that black loan applicants will be treated as well as comparable white individuals. Abundant anecdotal evidence describes qualified black loan applicants who have had great difficulty in obtaining loans. Virtually every congressional hearing and every journalistic treatment of lending disparities (including the aforementioned Atlanta series and a June 1992 PBS "Frontline" documentary) have described individual cases in which discrimination seems clearly to have occurred.

In addition, several types of statistical evidence are consistent with the existence of discrimination and inconsistent with alternative possibilities suggested by bankers. In the first serious study of racial lending disparities conducted by any of the federal banking regulators, researchers at the Federal Reserve Bank of Boston found that the smaller numbers of mortgage loans in neighborhoods with at least 80 percent black residents than in neighborhoods with fewer than 5 percent black residents could not be accounted for in a multiple regression analysis, even when each neighborhood's income, wealth, average house value, vacancy rate, number of bank branches, new housing development, and 10 other variables were taken into account. They were left with no explanation other than race itself for a 24 percent shortfall in mortgage lending in predominantly minority neighborhoods (Bradbury, Case, and Dunham, 1989).

Second, the "new" HMDA data disproved the claim that the small number of mortgage loans in minority census tracts was solely a result of low demand (small numbers of loan applications) rather than differential denial rates for blacks and whites. Third, in response to the political pressures resulting in the initial release of the "new" HMDA data in late 1991, the U.S. Justice Department for the first time undertook serious, detailed examination of the lending files of a number of banks whose HMDA reports suggested possible racial discrimination in lending. As a result of a careful statistical investigation of more than 4,000 mortgage applications, Decatur (Georgia) Federal Savings & Loan became in September 1992 the first bank ever charged by the U.S. Justice Department with racial discrimination in mortgage lending. The bank denied the charges but agreed both to pay an average of more than $20,000 to 48 black applicants who had been denied loans and to change a number of its banking practices (Canner and Smith, 1992, pp. 807–8).

Finally, evidence of racial discrimination against black loan applicants has been provided by a method called "testing," in which a matched pair of applicants—one white and one black, but substantially identical in terms of the criteria legitimately used in lending decisions—separately approach the same lender and record their experiences; because the situation is structured in such a way that systematic differences in responses can be attributed only to the different races of the applicants, the method is able to confirm the existence of discriminatory behavior.[16] The use of testing on a wide scale has clearly established the existence of discrimination in the housing market itself, as opposed to the market for housing credit (Turner, 1992). While testing in the mortgage loan area has not been employed on a large enough scale to produce statistically valid findings, pilot studies have strongly suggested significant discrimination during the initial stages of seeking mortgage loans (Galster, 1991a, pp. 23–36).

Regulatory Failure

Although banks must bear primary responsibility for their own poor performance in meeting community needs, the federal bank regulatory agencies have contributed to that poor performance by failing to fulfill their responsibilities to enforce the CRA. By acting more as consultants to the industry than as agents of the public, they compiled a long record fully justifying bank managers' conclusion that they would face no serious regulatory consequences for flouting the law.[17] If regulators had applied an appropriate combination of pressure and guidance, banks would certainly have performed better.

The sorry record of the bank regulatory agencies in enforcing the CRA during the first decade of its existence was well documented during two sets of Senate Banking Committee hearings in the aftermath of the *Atlanta Journal and Atlanta Constitution*'s "Color of Money" series. Testimony revealed that in the deregulatory fervor of the 1980s, the federal agencies charged with enforcing the CRA acted essentially as if it didn't exist. Regulators testified that only about 3 percent of all banks received unsatisfactory CRA ratings. They testified further that only 9 of more than 50,000 bank applications requiring regulatory approval during the decade since passage of the CRA had been denied on the grounds of inadequate CRA performance. Community advocates pointed out that although the U.S. General Accounting Office in a 1981 report to Congress had rebuked the regulatory agencies for inadequate CRA examinations, regulators actually reduced the total hours annually devoted to CRA exams by 68 percent between 1981 and 1984 (from 915,000 to 290,000 hours). And it was noted that the federal government had not brought a single case alleging loan discrimination against any bank, despite all the suggestive evidence. Mildred Brown, president of the Association of Community Organization for Reform Now (ACORN), summed up the situation as follows: "Banks are breaking the law and the regulators are their accomplices" (U.S. Senate Banking Committee, 1988).

Four years later, after that testimony had helped to achieve passage of the 1989 amendments to the CRA and the HMDA, a detailed investigation by a subcommittee of the Senate Banking Committee found that there had been little improvement in regulatory performance. Witnesses testified to the low quality of the publicly released CRA evaluations, pointing out that while regulators' CRA examinations had become somewhat more aggressive (the number of banks receiving less than satisfactory ratings had risen from 3 percent to 11 percent), regulators' disapproval too often targeted issues of process and of documentation rather than substantive aspects of CRA performance. Such supervisory behavior seemed almost designed to provoke strong protests from the banks; the industry's outcry against the "regulatory burden" imposed by CRA was provoked and fueled by inappropriate regulatory behavior (U.S. Senate Banking Committee, 1992a; see especially testimony of Bradford [1992a] and Goldberg [1992]). The subcommittee's report emphasized "[t]he supervisory agencies' record of inconsistent and lax enforcement" and concluded that "the agencies bear significant responsibility for the poor performance of many of the financial institutions. . . . *If the agencies were rated today on their overall performance, the Subcommittee would give them a 'D'"* (U.S. Senate Banking Committee, 1992b, p. 5; emphasis in original).

Financial Restructuring and Deregulation

The banking industry has been experiencing changes so extensive that former Fed Chairman Arthur Burns (1988) termed them an "ongoing revolution in American banking." This "ongoing revolution" has provided a changing context for CRA struggles in recent years. However, firm conclusions cannot yet be reached about the net impact of changes in banking structure—particularly, the trends toward consolidation and toward geographic expansion—on bank CRA performance.

It must be remembered that the period preceding deregulation and restructuring was far from a golden age of community reinvestment. Indeed, the community reinvestment movement grew up in response to widespread disinvestment during the late 1960s and early 1970s. The form taken by poor community investment performance has changed substantially, but it would be inappropriate to conclude that deregulation and restructuring explain banks' failure to meet community needs.

In addition, whatever negative effects the wave of bank mergers and interstate expansions may have had, these developments have provided the principal means by which communities have won bank agreements for improved reinvestment performance. Because every merger and every interstate bank acquisition require regulatory approval and because regulators are legally required to consider a bank's CRA performance in deciding whether to grant their approval, the process of bank expansion and consolidation has provided community groups with attractive opportunities to challenge applications on the grounds of inadequate CRA performance. In hundreds of cases, such challenges have resulted in agreements between banks and community groups.

On the question of bank size, there is no systematic evidence that larger banks perform more poorly in meeting local community needs. The situation appears to be analogous to the relationship between bank size and operating efficiency; the literature on economies of scale in banking indicates that the overall trend, if any, is far outweighed by substantial variation in efficiency at any given bank size (Clark, 1988; Humphrey, 1990). Not all small banks are community oriented (in cinemagraphic terms, for every heart-of-gold Jimmy Stewart character there may be a greedy and despicable Lionel Barrymore). Indeed, there are some indications that the community reinvestment performance of small banks may be, on average, worse than that of large ones: small banks have significantly lower loan-to-deposit ratios than larger banks (U.S. House of Representatives, 1992, p. 14), and have received a disproportionate share of poor CRA performance ratings from federal bank supervisors.[18]

By contrast with the ambiguous evidence for bank size, the elimination of barriers to the geographic expansion of banking firms appears to have very negative implications for local communities. The increasing expansion of banks within state borders and—through networks of banks controlled by bank holding companies—across state lines means that an increasing number of local communities, even in major metropolitan areas, are forced to deal with banks whose headquarters are located in distant cities. Systematic evidence on this issue does not yet exist. However, it seems reasonable to suppose that when decisionmaking power is concentrated in distant headquarters, local communities will find banks less knowledgeable about local circumstances, less concerned with solving local problems, and, especially, less susceptible to the local organizing campaigns that have been vital in bringing about agreements for improved CRA performance. In addition, the increased size and spread of the largest banking companies may be associated with greater political influence over elected officials and regulatory agencies, placing local community advocates at an even greater disadvantage than heretofore.

Factors Beyond the Control of Individual Banks

Finally, there are several circumstances in which individual banks are correct in holding back from undertaking community-oriented lending on the grounds that such lending would not be profitable. In at least three cases, poor community reinvestment performance may result from factors beyond the control of individual banks. In each case, however, appropriate public policy measures can change circumstances sufficiently to make the lending in question profitable.

First, there are cases in which reinvestment is blocked by a collective action problem. For example, a single bank may correctly decide that making a loan in a depressed community entails too great a risk of default, whereas if all banks began making loans there, the result would be an overall level of community prosperity that makes it possible for all loans to be repaid.[19] Another example concerns a bank's decision about whether to cash government (welfare) checks for non–account holders. A bank that does so unilaterally could find itself faced with heavy demands on its offices and staff, whereas the burden on any individual bank would be much less if all banks agreed to provide this service. In such cases, the policy prescription is to encourage, if not require, community-oriented behavior by all banks.

Second, there are cases in which individual bank lending is seriously constrained by the lack of an adequate or appropriate secondary market. This is most obviously true in the case of mortgage lending. As an ever-increasing portion of residential mortgage loans are made with the intention of being sold immediately in the secondary market, the underwriting standards and operating practices of Fannie Mae and other secondary market institutions have a growing impact on which loans the banks will originate. The result has been to encourage "plain vanilla" lending that does not respond to the particular circumstances of many low-income and minority potential homebuyers (Canner and Gabriel, 1992). Permanent financing for affordable housing developments and community-based businesses would also be greatly enhanced by creating appropriate secondary markets. In these cases, banks can join with others in advocating enhanced secondary markets that will enable them to increase their community-oriented lending.

Finally, there are cases in which the total benefits to society from the extension of additional credit outweigh the repayment costs, but too few of the benefits will flow back to borrowers to allow them to make the required loan payments. In these cases, which include much that is proposed and undertaken to meet the needs of low-income communities, public or private financial support is necessary. The role of public policy here is to provide the appropriate programs and subsidies and then to ensure that banks play an appropriate role within the framework established.

An Agenda for Community Reinvestment Policy

This section outlines a set of public policy proposals designed to improve bank performance in providing flows of credit and financial services for low-income and minority individuals and neighborhoods. These proposals are made in the three substantive areas in which inadequate performance was documented in the section titled Bank Performance in Meeting Community Needs: residential mortgage lending, basic banking services, and small-business lending.

The policies proposed here are best viewed as part of the broader set of financial reform proposals made in this volume; community reinvestment represents just one way in which the credit flows in this country must be redirected to enhance economic development and promote human welfare. Considering proposals for reinvestment together with proposals for other dimensions of financial reform can, at a minimum, ensure that policy responses to the banking industry's insolvency crisis do not end up worsening the industry's already dismal record of community reinvestment activity. More positively, political leverage for obtaining advances in this area may be greatest when improvements in community reinvestment legislation are integrated into an overall legislative package that includes changes eagerly sought by the banks. Further, community reinvestment objectives may be implemented through changes in capital requirements, deposit insurance provisions, supervisory organization and procedures, or other subjects of the more general reform and restructuring effort.

Some of the proposals offered here are clearly of zero or modest cost. Others, such as the creation of new not-for-profit lending institutions, might require substantial funding. Actual estimation of how much specific proposals might cost, detailed discussion of how these costs might be covered, and quantitative assessment of program benefits are all important tasks beyond the scope of this chapter.

The primary focus of this section will be on federal-level measures to improve banks' performance in meeting local community needs. This focus is entirely justified by the central role that banks must play in this area. At the same time, bankers and community advocates alike agree that it is unfair and unrealistic for banks to bear sole responsibility for reinvestment. A comprehensive program of measures for enhancing financial services and credit flows in underserved communities requires at least three other components.

First, appropriate community reinvestment obligations should be legally mandated for all the nondepository financial institutions that compete with banks—insurance companies, brokerage firms, mutual fund companies, mortgage banks/companies, and finance companies.[20] This step would remove banks' concern about being placed at a competitive disadvantage due to their special responsibilities in this area. At the same time, the total resources brought to bear on the pressing needs in underserved communities would be substantially increased.[21]

Second, obligations for improved community reinvestment performance should be imposed on government-sponsored enterprises such as Fannie Mae and Freddie Mac. One significant step in that direction is the obligation, embodied in legislation enacted in late 1992, that at least 30 percent of all mortgages purchased by Fannie Mae and Freddie Mac must be secured by property in central cities and that at least 30 percent must be for borrowers with less than the median income, with additional provisions that target some of this lending directly on lower-income borrowers. More precise targeting on mortgages for property located in low-income or minority neighborhoods, on mortgages made to minority or low-income borrowers, or on certain categories of mortgages such as multifamily housing produced by nonprofit developers would be a desirable further step. Moreover, given the impact of secondary-market underwriting standards on the types of loans that lenders are willing to originate, Fannie Mae and other substantial secondary market purchasers should expand the use of flexible underwriting standards that encompass the needs of borrowers from low-income and minority communities. Such support from secondary market institutions could significantly facilitate increased mortgage originations in underserved communities.

Third, one of the most promising approaches to community reinvestment is the creation of a special class of dedicated financial institutions. Such institutions might be patterned on the highly successful South Shore Bank in Chicago (Osborne, 1989) or built on the model of community development credit unions (Isenberg, 1991)—perhaps based in closed bank branches (Green and von Nostitz, 1992, pp. 83–84). Individual institutions might concentrate on one particular need such as providing microloans for community-based entrepreneurs or financing for affordable housing. (Hanggi [1992] offers a proposal to transform the Federal Home Loan Bank Board into a sort of "central bank" for community-oriented housing lenders.) Alternatively, institutions might have a broad general mandate as public-purpose banks (Schlesinger, 1991; Financial Democracy Campaign, 1992) or as part of the "national network of small business community development banks" called for by candidate Bill Clinton (Clinton and Gore, 1992, p. 149). They could range in size from tiny (to meet the needs of a single small community) to huge (for example, to provide a national secondary market for CRA-related loans made by community-based institutions and/or traditional lenders). Whatever their precise size and scope, such institutions would generally be not-for-profit, supported by public or private subsidies, and democratically controlled.

Nevertheless, while nonbank financial institutions, government-sponsored enterprises, and community-oriented not-for-profit banks could all make significant contributions to needed community reinvestment, these contributions cannot substitute for substantially improved performance by banks themselves. At least five types of changes in federal policy toward the banks could help to bring about this improved performance: enhanced enforcement of laws prohibiting racial discrimination, mandated provision of basic banking services, improvements in the CRA examination and evaluation process, material incentives for improved bank performance, and increased disclosure of information on CRA-related lending.

Combating Racial Discrimination

The pathetic performance by regulatory agencies in investigating and prosecuting racial discrimination in lending was noted earlier. High priority ought to be placed on ensuring that bank regulators—as well as HUD and the Department of Justice—take this responsibility much more seriously in the future. An alternative approach is to concentrate responsibility for enforcement of fair lending laws in a single agency with a focused mission and specialized expertise. In either case, the primary need is for aggressive, adequately funded efforts to enforce existing laws, rather than for new legislation.

In support of these efforts, the method of paired testing (described earlier) is a potentially valuable tool that merits implementation by the regulatory agencies; bank regulators should be mandated to support or even conduct testing on a widespread basis. Regulators also should encourage banks to establish formal mechanisms for internal review of tentative decisions to deny mortgage applications from minority individuals or for homes located in minority neighborhoods. For a survey of actual and potential fair lending initiatives, see Canner and Smith (1992, pp. 812–19).

Basic Banking Services

To ensure that all members of society have access to elementary banking services that most Americans take for granted—safekeeping of money, the capacity to make long-distance payments with personal checks, and opportunity to cash government checks—all banks should be required to provide low-cost savings accounts, low-cost checking accounts, and check-cashing services for non–account holders. Legislation to this end has been introduced for many years by U.S. Senator Howard Metzenbaum and others. Regulators, in turn, should be required to factor in the potential loss of basic banking services when deciding whether to approve bank proposals to close branch offices.

Provision of basic banking services will entail some costs for banks; but it will also yield benefits. Information obtained through providing basic banking services can be useful in lending activities in local communities. In many cases, banks will be establishing business relationships with people whose current deposits are minimal but who will become profitable customers when their economic circumstances improve. This is one case in which banks have a clear interest in the government's requiring socially responsible behavior from all banks. Individual banks then need not worry that unilateral steps to offer basic banking services might result in a heavy surge of demands on their own staff and facilities.

Improvements in the CRA Examination and Evaluation Process

Community reinvestment is by its nature local. The CRA examination process would be much more socially useful if supervisory agencies prepared separate CRA public evaluations for each major metropolitan area in which a given bank operates.[22] Residents of San Diego are interested in how Bank of America is meeting its CRA obligations in their own community, not in an overall assessment based on some unspecified supervisory blending of performance in Los Angeles, San Francisco, and other areas of California; the current practice of carrying out CRA examinations only on a whole-bank basis is already inadequate for large banks that operate statewide. The need to require separate CRA evaluations for individual metropolitan areas will become imperative if banks win the right to branch nationwide.[23]

Other modifications in the CRA examination process are advisable in light of the legitimate complaints by both bankers and community advocates. In particular, priority must be given to substance over form. CRA examinations should be performance based, because the adequacy of bank performance in actually providing needed credit is a question of substance, not of form. Only if performance is weak should regulators have to investigate in any depth the process by which the bank pursues its CRA obligations. While examiners may reasonably request documentation of bank CRA activities, reports from the field indicate that documentation has in many cases been regarded as more important than the activities themselves. This is again a case of supervisory behavior almost designed to promote banker anger and cynicism rather than improved performance in the spirit of the Community Reinvestment Act itself.

It would also be productive to tailor CRA standards and criteria carefully to the size and type of banking institution. We saw earlier that there is no good theoretical or empirical reason to believe that small or rural banks perform better in meeting their community reinvestment obligations than larger or urban-based ones do, but it is surely the case that the nature of their obligations differs. The anger expressed by one Massachusetts banker—whose bank had no branch offices—who was scolded by his CRA examiner for not having a branch closing policy indicates the folly of applying a standardized CRA checklist to different types of banks. What is needed instead is an appropriate matching of standards to banking institutions.

A final important change in the CRA examination and evaluation process would be increased opportunities for public participation and input. For example, agencies should be required to actively solicit comments from community groups when conducting a CRA exam.

Incentives for Improved CRA Performance

At present, banks are rewarded or punished for their CRA performance in two ways: favorable (or unfavorable) publicity and favorable (or unfavorable) consideration in regulatory review of applications for new branch offices or for mergers or acquisitions. Supplementing these rewards and punishments with additional material incentives might improve CRA performance. Such financial incentives might take the form of varying reserve requirements, deposit insurance premiums, or fees to supervisory agencies in response to one or more indexes of CRA performance—perhaps the CRA ratings themselves or specified ratios based on qualifying assets (e.g., loans in targeted low-income or minority census tracts) or liabilities (e.g., deposits in low-cost basic bank accounts). One such set of financial incentives—reduced deposit insurance premiums for new deposits in low-fee checking accounts offered to the poor and for increased lending in poor neighborhoods— was included in the FDIC Improvement Act of 1991 but was not implemented because the required budgetary appropriation was not forthcoming.[24]

Increased Disclosure

In the area of community reinvestment, as elsewhere, public disclosure of information documenting unsupportable practices has proved to be a powerful tool for furthering social change. Indeed, public availability of information is vital if processes of "regulation from below" by citizens' groups and community advocates can serve as a necessary complement to the often ineffective "regulation from above" by the regulatory agencies (Fishbein, 1992). It is thus important that bank regulatory agencies be required both to expand the scope of information subject to disclosure and to make this information readily available.[25] This would represent a dramatic turnabout from the regulators' 20-year record of reluctant compliance with legislative mandates for disclosure.

It would be particularly useful to require banks to report on their commercial loans as well as their residential ones. Data on the location of small businesses receiving financing, and on the race of their owners, would make it possible to document—and design solutions for—problems in financing community-based economic development.

Data that are currently collected should be made more readily available to community groups in accessible and affordable forms. Continuing advances in computer hardware and software make it possible to provide user-selected HMDA data and customized reports based on that data, in either hard-copy or diskette form, for a modest fee. Given the resources spent on collecting and processing the expanded HMDA information, modest additional outlays would greatly facilitate the distribution of this information in accessible form to interested community groups and researchers.

In a similar spirit, the regulators should be required to provide public reports on how well banks fulfill the CRA-related commitments they make when applying for mergers. At a minimum, detailed reports should be included in the public CRA performance evaluations prepared periodically by each bank's federal regulator.

A Concluding Observation

Even implementing all of these proposals fully would not eliminate the need for ongoing assessment of community reinvestment needs. On one hand, U.S. capitalism in general and the banking industry in particular are in a period of dramatic change; they present now, even more than usual, a moving target for framers of progressive public policy proposals. To illustrate how much the banking industry has changed in less than two decades, recall that in the first wave of the community reinvestment movement, neighborhood bank branches were plentiful and interstate banking was largely unknown. Indeed, as late as 1979, 12 states—including Illinois, where Chicago activists spearheaded the development of the CRA movement—were unit banking states that prohibited all branching (Mengle, 1990).

On the other hand, no victory is ever final—past victories must be defended, successful legislative initiatives must be implemented, agreements reached must be monitored, and new measures must be designed and struggled for in response to new challenges. To aid the community reinvestment movement in defending past and future accomplishments against the never-ending counterattacks from the banking industry, the preceding proposals for increased lending information disclosure and performance monitoring are particularly important.

Notes

1. The author acknowledges helpful comments on earlier drafts of this paper from Deepak Bhargava, Gary Dymski, Gregory Squires, Anne Shlay, and the participants in the June 1992 conference of the Economic Policy Institute's Working Group on Money and Financial Restructuring.

2. For simplicity, the term "bank" is used inclusively to refer to S&Ls and other thrift institutions as well as commercial banks. On the history of the community reinvestment movement, see Greenwald (1980, chs. 5–6), Campen (1990), Dreier (1991), Guskind (1989), and Squires (1992a). The last of these, the first book devoted entirely to the CRA movement, includes several extensive case studies of local community reinvestment struggles.

3. Although this chapter focuses on community reinvestment policies at the federal level, state and local policies also represent an important part of the overall picture. America's longstanding dual banking system of mixed federal and state regulation of banks is being eroded as banking supervision becomes increasingly concentrated at the federal level (due to the FDIC's role as insurer of state chartered banks). Nevertheless, approximately two-thirds of commercial banks and half of thrift institutions remain state-chartered. Thus there is considerable scope for state (and local) policy to promote community reinvestment. For an admirable (although by now somewhat dated) compilation of state government efforts in the areas of state-level community reinvestment acts, interstate banking laws, and linked deposit programs, see National Center for Policy Alternatives (1987).

4. An excellent compilation of CRA and HMDA documents, including the amended laws themselves plus the implementing regulations and other significant statements by the supervisory agencies, is contained in the appendixes of the National Training and Information Center's *Community Reinvestment Handbook* (1991).

5. These laws were preceded by more than a century by the Civil Rights Act of 1866, which prohibits racial discrimination in all forms of contracts, including those for loans (Wienk, 1992, p. 219). Discrimination on racial grounds is singled out from among the several prohibited characteristics specified in fair lending statutes (e.g., age, sex, and religious belief) because no body of evidence suggests widespread discrimination by banks on any basis other than race.

6. For an overview of this destructive phenomenon, and a guide to the literature, see Bradford (1991, pp. 9–11). Levine and Harmon (1992) eloquently describe one dramatic example of how such lending resulted in widespread foreclosures, loss of money and homes for the unfortunate borrowers, and rapid deterioration of a targeted neighborhood in Boston in the late 1960s.

7. This was not the first time that lending disparities had been systematically documented; for information about the previous (1970s) generation of studies of unequal patterns of mortgage lending, see Greenwald (1980) and Schafer and Ladd (1981).

8. Shlay and Goldstein (forthcoming) have prepared an excellent critical and historical survey of mortgage lending studies, including a systematic comparative analysis of the coverage, methodology, and findings of 26 post-1980 studies. Shlay (1989) also has provided an informative critical exposition of the nature and limitations of available data and of alternative research methods in this area.

9. Census tracts are areas a few blocks square, containing a few thousand people, for which detailed demographic and socioeconomic data are available. Boston, for example, contains approximately 160 census tracts, with an average area of 26 city blocks and an average population of about 3,300.

10. The *Atlanta Journal-Constitution* obtained these data from the Federal Home Loan Bank Board only by means of a Freedom of Information Act request; that now-defunct regulatory body had never done any analysis of the data it was compelled to collect under the terms of a 1979 settlement of a civil rights lawsuit.

11. For example, the Massachusetts Community Action Program Directors Association, after a statewide survey of the clients of community action agencies, reported that "The findings were startling. First, the concerns of our clients [are] almost exclusively in the area of basic services" (1989, p. 4).

12. Some of this evidence was presented at the June 1992 hearings of the Senate Banking Committee which included the just-cited testimony by Bhargava (1992); more was offered in a front-page *Wall Street Journal* article bearing the headline, "Small Businesses, Key to Urban Recovery, Are Starved for Capital: Situation Seems to Worsen; Usurious Lenders Thrive as Banks Shun Inner City" (Thomas, 1992b).

13. When the 1990 HMDA data, originally released in October, were revised the following January, a purchaser of the original data who wanted the revisions had no option but to purchase another complete set of tapes—for another $500.

14. For an account of the debate surrounding implementation of the act, including contemporaneous testimony before the regulators that "it was absolutely essential that bank examiners' comments about a bank's reinvestment performance be made available to the public," see Greenwald (1980, pp. 171–78).

15. For example, Atlanta's Citizens Trust Bank, a black-owned bank that made nearly all of its housing loans in minority neighborhoods, had the lowest default rate on real estate loans of any bank its size in the nation in 1986 (Dedman, 1988).

16. One goal of such testing is to discover the extent of "screening" of potential minority borrowers before a formal loan application is ever made—and therefore entered into the HMDA database.

17. If the banks' poor CRA performance can be understood partly as a consequence of the racial composition of their executives, this same factor may be playing a role in accounting for the related regulatory failure. A recent study by the House Banking Committee found that three of the four federal bank regulators (the Office of the Comptroller of the Currency, the Office of Thrift Supervision, and the Federal Deposit Insurance Corporation) had no minority individuals in any of their 10 highest-paid positions (*Wall Street Journal*, June 2, 1992).

18. For example, banks with assets of less than $25 million made up 34 percent of the

banks that received public CRA ratings as of mid-1992 but had received 44 percent of the ratings of substantial noncompliance (Goldberg, 1992, p. 201).

19. See Dymski (1990 and this volume) for an analysis of situations characterized by such lending spillovers.

20. Consideration should also be given to federal regulation of firms—such as check-cashing stores and pawnbrokers—that operate in the fringe banking industry noted on pp. 228–29, above.

21. On the extension of CRA obligations to other institutions, see the chapter by Dymski in this volume; on the more general need for greater uniformity in the regulation of different types of financial institutions, see the chapter by D'Arista and Schlesinger.

22. For an excellent set of recommendations for strengthening the CRA evaluation process, see U.S. Senate (1992b, pp. 9–13).

23. It may make little substantive difference in local operations whether the Dallas-area operations of NationsBank are conducted by a separately chartered Texas bank subsidiary of the North Carolina parent corporation or as branches of a nation-wide bank headquartered in North Carolina—in both cases, top management and real control are hundreds of miles away. However, in the absence of the proposed change in the geographic scope of CRA evaluations, the introduction of interstate branching would greatly reduce the available information about Dallas-area CRA performance. The Office of Thrift Supervision's approval of nationwide branching for the federally chartered thrifts, effective in mid-1992, did not include any provision for anything other than whole-bank CRA examinations for thrifts operating in more than one state.

24. For a much broader proposal that would tie each bank's reserve requirements to the social value of the activities financed by its loans, see the chapter by Pollin in this volume.

25. One benefit of increased federal provision of information about bank CRA-related performance would be more effective implementation of state- and local-government-linked deposit programs. Under some of these programs, the awarding of public deposits and of other banking business depends, at least partially, on an evaluation of bank performance in meeting local community reinvestment needs. For recent surveys of linked deposit banking programs, see Campen (1991) and Flax-Hatch (1991). For a detailed recommendation for a linked deposit banking program for the city of Los Angeles, see Dymski, Veitch, and White (1991, pp. 194–203). Although their implementation so far has been disappointing, such programs offer a promising avenue for promoting bank CRA performance at the subnational level.

Bibliography

Bates, Timothy. "Commercial Bank Financing of White- and Black-owned Small Business Start-Ups." *Quarterly Review of Business and Economics*, Vol. 31, Spring 1991, pp. 64–80.

Bhargava, Deepak. "Credit Availability for Minority-Owned and Inner-City Businesses." Statement at Hearings on Impediments to Access to Capital for Minority-Owned and Inner-City Businesses. U.S. Senate Committee on Banking, Housing, and Urban Affairs, June 23, 1992.

Blossom, Teresa, David Everett, and John Gallagher. "The Race for Money." *Detroit Free Press*, July 24–27, 1988.

Bradbury, Katharine L., Karl E. Case, and Constance R. Dunham. "Geographic Patterns of Mortgage Lending in Boston, 1982–1987." *New England Economic Review*, September/October 1989, pp. 3–30.

Bradford, Calvin. "Never Call Retreat: The Fight Against Lending Discrimination." Part 1 of *Credit by Color: Mortgage Market Discrimination in Chicagoland*. Chicago: Chicago Area Fair Housing Alliance, 1991.

Bradford, Calvin. " 'We Trust Our Banks'—15 Years After the CRA." Statement Before the U.S. Senate Committee on Banking, Housing, and Urban Affairs, Subcommittee on Housing, September 15, 1992a, pp. 149–80.

Bradford, Calvin. "The 20-year Effort to Secure Data on Race and Home Lending: A Review of HMDA, FIRREA, and the Fed." Unpublished paper. Des Plaines, IL: Community Reinvestment Associates, 1992b.

Burns, Arthur F. *The Ongoing Revolution in American Banking*. Washington, DC: American Enterprise Institute for Public Policy Research, 1988.

Campen, Jim. "Payment Due: Communities Win Bank Commitments." *Dollars and Sense*, No. 155, April 1990, pp. 12–14.

Campen, James T. "The Political Economy of Linked Deposit Banking Programs." Working Paper No. 91–02. Boston: Department of Economics, University of Massachusetts at Boston, 1991.

Canner, Glenn B. and Stuart A. Gabriel. "Market Segmentation and Lender Specialization in the Primary and Secondary Mortgage Markets." *Housing Policy Debate*, Vol. 3, No. 2, pp. 241–329.

Canner, Glenn B. and Ellen Maland. "Basic Banking." *Federal Reserve Bulletin, April 1987, pp. 255–69.*

Canner, Glenn B. and Dolores S. Smith. "Home Mortgage Disclosure Act: Expanded Data on Residential Lending." *Federal Reserve Bulletin*, November 1991, pp. 859–81.

Canner, Glenn B. and Dolores S. Smith. "Expanded HMDA Data on Residential Lending: One Year Later." *Federal Reserve Bulletin*, November 1992, pp. 801–24.

Caskey, John P. "Bank Representation in Low-Income and Minority Urban Communities." Unpublished paper, 1992.

Caskey, John P. "Check-Cashing Outlets in the U.S. Financial System." *Economic Review*, Federal Reserve Bank of Kansas City, November/December 1991a, pp. 53–67.

Caskey, John P. "Fringe Banking: The Shape of Things to Come." Paper presented at Jerome Levy Institute Conference on "Restructuring the Financial System for Economic Growth," November 1991b.

Center for Community Change. *New Research Shows S&Ls Shun Lower Income and Minority Neighborhoods*. Washington, DC: Center for Community Change, 1989.

Clark, Jeffrey A. "Economies of Scale and Scope at Depository Financial Institutions: A Review of the Literature." *Economic Review*, Federal Reserve Bank of Kansas City, September/October 1988, pp. 16–33.

Clinton, Bill and Al Gore. *Putting People First: How We Can All Change America*. New York: Times Books, 1992.

Community Investment Coalition. *Community Investment Plan: A Plan to Build and Preserve Affordable Housing and Improve Banking Services in North Dorchester, Roxbury, and Mattapan*. Boston: CIC, 1989.

Dedman, Bill. "The Color of Money." *Atlanta Journal and Atlanta Constitution*, May 1–4, 1988.

Dedman, Bill. "Blacks Turned down for Home Loans from S&Ls Twice as Often as Whites." *Atlanta Journal & Atlanta Constitution*, January 22, 1989.

Dreier, Peter. "Redlining Cities: How Banks Color Community Development." *Challenge*, Vol. 34, November/December 1991, pp. 15–23.

Dymski, Gary A. "Moral Hazard Versus Lending Spillovers: Paths into and out of the Dual Banking Crisis." Paper presented at the URPE/ASSA Conference on "The Crisis in Finance," Washington DC, December 1990.

Dymski, Gary, John Veitch, and Michelle White. *Taking It to the Bank: Poverty, Race, and Credit in Los Angeles.* A Report to the City of Los Angeles. Los Angeles: Western Center on Law and Poverty, 1991.

Elliehausen, Gregory and John Wolken. "Banking Markets and the Use of Financial Services by Small and Medium-sized Companies." *Federal Reserve Board Staff Study No. 160.* Washington, DC, 1990.

Financial Democracy Campaign. "Public Purpose Banking: Conceptual Outline" (undated pamphlet). Charlotte, NC: Financial Democracy Campaign, 1992.

Finn, Charles. *Mortgage Lending in Boston's Neighborhoods, 1981–1987: A Study of Bank Credit and Boston's Housing.* Boston: Boston Redevelopment Authority, 1989.

Fishbein, Allen J. "The Ongoing Experiment with 'Regulation from Below': Expanded Reporting Requirements for HMDA and CRA." *Housing Policy Debate,* Vol. 3, No. 2, 1992, pp. 601–36.

Flax-Hatch, David. *Banking in the Public's Interest: Promoting Community Development with the Public Deposits of Cities and States.* Chicago: Woodstock Institute, 1991.

Foust, Dean. "Bad Credit Doesn't Necessarily Mean No Credit." *Business Week,* November 9, 1992, p. 43.

Galster, George. "The Use of Testers in Investigating Mortgage Lending and Insurance Discrimination." In R. Struyk and M. Fix, eds., *Clear and Convincing Evidence.* Washington, DC: Urban Institute Press, 1992a.

Galster, George C. "Research on Discrimination in Housing and Mortgage Markets: Assessment and Future Directions." *Housing Policy Debate,* Vol. 3, No. 2, 1992b, pp. 639–83.

Goldberg, Deborah. "Enforcement of the Community Reinvestment Act." Statement Before the U.S. Senate Committee on Banking, Housing, and Urban Affairs, Subcommittee on Housing, September 15, 1992, pp. 180–203.

Green, Mark and Glenn von Nostitz. "Bank Mergers Are Taxing Consumers." *Nation,* January 27, 1992, pp. 81–84.

Greenwald, Carol S. *Banks Are Dangerous to Your Wealth.* Englewood Cliffs, NJ: Prentice-Hall, 1980.

Greider, William. *Secrets of the Temple: How the Federal Reserve Runs the Country.* New York: Simon and Schuster, 1987.

Guskind, Robert. "Thin Red Line." *National Journal,* October 28, 1989, pp. 2639–43.

Hanafin, Teresa M. "Bank Machines, Branch Offices Scarce in Boston Minority Neighborhoods." *Boston Globe,* February 7, 1989.

Hanggi, Elena. "The Public Purpose of the Federal Home Loan Bank System and Community Lending." Statement before the U.S. House Committee on Banking, Finance, and Urban Affairs, Subcommittee on Housing and Community Development, June 10, 1992.

Humphrey, David B. "Why Do Estimates of Bank Scale Economies Differ?" *Economic Review,* Federal Reserve Bank of Richmond, Vol. 76, October 1990, pp. 38–50.

Isenberg, Dorene. "Financial Institutions After the S&L Crisis: A Community-Based Credit Union." *Review of Radical Political Economics,* Vol. 23, Nos. 1 & 2, 1991, pp. 155–60.

Levine, Hillel and Lawrence Harmon. *The Death of an American Jewish Community: A Tragedy of Good Intentions.* New York: Free Press, 1992.

Massachusetts CAP Directors Association, Inc. "Analysis and Recommendations Regarding Basic Banking Services." Fitchburg, MA: 1989.

Mengle, David L. "The Case for Interstate Branch Banking." *Economic Review,* Federal Reserve Bank of Richmond, November/December 1990, pp. 3–17.

Munnell, Alicia H., Lynn E. Browne, James McEneaney, and Geoffrey M. B. Tootell. "Mortgage Lending in Boston: Interpreting HMDA Data." Working Paper No. 92–7. Federal Reserve Bank of Boston, 1992.

National Center for Policy Alternatives. *Legislative Sourcebook on Financial Deregulation*. Public Capital Series. Washington, DC: NCPA, 1987.

National Training and Information Center. *The Community Reinvestment Act (CRA) Handbook*. Fourth Edition. Chicago: National Training and Information Center, 1991.

Osborne, David. "A Poverty Program That Works." *New Republic*, May 8, 1989, pp. 22–25.

Pollin, Robert. *Deeper in Debt: The Changing Financial Condition of U.S. Households*. Washington, DC: Economic Policy Institute. Armonk, NY: M. E. Sharpe, Inc., 1990.

Schafer, Robert and Helen Ladd. *Discrimination in Mortgage Lending*. Cambridge, MA: Massachusetts Institute of Technology Press, 1981.

Schlesinger, Tom. "A Democratic Program for Financial Reform." Paper presented to Fannie Mae Colloquium Series, University of Rhode Island, November 21, 1991.

Shlay, Anne B. "Not in That Neighborhood: The Effects of Population and Housing on the Distribution of Mortgage Finance Within the Chicago SMSA." *Social Science Research*, Vol. 17, 1988, pp. 137–63.

Shlay, Anne B. "Financing Community: Methods for Assessing Residential Credit Disparities, Market Barriers, and Institutional Reinvestment Performance in the Metropolis." *Journal of Urban Affairs*, Vol. 11, No. 3, 1989, pp. 201–23.

Shlay, Anne B. and Ira J. Goldstein. "Proving Disinvestment: The CRA Research Experience." In Anne B. Shlay, ed., *The Politics of Community Reinvestment: Legislation, Organizing and Financial Reform*. Philadelphia: Temple University Press, forthcoming, 1994.

Squires, Gregory D., ed., *From Redlining to Reinvestment: Community Responses to Urban Disinvestment*. Philadelphia: Temple University Press, 1992a.

Squires, Gregory D. "Community Reinvestment: An Emerging Social Movement." In Gregory D. Squires, ed. *From Redlining to Reinvestment: Community Responses to Urban Disinvestment*. Philadelphia: Temple University Press, 1992b, pp. 1–37.

Squires, Gregory D. and William Velez. "Neighborhood Racial Composition and Mortgage Lending: City and Suburban Differences." *Journal of Urban Affairs*, Vol. 9, No. 3, 1987, pp. 217–32.

Thomas, Paulette. "Federal Data Detail Pervasive Racial Gap in Mortgage Lending." *Wall Street Journal*, March 31, 1992a.

Thomas, Paulette. "Small Businesses, Key to Urban Recovery, Are Starved for Capital." *Wall Street Journal*, June 11, 1992b.

Turner, Margery Austin. "Discrimination in Urban Housing Markets: Lessons from Fair Housing Audits." *Housing Policy Debate*, Vol. 3, No. 2, 1992, pp. 185–216.

U.S. General Accounting Office. *Government Check-Cashing Issues*. Washington, DC: U.S. Government Printing Office, 1988.

U.S. House of Representatives, Committee on Banking, Finance, and Urban Affairs. *Analysis of Banking Industry Consolidation Issues*. Staff Report. Washington, DC, 1992.

U.S. Senate, Committee on Banking, Housing, and Urban Affairs. Hearings on Community Reinvestment Act held March 22–23 and September 8–9, 1988, and July 31 and October 24, 1989.

U.S. Senate, Subcommittee on Housing. Hearings on Enforcement of the Community Reinvestment Act. September 15, 1992a.

U.S. Senate, Subcommittee on Housing and Urban Affairs, Report on the Status of the Community Reinvestment Act, Vol. I: Views and Recommendations, November 1992b.

Wienk, Ronald E. "Discrimination in Urban Credit Markets: What We Don't Know and Why We Don't Know It." *Housing Policy Debate*, Vol. 3, No. 2, 1992, pp. 217–40.

Williams, Peter, W. Brown, and E. Simmons. *Race and Mortgage Lending in New York City: A Study on Redlining*. Brooklyn, NY: Medgar Evers College, Center for Law and Social Justice, 1988.

PART III

Financial Markets and Productive Investment

CHAPTER TEN

Do U.S. Financial Markets Allocate Credit Efficiently? The Case of Corporate Restructuring in the 1980s[1]

JAMES R. CROTTY AND DON GOLDSTEIN

CHAPTER SUMMARY

Corporate acquisitions were big business during the 1980s. Their financing was an integral part of the revolution that took place in financial markets and practices and played a central role in creating the leverage mania of the decade. The 1980s corporate restructuring went beyond mergers *per se,* as a great many companies borrowed money to buy back stock or issue special dividends. The net effect of all this merger-driven activity was the same: equity was replaced with debt on corporate balance sheets on a massive scale.

The way for this leveraged restructuring boom was paved by the 1980s experiment with a radical laissez-faire approach to financial and antitrust policy. The results are now in, and they are devastating. Rather than mergers increasing productive efficiency, the search for speculative financial gain increasingly replaced production efficiency as their motive force as the decade evolved. And instead of pricing assets and allocating credit optimally, deregulated financial markets poured a trillion or so dollars of credit into this speculative asset shuffling.

It must be noted that in many cases and many ways, American corporations *are* in dire need of restructuring. Productivity growth has lagged; product quality has eroded; human resources are woefully mismanaged; and nowhere else in the industrialized world is the gulf in income and authority between top managers and those who actually produce the goods and services so wide. But the leveraged restructuring movement of the 1980s did not reduce the "short term-ism" underlying America's corporate woes—it made it worse:

• There were few systematic gains from mergers. While there were immense profits for some financial participants, others, such as acquiring-firm shareholders and the targets' bondholders, did not fare so well. And investor profits by themselves should not be interpreted as signs of enhanced productive efficiency.

The weight of the evidence suggests both that mergers brought ever-fewer economic benefits and that the corporate restructuring of the 1980s failed to achieve significant or lasting cost improvements.

• Significant and long-lasting costs were imposed on the American economy. The available evidence supports the public perception that workers, both blue and white collar, suffered major losses from leveraged mergers and acquisitions. Still needed is research into the spillover costs to families, communities, and the public sector. And instead of the lean-and-mean corporations that these cuts were supposed to buy, the leveraged restructuring movement left in its wake debt-constrained investment and R&D spending and a fragile financial structure.

• A regulatory rethinking is needed. Policy reforms are required in order to allocate credit away from the short-term speculation of the 1980s toward investments that are economically and socially efficient in the long run, as follows.

—Discourage lending by regulated financial institutions for highly leveraged restructuring, by manipulating existing policy levers (for example, deposit insurance coverage).

—Encourage long-term financial investment by taxing short term securities gains sharply and all secondary market trading modestly.

—Reform corporate governance to similarly tilt the playing field toward long-term-oriented behavior by recognizing the roles played by all corporate stakeholders and by encouraging pension funds as shareholders to ply their activism with an eye on the long term.

—End the tax advantage of corporate debt financing.

—Revitalize public investment in America's human, technical, and physical capital, providing examples and offering incentives to those firms willing to stake their own future on our country's.

Introduction

Why should a study of monetary and financial policy include a chapter on mergers? Corporate acquisitions were big business during the 1980s. Their financing was an integral part of the revolution that took place in financial markets and practices, and played a central role in creating the leverage mania of the decade. Thus the traditional product market question about mergers—How do they affect market power and operating efficiency?—must now be augmented by a serious investigation of their financial effects. In this chapter, we argue that the 1980s acquisitions left behind severe financial pollution,[2] which threatens the health of the suppliers of merger funds, and corporate anorexia, which saps the strength of the users of those funds. Because the scale of this merger-related activity in the 1980s was very large, the aggregate impact has already been felt economy wide.[3] Hence a policy concern for the financial market dynamics behind mergers is surely justified.

The 1980s merger wave provides an ideal experiment—a test case—for evaluating two of the theoretical pillars that supported the conservative, anything-goes, let-the-buyer-beware approach to financial regulation and antitrust policy in the past 15 years. The conventional academic wisdom in the late 1970s and early 1980s was that because mergers increase productive efficiency and because unregulated financial markets price assets and allocate credit optimally, neither mergers themselves nor their financing should be the subject of government regulatory activity. In the absence of government regulation, economists argued, private markets are "efficient."

The results of this experiment are now in, and they are devastating to the hands-off, laissez-faire approach to regulatory policy. We will show that a careful review of the relevant economic literature leads to two important conclusions. First, as the decade of the 1980s evolved, the search for speculative financial gain increasingly replaced production efficiency as the motive force behind the restructuring movement. And second—contrary to the predictions of the academic conventional wisdom—our deregulated financial markets proved to be shockingly inefficient as credit allocators. A radical departure from this disastrous laissez-faire regulatory philosophy in the coming years is imperative.

Just how massive the recent merger wave was may be glimpsed from a few numbers (*Mergerstat Review*, 1990). While the volume of mergers averaged just $16 billion yearly during 1970–77, in 1978–1983 that volume rose to an annual rate of $55 billion. It then climbed to $184 billion a year during 1984–89. For comparison purposes, consider the average annual volume of investment in new productive assets (net fixed nonresidential investment) for 1984–89: $84 billion (*Economic Report of the President*, 1992). Just during the years 1981–86, 18 percent of all mining and manufacturing assets changed hands, compared to 15 percent during the great turn-of-the-century merger wave (Markham, 1955; Ravenscraft, 1987). But the extent of 1980s corporate restructuring went beyond mergers *per se*. A great many companies "recapitalized," borrowing money to buy back stock or issue special dividends, often in response to the perceived threat of hostile takeover. Because 1980s mergers relied heavily on debt financing, the net effect of both kinds of restructuring was the same: Equity was replaced with debt on corporate balance sheets. Net equity financing (gross issues less retirements) plunged from $10 billion in 1980 to a negative $130 billion in 1988; by 1990, a net $622 billion in equity had been removed from corporate balance sheets. Meanwhile, the nonfinancial corporate sector's aggregate debt/equity ratio almost doubled, from .31 in 1980 to .56 in 1989.[4] At the same time, the fabulous fortunes made by all the big players in the leveraged restructuring game created a lust for leveraged gambling that permeated every segment of financial markets. The Federal Reserve Bank of New York (1991) estimates that the total increase in private-sector debt during the 1980s was about $2 trillion greater than would have been expected under more normal, less speculative financing practices.

It must be noted at the outset that in many cases and many ways, corporations in the U.S. *are* in dire need of restructuring. Productivity growth has lagged; product quality has eroded; human resources are woefully mismanaged. Nowhere else in the industrialized world is the gulf of income and authority so wide between top managers and those who actually produce the goods and services. But, for reasons that will be spelled out, the leveraged restructuring movement of the 1980s did not reduce the "short term-ism" underlying America's corporate woes—it made it worse.

We develop these points in subsequent sections, whose order and principal findings are as follows. The section entitled Stock Premiums from 1980s Mergers and Acquisitions: Speculation or Efficiency? reviews the arguments and evidence on the gains from mergers. While the merger wave was bestowing immense profits upon some financial participants, others—notably, acquiring-firm shareholders and the targets' bondholders—did not fare so well. And recent developments in the celebrated efficient financial markets debate show that investor profits by themselves should not be interpreted as signs of enhanced productive efficiency. Indeed, the weight of the evidence suggests that, on average, mergers brought ever-fewer economic benefits and that the corporate restructuring of the 1980s failed to achieve significant or lasting cost improvements.

The next section, What Are the Costs of the Merger Wave? finds although the trillion or so dollars of credit that financed the restructuring movement achieved little in the way of efficiency gains, it did impose significant and long-lasting costs on the American economy. First considered is the direct impact of mergers on employees. What evidence we now have supports the public perception that workers, both blue and white collar, suffered major losses from leveraged mergers and acquisitions (M&As). Still needed is research into the spillover costs to families, communities, and the public sector. The section then shows that instead of the lean and mean, state-of-the-art economic machine that this trillion dollars of credit was supposed to buy, the leveraged restructuring movement left in its wake debt-constrained investment and R&D spending and a fragile financial structure. The final section, Conclusions and Policy Implications, concludes that the evidence is clear and convincing: deregulation as financial policy is a disaster for the country even if a financial success for the takeover artists themselves. A complete rethinking of our regulatory philosophy is called for, and this final section of the chapter proposes a series of regulatory reforms designed to allocate credit away from the short-term speculation of the 1980s toward investments that are economically and socially efficient in the long run as follows:

• Discourage lending by regulated financial institutions for highly leveraged restructuring—by manipulating existing policy levers (for example, deposit insurance coverage);

• Encourage long-term financial investment by taxing short-term securities gains sharply and all secondary market trading modestly;

• Reform corporate governance in order to similarly tilt the playing field toward long-term-oriented behavior—by recognizing the roles played by all corporate stakeholders, and by encouraging pension funds as shareholders to ply their activism with an eye on the long term;
  • End the tax advantage of corporate debt financing; and
  • Revitalize public investment in America's human, technical, and physical capital—providing examples and offering incentives to those firms willing to stake their own future on our country's.

We look first at the question of who gains from mergers.

Stock Premiums from 1980s Mergers and Acquisitions: Speculation or Efficiency?

We will argue that the M&A boom was the driving force behind the leveraging of corporate America in the 1980s. The central policy question raised by this assertion is: Will the economic benefits of the merger wave exceed its costs to society over the long term? In this section, we review the debate about the sources of the impressive financial gains that accrued to the shareholders of acquired firms and to the takeover artists and the legions of specialists who assisted them. In the next section, we deal with the longer-term costs of the merger wave.

Sources of the Takeover Premium: Theory

The theoretical issue here is how to explain the origin of the immediate gains reaped by so many Wall Street participants in the 1980s merger wave. Were the gains generated by increases in corporate efficiency or by speculative excess in financial markets? As is by now well known, those gains were, on average, substantial (though, as noted below, there were also some losers). Most obviously and immediately, an array of financial market investors and professionals profited handsomely from the merger boom.

By far the largest category of such profits was target shareholders' stock premiums. Based on data from *Mergerstat Review* (1990), we estimate that premiums (the amount paid for a company beyond its original price) for the entire decade totaled $394 billion.[5] In addition, acquiring and acquired firms paid a variety of fees to investment and commercial bankers, attorneys, accountants, public relations firms, and others to arrange, advise, litigate, and defend in merger deals. Unfortunately, there is no readily available source of data on the aggregate size of those fees. To take an extreme case, the $26-billion leveraged buy-out (LBO) of RJR Nabisco in 1988 generated about $400 million in investment banking fees. The implied fee percentage in the RJR deal (1.5 percent) was actually rather low by LBO standards; Kaplan and Stein (1991) calculate that for large LBOs during the entire decade, fees rose from 2 to 6 percent of capital over the course of the decade. Adding in the legal fees would increase the totals significantly. For example, during 11 weeks in 1988, the struggle for Federated Department Stores produced more than $40 million in attorneys' fees, in addition to $160 million going to investment bankers (Cowan, 1988; Labaton, 1988).

Should these financial profits be interpreted as presaging rejuvenated performance for the underlying businesses and hence, gains for society, or merely as windfalls for the recipients? The conventional academic wisdom for much of the decade was that mergers are indeed efficiency enhancing and, therefore, create higher postmerger cash flows from the real assets of the acquired firms. This increased cash flow naturally causes a rise in the value of the stock providing ownership claims on those assets. Efficiency-enhancing acquirers are thus willing to offer large premiums to target shareholders, the story goes, and both parties gladly pay fees to the lawyers and investment bankers who make the transactions possible.

The dominant theory of the 1980s merger wave as an efficient restructuring of poorly managed corporations was the free-cash-flow theory of Michael Jensen (1986). The free-cash-flow hypothesis says that changing economic conditions left many American industries with cash flow arising from past investment that could not be profitably reinvested. If managers were too slow to react by paying out that free cash flow to shareholders—or even by shrinking the company— then various forms of leveraged restructuring could enforce such actions. Free cash flow is an example of a disciplinary merger explanation, in which efficient capital markets aid in correcting corporate inefficiencies (Marris, 1964; Manne, 1965). It figures prominently in the discussion to follow.

Of course, there are alternative explanations for why mergers take place that do not automatically assume increased economic efficiency and additions to social welfare. One theory of why mergers would occur in the absence of productivity gains holds that the hubris of acquiring managers, who overestimate their ability to enhance the efficiency of target assets, is to blame (Roll, 1986). Ravenscraft and Scherer's important study (1987) also suggests that uneconomic mergers may occur even in well-functioning capital markets; while on average, stock prices may be "right," at any time some will be underpriced (becoming vulnerable merger targets) and others overpriced (making them potential acquirers).

A different approach to theorizing nonefficient mergers—one that we find most persuasive—is to allow for the possibility of inefficiency in the capital markets themselves. In that case, various merger participants may be enriched by investors who overleverage or overpay for acquired firms or who do both, rather than facilitating improved efficiency.[6] In other words, if financial markets are subject to speculative booms and busts, then unwarranted optimism may induce buyers to pay more than the firm is really worth.

One way of thinking about such inefficiencies is in terms of a gap between the information available to merger "insiders" and that available to the public. DuBoff and Herman (1989) propose a theory in which investment bankers, top corporate managers, and others with promotional interests have both the ability and the incentive to inflate public expectations of prospective merger outcomes. These insiders then profit from the fees and security price run-ups that accompany the deals. In DuBoff and Herman's model, the gap between the public's and the promoters' information tends to be greatest during financial boom periods. A related theory (Goldstein, 1991) sees the financial sector's escalating willingness to finance debt as underlying the 1980s merger wave. In this view, American corporations became chips in a high-stakes game in which competitively pressed investors gambled on risky, leveraged restructuring assets supplied by similarly driven financiers, advisers, and raiders.

Which set of theories is right? The central problem in evaluating the academic conventional wisdom reflected in Jensen's free-cash-flow approach is that a corporation's future cash flows, and hence a current merger's efficiency effects, are *unobservable*. Thus, those who claim that 1980s mergers were driven by realistic or rational expectations of the potential for economic improvements have been forced to rely on the circular argument that the existence of target shareholders' gains proves that mergers were efficiency enhancing. That is, the *explanation* of merger stock profits rests on a prior *assumption* about what those profits represent.

In this vein, the great bulk of the evidence portraying the 1980s merger wave as an efficient restructuring process consists of stock market "event studies." Such studies demonstrate that during a short period around the merger event, target shareholders' returns exceed what could otherwise have been expected, based on past trends.[7] Others have pointed out that efficient mergers should benefit the shareholders of acquiring firms as well, but that over a longer time, acquirers' stock performance tends to deteriorate (Magenheim and Mueller, 1988). We will focus here on a different problem: *Any* attempt to acquire a target firm will force its market value to rise, no matter what the cause or effect of the takeover! If target stock prices cannot automatically be assumed to objectively reflect prospective corporate cash flows, then even the most positive event studies cannot provide adequate support for a laissez-faire merger policy.

That securities prices are in some sense accurate or objective estimates of the present value of future cash flows is known as the efficient market hypothesis. Some variant of the efficient market hypothesis is the intellectual core of the academic defense of the efficiency of the merger movement and of all arguments in favor of financial market deregulation. Thus, a critical evaluation of the efficient market thesis is a necessary prelude to any rethinking of financial market regulation policy. *If financial markets are not efficient, there is a prima facie case for government regulation.* While it has been the subject of a tremendous amount of discussion, a precise and widely recognized statement of the efficient market hypothesis is difficult to provide. Most definitions agree that in fully efficient markets, prices correctly reflect all existing information that is relevant to the returns expected from securities. This explanation goes hand in hand with the random walk theory of securities prices: In an efficient market, prices would change only when new information, which is by definition unpredictable and hence random, arrives.

But full market efficiency requires more than the random-walk property. Market prices must be an unbiased, objective estimate of the present value of the expected future cash flows associated with each security as determined by its so-called "fundamentals," untainted by speculation, fad, or market psychology. Because investors care about expected risk and return, the logic goes, freely functioning markets will price securities to channel resources to their best uses, taking full account of future returns (assumed, miraculously, to be known by investors) as well as the attendant future risks (assumed known as well). Should securities prices deviate from these fundamental values, informed speculators will profit by buying (selling) undervalued (overvalued) assets, thereby forcing prices back into line.[8]

Since it first emerged in explicit form during the 1960s, the efficient market hypothesis has generated heated academic debate. Early reviews were highly favorable; it was proclaimed by Jensen to be "the best established fact in all of social science" (1978).[9] However, the efficient market thesis has come under telling attack in recent years.

The now-widespread reconsideration of market efficiency by mainstream theorists began with studies of excess volatility undertaken independently by Shiller (1981 and 1984) and LeRoy and Porter (1981). These researchers argued that securities prices are far more volatile than warranted by the subsequent variability in the payments to which they give claim; hence, securities pricing must suffer from nonrational or nonfundamental influences. As Tobin put it: "Market speculation multiplies several fold the underlying fundamental variability of dividends and earnings" (1984, p. 6).[10]

A major, related critique of efficiency soon followed—that current securities prices are correlated with past ones: They exhibit cyclical fluctuations around their trend values. Yet according to the efficient market hypothesis, past prices, as currently available information, should not affect current price changes. There are no cycles in a random-walk market that smart investors can use to predict future changes in asset prices. It has long been known that over very short periods, stock prices tend to be positively, if weakly, cyclical. What has more recently been demonstrated is that over longer horizons—measured in years or even decades—returns on many securities in many countries are mean reverting. That is, they exhibit marked and persistent long-term deviations from trend (or speculative bubbles) before reverting to that average path.[11] Mean reversion is taken by many to indicate that securities prices undergo speculative booms and busts that depart from economic fundamentals.[12]

Noise trader theory has emerged as an alternative to the theory of efficient financial markets, one that is consistent with excess volatility, mean reversion, and many more specific empirical challenges to the efficiency approach (Shleifer and Summers, 1990). In the noise-trading framework, information is imperfect and imperfectly shared, and there are risks in going against the crowd, because even the best-informed professional traders (who are typically highly leveraged) cannot afford to wait forever for prices to return to fundamentals. Indeed, it will often pay arbitragers to go with rather than against the market as it pushes securities prices away from their fundamental values. Under these conditions, markets may significantly overreact to economic events. In deregulated financial markets, "fads" or seemingly irrational investor sentiment may drive prices away from what appear to be their fundamental values for years or even for decades.

Finally, it should be noted that these recent attacks from within neoclassical economics (broadly defined) fail to incorporate the most telling critique of the efficient financial markets thesis. This critique, associated with Keynes and Post-Keynesians such as Shackle, Vickers, and Davidson, can be summarized as follows. The fundamentals of neo-classical financial theory are embodied or reflected in agent expectations of future states of the economy. Efficient markets theory requires that agents with sufficient intelligence, resources, and energy will search for and eventually discover true or objective expectations of future outcomes and that the expectations of future risk and return discovered by such agents will determine the center of gravity for market prices.[13]

Put most starkly, the Keynesian attack on this theory is based on the argument that there is no objective predetermined future out there waiting to be discovered. Rather, the future remains to be *created* by the current and future decisions of economic agents. No one can possibly know the true future path of economy because no one can accurately predict the future actions of others. Because other people's future decisions are inherently unpredictable, future economic states are unknowable in principle; they are subject to fundamental uncertainty. In Shackle's words, "The future cannot be known before its time." Thus there is no objective foundation for the "rational" expectations that are the building blocks of the efficient market thesis—no objective center of gravity to anchor expectations and force market prices to some hypothetical efficient position. Expectations and market prices cannot help but be influenced by social conventions and fads (as described in the next section). Financial asset prices—by their very nature—must be "subject to waves of optimistic and pessimistic sentiment which are unreasoning, and yet in a sense legitimate where no solid basis exists for a reasonable calculation" (Keynes, 1936, p. 154). As a result, the efficient market thesis cannot possibly be sustainable.

A recent article by Peter Fortune in the Federal Reserve Bank of Boston's *New England Economic Review* (titled "Stock Market Efficiency: An Autopsy") summarized the current state of the debate over the efficiency of unregulated financial markets and its implications for policy as follows:

> This paper assesses the current state of the efficient market hypothesis, which was the conventional wisdom among academic economists in the 1970s and most of the 1980s. It reviews the empirical evidence and concludes that it provides an overwhelming case against the efficient market hypothesis. . . .

Our fundamental conclusion is that the efficient market hypothesis is having a near-death experience. . . . The fundamental implication of this conclusion is that security market inefficiency provides an economic foundation for public policy intervention in security markets. (1991, p. 34)

Sources of the Takeover Premium: Empirical Evidence

If the event study results are discounted and the efficient market hypothesis rejected, what kind of evidence about the alleged benefits of mergers can policy be based on? Here we will review two kinds of research on the operating characteristics of targets and acquirers that attempt to assess whether the economy gained from mergers. These studies examine either the characteristics of acquired firms before merger or the performance of the postmerger entity. Finally, we look at indirect evidence taken from the pricing of the securities that finance these transactions.

The purpose of premerger studies of firms acquired in the merger wave of the 1980s is to determine whether acquisition targets in general were poor performers that needed shaping up by new owners. Unfortunately, this literature presents a mixed and inconclusive set of results. In one study, Morck, Shleifer, and Vishny (1989) compare companies from the 1985 Fortune 500 purchased during the preceding five years with the nonacquired firms. They find that friendly (uncontested) merger targets tend to have top managers (often including founding or dominant families) with large equity stakes and thus personal financial incentives to sell unrelated to efficiency considerations. These cases provide no clues one way or the other about prospective efficiency gains.

Both Lehn and Poulsen (1989) and Long and Ravenscraft (1991) examine the before-the-fact characteristics of LBOs, reaching different conclusions about the kinds of companies involved. Lehn and Poulsen study 263 LBOs from 1980 to 1987, finding that the LBOs tended to suffer from free-cash flow problems—their undistributed cash flow was greater than required to finance the profitable investment opportunities available to the firm. By definition, this excess or free-cash-flow should have been paid out to shareholders. But their study is marred by the fact that the measure of the expected profitability of investment (which is unobservable) used by the authors is the rate of growth of sales, a poor proxy for expected profitability. In any case, the proxy was not able to distinguish LBO targets from nontargets effectively. Long and Ravenscraft, with a larger sample covering the same years, also find above-average cash flow prior to LBOs; however, they do not infer free-cash-flow problems or inefficiencies from this result. Indeed, their pre-LBO sample's below-industry average investment rate suggests an appropriate managerial response to declining investment opportunities. In a related study, Blair and Litan (1990) investigate aggregate data for the industry-level characteristics associated with heavy LBO activity. Their results suggest no connection between LBO activity *per se* and slow industry growth.

Research on 1980s hostile takeovers has also reached conflicting conclusions. Herman and Lowenstein (1988) find that early-1980s takeovers, unlike prior ones, appeared to target highly profitable firms hardly in need of the market for corporate control's discipline. But Morck, Shleifer, and Vishny, in the study previously cited, find that the hostile acquisitions in their sample are distinguished by low growth and investment, as well as a low stock market value for both the firm and its industry. They interpret these characteristics as indicative of poor premerger performance. Goldstein (1991) notes marginally lower profitability among hostile targets than for nonacquired firms, but in his sample, an equally strong predictor of takeover status (especially later in the takeover wave) is a high level of investment for firms with low current profitability, suggesting a conflict between short-horizoned securities holders and growth-oriented managers.

A compelling case for the efficiency theory of mergers, then, cannot be established on the basis of the premerger research. Most important, enough time has elapsed since the recent merger wave peaked so that studies of postacquisition performance are now appearing. (Most look at the effect of mergers on employees and on investment and research and development, which will be considered when we discuss the costs of mergers in the next section.) Two of these papers, both focusing on LBOs, directly investigate measures of operational efficiency. Lichtenberg and Siegel (1990) test for plant-level productivity before and after manufacturing buy-outs during the years 1981–86. Their results appear to show significant productivity gains, especially for LBOs during the later years. But Long and Ravenscraft (1991), using an overlapping sample from the same data source, reach very different conclusions. While they find substantial inventory cost savings, operating efficiency is not affected for the 1981–87 plant-level buy-outs surveyed. For reasons elaborated in endnote 13, we consider the Long and Ravenscraft study to be more reliable and its conclusions therefore more compelling.[14] LBOs in the 1980s on average have not demonstrated significant and persistent gains in efficiency.

Two studies related to acquisition financing suggest that speculation rather than efficiency considerations increasingly drove the merger wave as the decade wore on. The premiums achieved by the sellers seem to have derived increasingly from overoptimism on the part of the buyers. Kaplan and Stein (1991) directly examine the pricing and financing structures of 124 large management buy-outs during 1980–89, which accounted for three-fourths of the value of all LBOs during those years. They find ballooning purchase premiums and declining managerial equity investment later in the decade. Fees to commercial and investment bankers skyrocketed, from 2 percent of total capital at the decade's start to just under 6 percent by its end. Meanwhile, banks reduced their share of the financing. They also demanded earlier repayment of principal, which squeezed borrowing firms' cash flow to debt service ratios over the term of the loan. And the growing share of financing coming from new public debt (largely junk bond issues) was increasingly risky for the lender because interest payments were often deferred, while other, more senior, lenders had prior claim on the borrower's assets in the event of default. In sum, as public investors poured an ever-growing stream of capital into these deals, a variety of insiders began taking their cash out up front. Ultimately, the proportion of buyouts that defaulted on loans in Kaplan's and Stein's sample rose from zero for 1980–83 to a fourth during 1985–88. These results are consistent with those from Wigmore (1990), who finds that junk bonds' interest coverage at issue time fell steadily throughout the 1980s.

The picture that emerges from the postmerger evidence and the financing practices surveyed seems clear. By the middle 1980s, speculative or self-reinforcing financial profit expectations were coming increasingly unhinged from the efforts to raise efficiency that underlay many earlier deals. It is important to keep in mind that we do not argue that all mergers are undertaken for the same ill-founded reasons or that they come to the same unfortunate ends. It is not necessarily individual mergers, but merger waves, that have been associated historically with episodes of widespread speculative financial activity. The same holds true in spades for the 1980s.

We conclude that policymakers need not throw up their hands at the complexity of the arcane academic debate about the alleged efficiency of financial markets and its corollary, the free-cash-flow or efficiency-driven explanation of the sources of the huge fortunes created by the leveraged 1980s M&A boom. There are convincing reasons for accepting the strong and growing evidence that deregulated financial markets do not always allocate financial capital in a socially efficient manner and that financial markets perform their allocation function most poorly during speculative boom periods like the merger wave of the 1980s.

On one hand, there is no compelling evidence that the 1980s mergers targeted primarily inefficient or free-cash-flow firms or that the efficiency of the typical acquired firm did in fact significantly improve. On the other hand, we have empirical evidence of speculative bubbles in securities markets and realistic theoretical models of the behavior underlying these swings—behavior that cannot be convincingly portrayed as a rational response to changes in economic fundamentals. Both the noise trader and Keynesian theories are consistent with troubling events from recent financial history: the crash of 1987, the boom-and-bust junk bond cycle, the insurer insolvency scare, and the credit crunch in commercial banking, to name but a few. Both are compatible with what we know about people, whose decisions after all drive the markets. In an uncertain world, choices often suffer from judgment errors with respect to risk (taken too freely), past trends (expected to continue), and new information (greeted with overreaction).[15] And in an uncertain world, the deregulation of the financial markets that feed these speculative binges may be a recipe for disaster.

Now after examining the alleged benefits of the merger wave, we turn to a consideration of the possible losses to society.

What Are the Costs of the Merger Wave?

In this section, we fous on three major kinds of costs associated with the restructuring movement—costs to employees and their communities, to investment and R&D, and to the stability of the economic system.

The Human Dimension

Both proponents and critics of the 1980s merger wave agree that corporate restructuring has imposed hardships on certain individuals and groups. When operations are combined, or bureaucracy streamlined, or ancillary tasks contracted out, or facilities closed, or operating costs cut, people lose jobs or income or both. Nevertheless, almost all studies of the efficiency of corporate restructuring implicitly assume that all of the cost reductions achieved by these changes represent net gains to society, which in turn logically requires the following prior assumptions: It is implied that fired workers were making no contribution to firm revenue (i.e., that these "employees were purely deadwood and all of [their] labor costs [should be] treated as an efficiency improvement" [Summers, 1990, p. 77]), that they were able to find equivalent employment elsewhere, that there are no negative externalities—costs borne by parties not directly involved in the transaction, and that there will be no future costs associated with the breaking by the new owners of implicit contracts between the firm and its employees and suppliers. Typically, none of these assumptions is true.

The importance of negative externalities and the widespread rupture of implicit contracts are stressed in an influential paper by Shleifer and Summers (1988), who point out that substantial costs have been borne by various segments of the communities in which affected firms are located. Other businesses lose revenue as a result of the layoffs and wage cuts, local governments suffer erosion in their tax base, and homeowners may suffer substantial losses as the residential real estate market sags.

Although numerous journalistic accounts report the devastation wrought in particular communities as the result of layoffs and plant closings associated with specific corporate restructurings, to our knowledge there have been no careful academic studies assessing these indirect effects of the recent merger wave. Yet such negative externalities are surely crucial to any assessment of its social costs and benefits, and government policy must be cognizant of those externalities.[16] Moreover, Shleifer and Summers argue that the transfer or redistribution of existing wealth from stakeholders in the target firms (employees, suppliers, and local communities) to owners, rather than resulting in increased efficiency, may be the major source of the takeover premiums attained in hostile takeovers in particular and "disciplinary" mergers in general. For example, they argue that the "transfer" from the unions to Carl Icahn in the TWA takeover "amounted to one and a half times the takeover premium" (1988, p. 50). The most important source of these transfers, according to Shleifer and Summers, consists of the existing implicit contracts between workers and suppliers and the target firms. In these contracts, the firm has promised job security and future wage increases to workers and reasonable long-term profit margins to suppliers in return for their willingness to engage in costly and potentially risky firm-specific investments in human and physical capital. Such investments increase firm profits in the short to intermediate run but may prove worthwhile to employees and suppliers only over the long term.

In disciplinary mergers, then, new managers who feel no loyalty to stakeholders can reap a windfall for shareholders by laying off older workers (who have fulfilled their end of the contract but have not yet received full payment), cutting the wages of those who remain, and squeezing supplier profits. Whereas it was profitable before the fact for the target firm to agree to these implicit contracts, it is profitable after the fact for the new management to renege on them.

However, the long-term costs of these shortsighted practices could turn out to be enormous. If workers and suppliers no longer believe that firms can be trusted to hold up their end of the implicit contracting process, they will not be willing to undertake productivity-enhancing investments. "Potential suppliers will not invest in relationship-specific capital [and] the young will shirk if they expect no raise in the future" (Shleifer and Summers, 1988, p. 45). Over the past decade or so, the corporate restructuring wave, in combination with layoffs, union busting, and takeaway contracts among much of U.S. industry, has created a widespread belief among both blue- and white-collar workers that corporations cannot be trusted to reward hard work, extra effort, and firm-specific training with job security or wage increases. Yet the ability to make implicit contracts with workers—contracts that offer job security and enhanced future income in return for training and a commitment to improve firm productivity—is the foundation of the management philosophy used by our most successful international competitors. Thus, the lust for takeover transfers may have helped to destroy an essential condition for long-term productivity gains. In the end, this may prove to be the most long-lasting and destructive legacy of the 1980s takeover wave.

Lacking any serious analysis of the cost of negative externalities and the likely long-term effect of the collapse of implicit contracting, we turn instead to more narrow studies of how restructuring directly affects employees of acquired firms. The limited evidence now available indicates that there are employee losses after mergers. Rosett (1990) studies union wage settlements during 1976–1987, using his finding of reduced real wage growth after merger to estimate that workers lose only about 1 to 5 percent as much as shareholders gain. But in the absence of the efficient markets assumption, the interesting question is not what portion of stock premiums worker losses "explain," but rather what the extent of those losses has been. Converting Rosett's present-value estimate of a union wealth loss of $490 million (during six postmerger years) into cumulative terms, we infer very roughly that the union members in his sample lost a total of $600 million in reduced wage growth. Adjusting this figure—again, very roughly—to reflect the large number of U.S. workers not covered in his study, we come up with wage losses on the order of $6–12 billion.[17] If indeed, following mergers, worker incomes were reduced by billions of dollars, then the ripple effects on their local communities must have been substantial.

While Rosett focuses on wage settlements, Bhagat, Shleifer, and Vishny (1990) study post-takeover layoffs (and other effects) in a sample of large, hostile take-overs. For firms reporting layoffs, blue-collar cuts averaged 6.5 percent of the total labor force, and white-collar cuts 3.2 percent. Because there are far fewer white-collar workers, their layoffs appear to have been proportionately heavier. Similarly, in the Lichtenberg and Siegel (1990) study already discussed, LBOs are followed by substantial cuts in white-collar employment and compensation.

Bhagat, Shleifer, and Vishny note that they do not track layoffs at business units divested after takeover, yet such divestitures constitute about 30 percent of the value of target firms on average, with well over two-thirds of the take-overs followed by selloffs. But since purchasers of large business units also debt-finance, the same problems reappear at divested companies. For example, the Safeway LBO is listed in Bhagat, Shleifer, and Vishny as resulting in 300 layoffs, or 0.1 percent of the firm's labor force. But the spinoff of its Dallas division to nonunion operators resulted in the loss of 9,000 union jobs (although an undetermined number of lower-paid nonunion jobs replaced them). The re-sulting furor led to a union-Safeway agreement that unions at Safeway or its divestitures would be retained, but in return for wage cuts. A *New York Times* article at the time (Fisher, 1988) called "reduced labor costs ... the greatest factor" behind the "success" of the Safeway restructuring. A union official in-volved in the case put this leveraged "success" in human perspective: "It's kind of like contracting a dread disease for which the cure is very, very painful, and you're never the same afterward, but you survive" (Fisher, 1988, p. 32).

The evidence now available thus raises the disturbing possibility that while shareholders gained from mergers, workers lost, and these losses did not on the whole serve any efficiency-enhancing purpose. Employee costs can always be cut in the short run to make room for debt servicing. But sustainable productivity gains, of the kind required to buttress long-term competitiveness, are not so easily achieved. State-of-the-art managerial theory and practice suggest that truly productive restructuring must elicit worker loyalty and induce worker participa-tion in the struggle for efficiency. The chances of accomplishing this kind of transformation via the meat cleaver effect of leveraged restructuring are nil; whatever short-run contributions restructuring may have made, they have been overwhelmed by the impediments to the long-term productivity growth that it has created.

Merger Debt in the Longer Run: Investment and R&D Instability

As we have seen, the short-term effect of the M&A boom of the 1980s on the cost structure of affected firms has been the subject of some debate. However, short-term changes in costs are not our main concern. The question of whether or not from a longer-term societal perspective, the free-wheeling, deregulated financial markets of the era created and allocated efficiently or wisely the credit generated by the leveraged restructuring boom is of greater interest. In the previous section, we raised the possibility that the costs of mergers to workers and their communities have, in addition to their immediate human impact, long-term economic consequences as well. Here we will argue that leveraged restructuring has adversely affected investment, R&D, and economic stability and will continue to do so for some time to come.

No one denies that the M&A movement of the 1980s oozed debt from every pore. For the period 1980–89, net credit market borrowing by nonfinancial corporations totaled $1289 billion. But such massive borrowing was not required to finance capital investment; fixed investment exceeded corporations' internally available funds by a scant $99 billion during that span. Our rough estimate of the portion of 1980–89 restructuring (mergers and share repurchases) that was financed by debt is $1242 billion. In fact, most of the borrowing and most of the restructuring—about a trillion dollars in each case—took place from 1984 to 1989, when corporate internal funds actually exceeded their investment outlays.[18]

In the introduction, we reported one measure of this leveraging—the nonfinancial corporate debt/equity ratio. The debt/equity ratio reflects the firm's vulnerability to a decline in cash flow, a rise in interest rates, or the appearance of a credit crunch over the longer run. Unfortunately, as we noted, there is disagreement about how the value of equity (or of assets) should be measured. We reported the replacement cost of asset net worth. Some prefer market value, but market value is an acceptable measure only if one accepts the axioms of efficient market theory. Because market value is subject to speculative booms and busts, the market value measure of the debt/equity ratio is also extremely unstable. For these reasons, analysts generally measure financial vulnerability using some variant of the interest coverage ratio—the ratio of internal funds flow to interest payments, an index of the short-term financial security of the firm. Friedman's (1992) estimate of the impact of leverage on the interest coverage ratio of nonfinancial corporations in the 1980s is representative of most such studies. Friedman found that interest payments constituted 16 percent of before-tax profits plus interest payments in the 1950s and 1960s, rose to 31 percent in the 1970s, then elevated to 60 percent in the 1980s.[19] Friedman has also noted that the ratio of the debt of nonfinancial corporations to gross national product "fluctuated narrowly around 30 percent from 1960 through 1980. By year-end 1989, before the recession began, it stood at about 39 percent" (1991, p. 4).

Of course, debt mania was not confined to corporations directly involved in restructuring or to firms forced to substitute debt for equity to avoid a takeover. Nor, for that matter, was it confined to the nonfinancial corporate sector. According to the Federal Reserve Bank of New York,

> The 1980s in fact witnessed a widespread leveraging of the U.S. economy. The traditionally stable linkage between private sector debt and GDP [gross domestic product] broke down completely in the last decade and by 1991 an extra $2 trillion of private sector debt had been created over and above what would have been expected on the basis of the past relation between private sector debt and GDP. (1991, p. 11)

It is important to note that much of the debt buildup outside the nonfinancial corporate sector was directly or indirectly related to leveraged restructuring. The spectacular fortunes made in the takeover movement by those directly involved and by those, such as Michael Milken, involved in the financing of takeovers created a culture of leverage worship on the Street, a culture that academic gurus such as Michael Jensen assured us was efficiency enhancing and socially productive. M&As and stock buy-backs drove the stock market to ever-greater heights; junk bonds and bridge loans brought riches to everyone who touched them. The lesson from all this seemed clear; gambling on financial markets with borrowed money was the smart and quick path to wealth. The belief that high leverage was good for stockholders, financial institutions, and the economy, as well as the path to individual fortune became the conventional wisdom. The success of those who engaged in personal and corporate leveraging turned high leverage into a group norm and induced herd behavior—a tendency for individual decisions to conform to the collective conventional wisdom.[20]

The facts thus seem clear: corporations became significantly more indebted in the 1980s; the bulk of this debt was not needed to finance capital accumulation; and the merger wave, through its direct and indirect effects, was the single most important cause of this corporate leveraging process as well as a major contributor to the debt explosion outside the nonfinancial corporate sector. "The heart of the problem is the increased financial fragility that has resulted from the massive borrowing campaign upon which American corporations have embarked since the current economic expansion began in 1983" (Friedman, 1988, p. 126). These facts raise a key policy question: what have been, and what are likely to be, the effects of this debt burden on economic performance at the micro and macro levels?

Not surprisingly, different economic theories offer different answers. For those who cling to the increasingly discredited theory of efficient financial markets, high debt is an effective device with which to discipline managers; it forces capital out of inefficient companies into those with the most profitable investment opportunities. Debt is the sine qua non of the market for corporate control. However, once we leave the fairy-tale world of efficient markets and all-knowing expectations and return to the world as it really is, high leverage has its dangers and downsides, and they can be threatening. We focus our discussion on the likely effects of excessive corporate leverage on long-term investment and R&D

spending, but we address the related issues of the effect of indebtedness on macroeconomic instability and on the likelihood of a financial crisis as well.

Leverage, Long-Term Investment, and R&D Spending: Theory

Is it true, as is widely believed by corporate executives, financiers, and observers of the business scene, that the shaky financial structures and aggressive restructuring practices of the 1980s substantially shortened the horizons of business decisionmakers, causing them to shy away from long-term investments of all kinds—in capital goods, R&D, and worker education and training? Traditional neo-classical financial theory says no. According to the famous (or infamous) Modigliani-Miller theorem, under efficient markets, the decision to invest in capital goods should be independent of the firm's financial structure.[21] This independence property is alleged to hold "under reasonably general conditions" (Blanchard and Fischer, 1989, p. 295).

We have already discussed the arguments against the efficient market hypothesis. There are two important alternatives to efficient markets theory that provide solid analytical foundations for the proposition that excessive leverage will restrict investment spending. We consider in turn the increasingly influential New Keynesian (NK) theory and the more venerable Post-Keynesian (PK) theory.[22]

The basic NK innovation in the neo-classical theory of the relation of capital structure to investment can be easily understood using the model of bank lending presented in the seminal paper by Stiglitz and Weiss (1981).[23] Consider a competitive market in which firms use bank loans to finance investment projects. Assume that loans are risky for banks because the loans are not fully collateralized. Assume further that firms know the "true" expected risk and expected return associated with each of their potential investment projects but that banks do not. As a result of this information asymmetry, banks cannot distinguish before the fact between "bad" loans (high risk relative to expected return) and "good" loans (low risk relative to expected return). The expected return on the bank's loan portfolio consists of expected interest payments on successful projects and expected losses due to default on failed projects.

Stiglitz and Weiss show that under these conditions, banks must charge all borrowers—good and bad—a common lemons premium to compensate for the expected losses from defaults. The cost of borrowing for good investment projects will thus exceed the cost of internal funds because the rate charged for external funds will contain a lemons premium reflecting the high default risk of bad projects. Switching from internal to external funding will raise the cost of capital, causing some socially optimal investment projects to be rejected by the firm. Other things being equal, less-indebted firms (which can rely more heavily on internal funds and have more collateral to support their loan applications) will spend more on capital investment. Moreover, as banks raise interest rates, the proportion of bad projects in their loan portfolios will rise both because it is only the high-risk projects that remain profitable to the borrower under the higher rates (a sorting or adverse selection effect) and because firms' incentive to substitute bad for good projects rises with the interest rate (an incentive or moral hazard effect). Therefore, the expected return to banks may not rise at the same rate as the interest rate; beyond some point, it may actually fall. Thus, "under not implausible assumptions," credit rationing may take place (Stiglitz and Weiss, 1981, p. 394). Under credit rationing, a subset of socially optimal investment projects will not be undertaken. These sorting and incentive effects have been modeled for all forms of external funds.[24]

The upshot of these asymmetric information arguments is this. First, the greater the firm's net worth or the lower its debt/equity ratio, the greater the collateral it can use to obtain loans, the lower the lemons premium it will face, the lower the likelihood that it will be credit rationed, and, therefore, the higher its level of investment spending. Second, the more the firm can rely on internal financing for its investment projects, the lower will be the hurdle rate of return its investment projects must pass. In stark contrast with neo-classical theory, NK theory predicts *that investment should be inversely related to the firm's debt/equity ratio; and that investment spending by highly leveraged firms will be "excessively sensitive" to changes in current cash flow* (Gertler, 1988, p. 573).

This cash-flow sensitivity in turn creates a situation in which any shock to the level of income and profit in the economy will trigger a change in investment that will magnify the initial shock. Therefore, high leverage creates a more unstable macroeconomy. In a financially fragile environment, such instability could contribute to the initiation of a financial crisis.[25]

Note that in NK theory, the effect of debt on investment is transmitted exclusively through the cost of external finance. In PK theory, increased debt makes firms less willing to invest even in the absence of any lemons premium in the cost of external capital.[26] Thus, NK and PK theories should be seen as providing complementary reasons to believe that leverage restricts investment.

The basic PK argument is as follows. The firm operates under conditions of "fundamental" or Keynesian uncertainty. Since the future is unknowable in principle, agents never believe that they have complete and accurate knowledge of the likelihood of all possible future economic outcomes. In such an environment, forecasting and decisionmaking are appropriately described as conventional in character, based on custom, habit, tradition, rules of thumb, instinct, and other socially constituted practices. As such, they will be influenced by market fads and fashions and will respond to the ever-changing mood of the Street.[27] Because they can never have complete confidence in their forecasts, managers will want to maintain a financial cushion or margin of safety to protect themselves from creditors or irate stockholders in the event that future profits turn out to be lower than expected. This margin of financial safety required by the firm (represented by the inverse of the debt/equity ratio or by the interest coverage ratio or by both) is itself conventionally constituted and will, therefore, rise and fall with the boom-and-bust cycles of financial markets.[28]

At any time there will be a safety margin that conventional wisdom suggests is prudent; imprudent debt/equity or interest coverage ratios will be understood to threaten the firm with potential financial distress or even bankruptcy. Holding the cost of capital constant, higher leverage will diminish the firm's desire to invest, because additional long-term investment will place the firm in a position deemed to be imprudent or excessively risky. In the euphoria of a speculative financial boom such as took place in the 1980s, managers' perception of what constitutes a prudent or acceptable degree of leverage may rise as fast as, or even faster than, actual leverage, so that—temporarily—investment spending may not be debt restrained. But as the euphoria of the boom first levels off and then, with the first signs of financial distress, evaporates, more firms will come to see themselves as excessively or dangerously leveraged. And when, as in the past few years, degrees of leverage once conventionally certified as prudent become exposed as objectively dangerous to the survival of the firm and the decisionmaking autonomy of its management, then *the high leverage inherited from the speculative boom will severely restrict the firm's willingness to commit funds to risky and illiquid long-term investment projects.*

In sum, both NK and PK theory suggest that, *ceteris paribus*, the debt mania of the 1980s should have lowered the level of investment spending and increased investment instability, increased the instability of the macroeconomy, and raised the likelihood of a financial crisis. The two theories also imply that these effects will continue to plague the economy for as long as the debt overhang remains.

Leverage, Long-Term Investment, and R&D Spending: Empirical Evidence

For several decades, the neo-classical theorem that financial structure had no effect on investment decisions guided and constrained the econometric work on investment behavior that justified and reinforced belief in the empirical relevance of the theorem. However, concern about the rising indebtedness of the 1970s and especially the 1980s, in concert with the development of NK theory (which, because it is so close to neo-classical theory in assumptions and methodology, was treated with respect by mainstream economists), finally liberated empirical work from its neo-classical blinders. And, lo and behold, an impressive and ever-growing body of empirical evidence has developed that supports the NK-PK thesis that high leverage both restricts investment and R&D spending and makes them more unstable.[29]

Two kinds of empirical research are relevant here. The first studies the effect of leverage on the long-term commitments of firms acquired in the M&A boom. The second attempts to measure the effect of increased leverage on the investment spending of all firms, restructured or not.

Hall's 1990 econometric study found that while restructuring itself did not significantly depress R&D spending, the higher debt burdens associated with LBOs most certainly did: "the link between leverage and reduced R&D has been established" (p. 123). Hall observed that "R&D spending may be an unintended victim of the current trend in the United States to shift the source of financing toward debt" (1990, p. 123). Extending this research, Hall (1991) tested the broader question of whether the restructuring boom of the 1980s forced "managers to pay attention to short-term earnings at the expense of long-term investments" both in capital goods and in R&D (p. 1).[30] Her econometric evidence showed a "large negative impact on both kinds of investment from increases in leverage.... [T]hese are enormous effects, implying reductions in ... investment of the order of 50 percent [of the increase in debt]" (p. 11). Evaluating both regressions and case studies, Hall concluded that "massive changes in financial structure ... do appear to be accompanied by reduced investment of all kinds" (p. 23).[31]

As noted above, Long and Ravenscraft (1991) analyzed the most extensive data set on LBOs yet assembled. They found that LBOs raise "the amount of cash available to make interest payments by cutting capital expenditures. Capital expenditures/shipments drop by 9 percent" following a buyout (p. 20), and R&D spending declines by about 10 percent. Long and Ravenscraft also establish that these cuts in investment "are not temporary" (p. 21).

Finally, Kaplan and Stein (1991) found that for 124 management buy-outs between 1980 and 1988, the ratio of capital expenditures to sales declined on average by 38 percent in the year after the purchase (p. 31 and Table 10).[32]

Of the econometric work on this question not limited to the population of acquired firms, the micro data studies done by Steve Fazzari and associates have had the most impact.[33] For example, Fazzari, Hubbard, and Petersen (1988) show that decreases in internal funds flows have a significant negative effect on investment spending, especially for the small- and medium-sized firms that NK theory suggests should be faced with the largest lemons premium. Their results, which are consistent across various alternative specifications of the investment equation, suggest that a one-dollar decline in cash flow (caused by a one-dollar increase in interest payments) lowers investment spending by 23 cents.

In work similar in design to Fazzari's, Cantor (1990) demonstrated that highly leveraged firms exhibit greater cyclical sensitivity of investment spending (and of employment) because of the dependence of investment on internal funds. His work suggests, for example, that a firm with a 50 percent debt/asset ratio spends only half as much of each extra dollar of cash flow on investment than a firm with a 25 percent debt/asset ratio. "When leverage increases are fairly widespread, the corporate sector is likely to become more volatile and more responsive to sales and cash flow fluctuations ... " (p. 41).[34]

Franke and Semmler (1990) and Crotty and Goldstein (1992) get similar results using aggregate time series data for nonfinancial corporations and manufacturing firms, respectively. Two additional links between the debt explosion of the 1980s and reduced investment spending should be mentioned. First, Federer

(1991) demonstrated econometrically that investment spending declines when general macroeconomic uncertainty rises. Because NK empirical work shows that rising leverage increases macroeconomic instability and because the degree of uncertainty rises with instability, Federer's results establish yet another channel through which high leverage impedes investment. Second, if, as it seems reasonable to assume, the massive demand for credit associated directly and indirectly with the M&A boom put upward pressure on real interest rates in the mid to late 1980s, it also shortened corporate time horizons and decreased both investment and R&D spending through standard neo-classical channels.

Friedman's recent assessment of the empirical work on this question seems sensible.

> There is ample evidence indicating that highly indebted firms undertake less research and development than otherwise comparable firms with lower leverage. Similarly, there is evidence that highly leveraged firms do less capital spending than their less leveraged counterparts. Given the links connecting both research and investment to productivity, these developments suggest that the widespread leveraging U.S. corporations did in the 1980s left not a strengthened but a diminished basis for the economy's growth in the 1990s. (1991, p. 8)

A final aspect of the 1980s acquisition-related debt binge remains to be mentioned—its effect on the fragility of the financial system. Overeager lending by a range of financial institutions has left them weighted down with bad debts arising from the merger boom.

• Investment banks were caught with "hung" bridge loans when the 1989–1990 junk bond collapse made refinancing impossible and the banks had to be rescued with capital infusions; First Boston and its bailout by Crédit Suisse is one example.

• Commercial banks' troubled, highly leveraged transaction loans posed capital and regulatory problems for many of them and contributed to the credit crunch and thus to the length of the recent recession. An informal Fed study found that by 1988, several of the big New York banks were channeling as much as 40 percent of their new commercial and industrial lending into LBOs.[35]

• Before the junk bond market imploded in late 1989 and early 1990, savings and loan institutions (S&Ls) held about 9 percent of all outstanding junk; by that time, the great bulk of new-issue junk volume was being floated to finance mergers and restructurings (Altman, 1990). The thrifts' holdings were highly concentrated in just a few risk-plunging S&Ls, contributing both to their own demise and to the taxpayer bill arising therefrom.

• Even the continuing tremors in the insurance industry owe something to the merger boom; while the bulk of the bad debts that afflict insurers are in commercial real estate, the four huge problem investments that triggered the collapse of Mutual Benefit Life in 1991 included two LBOs (Pulliam and Anders, 1991).

Mergers were not unique in contributing to the shakiness of financial institutions. They took their place alongside other speculative ventures such as commercial real estate loans, Third World debt, oil-patch lending, and other outlets for the financial institutions' bruising, competitive search for high-risk, high-return assets. Indeed, financial competition played an important role in stimulating the merger wave itself. For many of the acquiring firms on the borrowing side of this dynamic, it has meant financial distress. We have shown that corporate leverage increased dramatically during the 1980s, and that restructuring accounted for the bulk of it. When a company lives close to the edge, with cash flow barely sufficient to service debt, it takes little to push it over the edge. Not surprisingly, we are in the midst of a quiet bankruptcy epidemic. Rising swiftly from late-1970s levels, the business failure rate reached and maintained a 1980s plateau more than twice as high as any level since the Depression. And the increase is most striking for large bankruptcies. As a result, since 1984, there have been on the order of $30 to $40 billion in business failures every year (*Economic Report of the President*, 1992).

We conclude, based on an evaluation of both theoretical and empirical evidence, that the allocation of credit by the deregulated, speculative financial markets of the 1980s was not only inequitable in its distributional effects, but also grossly inefficient. The costs of this misallocation in the form of high default and bankruptcy rates, constrained investment and R&D spending, slow economic growth, high unemployment, low productivity, stagnant wages, and shattered communities have hit hard already and will continue to plague the economy for some time to come. The economic stagnation we experienced beginning in early 1989 may represent only the first downpayment on our mortgaged future.

Conclusions and Policy Implications

Out of a welter of arguments and evidence, then, a few simple conclusions about the 1980s merger wave can be extracted. The decade's restructuring movement was a driving force in a tremendous increase in corporate indebtedness. But unless one accepts the stock market evidence that *assumes* that shareholder profits indicate enhanced efficiency—and there are strong reasons not to accept this—there are few signs that corporate performance has been enhanced, and many that it has not.

In contrast, the evidence is mounting that the costs of creating and allocating credit through the deregulated financial markets of the 1980s are likely to be significant and persistent. In many cases, employees in merged firms suffered a direct loss of security, income, and/or jobs. The spillovers from these losses have been substantial; communities have suffered, and workers' commitment to productivity growth has been badly shaken. Productivity is threatened also by the constraining effects of debt on investment and R&D expenditures. And finally, the financial stability and flexibility of industrial and commercial companies and financial institutions throughout the economy has been impaired. Capital and credit crunches in the banking, investment, insurance, and thrift industries all have been bound up with high-risk merger lending; the restructuring of borrowers' woes has led to soaring, sustained bankruptcy rates. As noted in a recent edition of *Business Week*: "The death toll among U.S. businesses remains at epidemic levels. Dun & Bradstreet Corp. report that business failures were 12% higher in July [1992] than in July, 1991, and are up 16% so far this year" (October 12, 1992, p. 24).

The ballooning of merger debt and its potential drag on long-term economic performance thus place corporate control at the intersection of two major policy problems of the 1990s: the restructuring debate over the performance and competitiveness of the U.S. economy and financial market reform. In both areas the conclusions summarized suggest a basic rethinking of merger-related financial regulatory policy. In the short term, policymakers should act to penalize the most egregious restructuring abuses. They should adopt measures that tilt financial markets in general and the market for corporate control in particular away from leveraged speculation and toward long-term economic and social priorities. And they should begin now, when the cooling of merger fever permits action that is considered, purposeful, and strong. In the longer term, we need fundamental institutional change in the way we create and allocate credit—change that will retard financial speculation and promote productive investment in human and physical capital. We urge consideration of the following:

• Discourage lending for highly leveraged restructuring. One step toward dampening pressures for short-term speculation in the financial markets could be taken by providing regulated banks and thrifts with disincentives against the lending that destabilizes their own and their business borrowers' financial positions. One targeted lending behavior would be borrowings used to finance mergers and recapitalizations (share repurchases and special dividends) rather than real investment. Included in this definition should be holdings of securities issued for those same purposes; for example, restructuring-related junk bonds. Given the existing regulatory structure, the most effective sanction would be denial of deposit insurance. Alternatives would include rising reserve or capital requirements or both.

• Encourage long-term financial investment. While regulated intermediaries' lending had a role in creating the climate for 1980s restructuring, stock and bond trading played a crucial part as well. Both merger and leverage mania thrive on short-term, speculative debt and equity markets. Congress should rein in casino investing behavior with two kinds of taxes. First, short-term capital gains—on holdings of less than a year—should be taxed at a significantly higher rate (not less than 50 percent). And second, as Keynes himself suggested, securities transactions in the secondary markets should be subject to a modest trading tax. Together these measures would lessen the markets' focus on short-term performance, weaken incentives for speculating in restructuring situations, and slow the erosion of the concept of "ownership" in the corporate sector.

• Reform corporate governance. The speculative financial market practices addressed by the preceding proposals have had a profound impact on corporate governance, especially with respect to corporate control. On the state, national, and private levels, the policy framework for mergers needs to address both recent patterns in short-term stockholding behavior and the complex interdependence of the corporation's profitability and its constituencies' interests. First, strengthened state laws regulating hostile takeovers—whose threat often spurred various kinds of leveraged restructuring—should be supported where they exist (e.g., Pennsylvania) and adopted where they do not. Such legislation should protect the rights of employees, restrict green-mail and other put-in-play investor profits, and give longer-term shareholders more of a voice in corporate control matters.

Second, socially responsible long-term shareholding should be mandated for the pension funds that increasingly dominate the equity markets. Up to now, pension funds' "shareholder activism" has been limited mainly to maximizing short-term capital gains, including support for high-premium restructurings, sacrificing a long-term climate conducive to growth and stability for the immediate gains of their beneficiaries. Yet it is employees who often pay the price in leveraged restructuring. Labor unions must explore ways of gaining more of a voice in the policies of their members' pension funds. And Empoyee Retirement Income Security Act law should be scrutinized for the incentives it provides for pensions' investing behavior.

• End the tax advantage of corporate debt financing. The perverse incentives of existing policy extend beyond corporate governance *per se*. By taxing corporate income used for dividends but not for interest payments, the federal government encourages and subsidizes both aggressive financing in general and leveraged restructuring in particular. The solution that is simplest and fiscally least problematic is to end the tax deductibility of interest. This could be phased in over several years to minimize disruption of corporate planning, and the corporate income tax could be adjusted to maintain a desirable overall corporate tax burden. Short of that, policymakers should consider excluding from tax deductibility the interest on high-yield debt (defined in terms of a spread above investment grade) or on debt issued for the retirement of equity or on both.

• Strengthen and democratize public investment. In attempting to discourage leveraged speculation and encourage long-term, economically and socially productive investment, it is crucial that we not ignore the power of public credit creation and allocation. Some of the most impressive national economic performances in recent decades, including those achieved by Japan, Germany, South Korea, and Taiwan, have relied heavily on the public and semipublic allocation of credit for industrial growth and development. In the U.S., federally channeled credit flows are already massive, but they have not in recent decades targeted investment outside the farm and housing industries. To influence the path of business restructuring, policymakers could, through careful use of publicly guided credit, sharpen the financial incentives offered to corporate leaders.

Such credit should flow in directions determined by the urgency of democratically registered social needs. Markusen and Yudken (1992) focused on the possibilities inherent in military conversion, and Pollin (this volume) on building environmental sustainability into our productive capacity. Surely other initiatives could deliver similar social benefits and economic spillover effects if nurtured through public credit flows. Proposals for specific mechanisms to create and allocate these flows are beyond the scope of this chapter, but they might include credit guarantees or subsidies, as well as creation of new public institutions or the development of new functionsfor existing ones. Over the longer term, the creation of a public investment bank (such as the one proposed by Robert Pollin in this volume) may be the key step in the construction of a financial system that is equitable as well as efficient.

All of these proposals grow out of a recognition that the 1980s merger wave was part and parcel of a much wider pattern of speculative financial excess. Thus our policy proposals are not (and cannot be) restricted to mergers *per se*. All are aimed at helping to shift our system of corporate finance away from its speculative focus on deals and asset turnover (reminiscent of the kind of finance called "capital market based" by Zysman [1983] and "fluid" by Porter [1992]) toward a system based on commitment to socially productive investment over the long haul (as in Zysman's "credit market based" and Porter's "dedicated" alternatives). Such a shift must build in greater decisionmaking accountability to worker and community interests, because companies' employee and community constituencies are crucial to and vitally affected by long-term corporate performance.

We have suggested that the effects of the 1980s' merger wave will include a kind of corporate anorexia: With debt-induced cost-cutting in employment, investment, and R&D, ash flow can be boosted in the short run, but the prognosis for long-term vitality is gloomy. We thus come full circle with the question of what kind of restructuring the American corporate economy needs.

Corporations and their managers do need to be pressed to be flexible and competitive and to invest for the long term in worker education and training, capital goods, improved technology, R&D, and product quality. But the financially driven restructuring of the 1980s pushed corporate America in the wrong direction. It is ironic that the academic defenders of this movement have rationalized the constrictive effects of leverage by essentially claiming that our economy suffers from too much investment, too benign treatment of employees, and too little attention to today's stock price.

We need a better basis for policy than that.

Notes

1. The authors wish to thank Ed Herman and Paul Burkett for their helpful comments on an earlier draft.

2. This term, for the unintended financial market spillover effects of risky merger lending, is due to Charkham (1989).

3. To take but one example, the economy's difficulty in rebounding from the 1990–

91 recession has often been interpreted as evidence that bank lending, business spending, and their contributions to economic activity have been weighed down by merger-related debt.

4. Data are from Pickering (1991) and from the Board of Governors of the Federal Reserve System, *Flow of Funds Accounts* and *Balance Sheets for the U.S. Economy*. Debt/equity is credit market borrowing over tangible net worth at replacement cost. It is often argued that debt-equity should use the market value of equity in the denominator. Doing so appears to remove the 1980s rising leverage trend, as the post-1982 bull market swamps growing borrowing. But that is symptomatic of the problems caused by the sensitivity of this measure to the stock market; for example, debt/equity so defined jumped from about 55 percent to over 80 percent between August 25 and October 19, 1987. Almost all such indicators show rising indebtedness during the decade.

5. We used each year's reported dollar value of M&As and the average percent premium paid over market in that year to calculate annual dollar premiums. The fact that not all deals report a price may bias this estimate downward. But there may be an opposite bias as well. In general, premiums are known only for public companies purchased, and that is where the "average percent premium" comes from. We have applied that percentage to the equity values of all mergers, public and private. If it is applied only to the value of public acquisitions, then the aggregate premiums estimate is $238 billion. (The years covered are off by one: 1980–89 for all mergers and 1981–1990 for public deals, due to data unavailability for the latter series.)

6. See, for example, Kaplan and Stein (1991). Some analysts have suggested that the flow of wealth to financial market participants in mergers represents transfers from various "stakeholders" in acquired companies—especially employees and communities. Actually, this explanation could be consistent with either the efficiency or the speculation categories of merger theories described in the text. We will return to this question in the third section when considering the costs of mergers.

7. For favorable reviews of this literature, see Jensen and Ruback (1983) and Jarrell, Brickley, and Netter (1988).

8. According to this view, for example, the thrift and banking crises arose because policy distortions (deposit insurance) reduced the need for depositors and therefore bankers to balance the rewards of asset choices against their risks.

9. One such favorable review is Fama (1970). It should be noted that many of the econometric tests used to support market efficiency were of low statistical power, meaning that the efficiency hypothesis was quite likely to pass the test even if it were not true. See Zeckhauser, Patel, and Hendricks (1991), pages 3 through 7, for a clear explanation of why this is so.

10. Although criticized on statistical grounds by efficient markets supporters (e.g., Kleidon, 1988), these studies continue to be influential.

11. Major studies are by Fama and French (1988) and Poterba and Summers (1988). A nontechnical review is contained in De Bondt and Thaler (1989). Although long-term mean reversion seems to be a much larger effect than short-horizon positive autocorrelation, by their very nature there are not many long periods to work with, and therefore the statistical precision of these tests tends to be low.

12. Although much of the growing debate over market efficiency has revolved around statistical issues, supporters of the efficiency hypothesis have countered with a variety of substantive responses to their critics. Probably the most central is the assertion that the apparently speculative swings in asset prices documented by critics are in fact driven by changes in the rates of return investors require, which are in turn tied to changing economic fundamentals. Recall that a security's price may be thought of as the discounted value of the stream of expected payments to which it gives claim. Rather than reflecting

irrational expectations about future payments, price trends may instead indicate that the discount rate being applied to those payments is changing. According to efficient market defenders, shifts in investor discount rates rationally reflect the impact of technological development, or of basic (though unobservable) changes in investor preferences for present versus future consumption (Fama, 1991).

But, again, this line of reasoning is circular. To argue that swings in market prices must be a reflection of swings in unobservable but rational discount rates is simply to assume what needs to be proved. Moreover, the idea that investor risk preference or time preference varies with broad macroeconomic conditions is perfectly consistent with theories of speculative bubbles. Speculative asset bubbles have often accompanied heated economic boom periods, as would be expected if overreaction and crowd sentiment color economic decisionmaking.

13. More technically, efficiency requires that agents have conditionally correct subjective probability distributions over future economic outcomes.

14. Because these two are the largest studies of the actual impact of 1980s leveraged acquisitions, it is important to consider the source of their differences. Long's and Ravenscraft's sample is larger, is more carefully screened and constructed, and covers an additional year. Another likely cause of the conflicting results is the difference in the efficiency measures used. Lichtenberg and Siegel measure productivity by the unexplained variation (residual) in each plant's dollar output in a regression using the inputs as explanators. Two of the three inputs used—plant capital stock and materials costs—are unlikely to change much after a buy-out. But their measure of the labor input is highly sensitive to how total wages and salaries are split between white-collar and blue-collar workers. The labor proxy declines when the portion of the payroll going to white-collar employees declines. In fact, the white-collar/blue-collar ratio in total compensation does drop significantly after the event for the buy-out firms in their sample. So all else being equal, LBO plants' output residual will rise post-buy-out. On the other hand, Long's and Ravenscraft's efficiency measure is a "price-cost margin" ratio—the values of shipments less total wages less materials, all over value of shipments. The straightforward labor compensation in this measure is not sensitive to the blue-collar/white-collar mix, and at least in that respect may be a more reliable efficiency indicator.

Another aspect of Lichtenberg's and Siegel's results that deserves scrutiny is the time pattern of the apparent productivity gains, which they find to be strongest for the later LBOs. What is puzzling is that the buy-outs done later in the decade are the ones that have proved to be most subject to financial distress. Indeed, in Long's and Ravenscraft's study, the later LBOs showed sharper bidding competition, higher prices and premiums, and lower equity participation by top managers in the buy-out entity. These characteristics seem more consistent with speculative fever, with a growing overpayment by eager outside investors, than with increasingly efficient managerial control of production costs.

15. For a selection from this rich literature, see Kahneman, Slovic, and Tversky (1982).

16. See Bluestone and Harrison, 1982, Chapter 3, for a discussion of the dimensions along which these costs should be measured.

17. We took Rosett's (1990) estimate of a $490-million real wealth loss to be the present value of a six-year annuity, at a real interest rate of 6 percent (the average difference between Baa bond rates and changes in the CPI over 1976–1987). The implied annual loss is about $100 million in constant dollars, for a cumulative (undiscounted) loss of $600 million. This figure is adjusted upward to reflect his sample coverage of only 25 percent of the private unionized labor force and the inclusion of only a fraction (we assumed 20 percent) of the total labor force in the unionized sector, that is, a sample coverage of roughly one-twentieth of the labor force. The implied losses are then $12 billion rathe than $600 million. We also present an estimate of half of that, since the

numbers are very rough and mergers are not evenly distributed across the economy; they occur more frequently in manufacturing, where unions are disproportionately represented (hence a smaller coverage adjustment would be required).

18. Data on net credit market borrowing is from the Board of Governors of the Federal Reserve System, *Flow of Funds Accounts*. The debt-financed restructuring estimates start with Table 1 in Pickering (1991), giving totals for leveraged buyouts, other non-stock financed mergers, and share repurchases. We then add the dollar value of divestitures from *Mergers & Acquisitions* magazine, as reported in Pickering; divestitures are omitted in the Pickering data, and are rarely stock-financed. The resulting estimate of debt-financed restructuring has an upward bias, because some non-stock-financed acquisitions are paid out of the buyer's cash on hand rather than by borrowing. But there are still omitted transactions which bias the estimate downward—e.g., leveraged dividend recapitalizations and acquisitions by U.S. companies of foreign firms. See also the relevant data in Henderson (1990, p.17) and Kopke (1989, pp. 39–40).

We do not mean to suggest that corporate investment should be exclusively financed through internal funds. The point is that sensible financing of investment spending during the 1908s would have required only a small fraction of the corporate borrowing that in fact took place.

19. See also the estimates in Bernanke and Campbell (1988), Bernanke, Campbell, and Whited (1990), Estrella (1990), Friedman (1991), Frydl (1990), Henderson (1990), and Ryding (1990). Bernanke and Campbell conclude that "all measures of interest expense [relative to cash flow] have risen significantly [in the 1980s]. The increase is particularly striking for real interest expense. Even at the median [of a large sample of public corporations] the current burden of real interest payments has approximately quadrupled since the late 1970s" (1988, p. 107). Bernanke, Campbell, and Whited show that even in the buoyant cash flow years of 1987 and 1988, the "leverage of the most highly leveraged firms continued to increase . . . " (1990, p. 258).

20. For example, Zeckhauser, Patel, and Hendricks report that "the evidence suggests that corporate executives determining debt/equity ratios are strongly influenced by the choices of their peers within the industry. Three reasons may be posited: (1) decision makers gain information from what similar firms are doing; (2) they secure protection from criticism (including self-criticism); (3) participants on the other side of the market (such as lending institutions or the buyers of new issues) are engaging in herd behavior, thereby inducing observed clustering among participants on this side" (1991, p. 21).

21. As noted by Gertler in a recent survey of financial theory:

> The MM theorem was attractive because it provided researchers with a rigorous justification for abstracting from the complications induced by financial considerations. For example, the developers of neoclassical investment theory (e.g. Hall and Jorgenson 1967) . . . used the MM theorem as a convenient rationale for ignoring capital market considerations when solving the firm's intertemporal investment choice problems. For similar reasons, financial variables started disappearing from empirical investment equations. (1988, p. 565)

22. For a survey of New Keynesian theory, see Mankiw and Romer (1991). The most influential Post-Keynesian analysis of the influence of leverage on investment spending is that of Minsky (1975 and 1986).

23. The New Keynesian theory of credit markets is also discussed in the chapter written by Steve Fazzari in this volume.

24. See, for example, Myers and Majluf (1984) and Greenwald, Stiglitz, and Weiss (1984).

25. Of course, excessive household leverage will also increase the likelihood of a financial crisis, and household leverage grew alongside corporate leverage in the "roaring 80s." From early 1983 through late 1990, the household debt-to-income ratio rose from 73

percent to 99 percent (Altig, Byrne, and Samolyk, 1992, p. 3). The greater the level of indebtedness of economic units in general, the greater the probability that a decline in income flows will trigger a financial implosion.

26. Note that the NK reduced-form econometric studies surveyed below cannot distinguish between the magnitude of the NK supply of credit and the PK demand for credit effects of leverage on investment.

27. See Crotty (1991) for an analysis of conventional decisionmaking and the characteristics of macrotheory under conditions of true uncertainty.

28. See Crotty (1991) for an analysis of conventional expectation and confidence formation and their relation to instability in the macroeconomy.

29. In an article entitled "Why Financial Structure Matters," Stiglitz made the following observation.

> [Neo-classical] theory drove the econometrics: financial structure variables were excluded [from econometric investment equations] because "economic theory"—that is, Modigliani and Miller—said they should be excluded. Only recently, as a developing and substantial body of economic theory says once again that such variables should be included, have econometricians included [financial] variables again in their specifications of the causes of investment. And lo and behold, they appear to be significant! (1988, pp. 121–22)

30. In a recent contribution to this debate on the alleged shortening of corporate horizons, Shleifer and Vishny (1990) argue that it is perfectly rational for enterprise managers to adopt short-term planning horizons, because the penalties to them of poor stock price performance outweigh the benefits of good stock price performance, and arbitrage can correct inefficient market valuations of short-term assets more quickly and completely than it can inefficient market valuations of long-term assets. "This reasoning suggests that managers will choose short over long-term investment projects, since picking the latter allows their equity to be more mispriced in equilibrium, *ceteris paribus*, and threatens their jobs" (p. 151).

31. Hall (1990) also questions the general efficacy of the market for corporate control as an institution through which stockholders resolve their agency problems with management: "[T]here is a strong feeling that long-term strategies are difficult to implement in an environment where managers fear losing their jobs or firms if they experience bad draws for a couple of years" (p. 33).

32. See also the related studies cited on page 3 of Long and Ravenscraft (1991).

33. See Fazzari (1992), Fazzari, Hubbard, and Petersen (1988), Fazzari and Mott (1986–87), and Fazzari and Petersen (1991).

34. In a similar vein, Sharpe's recent econometric study concludes that "employment at firms with higher leverage is . . . substantially and significantly more sensitive to demand-induced fluctuations in sales than employment at firms with lower leverage" (1991, abstract).

35. Details are available from the authors.

Bibliography

Altig, S., S. Byrne, and K. Samolyk. "Is Household Debt Inhibiting the Recovery?" *Economic Commentary*, Federal Reserve Bank of Cleveland, February 1992.

Altman, Edward. *The High Yield Debt Market*. Homewood, IL: Dow Jones Irwin, 1990.

Bernanke, Ben and John Campbell. "Is There a Corporate Debt Crisis?" *Brookings Papers on Economic Activity*, Vol. 1, 1988, pp. 83–139.

Bernanke, Ben, John Campbell, and Toni Whited. "U.S. Corporate Leverage: Developments in 1987 and 1988." *Brookings Papers on Economic Activity*, Vol. 1, 1990, pp. 255–86.

Bhagat, Sanjai, Andrei Shleifer, and Robert Vishny. "Hostile Takeovers in the 1980s: The Return to Corporate Specialization." *Brookings Papers on Economic Activity, Microeconomics*, 1990, pp. 1–72.

Blair, Margaret and Robert Litan. "Corporate Leverage and Leveraged Buyouts in the Eighties." In John Shoven and Joel Waldfogel, eds., *Debt, Taxes, and Corporate Restructuring*. Washington, DC: The Brookings Institution, 1990, pp. 43–80.

Blanchard, Olivier and Stanley Fischer. *Lectures on Macroeconomics*. Cambridge, MA: Massachusetts Institute of Technology Press, 1989.

Bluestone, Barry and Bennett Harrison. *The Deindustrialization of America*. New York: Basic Books, 1982.

Board of Governors of the Federal Reserve System. *Flow of Funds Accounts; Balance Sheets for the U.S. Economy*. Washington, DC: Board of Governors of the Federal Reserve System, various years.

Cantor, R. "Effects of Leverage on Corporate Investment and Hiring Decisions." *Quarterly Review*, Federal Reserve Bank of New York, Summer 1990, pp. 31–41.

Charkham, Jonathan. "Corporate Governance and the Market for Companies: Aspects of the Shareholders' Role." Bank of England Discussion Paper. London: Economics Division, Bank of England, 1989.

Cowan, Alison. "Investment Bankers' Lofty Fees." *New York Times*, December 26, 1988, p. D1.

Crotty, James. "Are Keynesian Uncertainty and Macrotheory Compatible? Conventional Decision-Making, Institutional Structures and Conditional Stability in Keynesian Macromodels." Working Paper No. 1991–17, Department of Economics, University of Massachusetts, Amherst, 1991.

Crotty, James and Jon Goldstein. "A Marxian-Keynesian Theory of Investment Demand: Empirical Evidence." In Fred Moseley and Edward Wolff, eds., *International Perspectives on Profitability and Accumulation*. Brookfield, VT: Edward Elgar, 1992, pp. 197–234.

De Bondt, W. and R. Thaler. "A Mean-Reverting Walk Down Wall Street." *Journal of Economic Perspectives*, Vol. 3, No. 1, 1989, pp. 189–202.

DuBoff, Richard and Edward Herman. "The Promotional-Financial Dynamic of Merger Movements: A Historical Perspective." *Journal of Economic Issues*, Vol. 23, No. 1, 1989, pp. 107–134.

Economic Report of the President. Washington, DC: U.S. Government Printing Office, 1992.

Estrella, Arthur. "Corporate Leverage and Taxes in the U.S. Economy." In E. Frydl, ed., *Studies on Corporate Leverage*, Federal Reserve Bank of New York, September 1990, pp. 29–44.

Fama, Eugene. "Efficient Capital Markets: A Review of Theory and Empirical Work." *Journal of Finance*, May 1970, pp. 383–417.

Fama, Eugene. "Efficient Capital Markets: II." *Journal of Finance*, Vol. 46, No. 5, 1991, pp. 1575–1617.

Fama, Eugene and Kenneth French. "Permanent and Temporary Components of Stock Market Prices." *Journal of Political Economy*, Vol. 96, 1988, pp. 246–273.

Fazzari, Steven. "Monetary Policy, Financial Policy, and Investment." This volume, 1993.

Fazzari, Steven, R. Glenn Hubbard, and Bruce Petersen. "Financing Constraints and Corporate Investment." *Brookings Papers on Economic Activity*, Vol. 1, 1988, pp. 144–95.

Fazzari, Steven and Tracy Mott. "The Investment Theories of Kalecki and Keynes: An Empirical Study of Firm Data." *Journal of Post Keynesian Economics*, Vol. 9, No. 2, Winter 1986–87, pp. 171–87.

Fazzari, Steven and Bruce Petersen. "Working Capital and Fixed Investment: New Evidence on Financing Constraints." Department of Economics, University of Washington, St. Louis, MO, November 1991.

Federal Reserve Bank of New York. *Annual Report*, 1991.

Federer, J. P. "The Impact of Uncertainty on Aggregate Investment Spending." Department of Economics, Clark University, Working Paper No. 1991–2, Worcester, MA, 1991.

Fisher, Lawrence. "Safeway Buyout: A Success Story." *New York Times*, October 21, 1988, First Business Page.

Fortune, Peter. "Stock Market Efficiency: An Autopsy." *New England Economic Review*. Federal Reserve Bank of Boston, March/April 1991, pp. 17–40.

Franke, R. and W. Semmler. "Finance, Profit Expectations and Investment in the Business Cycle: Theories and Empirical Evidence." Paper presented at the Jerome Levy Institute, September 1990.

Friedman, Benjamin. "Comment on Bernanke and Campbell." *Brookings Papers on Economic Activity*, Vol. 1, 1988, pp. 126–30.

Friedman, Benjamin. "Financial Impediments to Economic Prosperity." Department of Economics, Harvard University, Cambridge, MA: December 1991.

Friedman, Benjamin. "Risks in Our High Debt Economy: Depression or Inflation?" In Steven Fazzari and Dimitri Papadimitriou, eds., Financial Conditions and Macroeconomic Performance: Essays in Honor of Hyman P. Minsky. Armonk, NY: M. E. Sharpe, Inc., 1992.

Frydl, E. "Some Issues in Corporate Leverage: An Overview." In E. Frydl, ed., *Studies on Corporate Leverage*, Federal Reserve Bank of New York, September 1990, pp. 1–28.

Gertler, Mark. "Financial Structure and Aggregate Economic Activity." *Journal of Money, Credit and Banking*, Vol. 20, No. 3, Part 2, August 1988, pp. 559–88.

Goldstein, Don. "Takeovers and the Debt Assessments of Firms and the Stock Market." Unpublished Ph.D. dissertation, University of Massachusetts, Amherst, 1991.

Goldstein, Don. "Debt and Takeovers: What Makes Cash Flow 'Free'?" Allegheny College, Meadville., PA, 1992.

Greenwald, Bruce, Joseph Stiglitz, and Andrew Weiss. "Information Imperfections in the Capital Market and Macroeconomic Fluctuations." *American Economic Review*, Vol. 74, May 1984, pp. 194–99.

Hall, Bronwyn. "Corporate Restructuring and Investment Horizons." National Bureau of Economic Research Working Paper No. 3794, July 1991.

Hall, Bronwyn. "The Impact of Corporate Restructuring in Industrial Research and Development." *Brookings Papers on Economic Activity, Microeconomics*, 1990, pp. 85–133.

Henderson, Y. "Is Leverage a Tax Dodge—or Not?" *New England Economic Review*, Federal Reserve Bank of Boston, March/April 1990, pp. 11–32.

Herman, Edward and Louis Lowenstein. "The Efficiency Effects of Hostile Takeovers." In John Coffee, Louis Lowenstein, and Susan Rose-Ackerman, eds., *Knights, Raiders, and Targets*. New York: Oxford University Press, 1988, pp. 211–40.

Jarrell, Greg, J. Brickley, and J. Netter. "The Market for Corporate Control: The Empirical Evidence Since 1980." *Journal of Economic Perspectives*, Vol. 2, No. 1, 1988, pp. 49–68.

Jensen, Michael. "Some Anomalous Evidence Regarding Market Efficiency." *Journal of Financial Economics*, Vol. 6, 1978, pp. 95–102.

Jensen, Michael. "Agency Costs of Free Cash Flow, Corporate Finance, and Takeovers." *American Economic Review*, Vol. 76, No. 2, 1986, pp. 323–29.

Jensen, Michael and Richard Ruback. "The Market for Corporate Control: The Scientific Evidence." *Journal of Financial Economics*, Vol. 11, 1983, pp. 5–50.

Kahneman, Daniel, Paul Slovic, and Amos Tversky. *Judgment Under Uncertainty: Heuristics and Biases.* New York: Cambridge University Press, 1982.

Kaplan, Steven and Jeremy Stein. "The Evolution of Buyout Pricing and Financial Structure in the 1980s." National Bureau of Economic Research Working Paper No. 3695, May 1991.

Keynes, J. M. *The General Theory of Employment, Interest and Money*. London: Macmillan, 1973 (1936).

Kleidon, Allan. "Bubbles, Fads and Stock Price Volatility Tests: A Partial Evaluation: Discussion." *Journal of Finance*, Vol. 43, 1988, pp. 656–59.

Kopke, Richard. "The Roles of Debt and Equity in Financing Corporate Investments." *New England Economic Review*, Federal Reserve Bank of Boston, July/August 1989, pp. 25–48.

Labaton, Stephen. "$200 Million in Wall St. Fees Seen From Federated Deal." *New York Times*, April 5, 1988, p. D1.

Lehn, Kenneth and Annette Poulsen. "Free Cash Flow and Stockholder Gains in Going Private Transactions." *Journal of Finance*, Vol. 44, No. 3, 1989, pp. 771–87.

LeRoy, Steven and Roy Porter. "The Present-Value Relation: Tests Based on Implied Variance Bounds." *Econometrica*, Vol. 49, No. 3, 1981, pp. 555–74.

Lichtenberg, Frank and Donald Siegel. "The Effects of Leveraged Buyouts on Productivity and Related Aspects of Firm Behavior." *Journal of Financial Economics*, Vol. 27, 1990, pp. 165–94.

Long, William and David Ravenscraft. "Decade of Debt: Lessons from LBOs in the 1980s." *Brookings Discussion Papers No. 91–6*. Washington, DC: The Brookings Institution, 1991.

Magenheim, Ellen and Dennis Mueller. "Are Acquiring-Firm Shareholders Better off After an Acquisition?" In John Coffee, Louis Lowenstein, and Susan Rose-Ackerman, eds., *Knights, Raiders, and Targets*. New York: Oxford University Press, 1988, pp. 171–93.

Mankiw, N. Gregory and D. Romer. *New Keynesian Economics*. Cambridge, MA: Massachusetts Institute of Technology Press, 1991.

Manne, Henry. "Mergers and the Market for Corporate Control." *Journal of Political Economy*, Vol. 73, No. 2, 1965, pp. 110–20.

Markham, Jesse. "Survey of the Evidence and Findings on Mergers." In National Bureau of Economic Research, *Business Concentration and Price Policy*. Princeton, NJ: Princeton University Press, 1955, pp. 141–212.

Markusen, Ann and Joel Yudken. *Dismantling the Cold War Economy*. New York: Basic Books, 1992.

Marris, Robin. *The Economic Theory of "Managerial" Capitalism*. New York: The Free Press of Glencoe, 1964.

Mergerstat Review. Chicago: Merrill Lynch, 1990.

Minsky, Hyman. *John Maynard Keynes*. New York: Columbia University Press, 1975.

Minsky, Hyman. *Stabilizing an Unstable Economy*. New Haven, CT: Yale University Press, 1986.

Morck, Randall, Andrei Shleifer, and Robert Vishny. "Characteristics of Hostile and Friendly Takeover Targets." In Alan Auerbach, ed., *Takeovers: Causes and Consequences*. Chicago: University of Chicago Press, 1989, pp. 101–36.

Myers, Stewart and Nicholas Majluf. "Corporate Financing and Investment Decisions When Firms Have Information That Investors Do Not Have." *Journal of Financial Economics*, Vol. 13, June 1984, pp. 187–221.

Pickering, Margaret. "A Review of Corporate Restructuring Activity, 1980–1990." Staff Study No. 161. Washington, DC: Board of Governors of the Federal Reserve System, 1991.

Pollin, Robert. "Public Credit Allocation through the Federal Reserve." This volume, 1993.

Porter, Michael. "Capital Disadvantage: America's Failing Capital Investment System." *Harvard Business Review*, September-October 1992, pp. 65–82.

Poterba, James and Lawrence Summers. "Mean Reversion in Stock Prices: Evidence and Implications." *Journal of Financial Economics*, Vol. 22,1988, pp. 27–59.

Pulliam, Susan and George Anders. "Mutual Benefit Life Took Plenty of Risks, and Is Paying the Price." *Wall Street Journal*, July 26, 1991, p. A1.

Ravenscraft, David. "An Industrial Organization Perspective." In Lynn Browne and Eric Rosengren, eds., *The Merger Boom*: Boston: Federal Reserve Bank of Boston, 1987, pp. 17–37.

Ravenscraft, David and F. Michael Scherer. *Mergers, Sell-Offs, and Economic Efficiency*. Washington, DC: The Brookings Institution, 1987.

Roll, Richard. "The Hubris Hypothesis of Corporate Takeovers." *Journal of Business*, Vol. 59, No. 2, 1986, pp. 197–216.

Rosett, Joshua. "Do Union Wealth Concessions Explain Takeover Premiums?" *Journal of Financial Economics*, Vol. 27, 1990, pp. 263–82.

Ryding, J. "The Rise in U.S. Corporate Leveraging in the 1980s." In E. Frydl, ed., *Studies on Corporate Leverage*, Federal Reserve Bank of New York, September 1990, pp. 45–84.

Sharpe, Steven. "Debt and Employment over the Business Cycle." Finance and Economics Discussion Paper Series Number 172, Washington, DC: Federal Reserve Bank, October 1991.

Shiller, Robert. "Do Stock Prices Move Too Much to Be Justified by Subsequent Changes in Dividends?" *American Economic Review*, Vol. 71, 1981, pp. 421–36.

Shiller, Robert. "Stock Prices and Social Dynamics." *Brookings Papers on Economic Activity*, Vol. 2, 1984, pp. 457–98.

Shleifer, Andrei and Lawrence Summers. "Breach of Trust in Hostile Takeovers." In Alan Auerbach, ed., *Takeovers: Causes and Consequences*. Chicago: University of Chicago Press, 1988, pp. 33–68.

Shleifer, Andrei and Lawrence Summers. "The Noise Trader Approach to Finance." *Journal of Economic Perspectives*, Vol. 4, No. 2, 1990, pp. 19–33.

Shleifer, Andrei and Robert Vishny. "Equilibrium Short Horizons of Investors and Firms." *American Economic Review*, Vol. 80, No. 2, May 1990, pp. 148–53.

Stiglitz, Joseph. "Why Financial Structures Matter." *Journal of Economic Perspectives*, Vol. 24, No. 4, Fall 1988, pp. 121–26.

Stiglitz, Joseph and Andrew Weiss. "Credit Rationing in Markets with Imperfect Information." *American Economic Review*, Vol. 71, June 1981, pp. 393–410.

Summers, Lawrence. "Comment on Bhagat, Schleifer and Vishny." *Brookings Papers on Economic Activity, Microeconomics*, 1990, pp. 75–81.

Tobin, James. "On the Efficiency of the Financial System." *Lloyds Bank Review*, Vol. 153, July 1984, pp. 1–15.

Wigmore, Barrie. "The Decline in Credit Quality of New-Issue Junk Bonds." *Financial Analysts Journal*, September-October 1990, pp. 53–62.

Zeckhauser, R., J. Patel, and D. Hendricks. "Non Rational Actors and Financial Market Behavior." National Bureau of Economic Research Working Paper No. 3731, June 1991.

Zysman, John. *Government, Markets, and Growth; Financial Systems and the Politics of Industrial Change*. Ithaca, NY: Cornell University Press, 1983.

CHAPTER ELEVEN

Pension Funds, Capital Markets, and the Economic Future[1]

RANDY BARBER AND TERESA GHILARDUCCI

CHAPTER SUMMARY

There are practical and political reasons that the reform of pension investment practices is urgently needed. U.S. capital markets are increasingly short term and speculative, and pension funds increasingly contribute to this bias. In 1992, pension funds became, for the first time, a larger source of finance than commercial banks. At the same time, pension regulators ignore this role of the pension funds and the potential for pension funds to invest long term, a goal that is appropriate because pension funds have naturally long-term and predictable liabilities—workers' future pension benefits.

The regulators also ignore workers' needs for pension funds to be invested in ways that take into account their needs as participants, not just as future recipients of a pension check. To be sure, pension fund participants need their pensions to be wisely invested, but they also need continued employment to accrue pension credits. Pension investments can both earn a market rate of return and contribute to economic revitalization.

In addition, taxpayers should demand more from pension fund investments, because without government tax favoritism, most funds would not exist. Tax exemptions for pension fund earnings and contributions are the largest tax expenditure (loss of tax revenue) in the federal budget—$51 billion in 1992.

This chapter describes the role of pension funds in capital markets and the promising development in economically targeted investments (ETIs). Although we make policy recommendations for the federal government, we also encourage the maturation and fine-tuning of economically targeted investments on the state and local levels. We propose four regulatory changes that encourage fiduciaries both to develop a whole-participant, life-cycle portfolio strategy and to help move capital markets away from a short-term investment mentality as follows:

- Mandate participant representation on corporate pension fund boards;
- Provide strong incentives for long-term investing by taxing pension funds' short-term gains and providing credits for long-term holdings;

287

• Develop rules and safe-harbor guidelines that encourage job-creating pension investments;

• Via the Department of Labor, develop an intermediary, "broker" unit to make information available to pension fund managers about investment projects that promote long-term development.

Overview: Pension Funds and the Economic Future

Pension funds will play a central role in financing the economic future. With more than $4 trillion in assets, pension funds represent the largest source of savings in the economy, accounting for 74 percent of net individual savings during the first three quarters of 1992 (Board of Governors of the Federal Reserve System, 1992). Pension funds currently own about one-third of all corporate equities (Employee Benefits Research Institute [EBRI], 1992b, p. 55) and about 40 percent of corporate bonds.

No serious U.S. industrial policy can ignore the impact of pension fund investment decisions: pension funds hold almost one-third of the total financial assets in our economy (Board of Governors, 1992; also see Tables 11.1 and 11.2). In 1993, pension funds will make between $1 trillion and $1.5 trillion in new investment decisions (allocating new contributions and reinvesting earnings in addition to the normal 25–35 percent annual turnover of existing assets). In addition, the funds are gaining rapidly on banks and savings institutions as a source of credit in the financial markets. Indeed, pension assets now exceed those of commercial banks alone by over $500 billion.[2]

These massive pools of capital are uniquely suited to fund long-term investments because their liabilities are stable, predictable, and extended over many decades. However, over the past two decades, pension funds often invested very differently in capital markets as their mostly futile pursuit of above-average returns contributed heavily to "short term-ism" and speculation in the economy as a whole (Cosh, Hughes, Singh, 1990). Arguably, their behavior was one of the main detriments to prospects for long-term economic growth, employment creation, and increases in real incomes.

Pension funds are in large part creatures of the tax code, which permits employers to deduct contributions from their taxable income and permits pension trusts to receive contributions and investment income free of taxation. (Pension benefits are taxed only as current income to recipients, usually at a lower tax rate than when they were employed, since retirees usually have a lower income.) The value of pension funds' tax-exempt status during 1992 alone was $51 billion in forgone tax revenues (Munnell, 1992) and, although estimates vary widely, it is clear that a significant portion of total pension assets represent public tax expenditures accumulated over many decades.

Because of pension funds' tax-favored status, it is entirely appropriate for public policy to enunciate goals for pension funds' investment practices and appropriate functions in the nation's capital markets. Indeed, any government industrial and capital market policy will have to address the role of pension capital in such a policy.

Classifying investments as long or short term can be difficult. For instance, equities are textbook defined as long-term investments. But institutional stock purchasers have increasingly turned into traders and speculators. Moreover, the technologically driven investment techniques that have evolved over the past decade attempt to make a science of knowing not only when to buy but also when to sell.

For the purposes of our discussion and for public policy considerations, we define long-term investments in both conceptual and practical terms. Conceptually, we define a long-term investment as an asset purchased with the expectation either of deriving income (dividend or interest) over time or of realizing gain from the appreciation of the productive asset (normally a corporation), rather than from price changes driven by trading markets. Practically, we define a long-term investment as an asset held for a period of five to seven years, the typical payout cycle for venture capital investors (who obviously rely on significant growth in the real productive assets of their investment). This period is shorter than the average maturity of corporate and government bonds.

The financial markets of the 1980s—into which pension funds poured trillions of dollars—valued speculative activity over investments, much to the detriment of workers, their communities, and the economy as a whole. Pension funds, acting as traders and speculators instead of long-term investors, were significant players in the casino economy of the 1980s.

Federal pension regulators have adopted the view that the capital markets are perfect and efficient allocators of resources. This theory holds that pension funds are neutral actors on Wall Street and can best serve participant interests by being unfettered by any considerations other than the pursuit of high investment returns.

Since the 1974 enactment of the Employee Retirement Income Security Act (ERISA), federal regulators have treated pension funds like any other kind of trust whose only income source is investment returns, for example, a bank that is the fiduciary for an incompetent heir. The fiduciary's duty, thus simplified, was to obtain risk-adjusted maximum rates of return in capital markets that regulators viewed as free and efficient.

However, this approach ignores crucial real-world characteristics of pension funds. These characteristics are described as follows:

• Pension funds provide benefits that evolved from, and are still largely driven by, labor/management relations in industries characterized by unionized, higher-wage workforces (particularly the public sector, manufacturing, transportation, and telecommunications).[3]

• Pensions are specifically favored by tax law to meet compatible but different goals—retirement income security, employment stability (employee retention), long-term economic growth, increased savings, and capital formation.

• Pension funds have predictable and exceedingly long term liabilities, but their assets have not at all been well matched with these liabilities. Rather, pension funds accumulate highly liquid assets that they can, and too often do, sell within a year or two of acquiring them.

• Pension funds are too large and active to be in neutral financial markets. Yet pension sponsors, managers, and regulators in effect take the position that the movement of pension dollars through the markets somehow has a neutral impact on those markets.

• The pension industry (those who manage and provide other services for pension funds) has evolved a trading mentality that bears little resemblance to an investing ethos. Long-term considerations are effectively crowded out by short-term speculative considerations. Under extreme pressure to produce above-average short-term results, pension managers are fundamentally traders seeking the highest achievable current yields and not investors seeking sustained returns from a stable investment.

• Pension funds are increasingly invested globally (about 5 percent of their assets were in direct international investments at mid-1991). Their assets are extremely footloose, unlike those of many banks that focus on local and regional projects, either voluntarily or because of the requirements of such measures as the Community Reinvestment Act.

• While some pension funds are becoming active shareholders, most are not behaving like committed owners. Pension funds date companies, they do not marry them. They often side with corporate raiders, and they benefited from the hostile takeover and leveraged buy-out (LBO) activity of the 1980s. Moreover, LBO pension funds are rapidly adopting highly automated portfolio management and trading techniques that permit them not only to buy and sell large volumes of securities but also to make heavy use of various "synthetic" or "derivative" financial products such as stock index futures and options on stock indexes (Twentieth Century Fund, 1992, p. 40). Thus their trading technologies are removing them even further from the role of patient, involved investors.

• Federal law provides no role for participant representatives in the investment and administration of pension funds, with one exception: in 1947, the Taft-Hartley Act required union pension boards to include equal numbers of employer representatives. However, no comparable law requires employer sponsors to share control of their pension boards with participant representatives.

• A double standard privileging employers over workers developed in the 1980s. It tacitly permits firms to use pension funds for their own interests despite ERISA's exclusive-purpose rule. Corporations routinely incorporate a range of pension-related considerations in their overall strategic planning. Contribution levels are often driven by companywide net present value calculations, and many corporate sponsors structure pension portfolios to behave in complementary ways with their other assets. Meanwhile, economic returns—for both participants and the society at large—not captured by a purely trading-oriented market cannot be considered as part of returns.

Thus, pension regulators have failed to recognize participants' whole identities: as workers who need employment to accumulate retirement income, as citizens whose quality of life depends on the economic health of their communities, as parents who want their children to have as much or more opportunity than their parents have had, as future retirees who need assurances that the economy will be able to deliver the goods and services their pension checks are supposed to provide, and as future retirees whose pension income must in good measure derive from investment earnings.

Under the Republican administrations, federal regulators discouraged even modest attempts by some pension funds to invest in ways that create employment for participants, benefit a local economy, or otherwise fill identifiable capital gaps. They have only grudgingly acknowledged that current pension law actually permits a range of innovative investment activities.

Clearly, regulators must rethink their oversight of pension investments. The nation is losing the productive use of this vast pool of potential long-term capital. Several federal agencies—including the Departments of Labor, Treasury, Commerce, and Housing and Urban Development—should take an active role in identifying and constructing long-term investment mechanisms and vehicles for pension funds and other patient investors. In addition, regulators must begin taking steps to correct the financial markets' bias against productive long-term investments.

A new regulatory philosophy, without any legislative action, could begin to change this economically destructive situation. Regulators should help pension funds to match their stable, long-term liabilities with productive long-term investment assets. In addition, certain legislative changes could do much to encourage pension funds to play a key role in revitalizing the economy.

Broad reform of pension investment practices must be addressed on four fronts:

• Adoption of a whole-participant life cycle regulatory framework for pension investments that takes into account feedback effects of investments on continued participant employment and pension contributions, as well as the sustained needs of the economy;

• Enactment of legislation mandating joint participant representation on all benefit funds;

• Changes in financial market regulations and tax policies to encourage long-range investment and simultaneously discourage short-term speculation;

• Creation of new long-term investment vehicles and intermediaries (e.g., federal infrastructure bonds, secondary markets for ETIs and community development loan funds, well-staffed broker units to help structure viable investment projects for pension funds, mechanisms to creatively package subsidy and guarantee monies for use by pension funds, etc.).

The Structure and Control of Pension Funds

Types of Pension Plans

One important way to look at pension plans is to distinguish them by their governance and regulation.[4]

In the private sector, there are two forms of control: unilateral employer control of single-employer plans and joint union/employer control of multi-employer plans.

The 1947 Taft-Hartley Act restricted unions to a maximum of half the trustees on any pension plan with union representation, but the law does not require employers to share control with employee representatives. While unions negotiate over pension benefits in many single-employer plans (which account for about 90 percent of the assets of all private-sector plans), they have only an investment role in the multiemployer plans.

Private-sector plans are governed by ERISA, which establishes a regulatory regime for all aspects of private employee benefit plans.[5] With respect to investments, ERISA establishes a duty of loyalty, a duty of prudence, an asset diversification requirement, and various prohibitions against transactions involving potential conflicts of interest or self-dealing.[6] The U.S. Department of Labor (DOL) is charged with enforcing most investment-related aspects of ERISA (the Internal Revenue Service has a role as well).

Following the enactment of ERISA, the DOL issued a series of regulations and advisory opinions, among the most important of which were rules for judging the prudence of a plan's investments. In 1979, the DOL issued a regulation that provides that the prudence of a portfolio will be judged in its totality rather than by each investment (Lanoff, 1981). Thus, pension fund managers who follow current investment industry practices and do not practice self-dealing are not subject to sanction under the law, even if individual investments—or even their entire portfolio strategies—fail miserably. The DOL's whole-portfolio standard has been widely credited with encouraging pension funds to increase their investments in equities (and other assets with higher levels of risk than traditional, fixed-income securities). It also clearly contributed to pension funds' much more active trading patterns during the 1980s.

In the public sector, pension plans for state and local government employees are regulated by state, county, or municipal legislation. Although restrictions on their investment practices vary widely (and often include specifically permitted and prohibited investment classes), most public employee plans now invest their assets under an approximation of the federal prudent-expert rule. In addition,

some states explicitly permit, or even require, trustees to seek in-state investments such as housing and economic development. Others provide a "basket
clause," which exempts a portion of the plan's assets from otherwise applicable
provisions explicitly restricting various investment classes.

Most of these plans have at least some elected or appointed participant representation (often including retirees and designees of public employee unions),
although such representatives are almost always in the minority. Some state and
local government plans, however, are still unilaterally controlled by the employer; for example, the $50 billion New York State and Local Retirement
Systems—which excludes New York City—is controlled by just one trustee, the
elected comptroller of the state.

At the end of the third quarter of 1992, private-sector pension plans had
almost $3.2 trillion in assets, and state and local plans had $949 billion (Board of
Governors, 1992). State and local funds are managed in a variety of ways and are
subject to political scrutiny and restrictions. However, these plans have more
than doubled their equity holdings (as a proportion of their portfolios) as regulations restricting equity investments were gradually revised during the late 1970s
and 1980s (EBRI, 1992a).

The Management of Pension Plan Assets

A whole industry has grown up around the management of pension plans. The
typical plan uses the services of money managers, brokers, bank custodians, bank
master trustees, lawyers, actuaries, accountants, record keepers, and appraisers as
well as a range of specialized financial and technical data providers. Most plans also
use an outside consulting firm to help make portfolio design decisions, select investment managers, and track the performance of these money managers over time.

Commonly, employers integrate their pension funding and investment decisions with broader analyses of corporate finance, cash flows, and ability to
absorb risk (Ghilarducci, 1992). Companies also often use the pension management function as a window into the financial markets and a training ground for
corporate finance personnel.

Pension funds are still largely passive—or secondary—investors, buying and
selling previously created securities on the highly liquid public markets. With
notable exceptions, most pension funds do not negotiate or structure their own
investments, nor do they assume an active ownership role. Even plans that invest
some assets internally still rely heavily on outside asset managers.

There are three basic types of money managers: bank trust departments, insurance companies, and independent investment counselors. Insurance companies
and bank trust departments—the more traditional types of pension managers—
each manage about one-quarter of all externally managed pension assets: independent money managers control about one-half of externally managed assets
(*Pensions and Investments*, May 18, 1992).

During the past decade, there have been much specialization and attempted market differentiation among competing investment managers. Some present themselves as bottom-up value stock pickers: others tout a sectoral top-down approach to equity investing or advertise their ability to time their trades properly and add value by adjusting allocations among asset classes. Money managers specialize in various degrees of riskiness inherent in different investment styles: small capitalization or blue chip stocks, triple-A or non-investment-grade bonds. They also specialize by investment category: stocks, bonds, international investments, mortgages, equity real estate, insurance products, and the like. Many offer technologically driven products, such as a multitude of index-fund variations and hedging devices.

Even with all this competition, the management of pension assets is still very concentrated. The 10 largest managers control about 20 percent of all externally invested pension assets, and the top 50 control 53 percent (*Pensions and Investments*, May 18, 1992).

Basic Issues in the Investment of Pension Funds

Arguably, the independent pension consultant is the most important single actor in today's pension investment industry. Most plans of any size hire a pension consulting firm to provide multiple services, including basic advice on portfolio design and asset allocation decisions; screening, measurement, and selection of prospective investment managers; and continued monitoring of the plan's money managers in the areas of performance and the managers' ability to stick to their assigned task. (Funds do not want pure equity managers to "cheat" by going heavily into cash during a down market, because is an asset allocation job that should be left to the trustees and their advisers.)

Much has been written about the "quarterly performance sweepstakes" among money managers competing for billions of dollars in pension fees. However, this phenomenon has recently produced absurd new extremes such as the window dressing that is increasingly being observed at the end of each quarter, in which money managers sell off their embarrassing "dogs" and load up on the quarter's best-performing stocks to improve the cosmetics of their portfolios (Bodie, 1989). Other managers, having achieved above-average results during part of a year, use various techniques to lock in this superior performance during the year (restructuring the portfolio to mimic the market, or purchasing Standard & Poor's [S&P] 500 futures), in effect guaranteeing the results they will report at the end of the year (Lakonishok, Shleifer, and Vishney, November 1991, p. 25).

Studies dating back well over a decade have concluded that no intensive research or skilled stock-picking does better than a blind market portfolio or index, and in fact, when adjusted for administrative fees, this activity does worse (Langbein and Posner, 1980; Lakonishok et al., November 1991).[7]

Another issue concerning pension funds' relationship to the stability of financial markets deals with money managers' financial incentives. An agency problem arises so that the owners have different needs from those of the agents that represent them. Workers and retirees may have a long-term view, but money managers depend on short-term performance to keep their jobs and maintain their fees (Speidell, 1990, p. 9). Also, Lakonishok et al. suggest that corporate pension personnel may be as interested in the nonfinancial services provided by money managers ("hand-holding," meaning, a good story to explain poor performance) as they are in superior investment returns (Lakonishok et al. November 1991, pp. 22–25).

In response to evidence that active money management actually hurts performance, a new category of investment product emerged in the 1970s—the index fund. A "pure" index fund simply emulates the stock (or bond) market as a whole, often using the S&P 500 as a proxy for the entire market. In theory, an index fund should proportionately hold all of the securities in the market.

The advantage of an index fund, according to its advocates, is that it guarantees market-level returns with much lower management and transaction costs. The index fund sponsor needs fewer in-house professionals and outside consultants to keep track of money managers' performance; the managers can charge much lower fees, since they are little more than caretakers of a relatively static portfolio; and, because index funds just mimic the market, they do not incur trading costs once a portfolio has been constructed. In addition, advocates argue, since index funds do not try to beat the market by constantly trading in and out of positions, the opportunities for money managers to make costly errors in judgment are eliminated. Of course, advocates of value-added investment managing argue that the opportunity for above-market gains is foreclosed as well.

Most of the larger funds and money managers use some form of core index fund, around which various asset allocation or stock-picking strategies are pursued. In fact, this technique is so prevalent that some industry observers charge that many supposedly active money managers are actually closet indexers.

Ironically, the technology behind index funds is a close cousin to some of the capital market's most aggressive trading tools. Most index mechanisms consist of highly computerized systems that track a large number of securities, many of which are used for active investment management purposes as well. Even if they are not explicitly program-trading mechanisms, these automated systems are frequently used to generate buy-and-sell orders based on a combination of factors, including anticipated price ranges of a security, trading volumes, unusually large fluctuations in price, target prices, stop-loss provisions, and movements in the stock futures and options markets. Often, these systems also actively trade in the stock futures and options markets to hedge risks and lock in gains.

From the perspective of having pension funds become more committed long-term investors in our economy, both of these approaches lead pension funds farther away from an investing mentality and toward a trading mentality. The active manager, who in the study by Lakonishok et al. had a 45 percent annual turnover in stocks, is simply looking for the highest immediate return. But even the passive, indexed funds implicitly depend on an active trading market to bid up share prices generally. In effect, they are free riders, and as the ultimate mechanical investor, they pay little or no direct attention to the companies in their portfolios. Further, since many indexing strategies actually involve significant use of synthetic securities as hedging devices or market proxies, even these passive investors contribute in their own way to the market's volatility and short-term focus.

A Profile of Pension Funds in the U.S. Capital Markets

At the end of the third quarter of 1992, the $4.1 trillion in pension fund assets almost equaled the total value of common shares traded in the stock markets. Moreover, they surpassed commercial bank assets at the beginning of the 1990s and now exceed them by more than $500 billion (Board of Governors, 1992). Another measure of pension funds' impact is seen by their flows through the capital markets. As noted previously, pension funds will make between $1 trillion and $1.5 trillion in new investment decisions during 1993.

Moreover, pension funds' importance as the ultimate source of credit and equity capital has been gaining relative to all other financial sectors, even those that have experienced growth themselves (Tables 11.1 and 11.2). Pension funds' share of total financial assets in the U.S. economy rose from 15 percent in 1966 to more than 32 percent in 1992 (an increase of about 115 percent). Pension funds' growing control of the economy's financial assets matches the decline in importance of commercial banks (whose share of total financial assets has declined by 27 percent since 1966), savings and loans (declining by 52 percent), and the nonpension portion of the insurance industry (declining by 28 percent). Only mutual funds gained at a rate approaching that of pension funds (a 100 percent increase in share of total financial assets from 1966 to 1992), and mutual fund assets are still only about one-quarter the size of pension funds.

Thus, pension funds are becoming the ultimate provider of finance capital in the economy. The characteristic of an ultimate capital provider is to have a significant influence over allocation trends throughout the markets and to have a major impact on the kinds of projects funded. As pension funds are highly centralized, secondary investors, they are unlikely to duplicate the functions of the relatively more decentralized, less volatile, and liquid financial sources they have displaced.

The increasing volatility and accompanying short-term focus of the capital markets result in large measure from the increased velocity of holdings in those markets. For example, in 1960, the average holding period for stocks was seven years; today it is less than two years and falling. This dramatic rise in turnover can be tracked precisely with the growth of institutional domination of the stock markets, which increased from 8 percent in 1950 to almost 60 percent in 1990 (Porter, 1992, pp. 5–6).

Table 11.1

Assets by Financial Sector, Selected Years, 1966–1992(3)
(Trillions of dollars)

Sector	Year					
	1966	1972	1978	1984	1989	1992:3
Commercial banks[a]	$.363	$.663	$1.221	$2.131	$3.231	$3.576
Savings institutions[b]	.204	.359	.731	1.290	1.716	1.356
Insurance[c] (net of pension reserves)	.171	.258	.397	.617	1.140	1.282
Pension reserves (LI)[d] (of life insurance companies)	.029	.052	.122	.332	.711	.935
Private pension funds[e]	.076	.165	.386	.880	1.536	2.259
State, local pension funds	.038	.088	.154	.357	.735	.949
Finance companies	.047	.081	.160	.371	.719	.789
Mutual funds[f]	.035	.059	.056	.370	.994	1.567
Real estate investment	—	.011	.003	.006	.013	.015
Security brokers[g]	.011	.023	.032	.118	.236	.698
Totals	$.974	$1.759	$3.262	$6.472	$11.031	$13.426

Sources: Flow of Funds Accounts and Liabilities Year-End, 1966–1989 and the *Flow of Funds Accounts (Flows and Outstandings), Third Quarter 1992*. Washington, DC: Board of Governors of the Federal Reserve System.
Notes:
[a]U.S. chartered banks, foreign banking offices in the United States, domestic affiliates (bank holding companies), and banks in U.S. possessions.
[b]Includes savings and loan associations, mutual savings banks, and credit unions.
[c]Life and other insurance without pension reserves.
[d]Pension reserves of life insurance (LI) companies, includes separate accounts.
[e]Includes the Federal Employees' Retirement System Thrift Savings Plan.
[f]Includes open-ended investment company and money market mutual funds.
[g]Includes dealers and issuers of securitized credit obligations trusts.

Lakonishok et al. (November 1991, p. 13) studied the database of the firm of SEI and report that for the five-year period ending in 1990, the 250 money managers in the database (managing $540 billion in tax-exempt equities) had a median turnover rate of 45 percent annually, whereas managers in the 75th percentile of turnover had a rate of 70 percent. Another source reports that "the average institutional investor sells 40 percent of its stock holdings within a year's time from purchase" (Brancato, cited in Twentieth Century Fund, 1992, p. 76; Turner and Beller, 1990).

The increasingly rapid equity turnover rate of institutions has profound implications well beyond the performance results of those investors. This behavior has created a dynamic that is itself an economic vicious cycle, with a perverse

Table 11.2

Percent Share of Assets by Financial Sector, Selected Years, 1966–1992 (3)

Sector	Year					
	1966	1972	1978	1984	1989	1992:3
Commercial banks	37.3%	37.7%	37.4%	32.9%	29.3%	26.6%
Savings institutions	20.9	20.4	22.4	19.9	15.6	10.1
Insurance (net of pensions reserves)	17.6	14.7	12.2	9.5	10.3	9.5
Pension reserves (of life insurance companies)	3.0	3.0	3.7	5.1	6.4	7.0
Private pensions	7.8	9.4	11.8	13.6	13.9	16.8
Public pension	3.9	5.0	4.7	5.5	6.7	7.1
Finance companies	4.8	4.6	4.9	5.7	6.5	5.9
Mutual funds	3.6	3.4	1.7	5.7	9.0	11.7
Real estate	—	0.6	0.1	.1	.1	.1
Security brokers	1.1	1.3	1.0	1.8	2.1	5.2
Total	100.0%	100.0%	100.0%	100.0%	100.0%	100.0%

Sources: Flow of Funds Accounts and Liabilities Year-End, 1966–1989 and the *Flow of Funds Accounts (Flows and Outstandings), Third Quarter 1992.* Washington, D.C.: Board of Governors of the Federal Reserve System. See data in Table 1.
Note: Totals may not add to 100 percent due to rounding.

echo effect on the long-term investment prospects of institutions themselves.

Two studies published in 1992 analyze the destructive effects of market speculation and short term-ism. Both studies conclude that the behaviors threaten the economic well-being of our nation. A Twentieth Century Fund report concludes that short-term focus "is part of a larger pattern in which finance flourishes while our real economic foundation slowly erodes" (Twentieth Century Fund, 1992, p. 3).

Another recent report, by Harvard Professor Michael E. Porter, makes an even stronger case: "The U.S. system of allocating investment capital is threatening the competitiveness of American firms and the long-term growth of the national economy" (Porter, 1992, p. 3). Management, he argues, takes its signals from the behavior of the external markets and works to maximize current stock prices to the exclusion of fundamental long-term prospects.[8]

The Debate over Economically and Socially Responsible Investments

The Evolution of Economically Targeted Investments

Although the expression "economically targeted investments"[9] (ETIs) dates only to the late 1980s, the idea has been around for decades, the basic concept being that since capital markets do not automatically meet the needs of all people (i.e., they create "finance gaps")—especially working-class and poor people—new mechanisms should be created to do so. As far back as the 1920s, labor unions were creating banks and insurance companies to provide services and make loans to working people who could not gain access to established credit and insurance markets.

During the 1950s, both union pension funds and churches became involved in financing moderate- and lower-income housing projects, individual mortgages, and medical facilities. During the 1960s, the AFL-CIO established a pooled investment fund, called the Housing Investment Trust, which was designed explicitly to invest pension funds in mortgages on union-built single-family structures.

In the 1970s and 1980s, a myriad of what we now call ETIs were created by state and local governments, union-related pension funds, churches, foundations, "progressive" financial advisers and bankers, and even a few corporations.

Many of the initial ETIs were not particularly well designed, and often they involved unrecognized financial concessions. For one thing, most of the key actors in their creation had little or no experience in finance and were unfamiliar with many of the traditional investment design mechanisms that are available.[10]

During the late 1970s and early 1980s, a series of studies and books dramatically altered this situation. Probably the most influential was a series of books published under the auspices of the National Governors Association. Covering the areas of development finance, venture capital, and pension fund investments, these works provided the intellectual as well as operational framework for ETIs.

At roughly the same time, a number of other studies also took a much more rigorous approach to evaluating ETIs. In addition, the first critical surveys were published that, correctly in many cases, pointed to the financial and design flaws in some of the initial ETIs (Kieschnick, 1979; Kirshner, 1979; Litvak and Daniels, 1979; Smart, 1979; Peterson, 1980; Salisbury, 1980; Hansen, 1981; Harrington and Gardels, 1981).

Several other developments during this period had an important impact on the evolution of ETIs. In 1975, New York City faced bankruptcy. In what proved to be a successful effort to save the city from financial catastrophe, the municipal unions agreed to have city employee pension funds invest about one-quarter of their total assets ($3.1 billion) in newly issued municipal bonds (the so-called "Big MAC" bonds). At the time, no one doubted that under normal circumstances, this would have been an imprudent investment, by virtue both of its magnitude and of the fact that the bonds were arguably below the risk-adjusted market rates the funds could have obtained elsewhere. It was also the judgment of both the city's elected leaders and the municipal union leaders that there was no alternative but disaster.

In the early 1980s, California Governor Jerry Brown initiated one of the most comprehensive ETI efforts at the time. Following a study by a governor-appointed task force, a Pension Investment Unit (PIU) was created within the governor's office. The purpose of the entity was not to make investments but to broker them. Striving to address one of the most critical problems facing the growth of ETIs, it sought to structure or act as a catalyst to new investment vehicles. The PIU served as an intermediary among entrepreneurs, developers, labor unions, and community groups to develop investment ideas that met both public policy goals—such as dampening real estate speculation—and pension funds' need to earn market rate returns.

Ten years later, a New York State pension task force commended the program for being the most important model available for state involvement in encouraging successful ETIs (New York State Industrial Cooperation Council, 1990, p. 30). Indeed, the investment-brokering functions of the Industrial Cooperation Council (described later) are directly modeled after those of the PIU.

Also during the late 1970s and early 1980s, unions and their pension funds were developing a series of new approaches and investment pools to target pension investments for job creation. Commercial and residential construction projects were by far the prevalent type of investment on which the unions focused. Since the building trades are almost always involved in joint trustee plans, the motivation was obvious. A number of nationwide pooled mechanisms were either created or reinvigorated; they have grown subsequently to over $2 billion. These include the AFL-CIO's Housing Investment Trust (and subsequently created Building Investment Trust), Union Labor Life Insurance Company's (ULLICO's) "J for Jobs" Separate Account (ULLICO is owned by a group of labor unions), and the Multi-Employer Property Trust. The first two are pooled mortgage funds; the third is an equity real estate investment fund. All have requirements that they will finance or invest in new construction using only 100 percent union labor.

Other similar pooled investment products were launched by private insurance companies during the 1980s. These funds have not only grown significantly in size but also outperformed their non-ETI competitors in virtually every measurement period, including those from the funds' inception through year-end 1991 (Marco Consulting Group, 1992).

It is important to acknowledge that ETI is still in its infancy and has yet to mature in a number of crucial ways. As many have noted, this market is very "thin" and lacks broadly accepted standards and measurements. In addition, many potential ETI investors are hesitant to act alone or to bear the expense of creating a new investment vehicle.

The Current Status of Economically Targeted Investments

Today there are many types of ETIs. Some are designed to provide an additional benefit for participants directly (such as continued employment or lower-rate mortgage loans); others are geared to enhancing the economic environment in which participants, beneficiaries, and their dependents live.

The concentration of ETIs in housing and other forms of real estate is not an indication of limited demand or social or economic utility. Quite the contrary. The concentration represents a rational initial choice, given the opportunities in this market to structure transactions appropriately and achieve at least a modicum of effective targeting. The challenge is to develop comparable techniques for financing economic activity outside the housing and real estate markets.

Two good examples of efforts to broaden the range of ETIs are the AFL-CIO's Building Investment Trust (BIT) and the New York State Urban Development Corporation's Excelsior Capital Corporation (ECC).

The BIT is a relatively new, $200-million fund designed to invest in commercial and industrial real estate and provide both immediate construction industry jobs and long-term commercial and industrial employment. The AFL-CIO also has an older fund, the Housing Investment Trust, which is limited to government-guaranteed residential mortgages. In contrast, BIT invests in nonguaranteed mortgages and is even willing to let participating mortgages and take an equity position in the project. It has financed a number of commercial projects as well as a new biotechnology laboratory in Massachusetts.

The ECC, a nonprofit subsidiary of the Urban Development Corporation, structures new pension investment vehicles that provide pension investors with market-level returns while contributing to economic development in New York State and the surrounding region. The basic purpose of ECC is to create new investment intermediary mechanisms to provide capital in ways that would otherwise be unavailable. ECC's first project, in 1992, was the launching of the Excelsior Fund, which was designed to invest in privately structured debt and equity instruments for middle market companies. At this writing, the Excelsior Fund had $150 million committed from numerous public and employer-sponsored pension funds, was actively raising additional funds, and was in the process of soliciting investment proposals from regionally based firms.

In another interesting development, the AFL-CIO began exploring the implications of *international* ETIs (AFL-CIO Employee Benefits Department, 1992) and one investment group—with close labor ties—has proposed the creation of a pooled fund for direct equity and debt investments in Poland. Over the past few years, the AFL-CIO has also undertaken in-depth analysis of corporate governance issues, state antitakeover legislation, national and international capital flow issues, and the status of ETI programs in general. In 1991, it published a guide for union pension trustees on pension investments and proxy voting (AFL-CIO, 1991).

State and local targeted investing is practiced by public funds in a majority of the states (Center for Policy Alternatives, 1992). For example:

• Alabama public funds have been involved in financing construction of a pulp mill, a chemical plant, an airplane factory, a pipe mill, and a retail distribution center. The funds have also made targeted in-state housing loans.

• New York City pension funds have $850 million committed to ETIs. For a number of years, these funds have invested in a range of targeted housing and small-business loan programs. Among these initiatives are several designed to relieve a liquidity crisis in the housing industry, especially in redlined areas (where the funds now provide more mortgage loans than all banks combined). The funds have structured programs that permit low- and moderate-income New Yorkers to purchase homes with as little as 5 percent down. To date, the funds have provided more than 4,000 mortgages and funded the rehabilitation of over 15,000 housing units (O'Cleireacain, 1992).

• The $65-billion California Public Employee Retirement System (CALPERS) and the $37-billion State Teachers Retirement System (CALSTRS) have been involved in a large number of targeted investment programs. For example, they have let more than $1.5 billion in direct-participant mortgage loans (with CALSTRS). CALPERS has committed $100 million to the AFL-CIO Housing Investment Trust and has proposed a $375-million program in which it would actually develop residential housing tracts—using labor paid at the "prevailing rate." Both funds also are reportedly evaluating making investments in the Rebuild LA effort.

Critics of economically targeted or "social" investments frequently charge that they can be viable only if they rely on government grants, subsidies, or guarantees on the one hand, or financial concessions by pension investors on the other. These opponents argue that this is proof that ETIs cannot stand on their own in the marketplace.

It is important, however, to distinguish among various types of capital gaps and how they can best be filled. Some needs, such as increasing the availability of moderate-income housing, are beginning to be filled by pension investors, using existing market mechanisms, without any additional subsidies or concessions. Other needs, such as providing decent housing for the poor, can be met only with a combination of private capital and public expenditures. Yet other capital gaps exist because the existing capital market infrastructure has not been created to fill them, either because the start-up costs are high or because the potential profits for the intermediaries are insufficient, even if the underlying investments could meet traditional riskreward criteria.

During the last year of the Bush administration, its Labor Department ERISA Advisory Committee Investment Work Group conducted an extensive investigation into ETIs. In November 1992, the work group issued its report. Among other things, it found:

> On the basis of the testimony, literature, and shared experiences, the Work Group concludes that many sound investments exist in areas not usually targeted by pension funds. In some cases, investing in projects which are of local or occupational interest to a pension fund's participants can create a primary benefit from competitive financial returns and a collateral benefit from the creation of jobs, wealth and other local economic ripple effects. In some cases, these benefits are measurable. In others, they are not measurable but can reasonably be presumed. (Erisa, 1992, p. 28)

Finding a widespread perception of Department of Labor resistance to ETIs, the group urged the DOL to explicitly allow fiduciaries to consider collateral benefits in making investment decisions: "As long as trustees are loyal to participants and invest for their exclusive benefit, they should be free to seek investments which generate economic benefits for their region or industry."

Recognizing that the capital markets have not been efficient in providing investments that can offer these additional economic benefits, the group recommended that the Department of Labor "take the initiative in gathering information and the investment performance and attributes of ETIs and making it available to the pension community to aid its investment decisions."[11]

Critiques of ETIs

Criticisms of economically targeted and socially responsible investing have ranged from tightly reasoned technical objections to broad condemnations of unions, ETIs, and "corporative-state panaceas."[12]

Some of the critiques, especially early in the evolution of ETIs, were not only correct but useful in fine-tuning what was, after all, a very new set of techniques and procedures. Many were based on a stated desire to improve the technical excellence of ETIs and socially responsible investments, and they emanated from individuals who were broadly supportive of the trend (see especially Feder, Ferguson, and Leibig in Salisbury, 1979; Smart, 1979; Leibig, 1981; Litvak, 1981).

Our view is that, from the beginning, ETI advocates were correct in their analysis of the problems in the capital markets, as the recent mainstream literature on market speculation and short-term investing makes clear. They were also on the right track with their proposed solutions. However, initially, their implementation was at times poorly executed.

Creating alternative investment mechanisms involves significant technical and legal issues, some of which have been more or less overcome or resolved (often in response to earlier criticisms); others have remained vexing. Many of the proposals in the final section of this chapter address a number of important remaining obstacles.

We concern ourselves here with criticisms grounded in the efficient market hypothesis. Although coming from a number of legal and economic perspectives, these criticisms all fundamentally revolve around the efficient-capital-market theory: the argument that it is impossible to target capital without either completely displacing other investors (in which case your efforts are futile) or making some form of concession to true market rates (in which case you are both foolish and imprudent).

The conventional critique of ETIs and "social" investing is best represented by Hutchinson and Cole (1979) and Langbein and Posner (1980), who view all investments along an efficient market continuum (Bruyn, 1987, p. 12). At one end, the highest earners (adjusted for risk) are the portfolios managed by professionals whose only concern is producing competitive returns. At the other end of this continuum are the lowest earners—investors who are willing to voluntarily incorporate externalities and accept "social rate of return" in lieu of cash. Social investing in this context is defined as "excluding the securities of certain otherwise attractive companies from an investor's portfolio ... and including the securities of certain otherwise unattractive companies because they are judged to be behaving in a socially laudable way" (Langbein and Posner, 1980, p. 84).

This concept is based entirely on the perfect-capital-markets hypothesis that every investment's return compensates for its risk and that the only way to reduce risk without sacrificing return is to diversify well. Furthermore, no intensive research or skilled stock-picking does better than a blind market portfolio and in fact, when adjusted for administrative fees, this activity does worse (Langbein and Posner, 1980, p. 82; Lakonishok et al., 1991).

A liberal critic of many social investment practices is Federal Reserve Vice-President Alicia Munnell, who argues against ETIs based on her surveys of state mortgage lending programs in the early 1980s. Munnell (1983) concluded that the majority of 31 in-state mortgage programs earned returns equivalent to an AA corporate bond, but at a higher risk than such a security entailed. Thus, she argued, the funds investing in these programs were being undercompensated for the risks they were taking on.

When comparing these mortgage programs with investments of comparable risk (such as the Ginnie Maes), Munnell (1983) found some funds earned as much as 1.2 percent less. She and Steven Sass (1992) argue that this subsidy of "worthy" investments should not be borne by pension funds (and implicitly by public employees and retirees).

Moreover, Sass argues, it is unlikely that pension funds are increasing capital in these mortgage markets because anyone meeting national standards can already obtain a mortgage. In this case, such pension-fund mortgage investments do not fill any capital gaps. Sass and Munnell agree that these public investment choices are more fairly and democratically made through taxes and explicit public expenditures.[13]

Critics of what they call "backyard investing" also point to two fiascoes in the late 1980s. Alaska's public pension funds policy for in-state investments caused over 30 percent of their loans to become nonperforming when oil prices collapsed in 1982. Recently, the Kansas Public Employee Retirement System (KPERS) suffered the largest losses in the history of ETIs in 1991, when a series of in-state investments suffered $200-million losses out of $360 million invested, in an S&L-like collapse of asset values (White, 1991, p. 1).

In spite of these clear instances of poorly designed ETIs (or investments parading as ETIs that stemmed from other, less commendable motivations), the argument that a majority, or even a significant number, of ETIs are concessionary is incorrect. New York City's pension funds report that, during the past five years, their returns on ETI investments have averaged 13 percent, compared with a 9.9 percent yield on the funds' fixed-income portfolio. The funds' ETI and fixed-income portfolios have very similar risk profiles (O'Cleireacain, 1992). It is worth emphasizing that, apart from the collateral benefits these ETIs provide through increased economic activity in the city, the ETI investments can stand on their own merits financially.

A dozen years ago, Equitable Life Insurance Company established a Community Mortgage Program in response to pressures for the insurance giant to become a better "corporate citizen." This program, which makes targeted investments in underserved urban areas, has actually had a slightly higher return than has Equitable's straight commercial mortgage portfolio. In addition, "this program's impact on [Equitable's] overall portfolio risk was slightly beneficial because its covariance with the rest of the real estate portfolio was very low, and in some cases, negative" (ERISA Advisory Council Work Group on Pension Investments, p. 35). In other words, the specific characteristics of the Community Mortgage Program tend to smooth the volatility of the overall portfolio.

Another argument made by ETI critics is that, because no formal market exists for many "worthy projects" that fall through capital gaps, pension funds have difficulty finding good projects. Moreover, the projects they do find typically entail much more structuring and monitoring than a traditional stock or bond investment. These higher transaction costs, the argument concludes, can lower investors' yields significantly.

We fully endorse this critique and believe that it describes the difficulties all too often encountered by willing ETI investors. Indeed, it is nothing short of remarkable that so many competitive ETIs have been created. This problem is reflected in the fact that some investors have been willing to commit more funds to ETIs than they have been able to place. This is yet another sign of the relative immaturity of this market and particularly of its intermediary and brokerage mechanisms. Indeed, this critique gets to the heart of the "capital gap" analysis: the markets simply have not, on their own, created vehicles that can effectively serve many important sectors of the economy.

The lack of a national information and brokerage ETI infrastructure is addressed by some of the proposals that follow.

A Policy for Encouraging Long-Term Investment Strategies

Toward an Industrial and Capital Market Policy for Pension Funds

In this section, we present recommendations for ways in which government can systematically encourage pension funds to pursue long-term, economically productive investment strategies.

Before moving to these specific proposals, however, we must put them into a broader context. The most effective policies for revitalizing our economy will be those that address the functioning of the capital markets as a whole by discouraging the short-term investment mentality prevalent today (see also the other chapters in this volume). With the market environment altered to favor long-term investment strategies, pension funds will be in a much better position to meet their multiple policy goals of providing secure retirement income and promoting increased savings, economic growth, and job creation.

Thus, it is not sufficient to encourage a significant expansion of discrete ETI activities; without changes in the capital market environment, ETIs will continue to swim upstream as other investors respond to market signals that encourage trading rather than investing.

With respect to increased public support for ETIs, the policies we recommend are designed to facilitate the creation of new, replicable mechanisms that themselves will make a contribution to broader capital market policy goals.

It is important to keep in mind that government's industrial and capital market policies should be based on an understanding of the unique or defining characteristics of pension funds listed below.

• Pension funds and other tax-exempt investors are not directly impacted by traditional tax-based incentives and disincentives;

• Unlike other financial institutions, pension funds are regulated under a law that is not primarily financial in nature and by a government agency with no other involvement in financial matters;

• Also, under the Department of Labor's "whole portfolio" interpretation of ERISA, pension funds are arguably the least regulated of any major financial institution;

• Pension funds are for the most part passive investors acting through agents (money managers) who invest in secondary markets (publicly traded securities);

• Traditionally, pension funds are not addressed as a separate Wall Street entity in government economic policy and financial policy;

• In addition, pension funds are too often not controlled by their beneficial owners or their representatives, and there are usually multiple layers of agency between participants and the pension asset.

Changes in and Regulation of Tax Policy to Encourage Long-Range Investment and Discourage Speculation

There are many ways—through regulation or tax policy—that government could encourage pension funds to take a much more long-term approach in its investment activities. From the perspective of their financial behavior, pension funds are among the least regulated of financial institutions. Therefore it would be worthwhile to explore ways in which the regulation of pension investments can be made consistent with regulations governing other major financial institutions (see Pollin and Crotty and Goldstein in this volume). For example, an extension to pension funds of the operating principles of a strengthened Community Reinvestment Act could do much to encourage these funds to reinvest their assets in the areas from which contributions originate. Also, the application of such devices as the reserve requirements used to regulate other financial actors could give the government a tool to affect pension fund investment practices directly.

With respect to tax policy, most measures designed to spur long-term investing behavior and discourage short-term speculation fail to take into consideration pension funds' unique characteristics. Pension and other tax-exempt investors are not directly influenced by traditional tax-based incentives or disincentives (e.g., raising, lowering, or sectorally focusing capital gains rates), although they and all other investors will respond indirectly to such measures' effect on companies in which they invest. Accordingly, tax code incentives and disincentives should be designed to affect taxable and tax-exempt investors equally.

For example, we believe that taxation of capital (i.e., trading) gains should be graduated, as well as based on holding period. At one extreme, gains on assets held for less than one year should be taxed at a higher rate than current income is. At the other extreme, gains on assets held for more than five years (the short end of the range for the typical holding period for venture capital) should be taxed at a rate lower than current income is. Gains on assets held for one to five year would be unaffected. This measure should be prospective only, applying to securities purchased after enactment of the legislation (or after the date the legislation is first introduced).

For such a measure to affect taxable and tax-exempt investors equally, two provisions must be added:

• Tax short-term pension fund gains at a level that equals the penalty imposed on short-term gains for taxable investors;
• Provide refundable credits for tax-exempt investors' long-term gains of an economic value equal to tax reductions for taxable investors.

The mechanics for both proposals are relatively straightforward. Pension funds—or their investment managers—already are required to maintain the documentation necessary to implement them. As to the short-term tax, funds are required to file an annual IRS form providing significant details of their operations. And mutual funds are currently required to keep track of their short-term transactions of less than three months. To avoid income taxation at the mutual fund level, these institutions can derive no more than 30 percent of their income from such short-term transactions; if they cross the 30 percent line, then the mutual fund's income is taxed directly (Twentieth Century Fund, 1992, p. 88).

A refundable tax credit is simply a mechanism through which the federal Treasury will issue a check to a taxpayer in the amount by which its tax credits exceed its tax liabilities. For example, a current investor should be willing to pay a premium—totaling the net present value of the future tax benefit stemming from holding the security for five years or more—for an investment with a likelihood of long-term appreciation. In addition, the market will begin to value information on the extended prospects of companies much more than it does today. The longer an investor holds, the more value in continuing to hold it. Conversely, the price imputed to securities that are purchased for quick turnover would have to be discounted by the value of the short-term trading penalty.

Taken together, these two measures would reduce all investors' incentives for short-term speculation while raising the present value of truly long term investments. They should also begin to alter the investment environment sufficiently to make ETIs both more attractive and more viable. It is important, however, that any such measure be carefully designed so that it will not spur the reemergence of the tax-shelter industry, which created its own perverse economic results.

Michael Porter (1992) has proposed rewarding long-term investment behavior (although he does not penalize speculation, as does our proposal). He would restrict the preferential treatment to investments in operating company equities, exclude preferences for equity investments in "non-operating companies holding real estate or other financial assets," and exclude preferential treatment for capital gains from the appreciation in bonds, real estate, collectibles, and other non-operating equity assets. We tend to agree but note that speculation in other assets must be addressed as well.

Porter also suggests that the lower tax rate on gains from long-term holdings be passed through to participants at the time they begin collecting their retirement checks and not credited at the fund level. We disagree. Such an approach would have a weak impact on investment manager behavior, since many participants are decades away from retirement. A direct cash incentive at the fund level (which, we stress, would be of the same value as reduced marginal taxes for taxable investors) would be much more effective. We would also like to see some preference for dividend income earned from long-term holdings (the tax loss for which could be made up from even steeper short-term capital gain taxes).

Adoption of a Whole-Participant Life-Cycle Regulatory Framework for Pension Investments

In regulating pension investment patterns, the Department of Labor must look to the relevant language in ERISA. However, in developing its regulatory framework and interpretation of ERISA, the DOL completely embraced modern portfolio theory and its underlying efficient capital market hypothesis. Thus, the DOL adopted a premise that holds that the use of any criteria beyond the signals provided by the trading markets will inevitably result in suboptimal performance.

This, we believe, explains the DOL's hostility toward ETIs and its reluctance to acknowledge the legitimacy of considerations outside the four corners of modern portfolio theory. Ironically, this narrow interpretation actually serves to stifle financial market innovation.

Although modern portfolio analysis, properly applied, can be a useful tool, it provides an insufficient framework from which to make investment decisions or to regulate pension funds' financial behavior. Pension funds should be invested in ways that consider the needs and interests of participants as a whole, not just as potential future recipients of a pension check. Pension participants are workers, parents, and citizens who live in a society in need of economic revitalization. To be sure, pension participants must ensure their pension funds are wisely invested. But they also have an interest in continued employment so that they can continue to accrue pension credits. And they have an interest in the future shape of the economy, which, after all, they will depend on to deliver the goods and services they hope to purchase with their retirement checks. Rather than focusing narrowly on pension investment returns in the present to the exclusion of any other consideration, the DOL should actively encourage fiduciaries to develop a whole-participant life-cycle portfolio strategy. Specifically, the Department of Labor should adopt the position that fiduciaries are explicitly permitted (if not actually required) to consider the nonportfolio impact of their investment decisions both on participants and on the economy as a whole. This should not undermine a fiduciary's duty of loyalty; rather, it should serve to broaden fiduciaries' range of tools to meet their duty.

ERISA may be overly legalistic and complex, but much can still be accomplished without amending this legislation. We believe that it is primarily an interpretive issue, which at most requires a recasting of certain DOL regulations. To conform with this new perspective, the Department of Labor should clarify its existing regulations and interpretations in the light of a whole-participant, life-cycle portfolio analysis, restating or revising its previous positions as required.

The market to date has not valued information about the collateral benefits of ETIs that may accrue to participants, so these data are generally unavailable, even though, as recognized by the ERISA Advisory Council Work Group, they are reasonable to presume. It can also be expensive to attempt a quantification of collateral benefits for an individual investment.

A much more effective approach would be for the DOL, in the words of the Work Group, to design "a 'safe harbor' process for evaluating, benchmarking and tracking performance (incorporating the collateral benefits to current participants through the plan to achieve a prevailing rate) and [specify] the plan structures for which such considerations may be suitable."

Such an approach would provide fiduciaries both with additional flexibility in designing ETI initiatives and with certainty about the DOL's interpretation of the prudence of their actions. Therefore, the DOL should develop safe harbor regulations that set forth specific and detailed procedures by which fiduciaries can make economically targeted investments and incorporate presumptions of collateral benefits to meet a prevailing-rate-of-return test.

Promoting ETIs and Creating New Long-Term Investment Vehicles and Intermediaries

As discussed earlier in this chapter, pension funds are more or less passive, secondary investors. They and their agents typically buy and sell securities on highly liquid public markets; they rarely structure transactions themselves. They are not market makers; they are market consumers.

There is a critical need for an ETI infrastructure that can handle a range of transactions tailored to specific types of investments. In many ways, the main problem that potential ETI investors face does not relate to the inherent riskiness or unprofitability of targeted investments. Rather, it involves the still-excessive information and transaction costs associated with an immature market that lacks established and well-understood intermediary vehicles and mechanisms.

These market-enabling mechanisms should be designed to facilitate and accelerate the evolution of innovative, new investment vehicles. The ETI capital market can evolve to stand on its own. To the extent that subsidies and seed capital are available for ETIs, they should be applied to help create self-sustaining financial intermediaries, vehicles, and mechanisms.

It is important to distinguish between these types of grants or subsidies—designed to create self-sustaining, market-enabling mechanisms—and public allocations of tax revenues (or private grants) for broad societal purposes such as affordable housing, regeneration of our inner cities, and industrial competitiveness.

Certainly, public and private expenditures for broader social and economic purposes can be blended with pension capital to make ETIs more effective and attractive. Obviously, the poorest among us cannot afford the market price for decent housing. We should be clear, however, that any subsidies for affordable housing represent a public allocation for those individuals and not for the pension investor and that the subsidies come from the public treasury, not from pension funds.

In such cases, all subsidies do is bridge the gap between a pension investor's need for a risk-adjusted market return and the financial means of the potential renter or buyer. As a recent General Accounting Office report on affordable housing makes clear, pension funds can play an important role in this area, given the appropriate assistance (GAO, 1991).

Likewise, in the context of a national industrial and capital policy, public expenditures (along with other forms of incentives and disincentives) are needed to steer pension investments in specific areas of the economy.

Until now, ETI efforts have been initiated almost exclusively by state or local governments, private-sector unions, and nonprofit organizations. The federal government has been remarkable for its absence in this entire area. It is past the time for the Department of Labor, and other federal agencies, to become actively involved in assisting in the evolution of ETIs. The federal government should take the lead in promoting ETIs. The government should undertake a range of specific functions:

• Collecting, analyzing, benchmarking, tracking, and disseminating information about experiences with existing ETIs;

• Supporting the creation of new investment origination and packaging intermediaries, of pooling and risk-sharing mechanisms, and of secondary markets for ETIs;

• Coordinating the expenditure of federal economic development funds (which rarely include pension investors as "private-sector partners") to target significant monies to financial guarantees and other subsidies needed to spur broader participation by pension funds;

• Providing education, training, and technical assistance for private groups, state and local governments, and pension investors who want to pursue the creation of new ETIs.

As discussed earlier, models for such a government role in encouraging ETIs have been created at the state government level. The California Pension Investment Unit under Governor Jerry Brown pioneered the use of the executive's bully pulpit to pull together disparate groupings from the public and private sectors for specific investment projects. More recently, New York State's Industrial Cooperation Council has performed similar functions and has even established a subsidiary to become more actively involved in structuring innovative pension investment programs. The federal government should emulate and expand upon these models.

Many economic revitalization proposals could involve pension fund investments. A federal ETI coordinating agency could help to evaluate these ideas, coordinate their implementation (at least with respect to pension investors), and promote them to the pension industry.

Areas for pension fund investments that a federal ETI coordinating agency could explore include housing, physical infrastructure, and what could be called the economic infrastructure (private-sector productive resources such as telecommunications networks, cutting-edge manufacturing technologies, and so forth).

Enactment of Legislation Mandating Joint-Participant Representation

Simply permitting fiduciaries to consider broader economic and societal factors is insufficient. Such individuals are still, for the most part, investment professionals with the worldview and the biases inherent in the calling. Pension investments can reflect the overall needs and interests of participants and beneficiaries only if they are represented in the pension fund decisionmaking process itself. More than 40 years ago, Congress mandated joint employer–employee control of multiemployer plans. Many state and local public employee systems have significant participant representation.

It is far past the time that participants and beneficiaries be represented on the decisionmaking bodies of all pension plans. Congress should apply the joint trusteeship standard in existence for multiemployer plans to all private pension plans, both defined benefit and contribution.

In 1990, U.S. Representative Peter Visclosky (D-Ind.) proposed legislation that would have mandated joint-participant representation on all private defined benefit and defined contribution pension plans. The bill was defeated on the House floor; it received 173 votes (a shift of 39 votes would have changed the outcome). With the increased interest in the role of pension funds in the economy, the Visclosky bill should be revived.

Interestingly, in the wake of the Robert Maxwell pension scandal in the United Kingdom (where more than $600 million in assets was stolen), even *The Economist* found itself urging editorially (November 14, 1992) that pension participants be given the right to elect directly "more than one" of their fund's trustees.

Conclusion: Investing in Ourselves

Our interest in pension funds is, in a sense, a function of their sheer magnitude. "The Largest Lump of Money in the World" is the way an NBC television documentary once characterized them. Indeed, it is impossible to comprehend how much wealth and potential productive power $4 trillion ($4,000,000,000,000) represents.

But our concern with pension funds is not simply a Willie Sutton–like attraction to these institutions simply because that's where the money is. Pension funds are the deferred wages—the savings—of 50 million American workers.

We have tried to show that these funds are being invested in ways that are detrimental to our nation's economic prospects and to the prospects of participants and beneficiaries themselves.

A primary function of government is to intervene in situations when the actions of private entities threaten the public good and when those entities have proved themselves incapable of moderating their own behavior. This is clearly the case with respect to the capital markets' technologically driven preoccupation with short-term trading and speculation.

The public, through government tax expenditures and various regulatory policies, has helped to create pension funds as we know them. And it is clearly appropriate for the public to impose certain policy goals on pension fund investors, especially when those investors do not appear capable of adopting such goals on their own.

Pension funds can play a key role in revitalizing our economy by virtue of their longtime horizon. They are the most appropriate source of private capital to provide truly "patient" capital for the economy. Beyond a more general shift to longer-term investment horizons, economically targeted investments can provide pension funds with the tools to make such commitments.

Pension funds are a practical—and essential—tool we can use both to invest in ourselves and to more effectively control our economic destiny.

Notes

1. Robert Pollin, Ann Markusen, Helen Bowers, Ian Lanoff, Meredith Miller, and Martin Wolfson provided useful comments, and Heather Grob and Bill Barnes provided research assistance.

2. This chapter relies on two basic sources for aggregate data on pension funds: the Federal Reserve Board's *Flow of Funds Accounts* and the Employee Benefit Research Institute's (EBRI's) *Quarterly Pension Investment Report* (QPIR). While the QPIR leans heavily on *Flow of Funds*, it disaggregates certain data and uses somewhat different definitions for certain asset classes. In addition, QPIR incorporates data from other sources, including the American Council on Life Insurance.

During 1992, the Federal Reserve significantly revised its methodology for calculating pension accounts, resulting in a sharp increase in reported pension assets of approximately $500 billion over the previous methodology. At the time of this writing, EBRI had not yet incorporated these revisions into its QPIR data series. Where possible, we have used the new Federal Reserve data. However, QPIR contains levels of detail unavailable from the published Federal Reserve data, and we continue to rely on it for certain measures. Given the probable upward revisions from incorporating the new Federal Reserve data, the QPIR data should be viewed as conservative measures of pension funds' importance in the economy.

Also, other types of retirement or saving plans are not included in this discussion: they are federal government retirement systems and Individual Retirement Account (IRA) and Keogh plans.

The federal government sponsors a number of retirement systems, including civil service, military, and other plans, that had $251 billion in assets at year-end 1990 (EBRI *Issue Brief*, September 1992). All but about $10 billion of these assets are invested in special issue Treasury bonds. With the exception of the $10 billion defined contribution Federal Employees' Retirement System Trust Savings Plan, which invests through private-sector investment managers, the federal retirement system assets are not included in numbers reported by the Federal Reserve.

IRAs and Keogh plans, which are savings mechanisms directed by individual participants, had $685 billion in assets at year-end 1991, an increase of 200 percent since 1985. These saving plans bear many resemblances to defined contribution plans but are not included in pension asset numbers reported by the Federal Reserve. These plans are maintained in individual accounts held (in descending order of importance) by mutual funds, brokerage firms, commercial banks, savings and loan associations, insurance companies, credit unions, and mutual savings banks (EBRI *Benefit Notes*, July 1992). The Federal Reserve does not disaggregate IRA and Keogh assets from these institutions' other assets.

3. In a 1992 survey of the largest pension plans, 17 of the 25 largest cover state and local government or university employees. Of the remaining eight, all but IBM have relatively high levels of unionization: AT&T, General Motors, General Electric, Ford Motor, du Pont, NYNEX, and Ameritech (*Pensions and Investments*, January 20, 1992).

4. Another way to view retirement plans is to evaluate the certainty of the benefits they provide.

In defined benefit plans, participants are guaranteed a monthly benefit based on a formula expressed as a percentage of their final average salary over a period of years, a certain amount per year of service, or some combination thereof. This is the traditional pension plan.

In defined contribution plans, benefit levels are not guaranteed but are based solely on participants' accumulated account balances at the time of retirement. This balance is either distributed to the participant in a lump sum or used to purchase an annuity from an insurance company. Employees are often required to make contributions to these plans in addition to employer contributions.

There are many types of defined contribution plans, including simple cash accrual plans, Employee Stock Ownership Plans (ESOPs), profit-sharing plans, 401(k) plans, and thrift and savings plans. Since 1983, defined contribution plan assets have grown at about twice the rate of those of defined benefit plans, although they still represent less than one-quarter of all pension plan assets (Employee Benefits Research Institute, September 1992; *Money Market Directory*, 1992).

5. A thorough discussion of the basic ERISA provisions and subsequent regulations promulgated by the U.S. Department of Labor is beyond the scope of this chapter. For several useful recent introductory discussions of these issues, particularly as they relate to ETIs, see AFL-CIO Guide, 1991; ERISA Policy Review, 1992; and Berger, 1992. For a recent discussion of these issues from a labor lawyer's perspective, see Zanglein, 1992. For a recent overview of employee benefit regulation in both the public and private sectors, see Irish, 1992.

6. The "prudent man" concept was legally established when Harvard College lost a suit in 1830 against an investment manager, Francis Amory. Harvard College sued Amory for bad faith when he lost 40 percent of the assets entrusted to him in risky manufacturing and insurance stocks, but the court ruled in Amory's favor.

The "prudent person" or "prudent expert" rule, which was codified in ERISA, takes the Amory principle and modifies it somewhat by requiring a fiduciary to manage funds with the "care, skill, prudence, and diligence that a prudent person in a similar situation would apply" (Litvak and Daniels, 1979, p. 129). The prudence standard was thus shifted from a reference to how fiduciaries would manage their "own affairs" to how other professional investment managers would behave under similar circumstances.

7. A recent preliminary report by three academics (Lakonishok, Shleifer, and Vishney, November 1991) produces some fascinating insights into this issue. Using two databases made available to them by a major consulting firm, SEI, they were able to analyze the relative performance of the equity investments of more than 700 different pension funds and 350 separate money managers over different time periods. For example, they found that from 1983 through 1989, these portfolios' pension funds and their managers underperformed the Standard & Poor's 500 stock index by 2.6 percentage points (on a value-weighted basis), even before subtracting the average money management fee of 0.6 percent of assets. Noting other studies that found that mutual funds actually outperformed the S&P, they concluded, "Taken together, the evidence from different sources for different subperiods indicates that pension fund managers' performance net of management fees may lag that for mutual funds by 200 basis points [2 percent] per year."

They also found contradictory evidence on the impact of portfolio churning, or turnover; one analysis indicated that churning hurt earnings by about 0.8 percent, and another demonstrated a positive correlation between active management and increased yields of about 0.6 percent per year over five years (although this still produced an average performance lower than the S&P index).

Interestingly, they found that picking investment managers based on a higher-than-average short-term performance (one year) is actually counterproductive: "Picking a loser gives a higher subsequent return than picking a winner." However, they found some correlation between superior longer-term results (three years' worth of performance data) and subsequent superior performance. The authors note, however, that "These particular results do not imply that the good money managers selected in this way can be expected to beat a passive investment strategy, since the expected returns net of management fees even for these good managers appears to be below the S&P 500 returns."

8. At President Clinton's preinauguration Economic Summit, George Hatsopolous, chairman of Thermo Electron, argued that companies were suffering from a "capital squeeze" brought on by "short-term traders." Hatsopolous told Clinton that during the past five years, American corporations had depleted more than $1 trillion from their

treasuries to fund dividends and stock repurchase programs to bolster stock prices and appease restless shareholders. During that same period, he argued, Japanese companies received net capital inflows of $200 billion (*The Washington Post*, December 16, 1992, p. F3).

9. There is more than a little confusion over the differences, if any, between ETIs and socially responsible investing (SRI). We do not want to make too fine a point of this, but for the purposes of our discussion, we make the following distinctions.

> Economically targeted investments are discrete investment initiatives—with a policy goal of economically benefiting a group, community, region, industry, or the economy as a whole—that are:
> • designed to make direct loans or equity investments outside established market mechanisms;
> • designed to establish new market mechanisms; or
> • designed to alter or modify the functioning of existing market mechanisms in some important way.

> Socially responsible investing is a portfolio management technique of applying what are traditionally considered to be noneconomic criteria to the investment management process, usually (but not always) involving publicly traded securities. A feature of this technique is support for, or the sponsorship of, shareholder resolutions concerning a corporation's actions as they affect employees, communities, the environment, and society in general.

Needless to say, an ETI can have an important "social" component; likewise, an SRI can have economic policy goals.

10. Particularly important in this series was Lawrence Litvak's 1981 *Pension Funds and Economic Renewal*. In this book, Litvak methodically analyzed economic development, venture capital, affordable housing, and job creation portfolio strategies, applying modern portfolio techniques. He detailed dozens of new and promising ETI mechanisms, and he systematized the application of risk analysis to ETI portfolios.

11. Work Group Chairman Ronald D. Watson, in a letter conveying the report, wrote that the group "was unanimous in agreeing that pension funds had grown too large to be indifferent to the possibility that narrow investment policies might be thwarting the access of some sectors of the economy to long-term capital. . . . Innovations in financial engineering and public/private partnerships for project finance hold great promise for addressing some basic investment needs without compromising fiduciary duties" (November 16, 1992, letter from Watson to Randy Barber).

12. See Vieira, 1984. Bruyn (1987) argues that much of the attack comes from those political and economic interests that are threatened by the potential power from more scrutiny and employee participation in pension fund investing.

13. Noting that the pension system represents the largest tax expenditure in the federal budget, Munnell has advanced an argument for a onetime 15 percent tax on existing pension assets and ongoing 15 percent income tax on pension plan revenues (Munnell, 1992). Munnell argues that tax expenditures for pension benefits disproportionately benefit higher-income individuals and that these tax losses could be better "spent" by the government in other ways (e.g., for deficit reduction and funding of other programs). Indeed, if Munnell's proposal were implemented, it would yield a onetime revenue of $600 billion. The ongoing levy would produce revenues that in 1990 would have been close to $55 billion.

Drawing on her previous conclusions that ETIs are by definition concessionary, Munnell argues that the proper purview for government is to use tax revenues for worthy projects and not allow pension funds to invest in them and risk retiree welfare.

We do not agree with Munnell's proposal to tax pension assets and revenues. Dorsey (1992) has argued that most of the value of pension tax expenditures accrues to families with an annual income between $30,000 and $50,000. The problem she correctly identifies is that effective pension coverage has been "stuck" at less than half the workforce. The answer, we believe, is to implement much stronger measures to extend coverage instead of giving up on the quest to provide meaningful, employment-based retirement income for all workers. Specifically, we support the enactment of an advance-funded mandatory universal pension system, which would require all employers to maintain, or make payments into, a retirement plan for all employees. Of course, a significant strengthening of the Social Security system will be important to address structural income distribution issues.

However, even if we agreed with Munnell's proposal to tax current pension fund assets and revenue, we would still not agree with her implicit assumption that the capital markets are efficient and immutable and that they should simply be left to their own devices. If her proposal were implemented, we would still be faced with the problems of short-term investment strategy and speculation.

If pension funds played a less significant role in the capital markets, perhaps there would be no need for public policies addressing their investment behavior. But pension funds are far too large and important to ignore, no matter what other retirement income policies may be desirable to adopt.

Bibliography

AFL-CIO. Committee on the Investment of Union Pension Funds. *Investment of Union Pension Funds*. Washington, DC: AFL-CIO, 1979.

AFL-CIO. Department of Employee Benefits. "Domestic and International Pension Investment Issues: A Report Prepared for the AFL-CIO Pension Investment Committee." *Investment of Union Pension Funds*. Washington, DC: AFL-CIO, 1992.

AFL-CIO. *Investing in Our Future: An AFL-CIO Guide to Pension Investment and Proxy Voting*. Washington, DC: AFL-CIO, 1991.

Berger, Marshall J. "Statement of the Solicitor." Before the Infrastructure Investment Commission, U.S. Department of Labor, October 30, 1992.

Bodie, Zvi. "Pension Funds and Financial Innovation." Working Paper No. 3101, Series. Cambridge, MA: NBER, September 1989.

Brancato, Carolyn Kay. "Institutional Investors and Corporate America: Conflicts and Resolutions: An Overview of the Role of Institutional Investors in Capital Markets and Corporate Governance." Exhibit 17, pp. 70–85. In *Impact of Institutional Investors on Corporate Governance, Takeovers, and the Capital Markets*. Hearing before the U.S. Senate Subcommittee on Securities of the Committee on Banking, Housing, and Urban Affairs, Washington, DC, 1990.

Bruyn, Severyn. *The Field of Social Investing*. Cambridge, England: Cambridge University Press, 1987.

Center for Policy Alternatives. "State Experiences with Economically Targeted Investments," December 7, 1992.

Congressional Research Service. "Joint Pension Trusteeship: An Analysis of the Visclosky Proposal." Hearings before the Subcommittee of Labor-Management on H.R. 2664, Washington, DC, February 21–28, 1990.

Cosh, A., A. Hughes, and A. Singh. "Takeovers and Short-termism: Analytical and Policy Issues in the U.K. Economy." In *Takeovers and Short-Termism in the UK Industrial Policy Paper No. 3*. London: Institute for Public Policy Research, 1990.

Dorsey, Stuart. "Taxation of Pensions." In John Turner and Daniel Beller, eds., *Trends in Pensions*. Washington, DC: U.S. Government Printing Office, 1992, pp. 577–88.

Durgin, Hillary. "Milrite Finds Opportunities Limited." *Pension and Investment Age*, Vol. 17, No. 25, November 17, 1989, p. 33.

Economist. "Protecting Pensions." November 14, 1992.

Employee Benefit Research Institute. *Retirement Security and Tax Policy.* Washington, DC: EBRI, 1984.

Employee Benefit Research Institute. *Issue Brief.* Washington, DC: EBRI, 1992a.

Employee Benefit Research Institute. *Quarterly Pension Investment Report.* Washington, DC: EBRI, September 1992b.

ERISA Advisory Committee. *Economically Targeted Investments: An ERISA Policy Review.* Work Group on Pension Investments, Advisory Council on Pension Welfare and Benefit Plans. Washington, DC: U.S. Department of Labor, November 1992.

Federal Reserve System, Board of Governors. *Flow of Funds, Financial Assets and Liabilities: Year-End 1966–1989.* Washington, DC: Board of Governors of the Federal Reserve System, 1991.

Federal Reserve System, Board of Governors. *Flow of Funds, Financial Assets and Liabilities: Third Quarter 1992.* Washington, DC: Board of Governors of the Federal Reserve System, 1992.

Ferguson, Karen. "The Advocates Arguments: A Review and Comment." In Dallas Salisbury, ed. *Should Pension Assets Be Managed for Social/Political Purposes?* Washington, DC: Employee Benefits Research Institute, 1980, pp. 94–105.

Ghilarducci, Teresa. *Labor's Capital: The Politics and Economics of Private Pensions.* Cambridge, MA: Massachusetts Institute of Technology Press, 1992.

Hansen, Derek. *Banking and Small Business.* National Governors Association, Council of State Planning Agencies. Washington, DC: NGA, 1981.

Harrington, John. *Investing with Your Conscience: How to Achieve High Returns Using Socially Responsible Investing.* New York: John Wiley and Sons, 1992.

Harrington, John and Nathan Gardells. *Interim Report: Governor's Public Investment Task Force (California)*, March 1981.

Harrington, John and Nathan Gardells. *Final Report: Governor's Public Investment Task Force (California)*, October 1981.

Hollister, Robert and Tunney Lee. *Development Politics: Private Development and the Public Interest.* National Governors Association, Council of State Planning Agencies. Washington, DC: NGA, 1981.

Hutchinson, James D. and Charles G. Cole. "Legal Standards Governing the Investment of Private Pension Capital." In Dallas Salisbury, ed., *Should Pension Assets Be Managed for Social/Political Purposes?* Washington DC: Employee Benefits Research Institute, 1980, pp. 28–93.

Institute for Fiduciary Education. *Economically Targeted Investments: A Reference for Public Pension Funds.* Sacramento, CA: Institute for Fiduciary Education, 1989.

Irish, Leon E. "Twenty Years of Employee Benefits." *Tax Notes*, November 12, 1992.

Jensen, Michael C. "Corporate Control and the Politics of Finance." *Journal of Applied Corporate Finance*, Vol. 4, No. 3, Summer 1991.

Kieschnick, Michael. "Venture Capital and Urban Development." National Governors Association, Council of State Planning Agencies. Washington, DC: NGA, 1979.

Kirshner, Edward. "The Effect of Housing-Related Securities on the Performance of Public Employee Pension Funds." Working Paper. Oakland, CA: Community Economics, Inc., 1979.

Lakonishok, Josef, Andrei Shleifer, and Robert Vishney. "The Structure and Performance of the Money Management Industry." Preliminary draft. University of Chicago, November 1991.

Langbein, John H. and Richard A. Poser. "Social Investing and the Law of Trusts." *Michigan Law Review*, Vol. 79, No. 72, November 1980, pp.72–111.

Lanoff, Ian. Department of Labor, Advisory Opinion 8112A. Letter to Robert Georgine. Washington, DC, January 15, 1981.

Leibig, Michael. "Social Investing and the Law: The Case for Alternative Investments." Conference for Alternative State and Local Policies. Washington, DC, 1981.

Litvak, Lawrence. *Pension Funds and Economic Renewal*. National Governors Association, Council of State Planning Agencies. Washington, DC: NGA, 1981.

Litvak, Lawrence and Belden Daniels. *Innovations in Development Finance*. Council of State Planning Agencies, National Governors Association. Washington, DC: NGA, 1979.

Luzzatto, Daniel. "Social Investing; the Protest for 1980s." *National Underwriter*, Vol. 91, No. 4, January 26, 1987, pp. 4–5.

Marco Consulting Group. "Survey Shows Targeted Investments Create Jobs, Outperform Competitors." Press release. Chicago, April 15, 1992.

Mitchell, Gina. "Social Investing of Public Pension Funds." National Conference on State Legislatures, Washington, DC. Monograph. November 1986.

Munnell, Alicia. "Pitfalls of Social Investing: The Case of Public Pension Funds and Housing." *New England Economic Review*, September/October 1983, pp. 20–41.

Munnell, Alicia. "Current Taxation of Qualified Pension Plans: Has the Time Come?" *New England Economic Review*, March/April 1992, pp. 12–25.

New York State AFL-CIO Task Force. *It's Our Money*. Edward Cleary, President, and Joseph E. McDermott, Chair, 1990.

New York State Industrial Cooperation Council. *Our Money's Worth: The Report of the Governor's Task Force on Pension Fund Investment*. Ira Millstein, Chair, and Lee Smith, Director and Editor, June 1989.

O'Cleireacain, Carol. Prepared remark for the Center for Policy Alternatives Conference on ETIs, Washington, DC, December 7, 1992.

Peirce, Neal, Jerry Hagstrom, and Carol Steinbach. "Economic Development: The Challenge of the 1980s." National Governors Association, Council of State Planning Agencies. Washington, DC: NGA, 1979.

Pension and Investments. "Managers Ranked by Pension Fund Assets," and "Profile Statistics at a Glance," May 18, 1992, pp. 1–3.

Pension and Investments. "Market Lifts Top 1000 Assets to $2.3 Trillion." January 20, 1992, p. 1.

Peterson, John S. "A Summary of State and Local Employee Retirement System Investment Practices and Policies." Government Finance Center, Chicago, IL, 1980.

Porter, Michael E. "Capital Choices: Changing the Way America Invests in Its Industry." Council on Competitiveness, Washington, DC: 1992.

President's Commission on Pension Policy. *Coming of Age: Toward a National Retirement Income Security Policy*, 1981.

Salisbury, Dallas, ed. *Should Pension Assets Be Managed for Social/Political Purposes?* Washington, DC: Employee Benefits Research Institute, 1980.

Sass, Steven. "Public Pensions: Dos and Don'ts." *Regional Review*. New England Federal Reserve Bank, Spring 1992, pp. 21–24.

Smart, Donald A. "Investment Targeting: A Wisconsin Center for Public Policy." Wisconsin Center for Public Policy, Madison, WI, 1979.

Smith, Lee, ed. and coauthor. "Competitive Plus: Economically Targeted Investments by Pension Funds." Prepared by the New York State Industrial Cooperation Council in cooperation with the Governor's Task Force on Pension Fund Investment, New York State, 1990.

Speidell, Lawrence S. "Embarrassment of Riches: The Discomfort of Alternative Investment Strategies." *Journal of Portfolio Management*, Vol. 17, No. 1, Fall 1990, pp. 6–11.

Turner, John and Daniel Beller. *Trends in Pensions*. Washington, DC: U.S. Government Printing Office, 1990.

Twentieth Century Fund. *The Report of the Twentieth Century Fund Task Force on Market Speculation and Corporate Governance*. Background paper by Robert J. Shiller. New York: Twentieth Century Fund, 1992.

U.S. Congress, Government Accounting Office. "Pension Plans: Investments in Affordable Housing Possible with Government Assistance." Report to the Chairman, U.S. House of Representatives, Committee on Government Operations, Washington, DC, 1991.

Vieira, Edwin, Jr. *"Social Investing": Its Character, Causes, Consequences and Legality Under the Employment Retirement Income Security Act of 1974*. Washington, DC: U.S. Department of Labor, Labor-Management Services Administration, 1984.

White, James. "Picking Losers: Back Yard Investing, Roils Kansas Pension System." *Wall Street Journal*, August 21, 1991.

Zanglein, Jayne Elizabeth. "Solely in Our Interest: Creating Maximum Benefits Through Prudent Pension Investments." The Labor Law Exchange, AFL-CIO Lawyers Coordinating Committee, Washington, DC, No. 11, 1992.

CHAPTER TWELVE

Public Credit Allocation through the Federal Reserve: Why It Is Needed; How It Should Be Done[1]

ROBERT POLLIN

CHAPTER SUMMARY

This chapter outlines a comprehensive restructuring program for the Federal Reserve System, giving it broad authority in the area of credit allocation. Undertaking a structural overhaul of the Federal Reserve in a period of pervasive financial problems is consonant with the evolution of central banking in the United States. In this proposal, the central bank would still be responsible for short-term money and interest rate management, but its relative focus would shift to long-term promotion of productive investment, financial stabilization, and sustainable growth. Equally important, the extent to which the Fed's activities are accountable to democratic processes would increase dramatically.

The chapter considers four systemic problems that, evaluated as a whole, demonstrate the need for the proposed transformation. These are the long-term pattern of deepening financial fragility, the bias for short-term over long-term investment and planning commitments, the lack of democratic accountability within both public and private institutions operating in the financial market, and the declining capacity of existing government policies to counter these systemically embedded fractures.

In addition, the proposal offers a vehicle for addressing somewhat separate, but equally serious, questions. The first is the need to undertake two long-term processes of industrial conversion—out of military production on the one hand and into environmentally benign production techniques on the other. The second is to increase opportunities for high-wage, high-productivity jobs in the United States, given the intensified downward wage pressure resulting from globalization of our labor and financial markets.

The specific features of the restructuring proposal are drawn entirely from programs that have been used or at least seriously considered in the United States or other market economies. They include:

• Increasing democratic accountability through direct election, within each region of the country, of the directors of the 12 Federal Reserve district banks;

• Increasing the role of discount-window reserve creation relative to open market operations. This will give district banks more direct regulatory authority over the lending activities of private intermediaries, enabling them to promote financial stability and the productive uses of funds. It will also redistribute downward Federal Reserve decisionmaking power, creating more effective channels for accountability;

• Establishing differential asset reserve requirements for all U.S. intermediaries. Preferred uses of credit, such as investing in environmentally benign technologies, will thus become significantly less costly for intermediaries than nonpreferred uses, such as mergers and buy-outs.

The chapter also addresses the practicality of these proposals in terms of historical experiences with government credit allocation policies, both in the United States and elsewhere. It then considers criticisms of credit allocation policies. It concludes that the program is feasible. Moreover, the program can be implemented within the existing U.S. institutional structure, with minimal demands on the federal budget and while maintaining substantial flexibility for the private sector in financial markets.

Introduction

The U.S. financial system faces pervasive structural problems: systemic instability, inadequate commitment to long-term productive investment, and the concentration of decisionmaking power within an unrepresentative and unresponsive elite. Moreover, the policy tools in place to address these problems—including fiscal, monetary, and regulatory policy—are evidently inadequate for reversing these patterns and promoting stability, long-term investment, and democratic accountability.

The proposal advanced here is to create a public credit allocation system within the Federal Reserve, thereby providing the Federal Reserve with new policy instruments for countering the tendencies toward fragility and inadequate productive investment. This transformation also involves substantially increasing democratic accountability over Federal Reserve activities, thereby creating a mechanism for extending democracy throughout the financial system.

It is possible to design a new public credit allocation authority that would operate separately from the Federal Reserve. However, transforming the existing central banking system rather than creating a new institution has the merit of minimizing both start-up problems and the growth of bureaucracies. Moreover, revamping the Federal Reserve during a period of pervasive financial problems is also consonant with evolution of central banking practices in the United States.

Throughout the 19th century, there was considerable resistance to the idea of creating a central bank at all in the United States. The Federal Reserve System was created in 1913 only after it became clear that the minimal regulatory structure organized around the National Bank Act of 1864 was incapable of preventing the severe financial panics of 1873, 1893, and 1907–9. Moreover, the political system could not continue to pay the high price of widespread social unrest that followed these financial crises.

But the initial Federal Reserve structure exercised little real influence. The heavy wave of financial speculation in the 1920s, culminating in the 1929 Wall Street crash and subsequent collapse of the banking system, demonstrated the incapacity of this initial central banking system to promote financial stability. This was true even though during the 1920s, open market operations were developed as a powerful new technique for conducting monetary policy.

The system was then revamped in 1935. The intention was to concentrate power within a newly created board residing in Washington and to give the board increasing authority in fixing reserve requirements and the discount rate. With these new powers, the new centralized Fed focused on influencing two policy targets—short-term interest rates and the growth of the money supply.

The intention of the present proposal is to shift the focus of Federal Reserve activities more than to increase its powers *per se*, as was done through the 1935 restructuring. The point here is to provide the means for the central bank to focus less on short-run money supply and interest rate targets and more on long-term measures to promote accountability, stability, and productive investment. At the same time, providing the Federal Reserve with new credit allocation policy instruments will not diminish its capacity to conduct short-term monetary policy. Indeed, the more stable financial environment, which the new policies are designed to achieve, will enhance the effectiveness of short-term policies as well.

The ideas advanced here borrow from the experiences of other advanced capitalist economies. Our specific models are those economies, such as Japan's and France's, where central banks and allied institutions traditionally have been active participants in the allocation of credit for large-scale investment projects. These relationships have diminished in recent years through financial innovation and deregulation, but the overall post-war experience nevertheless contains useful lessons.

What is of central interest about these countries is that large-scale investment financing has been planned through negotiations among various constituencies within the financial market—through the exercise of "voice," in Albert Hirschmann's (1970) terminology. I argue that the U.S. system suffers because long-term financing is dominated by arm's-length market relationships in which "exit" is the primary vehicle for seeking institutional changes.

At the same time, the standard operating procedure within the Japanese and French systems has been to limit accountability within their public investment institutions; the voice option was extended only to elite cadres of bureaucrats and businesspeople. By contrast, the proposal advanced here offers a strategy for developing credit allocation policies through extending, not circumscribing, democracy.

Finally, this proposal provides a vehicle for addressing separate, but equally serious, questions facing the U.S. economy. The first is the need to undertake two long-term processes of industrial conversion—out of military production on the one hand and into environmentally benign production techniques on the other. The second is to increase opportunities for high-wage, high-productivity jobs in the United States, given the intensified downward wage pressure resulting from globalization of our labor and financial markets. These problems are not specifically tied to issues of financial stabilization or restructuring. However, they are linked in the sense that grappling with all of them will entail a commitment to planning long term and to using financial resources productively.

Overall then, this proposal offers an approach toward implementing the long-standing Keynesian idea of socializing investment. There are strong reasons why public credit allocation policies deserve a place on the political agenda as an instrument for socializing investment: to promote financial stabilization and limit speculation, to support long-term investment commitments, to increase accountability over major finance and investment decisions, and to address structural problems in which private market solutions are not feasible or acceptable.

The organization of this paper is as follows. The second section surveys the basic problems within the existing financial structure as they are relevant to our immediate policy concerns. The third section proposes a set of new policy instruments that the Federal Reserve will need to adopt in order to promote long-term stabilization, productive investment, and democratic accountability. The fourth section considers the experience in both the United States and other market economies with credit allocation policies. The fifth section evaluates the critical literature on such policies. The brief concluding section addresses the issue of how the proposals advanced here could be implemented over time—some immediately within the existing legal framework and political climate, and others at later points as economic and political circumstances change.

A Financial System That Doesn't Work

We consider here four fundamental and systemic problems in the U.S. financial system that, evaluated as a whole, demonstrate the need for giving the Federal Reserve new powers in the area of credit allocation. The four problems are:

- the long-term pattern of deepening financial fragility;
- the bias for short-term over long-term investment and planning commitments;
- the lack of democratic accountability within both public and private institutions operating in the financial market; and
- the declining capacity of government policies to counter these systemically embedded fractures, so much so that government policies now appear to contribute to the problems.

We address these issues in turn, then consider the related issues of industrial conversion and globalization.

Financial Instability

There are different levels at which we can observe the tendency toward systemic financial instability. At the most apparent, we see the effects of instability through the set of interlocking crises and transformations taking place within financial institutions.

From the lenders' side of the market, the most obvious indicator of instability is the collapse of the savings and loan industry and the enormous public costs of paying for the collapse. A parallel phenomenon is the crisis of the banking system, as measured, for example, by the rise in bank failures from an average of 4 failures annually per 10,000 institutions between 1947 and 1979 to 78 annually per 10,000 institutions between 1980 and 1989, and with 169 failures occurring in 1990 (128 per 10,000 institutions). Another measure of instability is the disintegration of the financial regulatory structure constructed during the New Deal and the complete lack of direction as to what, if anything, should replace it.

From the borrowers' side of the financial market, we observe systemic financial instability through the patterns of accelerated rates of debt financing by businesses—especially nonfinancial corporations—and households. Figure 12.1 shows the rise in the debt/gross national product (GNP) ratios for nonfinancial corporations and businesses. After allowing for cyclical fluctuations, we see that in both cases, debt has been rising relative to GNP since the early 1960s. Also in both cases, the rate of increase accelerates sharply through the 1980s. Thus, from 1961 to 1990, the household debt ratio has risen from 46 to 75 percent. The rise of the corporate debt ratio, from 48 to 63 percent, is less steep but nevertheless substantial.

And because the rising debt/income ratios of the 1980s were accompanied by unprecedented high real interest rates, as we also see in Table 12.1, the debt-servicing burdens for both households and businesses became serious as the decade progressed, and they intensified as incomes tended to decline during the 1990–92 recession. Thus, the business failure rate rose from an average of 42.3 per 10,000 between 1947 and 1979 to 90.8 per 10,000 for the 1980s. The household sector again follows in a basically parallel fashion. The personal bankruptcy rate per 10,000 households rose from a remarkably stable rate of about 8–9 per 10,000 in the 1960s and 1970s to 19 per 10,000 in 1982–1990.

At the simplest level of accounting, the underlying source of financial instability must be that debt commitments are systematically outstripping the income flows necessary to service them. The challenge then is to explain the source of the mismatch between debt commitments and income flows. I have argued elsewhere (Pollin 1990, 1992) that the basic explanation for the systematic deviation between debt commitments and income flows is that borrowed funds have been

Figure 12.1. **Debt Ratios and Interest Rates, 1961–1990**

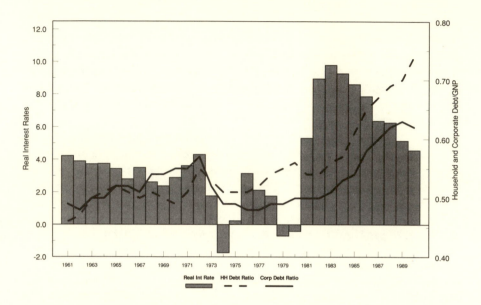

Source: Federal Reserve Board, *Balance Sheet for U.S. Economy.*
Note: Interest rate is average of Moody's average yield on corporate bonds and secondary market yield on FHA-insured mortgage loans minus change in CPI.

used disproportionately to finance speculative and compensatory spending, that is, borrowing to purchase existing assets with the expectation of capital gain and to compensate for declining income streams or other internally generated funds. At the same time, borrowed funds have been used insufficiently to finance productive spending, that is, spending that enhances the productive capacity of firms and individuals. When credit is extended for speculative and compensatory spending to a disproportionate degree relative to productive spending, the necessary result will be income streams inadequate to finance the growth of debt.[2]

Short-Term Bias

Part of the explanation for the rise in speculative activity is the bias toward short-term investment commitments embedded in the present financial structure. There are two basic sources for the short-term bias in the contemporary U.S. financial market. The first is contemporary profitability trends that have rewarded short-term asset transfers over long-term investments in asset creation. The second is an organizational structure that similarly rewards short-term measures to raise equity returns over long-term commitments to productive enterprise. These will be considered in turn.

Profit Rates and Market Values

For nonfinancial corporations on average, the pretax profit rate—i.e., profitability relative to the replacement cost of existing capital stock—declined from 12.2 percent in the 1960s to around 6 percent in the mid-1970s and early 1980s. Profitability rose to an average of 8.6 percent over the 1982–1990 business cycle, but it did so almost entirely through redistributive effects (from lower taxation and a falling wage bill—a redistribution from stakeholders to shareholders) with little overall gain in productivity.

During this same period, the average market value of the corporations relative to their assets at replacement cost (what we may call a proxy q ratio) fell dramatically, from 96.1 percent in the 1960s to a range of 41–44 percent between the mid-1970s and early 1980s. From 1982 to 1990, and especially before the 1987 stock market crash, the proxy q ratio rose along with stock prices, but only to an average of 63 percent. This meant that between 1982 and 1990, one dollar's worth of existing corporations' productive assets could be purchased on the stock market for only 63 cents.

As a result, the corporations' fixed investment growth stagnated, while the level of borrowing to finance speculative activity—mergers, acquisitions, and buy-outs of existing corporate assets—soared. Between 1982 and 1990, the growth of capital expenditures averaged only 2.2 percent, and *all* of that growth was due to a 35 percent increase in spending between 1983 and 1984, as the economy came out of recession. Otherwise, capital expenditures declined by an average of 1.5 percent annually. At the same time, spending on mergers and acquisitions in the 1980s totaled $1.3 trillion, which was one-third of the amount spent on fixed investment over the decade.[3]

Exit and Voice in Financial Markets

The U.S. financial system is organized primarily through arm's-length relationships in capital markets. It is, as John Zysman (1983) has put it, a "capital market" dominated system, similar to Great Britain's, in which "financial institutions tend to manage portfolios of stocks, spreading their risks across companies rather than investing in the future of specific companies that they nurture through hard times" (p. 63). This institutional structure encourages a short-term focus on dividends and capital returns rather than a long-term focus on nurturing investment projects.

Such an institutional arrangement contrasts sharply with the "credit market"–based systems that prevailed in Japan, France, and Germany prior to the 1980s wave of financial innovation and deregulation. Zysman argues that in those systems, financial firms interacted closely with nonfinancial firms and the state in forging commitments to long-term investment projects. The pressures for short-term profitability or capital appreciation were therefore substantially lower.

As Zysman puts it (p. 64), because Japan, France, and Germany had "more restricted capital markets and, in particular, a limited secondary capital market, it is harder for financial institutions to treat equity investments simply as a matter of financial portfolio balance."[4]

Zysman draws fruitfully on Hirschmann's exit/voice framework for analyzing economic interactions. The U.S./British system, as Zysman explains, is dominated by exit as a means of exercising influence. Thus, dissatisfied shareholders or bondholders will typically express their displeasure by selling their claims to the company. In contrast, the credit-based systems of corporate finance were premised on the exercise of influence by voice. Major financial institutions and state agencies have been actively involved in charting a nonfinancial firm's long-term plans and then committing themselves to the process of implementing those plans.

The point here is not that credit market systems necessarily encourage voice while the capital market system must rely on exit; rather, that in the current U.S. system, there is no institutional framework parallel to that which prevailed in Japan, France, and Germany for encouraging the exercise of voice. This absence—embedded within a capital market based system—has focused the U.S. financial structure on short-term thinking.

Lack of Accountability

The problems of accountability in the U.S. financial system have long been recognized, at least insofar as they reside within nonfinancial corporations. Berle's and Means's classic 1932 study was among the first to argue that the growth of the corporate form of organization would encourage a divergence in the interests of managers and owners—a "principal/agent" problem, in modern terminology. The problem is that managers, as agents of a dispersed and unorganized set of owners, will act in behalf of their own interests; and their interests are not necessarily identical to, or even compatible with, those of the firms' owners. Managers, for example, will frequently seek to maximize their own salary, security, power, and perquisites, even when a firm's resources could be more productively directed elsewhere.

In recent years, a version of the Berle-Means argument has been revived with an unusual twist by Michael Jensen (e.g., 1989). In his writings in defense of the market for corporate control, Jensen claims that the principal/agent conflict within corporations stems not from the natural evolution of the corporate form itself. It has rather resulted from the New Deal regulations that dramatically restricted the power of investment banks to participate as owners and overseers of investment projects for which they had raised money.

Jensen claims that prior to the New Deal laws, investment bankers took the lead in organizing financing for corporate investment, invested their own capital, and closely monitored the activities of firm managers. Jensen also says that J. P.

Morgan, residing at the top of the old system, also epitomized its best features. Morgan was able to coordinate finance and investment activity for the entire economy, and this forged even tighter relationships between financial and nonfinancial institutions. Government involvement was unnecessary. Jensen would therefore restore accountability to corporations by eliminating the legal barriers between investment banks, commercial banks, and corporate managers.

However, Jensen's solution to the problem of accountability in the U.S. financial system suffers from several problems. The first is that he takes too narrow a view of the problem of accountability. Many interests besides those of shareholders are badly represented in the present financial and corporate system. First among these are the many "stakeholders" of corporations and banks, including workers and communities whose livelihoods depend on the well-being of the corporations.[5] Banks' practice of neighborhood redlining is one indicator of the problem of accountability at the community level; the weak enforcement of the Community Reinvestment Act makes clear that this accountability problem has not diminished since the act's passage in 1977 (Campen, this volume).

In addition, a substantial percentage of the actual owners of corporations are contributors to pension funds. As of 1987, pension funds held 24 percent of the total publicly owned corporate and foreign equities as well as 39 percent of corporate and foreign bonds (Barber and Ghilarducci, this volume). However, pension fund holders exercise no influence over the ways their pension fund savings are invested. Thus, we observe such perverse activities as funds from unionized workforces investing in antiunion companies or in foreign countries even when such investment will mean the loss of high-paid domestic jobs and the decline of communities.

The final problem, overlooked completely by Jensen, is that no J. P. Morgan equivalent exists or could exist within the contemporary U.S. financial system. The reason is that U.S. financiers and corporate managers no longer stand in a relationship with the U.S. economy equivalent to that of J. P. Morgan. At present, U.S. corporate and financial interests operate in an integrated global market. They seek the highest rates of return wherever they may be found. Morgan, of course, would have followed an identical strategy; but given the opportunities and constraints available to him in the early part of the century, investment in the United States offered the greatest profit opportunities.

But the implication of the present circumstances is that the self-interest of capital stands more sharply in conflict with the interests of most U.S. savers—who are, after all, the suppliers of the raw material on which all investment and financial activities depend. Most U.S. savers are also people who seek decent employment and a stable community and who therefore place greater value than the financiers on investments that also increase domestic employment and enhance community. These interests as well are systematically excluded from the economy's major financing and investment decisions.

Policy Ineffectiveness

For much of the period after World War II, government fiscal, monetary, and regulatory policies all appeared to contribute to financial stability.[6] They also encouraged both long-term commitments—insofar as they contributed to financial stability—and the exercise of voice through the democratic procedures embedded in the regulatory system.

However, beginning in the 1970s, and especially in the 1980s, the positive effects of government policies appear to have seriously diminished. Of the three policy areas, regulatory policy has been weakest. What became clear in the 1970s was that the post-war regulatory structure was not capable of inhibiting the momentum toward financial innovation that had been gathering strength since the early 1960s. The deregulation laws that were passed in the early 1980s essentially only codified what had already become the de facto state of affairs.

Efforts to control monetary aggregates or the interest rates had become equally ineffective in the 1980s. The behavior of monetary aggregates lost any clear and consistent relationship to either nominal GNP or inflation targets that orthodox theory would have suggested.[7] And while the Federal Reserve's aggressive efforts to push down short-term interest rates in the early 1990s largely succeeded, it also became clear that the Fed could exert far less influence on long-term rates. Thus, by the end of 1991, after two years of rate cutting by the Federal Reserve, short-term rates were at their lowest point in 18 years but the yield curve was also at its steepest.

Lender-of-last-resort monetary policies have succeeded in contributing to financial stability during this period, but only in the narrow sense of preventing a fragile financial system from descending into a crisis. Moreover, over a longer time horizon, lender-of-last-resort interventions themselves contribute to instability through creating a moral hazard: knowing that the government safety net is beneath them, financial institutions have become more willing to pursue risky practices than would be otherwise prudent.

Federal deficit spending, over the long post-war period, has produced a result similar to that of lender-of-last-resort interventions. At base, the purpose of deficit spending is to establish a floor for effective demand during an economic downturn. And to the extent that such a floor has been created, it contributes to fending off the historical patterns of debt deflations and depressions that characterized the history of capitalist finance prior to World War II. But, precisely by contributing to the avoidance of debt deflations, deficit spending has acted to validate existing speculative practices: speculative behavior is not punished as it would be in the absence of deficit spending.

Thus, the effectiveness of deflation-prevention policies has deteriorated over time: government policy is called on increasingly to bail out the fragile system and thereby avoid a deflation, but this very policy encourages more fragility and thus increases the burdens placed on future policy interventions. Larger and more frequent interventions have become necessary to fend off deflations. The costs of policy interventions, in other words, have risen while their benefits diminish.[8]

Credit Policies for Managing Structural Change

In addition to the problems of systemic instability, short-term bias, and inadequate accountability concentrated in the financial sphere, the U.S. economy faces two other formidable challenges regarding the way financial resources should be allocated to long-term investment. These are industrial conversion and globalization. And while these questions are less focused on the financial structure as such, the need for credit allocation policies to address them is equally strong.

Industrial Conversion

Throughout the post–World War II period, the U.S. economy has always had a planned sector in the form of military spending. For all its bad features—and there are many, ranging from the wasteful to the nefarious—military spending has also promoted the stability of both aggregate demand and technical innovation.[9] We must, of course, seize the transcendent opportunity for disarmament. But economic policy then must reproduce elsewhere both demand stabilizers and a nurturing environment for nonmilitary research and development.

One obvious choice for absorbing both the large-scale public funds and the technical resources now devoted to the military is the environment—specifically, an epoch-defining project for restructuring our productive capacity into a system whose foundation is environmental sustainability. Barry Commoner (1990) has estimated that an environmentally benign productive system could be created in the United States within 20 years by spending about one-third of current levels of military spending. However, even if the funds for such a project were made available, implementation would involve enormous coordination problems. A central bank with credit allocation powers will be well situated to address these coordination problems, since it would be uniquely capable of observing the full range of interactions between industrial conversion and long-term investment.

Globalization

Integration of U.S. investment, finance, and labor into the global economy is proceeding apace. One central long-term implication of this tendency, should it continue in its current trajectory, is now clear: it will continue to exert downward pressure on the wages of U.S. workers, as they are forced to compete in a globally integrated labor market against substantially lower paid workers elsewhere. Thus, unskilled jobs continue to be exported to lower-wage countries. But even skilled jobs that involve technically sophisticated equipment are increasingly capable of being relocated within low-wage regions.

The major policy solution advanced thus far by liberals is to invest in education, so that U.S. workers will acquire a competitive advantage on the basis of their skills. But this strategy will not inhibit multinational firms from seeking a lower-paid, skilled labor force elsewhere.[10]

The need therefore is to establish an incentive structure for long-term investment and job creation in the United States. But this incentive structure would be most effective if implemented through means less heavy-handed than explicit capital controls and less expensive than tax advantages. Properly designed credit allocation policies should provide adequate instruments to address the problem most equitably and at the least cost.

Policy Instruments for Public Credit Allocation

This section discusses the various policy instruments that will be needed to establish effective credit allocation policies within the Federal Reserve.[11] Even though such a policy approach would represent a dramatic departure from present practices, the specific features of this proposal are taken entirely from programs that have been or are now in place in the United States or other market economies. The challenge is to develop the best combination of policies to maximize their chances for success.

Within the U.S. context, it is important to keep in mind that even in 1992, after 12 years of relentless anti-government rhetoric, the federal government was still the largest single creditor in the U.S. financial market (it was also, of course, the largest single debtor). The amount of direct lending, loan guarantees, and government-sponsored enterprise loans (Federal National Mortgage Association [Fannie Mae], Home Loan Bank System, Student Loan Marketing, and Farm Credit System) is shown in Table 12.1. Table 12.2 shows the major recipients of those funds. As can be seen, the percentage of federally assisted lending has varied between 15 and 36 percent from 1975 to 1991; the major recipients of loans have been the housing sector, agriculture, and education.

With government lending operating on so substantial a scale, the proposal offered here clearly does not represent a dramatic departure from the extent of government involvement in financial markets. It rather offers a new set of priorities and instruments for intervening.

In considering present federal government credit allocation programs, Bosworth, Carron, and Rhyne (1987) have argued that these programs serve three functions: to create more effective markets, to reallocate financial resources, and to redistribute income. They conclude that the present credit allocation programs are most successful when they seek to improve markets and are reasonably successful in reallocating resources. But they are ineffective at redistributing income, because more direct and efficient techniques of income redistribution will almost always be available.

Consistent with the conclusions of Bosworth et al. (1987), the present propos-

Table 12.1

U.S. Government Credit Allocations (Billions of dollars)

	1975	1980	1985	1991
Direct loans	$12.8	$24.2	$28.0	$26.6
Guaranteed loans	8.6	31.6	21.6	106.9
Government-sponsored enterprise loans	5.6	21.4	60.7	90.7
TOTAL Federally Assisted Lending	27.0	77.2	110.3	224.2
TOTAL Funds Loaned in U.S. Credit Markets	178.0	354.5	768.6	616.9
Federally assisted as percentage of total loans	15.2%	21.8%	14.4%	36.3%

Sources: Data for 1975, 1980, and 1985 from Bosworth et al., 1987, p. 5. Data for 1991 from *Budget of the United States*, Appendix 1, p. 123; and *Flow of Funds Accounts*, Federal Reserve System, fourth quarter 1991, p. 61.

Table 12.2

Federal Government Loans by Major Program Area Fiscal Year 1985 (percentage of total loans)

	Direct Loans	Loan Guarantees	Government-Sponsored Enterprises
Housing	11.4%	81.2%	80.7%
Agriculture	49.3	2.7	16.5
Education	6.3	8.7	2.8
Exports	6.6	—	—
Small business	3.7	2.2	—
Other	22.7	5.2	—

Source: Bosworth et al., 1987, p. 12.

als are aimed primarily at improving the functioning of financial markets and reallocating resources. The argument of the previous section was precisely that existing markets are failing because they generate systemic instability, a short-term bias, and inadequate accountability. The needed restructuring must inevitably entail a reallocation of financial resources: the favored activities will crowd out both the less desirable uses of credit and the existing inequitable allocational procedures.

We first consider means of democratizing the central bank and thereby dramatically increasing its accountability. Without democratization, efforts to increase the authority of the central bank will be interpreted correctly as an illegitimate grasp for more power by those already entrenched.

We then discuss various tools for shifting credit allocation, including substituting discount reserve lending for open-market operations, differential asset reserve requirements, loan guarantees, and interest rate subsidies.

Any effort to create new financial regulations must confront in some way the lesson that was learned so painfully in the 1970s—that profit incentives will always lead intermediaries to seek, and, through innovation, almost always find, techniques to avoid regulations. The solution to this problem is developed in the chapter by D'Arista and Schlesinger in this volume: to "level the playing field" by applying consistent (though not necessarily uniform) incentives and restrictions to all intermediaries, that is, to all business entities that, in some fashion, accept deposits and make loans.[12] New regulations will therefore create no disadvantages for banks or any other intermediaries. Practical problems undoubtedly will emerge in implementing consistent regulations, especially in the context of a globally integrated financial market. But these will not be insurmountable and, in any case, the need to adhere to this principle is evident. Thus, the assumption underlying all of the following proposals is that they will be implemented in ways that consistently affect all lending institutions.

Democratization

The demand for democratization of the Federal Reserve is not new. It has been advanced within mainstream political circles for a long time, through the efforts, among others, of Wright Patman and Henry Reuss, both former chairmen of the U.S. House of Representatives Banking Committee. More recently, Rep. Lee Hamilton and Sen. Paul Sarbanes, both recent chairs of the Joint Economic Committee, have offered proposals for Fed democratization. Rep. Henry Gonzales, current chair of the House Banking Committee, has also strongly supported such proposals.[13]

As an organizing principle, democratization should proceed through redistributing power downward to the 12 district banks of the Federal Reserve System. The guiding concept behind creating 12 district banks along with the headquarters in Washington was to disperse the central bank's authority broadly. This remains a valuable idea, but it has never been seriously attempted in practice. Right now, the district banks operate under anomalous circumstances: they are highly undemocratic and yet have virtually no power. I propose reversing the equation: democratizing and empowering the district banks.

Bank presidents are currently selected by the banks' boards of directors, who are unelected businesspeople, mostly commercial bankers. Democratization could therefore involve the direct election of district bank directors by residents of the relevant regions.

The district banks exercise power now only because 5 of the 12 bank presidents sit on the Federal Open Market Committee, along with the 7 members of the Board of Governors. One means of increasing their authority would be to create additional seats for them on the Open Market Committee. Another complementary approach would be to devolve authority from the headquarters to the regional banks. The board would then be responsible for setting general guidelines, while the district banks would have significant power in implementation. One means of increasing district bank authority is to allow an increased role for discount window operations. This would also give the district banks a greater role in monitoring and regulating institutions in their districts. I expand on this point below.

Another proposal would be to build upon an experiment attempted in the 1930s, when district banks formed committees of bankers and businesspeople to discuss financial market issues in a nonmarket setting. This model could now be extended to include labor, consumer, and community representatives in the discussions. One focus of such a committee could be the attainment of far greater success than achieved thus far in enforcing the Community Reinvestment Act.[14]

The final, crucial component of any plan for increasing democratic accountability is that a democratic Fed have the wherewithal to address the fundamental problems facing the financial system, including systemic instability, short-term bias, and utilizing resources for industrial conversion and managing globalization. If the Fed does have such power, the extension of democracy will be of symbolic significance only. Thus, along with democratization, it will be necessary to give the central bank new tools for addressing the problems at hand.

Increasing the Role of Discount-Window Reserve Creation

Under present Federal Reserve procedures, reserves are distributed to banks almost entirely through open market operations, i.e., when the Fed purchases government bonds owned by private banks. Thus, between 1953 and 1988, 97 percent of the reserves outstanding were created through open market operations (Pollin, 1991, p. 383). As a result, there is little direct connection between the creation of reserves and the monitoring and regulation of private bank activity under this technique.

A powerful shift in Federal Reserve procedures would entail a substantial increase in the extent to which it furnishes reserves through the discount window. The procedure for increasing the relative weight of discount-window lending has been outlined with typical insight by Hyman Minsky (1986, pp. 322–28). Minsky explains that under a discount-window-based system, bank reserves would be furnished when the Federal Reserve discounts bank loans that arise in the financing of short-term business activity. As such, bank reserves would rise in connection with specific lending activity, and, equally important, reserve balances would fall as loans fall due and are repaid.

This procedure would produce four important benefits relative to the present system:

First, it would connect the reserve creation process more tightly to the financing of business activity. To a much greater extent than at present, banks would obtain reserves when they are lending for specific purposes. The Federal Reserve could therefore either choose to refuse discount loans or charge penalty rates when banks seek reserves to finance speculative activity. Strong obstacles to speculative finance are thus created through relatively simple mechanisms.

Second, the discount-window procedure would create a more effective strategy for monitoring and regulating financial institutions. Intermediaries would have to submit to the central banks' scrutiny on a regular basis. Regulatory interventions would be more closely linked to the processes of financing investment.

Third, this procedure would give the Federal Reserve greater power in influencing market interest rates. The discount rate set by the Federal Reserve would be more directly embedded in the cost of funds for the private sector. This will include the penalty rates charged for speculative financing.

Finally, implementation of the procedure would be the best technique for devolving power to the district banks. Even though discount rates will necessarily have to remain uniform throughout the system, each district bank would have considerable authority in approving discount loans and monitoring bank compliance with regulations. This then will promote regional money markets and the decentralization of the financial structure. As Minsky puts it, "The regional reserve banks would then have a lender's relation with individual banks and with the district's money market" (1986, p. 326).

Minsky's specific proposal is essentially to supplant open market operations with discount-window lending. Though the logic of his argument would lead to that conclusion, such a sweeping change would be impractical. It would entail an enormous increase in central bank administrative responsibilities, especially because through creating a "level financial playing field," all intermediaries (as defined by D'Arista's and Schlesinger's proposal for "leveling the playing field")—not just banks alone—would be subject to reserve requirements and Federal Reserve oversight.

A more workable approach would be to increase the relative weight of discount window operations to an extent just sufficient to achieve the intended effects of increasing Federal Reserve oversight, raising the obstacles to speculative finance, and promoting regional credit markets. This would essentially entail holding a tighter rein on open market operations. The federal funds rate should be maintained at a level significantly higher—perhaps 1–2 full percentage points—than the discount rate. Intermediaries will therefore be compelled to seek funds regularly at the discount window. At the same time, the district banks will not be overwhelmed with administrative burdens.

As a possible supplement to this strategy that would reduce the administrative burdens of the district banks further, the Federal Reserve could begin conducting open market operations, as is done increasingly in Britain, through the commercial bills market (Bank of England, 1984). In Britain, central bank purchases of eligible bank bills have become the major vehicle for open market operations. Were the United States to adopt such an approach, it would require that bank bills eligible for Federal Reserve purchases be loans that met the same standards as those acceptable at the discount window. Such an innovation would require an amendment to the Federal Reserve's current governing laws.[15]

Asset Reserve Requirements

The basic features of a system of asset reserve requirements are straightforward. Various versions of this policy approach were outlined in the 1970s by economists such as Lester Thurow (1972) and former Federal Reserve Governors Andrew Brimmer (1975) and Sherman Maisel (1973). Their interventions were more or less closely linked to unsuccessful efforts by Sen. William Proxmire and Rep. Henry Reuss, then chairs of the Senate and House Banking Committees, respectively, to advance bills establishing procedures for Federal Reserve–directed credit allocation policies.[16]

The first and most important step would be for the policymaking process, either within a democratized Federal Reserve or through a broader dialogue, to determine the sectors of the economy to be given preferential access to credit. For example, I have proposed as priorities industrial conversion from military production to renewable energy and, more generally, productive investment within the United States. Once goals are established, then depository institutions' reserve requirements will be significantly lower for loans that finance these activities than for less desirable investment areas.

Thurow, for example, sketches the following arrangement:

> If national goals called for investing 25 percent of national savings in housing and other preferred sectors, each financial institution would have a 100 percent reserve requirement on that fraction of its assets. As long as it invested 25 percent of its assets in housing, however, it would not have to leave any reserves with the government. If it had invested 20 percent of its assets in housing, 5 percent of its assets would have to be held with the government as required reserves. If it invested nothing, 25 percent of its assets would be held as reserves. (1972, pp. 186–87)

It is not possible, *a priori*, to provide a reasonable estimate of what would be the appropriate level for the reserve requirement differential, given the enormous ongoing changes in financial markets and the still further changes that would accompany the implementation of a new Federal Reserve structure. However, econometric studies confirm that long-term changes in reserve requirements will significantly affect the profitability of intermediaries and are therefore capable of influencing lending patterns in desired directions (see, e.g., Kolari, Mahajan, and

Saunders, 1988). It follows that the less-desired activities would tend to be crowded out of the market.

This technique creates a means for significant social control over major finance and investment activities while still allowing considerable decisionmaking freedom for both intermediaries and businesses. The intermediaries, for example, would still be responsible for establishing the creditworthiness of businesses and the viability of their projects. The businesses would still be responsible for the design and implementation of their investments. Indeed, business would still be free to pursue nonpreferred projects and banks could still finance them. Financing costs would just be significantly higher. To some extent, then, this technique resembles a tax on banks that finance nonpreferred activities: the banks are effectively giving the government an interest-free loan, which the Fed can then use to purchase government bonds.

However, setting differential reserve requirements is preferable to a tax because it is more flexible. Depending on circumstances, asset reserve requirements could be changed periodically, just as, under current law, reserve requirements on deposits can be changed by Federal Reserve decree.[17] Under a democratized Federal Reserve, the ability to set differential reserve requirements would therefore create more room for voice as a means of exercising influence in finance and investment decisions, that is, greater opportunity for popular debate and negotiation uninhibited by the impediments of the tax code.

To bring additional flexibility, the requirements should be implemented as suggested by Maisel (1973), as a system of market auctions rather than quotas. Through an auction system, institutions would not be required to carry the specified proportion (say, 25 percent, following the Thurow example) in loans to preferred sectors. As with a marketable pollution permit system, intermediaries that exceed the limit would obtain a permit that they could then sell to institutions whose loans to preferred sectors are below the minimum. Individual institutions could therefore choose to maintain particular market niches. At the same time, the system would ensure that some niches carried an extra burden of either higher reserves or purchases of "preferred asset permits."

As to the practicality of the proposal, recall that the Federal Reserve has long set differential reserve requirements on deposits to promote financial stabilization. The underlying premise has been that the reserve requirements should increase as deposits are larger and more liquid. To a considerable extent, differential deposit requirements have been abandoned now, as they proved to be readily avoidable through financial innovation when the incentives for avoidance became sufficiently powerful.[18]

More to the point, the rough equivalent of asset reserve requirements has long been part of established practices in the United States. The original idea of savings and loans, after all, was that their loan portfolio be restricted to home mortgages exclusively.

Even now, a close equivalent to asset requirements operates through the international risk-based capital adequacy standards formulated at Basel in 1988. These standards are now administered in all Organization for Economic Cooperation and Development (OECD) countries. According to the Basel standards, banks' capital adequacy is determined by a system of assigning different weights to capital and assets according to their perceived riskiness. The system, for example, defines two tiers of capital—a first tier for permanent shareholders' equity and a second for noncommon equity items. One of four risk weights is then assigned to assets (as well as off-balance-sheet items) on the basis of broad judgments of relative credit risk. At the end of 1992, risk-based capital/asset ratios were set at 8 percent for both tiers of capital, and 4 percent for primary capital.[19]

Given the fact that the Basel system is already operating in the United States, it would be relatively easy to supplement this asset-weighting system with additional relative weights assigned to various assets. This would allow the U.S. financial system to pursue broader social goals than those sought through the Basel standards alone.

Other Credit Allocation Tools

Loan guarantees, interest rate subsidies, and outright government loans are all techniques that are presently in wide use in the United States, as seen in Tables 12.1 and 12.2. These policies could also be used to promote preferred credit allocations and the market restructurings previously described. There are, however, two clear disadvantages to these approaches relative to both the discount-window and the asset reserve requirement techniques. The first is that they are more expensive and would therefore add an additional strain to the federal budget. Loan guarantees are contingent liabilities of the federal government that must be paid to private lenders when borrowers default. But even in the absence of defaults, loan guarantees provide a subsidy equivalent to the fee that would be required to purchase private insurance against default. Direct government loan programs involve more government administrative burden than loan guarantees, but otherwise are equivalent, since they also imply that government absorbs the risks and costs of default. Interest subsidies, finally, involve direct costs to government, either through a government loan program or as attached to privately originated loans.

The second weakness of these programs is that they would require greater government involvement in downstream business activity. Rather than simply setting guidelines for lending institutions and monitoring them, government loans, guarantees, and subsidies entail substantial direct involvement with borrowers. This would increase administrative expenses for the government and probably reduce the efficiency of project monitoring relative to what could be done by private lenders.

To the extent possible, therefore, the discount-window and asset reserve requirements should be relied upon to promote the allocative ends sought. Loan guarantees, subsidies, and outright government lending should be recognized as less desirable and should be used primarily to buttress the discount window and asset reserve policies. These latter approaches on their own, however, may not be sufficiently powerful. This consideration may become especially significant as long as financial innovation and globalization continue to create obstacles to the enforcement of regulations in any single country, even one with a financial market as large as that of the United States.

Experiences with Credit Allocation Policies

Within the United States, we have seen that credit allocation policies control a substantial part of the U.S. financial market today, especially in the areas of agriculture, housing, small business, and export sales. But it also would be instructive to recall the origins of these present policies.

Before the 1930s Depression, the financial system was geared almost entirely toward commerce, industry, and the wealthy. Interventionist financial market policies were then initially created to stabilize the system after the disastrous events of the early 1930s. Their aim was initially to provide relief for individuals and institutions suffering losses.

Thus, as Bosworth, Carron, and Rhyne (1987) have written:

> The Reconstruction Finance Corporation loaned money to banks and helped them stay open. The Home Owners Loan Corporation purchased and rescheduled delinquent mortgages from banks, and the Federal Farm Mortgage Corporation provided a similar function for farmers. These agencies helped private financial institutions to stay afloat and kept families from losing their homes and farms.
>
> By the end of the 1930s, the relief functions of federal credit had dwindled, and most of the agencies that provided them were soon liquidated. The emphasis shifted toward correcting perceived failures of private capital markets and developing mechanisms to ensure that the financial system would be safe from another collapse. Among such programs were the Federal Deposit Insurance Corporation, the Securities and Exchange Commission, and such large credit programs as the Federal Home Loan Bank System, a government-sponsored enterprise empowered to lend to savings and loan institutions; Federal Housing Administration mortgage insurance to create lender confidence in long-term amortizing mortgages; and the Commodity Credit Corporation to provide crop financing to farmers. The Export-Import Bank opened its doors in 1934 to promote U.S. exports, and in 1938 the Federal National Mortgage Association (Fannie Mae) was created to develop a resale market for residential mortgages. A battery of federal programs to meet the special needs of agriculture included, besides the Commodity Credit Corporation, the Rural Electrification Administration; an expanded Farm Credit System, which furnished a range of services to creditworthy farmers; and the Farmers Home Administration, which served smaller, more marginal farmers. (p. 11)

In short, from the Depression to the present, credit allocation has been a major part of government policy. It has also achieved some notable successes, such as creating unprecedented access to homeownership for a high proportion of the nonwealthy.[20]

In other countries, financial market policies have relied even more heavily on public credit allocation techniques, through both their central bank and other institutions engaged in financing long-term investments. A study conducted on this question for the House Banking Committee in 1970 (Thurow et al., 1970) surveyed central bank practices in Germany, France, Italy, Israel, the Netherlands, Japan, Sweden, and Britain among the advanced capitalist economies. They reached this conclusion:

> Central banks in most countries designate certain sectors of the economy that are to receive favorable treatment from the central bank. This means either making loans in these favored sectors at below market rates of interest or making credit more available in these sectors than it would be if so-called market forces were allowed to operate. In some cases this is done to aid preferentially particular sectors and in some cases this is done to offset the uneven impacts of private money markets. (p. 1)

It is true that the most recent trends have been away from such policies, in favor of a more liberalized financial market.[21] These policy shifts reflect the pressures of financial globalization and other market innovations that have been gathering momentum since the late 1960s. This tendency is likely to be consolidated further as European economic integration proceeds. As such, it has become increasingly difficult to practice interventionist or regulatory policies when the market has created a formidable capacity to circumvent regulation.

Nevertheless, the need for such policies has not diminished. What is therefore required is that the policy targets be specified more sharply and that the tools for reaching the targets be strengthened. Let us consider some relevant experiences in more detail.

Japan

The Japanese case is the outstanding example of how an economy can use credit allocation techniques to promote financial stability and long-term growth. The wave of speculative finance in Japan culminating in the spring 1992 stock market crash in no way diminishes the long-term achievements of these policies. Indeed, at least in part, the recent financial instability has resulted from the tendency to liberalize the state-directed allocation system, which began in the mid-1970s and accelerated in the mid-1980s.

During the post–World War II period, the Japanese relied on three basic mechanisms for mobilizing private savings into long-term investment projects.

The first is control over small-scale individual savings. This was achieved first by way of the post office savings system, through which the government directly received the deposits of small-scale savers. But the government also restricted private branch banking, thereby limiting the competition for post office savings.

The second mechanism was the central bank policy of issuing short-term loans to commercial banks. Central bank lending to commercial banks is far greater than that in the United States, because it is able both to lend post office savings and to create new reserves. Moreover, discount-window borrowing was used much more extensively than open market operations as a technique for creating reserves.[22] In addition, commercial banks apply for loans in connection with the demand for credit attached to specific projects by industrial firms. This means that central banks are effectively making indirect loans to industrial firms. And since the loans are short term, the central bank is able to monitor commercial banks' portfolios—and indirectly the activities of the nonfinancial firms—at regular intervals.

The other key government agency involved in credit allocation policies is the Ministry of Industrial Trade and Industry (MITI), whose primary function has been to channel credit to large firms and industrial sectors that it had earmarked for long-term growth. MITI would direct both post office savings and private bank funds through special credit institutions such as the Export-Import Bank and Japanese Development Corporation into selected sectors.

Thus, although Japan has never had a formal planning system, the extensive use of credit allocation policies meant that MITI, the central bank, and other government agencies became the de facto central planners. The system was based around "dirigisme," indicative five-year planning, and a form of bargained corporatism.

Many analysts have correctly noted that the basis of Japan's success with a credit allocation–centered planning system was consensus within political elites and the absence of a strong opposition movement. This enabled MITI and allied institutions to mobilize savings in support of favored sectors and firms without having concurrently to accommodate competitive demands to support consumption, social welfare expenditures, or small business. At the same time, though, there have always been divisions within Japan's business class and bureaucratic elite. As Cox (1986) notes, MITI was pitted in the early post-war period in

> ceaseless political battles with the old Ministry of Finance and Bank of Japan to ensure that sufficient funds were available for industry in the face of the inherent financial conservatism for balanced budgets residing in these institutions. Similarly, MITI had to use indirect means to manipulate the privately-owned commercial banks to provide long-term loans to large firms that it had earmarked as the future driving force of the Japanese economy. (p. 18)

In short, even among the Japanese elite, support for credit allocation policies has never been monolithic, as, indeed, the recent moves toward financial liberalization confirm. In any case, the debates on credit allocation within Japan were fairly well confined to a form of bargained corporatism that included various factions of the business and bureaucratic elite. Labor and other popular groups were never included in the negotiations.

France

The credit allocation system that evolved in France after World War II had many features similar to that of Japan. And as with Japan, the French system has been substantially altered over the past decade through innovation, globalization, and deregulation.

Prior to this latest phase of deregulation, the French state took the lead after World War II in promoting economic modernization through financing productive investment. The state's principal policy instrument was credit allocation. The state had been actively involved in financial markets before the war, but never with the clear aim it had set for itself in the post-war period.

French credit allocation policies have been concentrated in the Treasury, and in particular the Trésor, the elite department of the Treasury that compares closely in function with MITI.

The Trésor's first major post-war task was to disburse Marshall Plan aid in a way that supported economic modernization. It faced, but ultimately defeated, substantial opposition in this project from traditional business interests. But the Trésor's influence over French financial markets continued long after the Marshall Plan ended. As Zysman (1983) observed, the Trésor has stood at the center of French economic policymaking throughout the post-war period.

> The Trésor is not simply a bank for the state but an instrument for intervention in the public sector and the private industrial sector. . . . A remarkable range of policy responsibilities concentrate here, including a concern with money supply, bank regulation, and control of government loans or grants to industry. The Trésor manages the finances of the central government, but it has used that power to manipulate the national economy as well. Government departments account for a substantial portion of total investment and the Trésor exerts power over investments made by the public entities. Moreover, the Trésor is itself a financial intermediary, intervening in the economy with loans and transfer facilities. (p. 114)

In conjunction with the Trésor's general leadership role, other institutional changes were made after the war to support the Trésor in implementing the state's credit allocation policy. For example, four major deposit banks and some insurance companies were nationalized after the war, and several government agencies were created to channel post office savings, social security funds, and pension funds into domestic industry.

Although the administrative apparatus of French credit allocation policies clearly resembled that of Japan, what is less clear is whether the French have enjoyed the same measure of success with these policies as the Japanese. There is no pretense, of course, that the French system promoted anything resembling a socialist agenda, either through the initial wave of nationalizations or under Mitterrand's socialist government, which involved additional nationalizations in its early stages.[23] The relevant question, rather, is: How successful have they been even at the more modest goal of mobilizing credit for long-term productive investment?

Zysman's endorsement circa 1983 is strong on this point. But other observers such as Cox (1986) argue that the performance of the French credit allocation system had weakened by the mid-1980s. This occurred, in Cox's view, precisely because the French, unlike the Japanese, could not sustain a consensus over the aims of credit allocation policies. Social welfare demands were much stronger within the French bureaucracy and so therefore was the competition for favored credit treatment. Thus, for example, the French were forced to a far greater degree than the Japanese to subsidize ailing industrial firms, because the short-term social costs of closing plants would be high.

Regardless of the accuracy of Cox's assessment,[24] the point Cox raises is important. He is suggesting that the more the state is a site of political conflict, the greater the likelihood that credit allocation policies will become an instrument for competing, rent-seeking constituencies. We will return to this issue later.

South Korea

One obviously cannot expect to draw direct lessons from South Korea's experience with public credit allocation policies, given the enormous differences between Korea and the United States or other advanced economies. Nevertheless, South Korea is an illuminating experience worth additional attention.[25]

According to the mainstream literature, a crucial feature of South Korea's successful growth beginning in the mid-1960s was the liberalization of its financial markets in 1965, following the recommendations of U.S. economists Ronald MacKinnon and Edward Shaw. This reform, it is argued, established a rational incentive structure in South Korea's financial system, producing in particular a rise in interest rates that accurately reflected market conditions. Interest rate increases were said to engender three fundamental market adjustments: they substantially increased the flow of savings into the market; they encouraged efficiency in investment by filtering out projects whose profit potential was below the interest-rate-determined hurdle rate; and they contributed to the establishment of an appropriate exchange rate. These factors, in turn, are said to be the foundations of South Korea's export-led success.

However, contrary to this standard perspective, more careful examination of South Korea's economic policies since 1965 makes clear that the liberalization law promoted a successful growth path through a quite different set of effects. In fact, as Harris (1988) has shown, the liberalization law *increased* the ability of the state to pursue selective credit allocation policies and in particular to channel subsidized credit to favored export firms.

Harris argues that the reforms notwithstanding, the state actually maintained decisive control over the two crucial variables in the financial system: saving flows and the interest rate. It controlled savings by running persistent budget surpluses after 1965. By 1971, the budget surplus accounted for 42 percent of total domestic savings.

With this supply of savings, the state then had the power to act as the economy's principal financial intermediary. In this role, the state was able to allocate credit to favored sectors at concessionary rates. The liberalization law did indeed lead to a rise in market interest rates. But it was precisely these high market rates that provided the state with wide latitude in offering below-market rates to its favored firms, those achieving success in penetrating export markets.

The political prerequisite for South Korea's success with credit allocation policies, like that in the Japanese experience, was the largely unchallenged authority of the bureaucratic elite. The state acquired this power, again like Japan, because the influence of the traditional landed gentry had been destroyed in the post-war land reform. Moreover, only a nascent modernizing capitalist class existed in South Korea at that time. The state was therefore able to stand in as surrogate modernizing capitalist.

Through this experience, we once again see that credit allocation policies can be extremely powerful tools. But success with these tools depends on the political configuration by which they are exercised.

Could It Really Work?

A range of criticism of credit allocation policies—much of it quite dismissive—has been advanced over the years, both as these policies are practiced in the United States and more broadly.

The most fundamental critique, of course, is that purely market arrangements will always be superior to any form of state intervention, on both efficiency and equity grounds. To reach this conclusion, some analysts rely on the strong assumption that actual functioning markets, including the financial market, approximate the model of how a perfect market allocates resources with unequaled efficiency and fairness. But it is also possible to begin from the somewhat weaker claim that although real-world markets operate imperfectly, their outcomes will usually be superior to those produced through state interference with the market mechanism.

However, if the criticisms of the contemporary U.S. financial market advanced in the first part of this chapter are valid—that the market fosters financial instability, that it promotes short-term thinking, and that it suffers from a lack of democratic accountability—then the implication is that market imperfections are deep and pervasive. Some forms of interventionist policies must at least be entertained. If we also recognize that the U.S. economy faces two additional fundamental challenges—to undertake a rational industrial conversion from military spending and into environmental sustainability and to gain control over the process of economic globalization—then this strengthens the case for interventionist policies that will restructure the market's operations.

The question then becomes not whether to intervene but what are the most effective instruments and targets of intervention. Mayer (1975) summarizes well much of the critical literature in advancing reasons that, even assuming market imperfections require intervention, credit allocation policies are still not justified because they are not an effective means of intervening.[26]

Mayer's first point is that credit allocation policies would be ineffective at achieving the ends sought. They would entail that special regulations be imposed only to a subset of intermediaries—primarily (if not exclusively) banks. Other intermediaries, unconstrained by the Federal Reserve's requirements, would then acquire a competitive advantage. For example, unregulated institutions would not face asset reserve requirements, so their cost of funds would be lower than that for banks. This fact would enable them to offer loans at lower rates and would drive the regulated banks out of the market.

This point is valid as far as it goes. But as was discussed earlier, the simple solution to this problem is to level the playing field, that is, create consistent regulations for all financial institutions along the lines of the proposal by D'Arista and Schlesinger (this volume). The successful implementation of such a regulatory approach would overcome this initial concern.

Mayer's second point is that credit allocation policies are inefficient relative to alternative policy tools. In fairness, Mayer made this claim with respect to some specific policy targets, such as providing more affordable housing, in which case his argument may have some validity. But for addressing the broad set of problems cited here, credit allocation policies are substantially less costly and more efficient than alternatives.

Fiscal policy measures, such as public investment, will unquestionably be crucial to promoting productive investment over speculation. But fiscal policy involves direct government expenditures and long lead times. Credit allocation policies can be implemented quickly and with greater attention to detail. Moreover, the policies developed here will provide substantial new opportunities for democratic participation in important economic policy decisions. As such, these policies provide an efficient way of solving the principal/agent problems prevalent in capital markets. Indeed, this approach is far more efficient than the solution endorsed by Jensen that prevailed in the 1980s, namely, the market for corporate control.

The final criticism of this approach is the most serious: such policies will inevitably degenerate into rent-seeking, through which the only winners are those who buy the best lobbyists. The historical record indicates that this problem was minimized in situations in which a consensus and a sense of purpose existed within the elite groups that controlled central bank policies. The outstanding examples here are Japan and South Korea.

The essentially dictatorial approach that was successful in Japan and South Korea is obviously unacceptable within the framework I am proposing. The challenge, then, is how to implement effective credit allocation policies by broadening, not narrowing, democracy. It is easy enough to design institutional structures that will promote democracy within the Federal Reserve. But in the end, the success of this approach will depend on a vigorous political movement that can fuse equally legitimate but potentially conflicting demands: for economic democracy on the one hand and for equitable and sustainable growth on the other.

This is undoubtedly a difficult task, and complete success will never be achieved—rents will inevitably be sought and obtained. However, this fact has to be considered within a broader perspective. Rent-seeking occurs through market exchanges as well as state-directed allocations. This becomes clear when we define rent-seeking as activities in which "private returns come from the redistribution of wealth and not from wealth creation" (Murphy, Shleifer, and Vishny, 1990, p. 5). Bhagwati (1982) has developed the more general term "directly unproductive profit seeking," meaning, activities that may be privately profitable but do not directly increase the flow of goods and services. From this perspective, for example, the entire mergers and acquisitions movement of the 1980s was, to a substantial extent, an exercise in rent-seeking for which $1.3 trillion of credit was privately allocated. Creating effective public credit allocation mechanisms will be aimed precisely at minimizing such private rent-seeking. It would be difficult to imagine a worst-case scenario under public credit allocation in which the opportunities for obtaining rents could approach the magnitude of the 1980s mergers and acquisitions experience.[27]

There is one further consideration that Mayer, writing in 1975, could not have anticipated: whether such policies would be sustainable in a globalized financial market. Globalization offers intermediaries the prospect of establishing legal residency wherever regulations are least costly, while still being able to conduct business anywhere in the global marketplace. Thus, without excessively cumbersome legal manipulations, intermediaries would likely be able to avoid new Federal Reserve regulations by establishing their legal residency outside the United States while still accepting deposits and making loans to U.S. residents. In recognizing just such prospects as this, the Basel international capital adequacy requirements were designed to create a uniform regulatory environment. This eliminates incentives for intermediaries to exploit regulatory differences between countries. How then could the United States successfully implement regulations more stringent than those accepted at Basel?[28]

Several incentives are in fact built into this proposal that should allow a restructured Federal Reserve System to counteract the leveling pressures of globalization.

The first is that non-U.S. institutions will not be eligible to receive reserves from the Federal Reserve. They would, of course, be able to borrow dollars in the private interbank loan (federal funds) market. However, as long as the costs of discount-window loans are kept significantly lower than the federal funds rate, intermediaries that do business primarily in the United States will want to remain within the U.S. legal framework. This consideration becomes even more important when one recognizes that during liquidity crises, U.S. institutions alone will be eligible for lender-of-last-resort support from the Fed.

In addition, only U.S. financial institutions will be able to participate in open market trading with the Fed—an arrangement that will give U.S. institutions still greater access to dollar reserves. This incentive can be strengthened further should the restructured Fed also adopt the British-style system of trading commercial bills in the open market. Under such an arrangement, only the paper issued by U.S.-resident institutions could be eligible for the Fed's open market purchases, a fact that would greatly widen their marketability relative to foreign issues.

Third, only U.S.-based institutions will be eligible to carry government-insured deposits. The specific means through which this feature is implemented will of course depend on how the system of deposit insurance itself is redesigned. If one follows D'Arista's proposal (Chapter 8 in this volume) that individuals rather than institutions will receive deposit insurance, one can easily attach to it the idea that individuals must deposit funds in U.S.-resident institutions to receive their insurance coverage.

In combination, these factors should carry sufficient weight to counteract the lures that intermediaries might otherwise feel about seeking residency in less-regulated countries. Those operating in the U.S. market will find strong incentives to declare U.S. residency, even if U.S. regulations are more stringent than the international norm. Moreover, these incentives will be achieved at virtually no cost to U.S. taxpayers.

Evolutionary Transformation

Creating a new Federal Reserve structure with a new set of credit allocation powers and with deep democratic moorings (or some variation on this, such as creating an institution parallel to the Fed that addresses credit allocational questions) will obviously not occur overnight. Nevertheless, the proposal outlined here is designed so that the transformation of U.S. central banking—and, more broadly, public intervention in financial markets and long-term investment activity—can unfold through an evolutionary process.

More specifically, the proposal is designed so that some elements of it can be implemented either immediately within the existing legal and institutional framework, or at least through achieving reforms that are feasible within the existing political climate. Four ideas advanced in this chapter would seem to qualify on these scores:

• Enforcement of the Community Reinvestment Act;
• Substantial increase in the use of discount-window lending and equivalently reducing that of open market operations as mechanisms for generating reserves for the banking system;
• Creation of a consistent regulatory environment for all intermediaries; and
• Democratization of the Federal Reserve through, for example, direct election of the district banks' boards of directors.

Following experience with these reforms, the project could move on to other proposals, such as channeling credit to priority investment areas through differential asset reserve requirements. But implementing this crucial reform will first require greater clarity as to what should be the preferred investment targets and, correspondingly, what types of investments should pay the implicit tax of higher reserve requirements. Reaching this point will also presume significant experience with a new set of democratic operating procedures within the Federal Reserve System.

Notes

1. This chapter was originally presented at the conference of the Monetary and Financial Markets Restructuring Working Group of the Economic Policy Institute, Washington, D.C. Comments from other group members, especially Gerald Epstein, are gratefully acknowledged. I also wish to thank Fred Block, Ilene Grabel, Laurence Harris, Chris Lewis, Thomas Mayer, and an anonymous referee for their extremely constructive comments and suggestions on a previous draft. All errors, unfortunately, remain my own.

2. Goldsmith (e.g., 1969) and others have long argued that increasing debt/national income ratios were a sign of an economy's "financial deepening" and overall economic development. But this is evidently true only if rising debt ratios are accompanied by increasing productive investments through which, over time, the capacity to service debts rises correspondingly.

3. This discussion is developed further in Pollin (1992).

4. This is essentially the same argument that Keynes makes in his justly famous Chapter 12 of *The General Theory* (1936). Keynes, for example, writes in that chapter:

> In the absence of security markets, there is no object in frequently attempting to revalue an investment to which we are committed. But the Stock Exchange revalues many investments every day and the revaluations give a frequent opportunity to the individual (though not to the community as a whole) to revise his commitments . . . .But the daily revaluations of the Stock Exchange, though they are primarily made to facilitate transfers of old investments between one individual and another, inevitably exert a decisive influence on the rate of current investment. (p. 151)

Recent studies by Porter (1992) and Poterba and Summers (1991) also support the view that the existing U.S. financial structure encourages shorter time horizons than other advanced economies. Porter writes that the U.S. financial system, despite its many strengths, "does not seem to be the most effective in directing capital to those firms that can deploy it most productively and, within firms, to the most effective productive investment projects" (p. 20). Poterba and Summers conducted a particularly interesting survey of CEOs of Fortune 1,000 firms in the United States as well as a more limited survey of CEOs in Japan, Germany, and the United Kingdom. They found that the U.S. and foreign CEOs agree that corporate time horizons are shorter in the United States. Also, most U.S. managers think that the U.S. equity market undervalues their long-term investments.

5. Shleifer and Summers (1989) presented the initial argument that corporate take-

overs represent a mechanism for redistributing welfare away from corporate stakeholders. The literature that developed around this issue is surveyed in Crotty and Goldstein's chapter in this volume.

6. Evidence that "big government" interventions created a more stable macroenvironment from the beginning of the post–World War II period through the 1970s is presented in Pollin and Dymski (1993).

7. Friedman (1988) and Friedman and Kuttner (1992) offer a devastating assessment of the capacity of monetary policy to affect financial markets in any of the ways orthodox theory would anticipate.

8. This is an abbreviated version of a central argument advanced in Pollin and Dymski (1993).

9. Markusen and Yudken (1992) provide an outstanding exposition of the effects of military spending on the U.S. economy and of strategies for disarmament.

10. The increasing integration of trade and finance is indicated by standard measures such as the trade/gross domestic product ratio and the proportion of foreign sources of credit in the U.S. financial market. It is true that by some measures, the extent of integration is no greater than that of the late 19th century and early part of this century (see, e.g., Gordon, 1988; Zevin, 1992). However, it is undeniably correct that integration has increased over the course of the post–World War II period. Moreover, even relative to the earlier period, the *character* of integration has changed dramatically. As MacEwan (1991) points out, in the 19th century, international trade and finance affected only a relatively small segment of most countries' economies, because in most cases, the links between the international sectors and the rest of the largely agrarian economies were weak. Now, however, linkages are much stronger as market relations have penetrated far more deeply. This then explains why the U.S. labor market faces competition from foreign labor to an unprecedented extent. The liberal response to this development is most extensively argued by Reich (1991). A formidable challenge to the Reich strategy comes from Shaiken's (1987) brilliant case study of the location of a cutting-edge-technology auto motor assembly plant in the Maquilladora region of Mexico.

11. Grabel (1989) provides a very informative discussion that pursues questions similar to those in this section.

12. D'Arista and Schlesinger (this volume) define entities that will fall under a consistent regulatory system as including any entity that "directly accepts funds from the public for investment; makes loans to the public or buys loans or securities using funds other than its own equity capital and retained earnings; or sells loans or third-party securities to financial institutions or investors."

13. The most extensive and rigorous work on the issue of accountability within the Federal Reserve is that of Gerald Epstein. His chapter in this volume offers an introduction to his approach and further references.

14. One change that would be necessary if the district banks were established as key sites for democratic accountability would be to redraw the district boundaries or something comparable. When the Federal Reserve System was established in 1913, the 12 district banks were allocated geographically to reflect the distribution of population and political/economic power at that time. At present, the district boundaries and locations of the 12 banks are a quaint vestige of that earlier era. Thus, for example, there are 2 district banks in Missouri—in St. Louis and Kansas City—but only 1—in San Francisco—for all the West Coast as well as Nevada, Arizona, Idaho, Alaska, and Hawaii. Epstein and Ferguson (1984) provide a description of the 1930s experiment in increasing accountability within the district banks.

15. Minsky says that the model for this approach was the Bank of England's money market operations prior to World War I. More generally, his ideas bear resemblance to the old "real bills doctrine" first developed in Adam Smith's *Wealth of Nations*. The central

proposition of the real bills doctrine is that bank notes that are lent in exchange for "real bills," i.e., titles to real value or value in the process of creation, cannot be issued in excess. Speculative finance and inflation would therefore be suppressed as long as central banks adhered to the doctrine (see Green, 1987).

This argument has had a spotted history in the annals of monetary theory. For example, it was adopted as a guiding idea when the Federal Reserve System was founded in 1913. But it was discredited and abandoned in the United States after inflation rose to 14 percent in the aftermath of World War I. What is clear from history is that reliance on the real bills doctrine is not a viable central banking policy. The reasons are that businesses that obtain loans for one purpose may still use them otherwise and that investment plans frequently go unfulfilled or fail. As Arnon notes, the doctrine could work only "as long as the borrower evaluated his business correctly, an evaluation that was based on the realization of what he planned at the time of the loan" (1991, p. 171). At the same time, the core idea of the doctrine—that central banks should seek to issue reserves in close concert with the nonfinancial sector's explicit needs for productive financing—remains valid, as Minsky's proposal conveys. Karl Marx, for one, supported this middle position (1973, p. 131), arguing that the "average measure of security" it affords is at least as successful as any alternative stabilization policy, including the types of quantity constraints advocated by the doctrine's critics.

16. See, for example, the hearings before the Subcommittee on Domestic Monetary Policy of the House Banking Committee addressing the bill H.R. 212, "An Act to Lower Interest Rates and Allocate Credit" (U.S. Government Printing Office, 1975).

17. The Federal Reserve would, of course, need to exercise prudence in contemplating changes in asset reserve requirements to avoid encouraging speculative activity around anticipated changes.

18. Only two requirements remain at present: 3 percent on transaction deposits up to $42.2 million and 10 percent on transaction deposits greater than that.

19. Alfriend (1988) provides a good exposition of the history and logic behind the international risk-based capital standards.

20. A separate but related issue is whether the existing credit allocation programs should continue at their current levels of support. A serious examination of this question would involve asking whether the basic premises underlying federal support for housing, agriculture, small business, and exports are legitimate; whether credit market preferences are appropriate instruments of support; and, finally, whether the extent of support is justifiable. All these issues are beyond the scope of this chapter. Nevertheless, to mention just one area, the extent of the housing subsidy flowing to affluent households through the government-sponsored secondary mortgage market as well as mortgage interest deductions is surely inconsistent with the initial purpose of these programs, which was to make a basic level of homeownership widely accessible.

21. The OECD Economic Surveys for France (1987) and Japan (1991) provide careful descriptions of the liberalization processes in these countries. Feldman (1986) offers a more in-depth study of the process of innovation, globalization, and liberalization in Japan.

22. The basic references for this discussion are Zysman (1983) and Eccleston (1986). Ruehl (1988) provides useful details on interest rate policy and credit rationing in Japan. Feldman (1986) points out that the relative importance of the two techniques is changing as a result of innovation and deregulation, since open market operations, in which central banks create reserves without directly monitoring commercial bank performance, are more consistent with financial market liberalization.

23. Lipietz (1988), for example, writes that the policy of nationalizing banks contributed absolutely nothing to a socialist economic agenda in France under Mitterrand. The reason is that the agendas of the directors of the nationalized banks were in perfect compliance with those of private bankers.

24. It is notable that Cox does not consider the effects of liberalization on the functioning of credit allocation policies.

25. This section relies heavily on Harris (1988).

26. Silber (1973) provides a relatively objective survey of the debate on this issue within mainstream U.S. circles. Gale (1991) is a more recent study that presents a formal model and econometric evidence on the negative effects of credit allocation programs.

27. Ilene Grabel's detailed comments on a previous draft and subsequent discussions of portions of her 1992 doctoral dissertation were extremely helpful in clarifying this point.

28. The imperative for even posing this question is conveyed powerfully in the following passage from William Greider's excellent work *Who Will Tell the People?* (1992):

> ACORN, the grassroots citizens' organization, discovered . . . that the prospect for financing low-income housing—a major priority for its members—had been seriously damaged by a new banking regulation that assigns an extremely high risk rating to bank lending for multi-family housing projects. . . . But the new credit regulation did not flow out of any legislation enacted by Congress and the president. It was a small detail in an international [Basel] agreement forged among the central bankers from a dozen industrial countries, including the United States. . . . America's representative (and leading promoter of the agreement) was the Federal Reserve, the nonelected central bank that enjoys formal insulation from political accountability. (pp. 387–88)

Bibliography

Alfriend, Malcolm C. "International Risk-Based Capital Standard: History and Explanation." *Economic Review*, Federal Reserve Bank of Richmond, November/December 1988, pp. 28–34.

Arnon, Arie. *Thomas Tooke: Pioneer of Monetary Theory*. Ann Arbor, MI: University of Michigan Press, 1991.

Bank of England. *The Development and Operation of Monetary Policy, 1960–1983*. Oxford, England: Clarendon Press, 1984.

Barber, Randy and Teresa Ghilarducci. "Pension Funds, Capital Markets, and the Economic Future." This volume, 1993.

Berle, Adolf A. and Gardiner C. Means. *The Modern Corporation and Private Property*. New York: Harcourt, Brace and World, 1932.

Bhagwati, Jadish. "Directly Unproductive Profit-Seeking Activity." *Journal of Political Economy*, Vol. 90, No. 5, October 1982, pp. 998–1002.

Bosworth, Barry P., Andrew S. Carron, and Elisabeth H. Rhyne. *The Economics of Federal Credit Programs*. Washington, DC: The Brookings Institution, 1987.

Brimmer, Andrew. "Central Banking and Credit Allocation." In W. H. Irons Memorial Lecture Series No. 2, Bureau of Business Research, Graduate School of Business, University of Texas at Austin, 1975.

Campen, James. "Banks, Communities, and Public Policy." This volume.

Commoner, Barry. *Making Peace with the Planet*. New York: Pantheon Books, 1990.

Cox, Andrew. "The State, Finance, and Industry Relationship in Comparative Perspective." In Andrew Cox, ed., *The State, Finance, and Industry*. Sussex, England: Wheatsheaf Books, 1986.

Crotty, James and Don Goldstein. "Do U.S. Financial Markets Allocate Credit Efficiently? The Case of Corporate Restructuring in the 1980s." This volume.

D'Arista, Jane. "No More Bank Bailouts: A Proposal for Deposit Insurance Reform." This volume.

D'Arista, Jane and Tom Schlesinger. "The Parallel Banking System." This volume.

Eccleston, Bernard. "The State, Finance, and Industry in Japan." In Andrew Cox, ed., *The State, Finance, and Industry*. Sussex, England: Wheatsheaf Books, 1986.

Epstein, Gerald. "Monetary Policy in the 1990s: Overcoming the Barriers to Equity and Growth." This volume.

Epstein, Gerald, and Thomas Ferguson. "Monetary Policy, Loan Liquidation, and Industrial Conflict: The Federal Reserve and Open Market Operations of 1932." *Journal of Economic History*, Vol. 64, No. 4, 1984, pp. 957–98.

Feldman, Robert Alan. *Japanese Financial Markets: Deficits, Dilemmas, and Deregulation*. Cambridge, MA: Massachusetts Institute of Technology Press, 1986.

Friedman, Benjamin. "Lessons of Monetary Policy from the 1980s." *Journal of Economic Perspectives*, Vol. 2, Issue 3, Summer 1988, pp. 51–72.

Friedman, Benjamin, and Kenneth Kuttner. "Money, Income, Prices, and Interest Rates." *American Economic Review*, Vol 82, Issue 3, June 1992, pp. 472–92.

Gale, William G. "Economic Effects of Federal Credit Programs." *American Economic Review*, Vol. 81, Issue 2, March, 1991, pp. 133–52.

Goldsmith, Raymond. *Financial Structure and Development*. New Haven, CT: Yale University Press, 1969.

Gordon, David. "The Global Economy: New Edifice or Crumbling Foundations?" *New Left Review*, March/April 1988, pp. 24–65.

Grabel, Ilene. *Financial Market Regulation and Economic Growth: A Consideration of Theories of Optimal "Repression."* Ph.D. dissertation. Amherst, MA: University of Massachusetts, 1992.

Grabel, Ilene. "Taking Control: An Agenda for a Democratic Financial System." Mimeo. Amherst, MA: Department of Economics, University of Massachusetts, 1989.

Green, Roy. "The Real Bills Doctrine." *The New Palgrave*, 1987, pp. 101–2.

Greider, William. *Who Will Tell the People? The Betrayal of American Democracy*. New York: Simon and Schuster, 1992.

Harris, Laurence. "Financial Reform and Economic Growth: A New Interpretation of South Korea's Experience." In Laurence Harris, Jerry Coakley, Martin Croasdale, and Trevor Evans, eds., *New Perspectives on the Financial System*. London: Croom Helm, 1988.

Hirschmann, Albert. *Exit, Voice, and Loyalty: Responses to Decline in Firms, Organizations, and States*. Cambridge, MA: Harvard University Press, 1970.

Jensen, Michael C. "Eclipse of the Public Corporation." *Harvard Business Review*, Vol. 67, Issue 4, September-October 1989, pp. 61–77.

Keynes, John Maynard. *The General Theory of Employment, Interest, and Money*. New York: Harcourt, Brace and World, 1936.

Kolari, James, Arvind Mahajan, and Edward Saunders. "The Effect of Changes in Reserve Requirements on Bank Stock Prices." *Journal of Banking and Finance*, Vol. 11, Issue 3, June 1988, pp. 183–98.

Lipietz, Alain. "The Limits of Bank Nationalization in France." In Laurence Harris, Jerry Coakley, Martin Croasdale, and Trevor Evans, eds., *New Perspectives on the Financial System*. London: Croom Helm, 1988.

MacEwan, Arthur. "What's New About the 'New International Economy'?" *Socialist Review*, Vol. 21, Nos. 3–4, July–December 1991.

Maisel, Sherman. "Improving Our System of Credit Allocation." In Federal Reserve Bank of Boston, *Credit Allocation Techniques and Monetary Policy*. Proceedings of a conference held at Melvin Village, New Hampshire, 1973, pp. 15–30.

Markusen, Ann and Joel Yudken. *Dismantling the Cold War Economy*. New York: Basic Books, 1992.

Marx, Karl. *Grundrisse*. New York: Vintage Books, 1973.

Mayer, Thomas. "Credit Allocation—A Critical View." In Karl Brunner, ed., *Government Credit Allocation: Where Do We Go from Here?* San Francisco: Institute for Contemporary Studies, 1975.

Minsky, Hyman P. *Stabilizing an Unstable Economy*. New Haven, CT: Yale University Press, 1986.

Murphy, K. M., A. Shleifer, and R. W. Vishny. "The Allocation of Talent: Implications for Growth." National Bureau of Economic Research Working Paper No. 3530. Cambridge, MA: NBER, 1990.

Organization for Economic Cooperation and Development. *OECD Economic Surveys: France*. Paris: OECD, 1987.

Organization for Economic Cooperation and Development. *OECD Economic Surveys: Japan*. Paris: OECD, 1991.

Pollin, Robert. *Deeper in Debt: The Changing Financial Conditions of U.S. Households*. Washington, DC: Economic Policy Institute, 1990.

Pollin, Robert. "Two Theories of Money Supply Endogeneity: Some Empirical Tests." *Journal of Post Keynesian Economics*, Vol 13, No. 3 Spring 1991, pp. 366–96.

Pollin, Robert. "Destabilizing Finance Worsened This Recession." *Challenge*, Vol. 35, No. 2, March–April 1992, pp. 17–24.

Pollin, Robert and Gary Dymski. "The Costs and Benefits of Financial Fragility: Big Government Capitalism and the 'Minsky Paradox'." In Robert Pollin and Gary Dymski, eds., *New Directions in Monetary Macroeconomics: Explorations in the Tradition of Hyman P. Minsky*. Ann Arbor, MI: University of Michigan Press, forthcoming, 1993.

Porter, Michael. *Capital Choices: Changing the Way America Invests in Industry*. Washington, DC: Council on Competitiveness, 1992.

Poterba, James and Lawrence Summers. "Time Horizons of American Firms: New Evidence from a Survey of CEOs." Washington, DC: Council on Competitiveness, 1991.

Reich, Robert. *The Work of Nations: Preparing Ourselves for 21st Century Capitalism*. New York: Alfred P. Knopf, 1991.

Ruehl, Sonja. "Interest Rate Policy and Credit Rationing in Japan: The Evidence." In Laurence Harris, Jerry Coakley, Martin Croasdale, and Trevor Evans, eds., *New Perspectives on the Financial System*. London: Croom Helm, 1988.

Shaiken, Harley. *Automation and Global Production: Automobile Engine Production in Mexico, the United States, and Canada*. La Jolla, CA: Center for U.S.-Mexican Studies, 1987.

Shleifer, Andrei and Lawrence Summers. "Breach of Trust in Hostile Takeovers." In A. Auerbach, ed., *Takeovers: Causes and Consequences*. Chicago: University of Chicago Press, 1989, pp. 33–68.

Silber, William L. "Selective Credit Policies: A Survey." *Banca Nazionale del Lavoro Review*, No. 3, 1973, pp. 329–51.

Thurow, Lester. "Proposals for Rechanneling Funds to Meet Social Priorities." In Federal Reserve Bank of Boston, *Policies for a More Competitive Financial System*. Proceedings of a conference held in June 1972, pp. 179–89.

Thurow, Lester, Peter Temin, Alan Blinder, Joseph Quinn, and Ernesto Tironi. "Activities by Various Central Banks to Promote Economic and Social Welfare Programs." Staff Report prepared for the Committee on Banking and Currency, House of Representatives, 91st Congress, 2nd Session, 1970.

U.S. House of Representatives, Subcommittee on Domestic Monetary Policy. *An Act to Lower Interest Rates and Allocate Credit: Hearings on H.R. 212*. Washington, DC: U.S. Government Printing Office, 1975.

Zevin, Robert B. "Are World Financial Markets More Open? If So, Why and with What Effects? In T. Banuri and J. Schor, eds., *Financial Openness and National Antonomy*. Oxford, England: Clarendon Press, 1992.

Zysman, John. *Government, Markets and Growth: Financial Systems and the Politics of Industrial Change*. Ithaca, NY: Cornell University Press, 1983.

INDEX

CONTRIBUTING AUTHORS

Randy Barber is President of the Center for Economic Organizing, a Washington, D.C.–based strategic financial consulting firm serving a union clientele with an emphasis in the areas of the investment and control of pension funds, analysis of corporate finance and operations, collective bargaining, and employee stock ownership plans. Mr. Barber is coauthor, with Jeremy Rifkin, of *The North Will Rise Again: Pensions, Politics and Power in the 1980s* (Beacon Press, 1978). He has spoken and written widely on pension investment issues during the past 15 years.

James T. Campen is Associate Professor of Economics at the University of Massachusetts at Boston. He is the author of *Benefit, Cost, and Beyond: The Political Economy of Benefit-Cost Analysis* (Ballinger, 1986) as well as many publications in the area of banks and community reinvestment.

James R. Crotty is Professor of Economics at the University of Massachusetts at Amherst and staff economist at the Center for Popular Economics.

Jane W. D'Arista is a former Congressional economist who lectures on international banking law at Boston University School of Law.

Gary A. Dymski received a Ph.D in economics from the University of Massachusetts at Amherst in 1987. He was Assistant Professor of Economics at the University of Southern California from 1987 to 1991 and is currently Assistant Professor of Economics at the University of California, Riverside. He and Robert Pollin have edited *New Perspectives in Monetary Macroeconomics: Explorations in the Tradition of Hyman P. Minsky* (University of Michigan Press). He is currently working on a book with John Veitch on the interconnections between banking, poverty, race, and community development in Los Angeles.

Gerald Epstein is Associate Professor of Economics at the University of Massachusetts at Amherst and staff economist at the Center for Popular Economics. He has published numerous articles about the Federal Reserve System and other central banks and conducts research on various topics in domestic and international money and finance. He is also a research associate with the macroeconomics projects of the World Institute for Development Economic Research of the United Nations University.

Steven M. Fazzari received a Ph.D. from Stanford University in 1982. He is Associate Professor of Economics at Washington University in St. Louis and research associate at the Jerome Levy Economics Institute. Professor Fazzari teaches macroeconomics and studies the link between macroeconomic activity and finance, particularly the financial determinants of investment spending and the impact of debt on macroeconomic stability. His recent publications include coediting *Financial Conditions and Macroeconomic Performance: Essays in Honor of Hyman P. Minsky* and articles in *Rand Journal of Economics* (forthcoming), *Brookings Papers on Economic Activity*, and *Review of Economics and Statistics*.

James K. Galbraith is Professor at the Lyndon B. Johnson School of Public Affairs and at the Department of Government, University of Texas at Austin. He holds a Ph.D. in economics from Yale and has served on the staff of the U.S. Congress, including as Economist for the House Banking Committee and as Executive Director of the Joint Economic Committee. He is coauthor of a new textbook, *Macroeconomics*, forthcoming from Houghton-Mifflin this year.

Teresa Ghilarducci is the author of *Labor's Capital: The Economics and Politics of Private Pensions* (MIT Press, 1992) and is Associate Professor of Economics at the University of Notre Dame.

Don Goldstein teaches economics at Allegheny College in Meadville, Pennsylvania. A 1974 graduate of Harvard College, he received his Ph.D. from the University of Massachusetts at Amherst in 1991. In between he worked for many years, including several as a machinist in the western Pennsylvania steel industry. Dr. Goldstein's interest in mergers led to a doctoral thesis on hostile takeovers, written partly while he was a Research Fellow at the Brookings Institution during 1989–1990.

Robert Pollin teaches economics at the University of California, Riverside, specializing in money and banking, macroeconomics, and political economy. He is coeditor (with Gary Dymski) of *New Perspectives in Monetary Macroeconomics: Explorations in the Tradition of Hyman P. Minsky* (University of Michigan Press) and author of the monograph *Deeper in Debt: The Changing Financial Conditions of U.S. Households*, published by the Economic Policy Institute. He has been a member of the Capital Formation Subcouncil of the Competitiveness Policy Council and a consultant to the Joint Economic Committee of the U.S. Congress and the United National Development Program. He is on the editorial boards of *Dollars and Sense* magazine and *International Review of Applied Economics*.

Tom Schlesinger is Director of the Southern Finance Project, an independent research center that monitors financial markets and policy issues. Founded in 1986, the project works with policymakers, grass roots organizations, unions, and journalists around the country.

Martin H. Wolfson teaches economics at the University of Notre Dame. Prior to coming to Notre Dame, he was an economist for six years at the Federal Reserve Board in Washington, D.C. He is the author of *Financial Crises: Understanding the Postwar U.S. Experience,* M.E. Sharpe, Inc.

The Economic Policy Institute was founded in 1986 to widen the debate about policies to achieve healthy economic growth, prosperity, and opportunity in the difficult new era America has entered.

Today, America's economy is threatened by stagnant growth and increasing inequality. Expanding global competition, changes in the nature of work, and rapid technological advances are altering economic reality. Yet many of our policies, attitudes, and institutions are based on assumptions that no longer reflect real world conditions.

Central to the Economic Policy Institute's search for solutions is the exploration of the economics of teamwork—economic policies that encourage every segment of the American economy (business, labor, government, universities, voluntary organizations, etc.) to work cooperatively to raise productivity and living standards for all Americans. Such an undertaking involves a challenge to conventional views of market behavior and a revival of a cooperative relationship between the public and private sectors.

With the support of leaders from labor, business, and the foundation world, the institute has sponsored research and public discussion of a wide variety of topics: trade and fiscal policies; trends in wages, incomes, and prices; the causes of the productivity slowdown; labor market problems; U.S. and Third World debt; rural and urban policies; inflation; state-level economic development strategies; comparative international economic performance; and the studies of the overall health of the U.S. manufacturing sector and of specific key industries.

The Institute works with a growing network of innovative economists and other social science researchers in universities and research centers all over the country who are willing to go beyond the conventional wisdom in considering strategies for public policy.

Founding scholars of the Institute include:

Jeff Faux—EPI President

Lester Thurow—Sloan School of Management, MIT

Ray Marshall—former U.S. Secretary of Labor; Professor at the LBJ School of Public Affairs, University of Texas

Barry Bluestone—University of Massachusetts-Boston

Robert Reich—U.S. Secretary of Labor

Robert Kuttner—Author; editor, *The American Prospect*; columnist, *Business Week*; and Washington Post Writers Group

EPI Reports, Working Papers, Briefing Papers, and Seminars are distributed by *Public Interest Publications*. For a publication list or to order, call 1-800-537-9359.

Other **EPI Books** are available from M. E. Sharpe at 1-800-541-6563.

For additional information contact the Institute / 1730 Rhode Island Ave., NW, Suite 200 / Washington, DC 20036 / 202-775-8810.